International Watercourses Law in the Nile Basin

The Nile River and its basin extend over a distinctive geophysical cord connecting eleven sovereign states from Egypt to Tanzania, which are home to an estimated population of 238 million people. The Nile is an essential source of water for domestic, industrial and agricultural uses throughout the basin, yet for more than a century it has been at the centre of continuous and conflicting claims and counter-claims to rights of utilization of the resource.

In this book the author examines the multifaceted legal regulation of the Nile. He re-constructs the legal and historical origin and functioning of the British Nile policies in Ethiopia by examining the composition of the Anglo-Ethiopian Treaty of 1902, and analyses its ramifications on contemporary riparian discourse involving Ethiopia and Sudan. The book also reflects on two fairly established legal idioms – the *natural* and *historical* rights *expressions* which constitute central pillars of the claims of downstream rights in the Nile basin; the origin, essence and legal authority of the notions has been assessed on the basis of the normative dictates of contemporary international watercourses law. Likewise, the book examines the *non-treaty* based claims of rights of the basin states to the Nile waters, setting out what the equitable uses principle entails as a means of reconciling competing riparian interests, and most importantly, how its functioning affects contemporary legal settings.

The author then presents the concentrated diplomatic movements of the basin states in negotiations on the Transitional Institutional Mechanism of the Nile Basin Initiative (NBI) – pursued since the 1990's, and explains why the substance of water use rights still continued to be perceived diversely among basin states. Finally, the specific legal impediments that held back progress in negotiations on the Nile Basin Cooperative Framework are presented in context.

Tadesse Kassa Woldetsadik, Ph.D, is Assistant Professor of Law and Human Rights, Addis Ababa University, Ethiopia.

International Watercourses Law in the Nile Basin

Three states at a crossroads

Tadesse Kassa Woldetsadik

Routledge
Taylor & Francis Group
LONDON AND NEW YORK

First published 2013
by Routledge
2 Park Square, Milton Park, Abingdon, Oxon, OX14 4RN

Simultaneously published in the USA and Canada
by Routledge
711 Third Avenue, New York, NY 10017

Routledge is an imprint of the Taylor & Francis Group, an informa business

British Library Cataloguing in Publication Data
A catalogue record for this book is available from the British Library

Library of Congress Cataloging-in-Publication Data
Woldetsadik, Tadesse Kassa, 1973–
International watercourses law in the Nile River Basin : three states at a crossroads / Tadesse Kassa Woldetsadik.—First edition.
pages cm
"Earthscan from Routledge."
Includes bibliographical references and index.
ISBN 978–0–415–65767–9 (hbk)—ISBN 978–0–203–07668–2 (ebk) (print)
1. Nile River Watershed—International status. 2. Water resources development—Law and legislation—Nile River Watershed. I. Title.
KQC660.N55.W65 2013
341.4'420962—dc23
2012032393

Typeset in Baskerville
by Swales & Willis Ltd, Exeter, Devon

MIX
Paper from responsible sources
FSC® C004839
FSC
www.fsc.org

Printed and bound in Great Britain by the MPG Books Group

Contents

Table of cases and advisory opinions

Arbitral Decision Rendered in Conformity with the Special Agreement Concluded on December 17, 1930, Between the Kingdom of Sweden and the United States of America Relating to the Arbitration of a Difference Concerning the Swedish Motor Ships Kronpris Gustaf Adolf and Pacific. AJIL (1932)

Arizona vs. California. 373 US Reports (1963)

Colorado vs. New Mexico. 467 US Reports (1984)

Competence of the ILO to regulate Agricultural Labor. Advisory Opinion 2. PCIJ (1922)

Competence of the Assembly regarding Admission to the United Nations. Advisory Opinion. ICJ Reports (1950)

Connecticut vs. Massachusetts. 282 US Reports (1931)

Continental Shelf (Tunisia/Libyan Arab Jamahiriya). Judgment. ICJ Reports (1982)

East Timor (*Portugal vs. Australia*). Judgement. ICJ Reports (1995)

East Timor (*Portugal vs. Australia*). Dissenting Opinion. ICJ Reports (1995)

Eritrea-Ethiopia Boundary Commission Decision Regarding the Delimitation of the Border between the State of Eritrea and the Federal Democratic Republic of Ethiopia. The Hague (13 April 2002)

Fisheries Jurisdiction (*Federal Republic of Germany vs. Iceland*). Judgment. ICJ. Reports (1973)

Fisheries Jurisdiction (United Kingdom/Iceland). Dissenting Opinion. ICJ Reports (1974)

Gabcikovo-Nagymaros Project (*Hungary vs. Slovakia*). Judgment. ICJ. Reports (1997)

Government of India, Krishna Water Disputes Tribunal, The Report of the Krishna Water Disputes Tribunal with the Decision. Vol II (1973)

Interpretation of Greco-Turkish Agreement of Dec. 1st, 1926. Advisory Opinion, August 28. PCIJ (1928)

Interpretation of Statute of Memel Territory (*UK vs. Lithuania*). Judgment, August 11. PCIJ (1932)

Kansas vs. Colorado. 206 US Reports (1907)

Kasikili/Sedudu Island (Botswana/Namibia). Judgment. ICJ Reports (1999)

Lake Lanoux Arbitration (France/Spain). Arbitral Tribunal set up under a compromise dated 19 November 1956 pursuant to an Arbitration Treaty of July 10, 1929 (1957)

Lepeschkin vs. Gosweiler et Cie, Swiss Federal Tribunal (1923)

Nebraska vs. Wyoming. 325 US Reports (1945)
North Sea Continental Shelf. Judgment. ICJ Reports (1969)
Oil Platforms (Islamic Republic of Iran/United States of America). Judgment. ICJ Reports (2003)
Territorial Dispute (Libyan Arab Jamahiriya/Chad). Judgment. ICJ Reports (1994)
The Report of The Cauvery Water Disputes Tribunal with the Decision in the Matter of Water Disputes Regarding the Inter-state River Cauvery and the River Valley. (2007)
Wyoming vs. Colorado. 259 US Reports (1922)

Table of treaties and selected international instruments

Act Regarding Navigation and Economic Cooperation between the States of the Niger Basin. Niamey (26 October 1963)

Agreement Between Great Britain, France, and Italy respecting Abyssinia. London (13 December 1906)

Agreement between Great Britain and the Independent state of Congo modifying the 1894 Agreement relating to their respective spheres of influence in East and Central Africa. (9 May 1906)

Agreement between the Belgian Government and the Government of the United Kingdom of Great Britain and Northern Ireland regarding water rights on the boundary between Tanganyika and Ruanda-Urundi. London (22 November 1934)

Agreement between the British and German Governments Respecting Africa and the Helgoland. Berlin (1 July 1890)

Agreement between the Federal Republic of Nigeria and the Republic of Niger Concerning the Equitable Sharing in the Development, Conservation and Use of their Common Water Resources. Maiduguri (18 July 1990)

Agreement on the Nile River Basin Cooperative Framework. Kampala (14 May 2010)

Colorado River Compact. Santa Fe, New Mexico (1922)

Convention between the USA and Mexico concerning the equitable distribution of the waters of the Rio Grande for irrigation purposes. Washington (21 May 1906)

Convention Relating to the Status of the River Gambia. Kaolack (30 June 1978)

Ethio-Egyptian Framework for General Cooperation. Cairo (July 1993)

Ethio-Sudanese Accord on Peace and Friendship. Khartoum (23 December 1991)

Exchange of Notes between the UK and Italy Respecting Concessions for a Barrage at Lake Tana and a Railway Across Abyssinia from Eritrea to Italian Somaliland. Rome (14 and 20 December 1925)

Exchange of Notes between his Majesty's Government in the United Kingdom and the Egyptian Government in regard to the use of the waters of the River Nile for irrigation purposes. Cairo (7 May 1929)

Institute of International Law. International Regulation Regarding the Use of International Watercourses for Purposes other than Navigation. Madrid (20 April 1911)

Institute of International Law. Resolution on the Use of International Non-Maritime Waters. Salzburg (11 September 1961)

International Law Association. Statement of Principles. Dubrovnik (1956)

International Law Association. Agreed Principles of International Law, Resolution on the Use of the Waters of International Rivers. New York (1958)

International Law Association. The Helsinki Rules on the Uses of the Waters of International Rivers. Helsinki (August 1966)

Protocol between the British and Italian Governments for the demarcation of their respective spheres of influence in Eastern Africa, from the river Juba to the Blue Nile. (24 March 1891)

Protocol between the British and Italian Governments for the demarcation of their respective spheres of influence in East Africa, From Ras Kasar to the Blue Nile. (15 April 1891)

Southern African Development Community Protocol on Shared Watercourse Systems. Johannesburg (28 August 1995)

Treaty Between Ethiopia and the United Kingdom Relative to the Frontiers between the Soudan, Ethiopia and Eritrea. Addis Ababa (15 May 1902)

Treaty Between the United Kingdom and the Independent State of Congo to Redefine their Respective Spheres of Influence in Eastern and Central Africa. London (9 May 1906)

Treaty between the USA and Great Britain Relating to the Boundary Waters, and Questions Arising Between the USA and Canada. Washington. US Treaty Series, No 548 (11 January 1909)

Treaty between India and Pakistan regarding the use of the waters of Indus. Karachi (19 September 1960)

Treaty on the River Plate Basin. Brasilia (23 April 1969)

The Treaty of Wuchiale concluded between Ethipia and Italy, May 1889

United Arab Republic and Sudan Agreement for the Full Utilization of the Nile Waters. Cairo (8 November 1959)

United Nations Convention on the Law of the Sea (10 December 1982)

United Nations, Vienna Convention on the Law of Treaties. Vienna (23 May 1969)

United Nations General Assembly, Resolution 523(VI). Integrated Economic Development and Commercial Agreements. (12 January 1952)

United Nations General Assembly Resolution 626 (VII). Right to Exploit Freely Natural Wealth and Resources. (21 December 1952)

United Nations General Assembly Resolution 1314 (XIII). Recommendation Concerning International Respect for the Right of Peoples and nations to self-determination. (12 December 1958)

United Nations General Assembly Resolution 1515 (XV). Concerted Action for Economic Development of Economically Less Developed Countries. (15 December 1960)

United Nations General Assembly Resolution 1803 (XVII). Permanent Sovereignty Over Natural Resources. (14 December 1962)

United Nations General Assembly Resolution 3281. Charter of Economic Rights and Duties of States. (12 December 1974)

United Nations General Assembly Resolution 51/229. Convention on the Law of the Non-navigational Uses of International Watercourses 1997. (21 May 1997)

List of abbrevations

BFO	British Foreign Office
CESCR	Committee on Economic, Social and Cultural Rights
CFA	Cooperative Framework Agreement
EEBC	Eritrea–Ethiopia Boundary Commission
EFANSPS	Ethiopia's Foreign Affairs and National Security Policy and Strategy
EWRMP	Ethiopian Water Resources Management Policy
ICJ	International Court of Justice
IIL	Institute of International Law
ILA	International Law Association
ILC	International Law Commission
ILO	International Labour Organization
JN-TANC	Joint Nile-Technical Advisory and Negotiators Committee
Nile-COM	Nile Council of Ministers
NRBC	Nile River Basin Commission
NWDPC	National Water Development Commission
PCIJ	Permanent Court of International Justice
PSNR	Permanent Sovereignty over Natural Resources
SADC	Southern African Development Community
TIM-NBI	Transitional Institutional Mechanism of the Nile Basin Initiative
UNCERDS	United Nations Charter of Economic Rights and Duties of States
UNECA	United Nations Economic Commission for Africa
UNECE	UN Economic Commission for Europe Convention for the Protection and Use of Transboundary Watercourses and International Lakes
UNESCO-WWAP	World Water Assessment Program
UNFAO	United Nations Food and Agriculture Organization
UNGA	United Nations General Assembly
WSDP	Water Sector Development Program
YBIL	*Yearbook of International Law Commission*

Foreword

International Watercourses Law and the Nile Basin – Three States at a Crossroad is a welcome and much-needed contribution to scholarship on the Nile. The topic could not be more timely, as transboundary cooperation on the Nile has reached an impasse, despite important development initiatives across the basin. How will the watercourse states along the Nile proceed within this context? What are the rules of law that govern the uses of shared Nile waters: what lessons might be learned from international law and international diplomacy? This work by Dr Tadesse Kassa Woldetsadik offers a fresh look at some of these questions and offers new insights on possible future solutions on the Nile.

The study is unique in many ways – through its examination of the historical underpinnings of the treaty regime and state practice regarding the Nile, and with its focus on international law and its application across the basin, honing in on the Blue Nile shared by Ethiopia, Sudan and Egypt. This case study offers ample opportunity for exploring hydro-diplomacy in the context of one of the world's most important river basins and provides a rigorous examination of the changing geopolitical settings and the origins and evolution of the legal regime from colonial times.

The Anglo-Ethiopian Treaty (1902) is selected for close and critical examination through historical, political and legal lenses. The authentic texts (the original Amharic and English versions) of the agreement are considered thoroughly and done here for the first time in an international legal study, using the Vienna Convention on the Law of Treaties as an analytical tool. State practice ('non-treaty-based claims') related to the Nile are identified and evaluated, with a reflective review of the 'natural and historical rights' concept, a notion that remains under-studied. The book covers a long time span, which helps a fuller comprehension of the current situation on the Nile.

At present the Nile Basin States continue their discourse around the Nile Basin Cooperative Framework Agreement (CFA) as a foundation for their basin-wide cooperation. Six States (Ethiopia, Tanzania, Rwanda, Uganda, Burundi, and Kenya) have endorsed the CFA, with the Democratic Republic of Congo, Egypt and Sudan still withholding their support, primarily as a result of disagreement over one provision: Article 14 on water security. Dr Tadesse reviews this issue and suggests that 'The Cooperative Framework Agreement presents the perfect setting, both diplomatically and legally, for rectifying entrenched perceptions of grave inequity in upstream Nile and for engaging cooperatively on the basis of recognized rules and principles of customary international law.' Giving much thought to how this might evolve, in view of the current impasse and in the light of his research, the author proposes that 'the long-term security to national riparian interests would very much depend in a fitting compromise volunteered today', emphasising the important role that the international obligation of cooperation might play in this context. The work also highlights the contribution of the rules of international law, in treaty practice and under customary norms, including those reflected in the 1997 UN Watercourses Convention and advanced by the International Law Association and Institute of International Law, to the development of the legal regime of the Nile basin. The author's analysis of 'all relevant factors' in determining 'equitable and reasonable use' of the Nile, elaborated in the last part of the study, provides insight on how contemporary issues (such as food security) might be addressed within a use-allocation framework.

Cooperation on the Nile continues to be a challenge with cascading impacts on regional development and security. Africa is home to a large number of the world's international watercourses and lessons from the experience on the Nile might assist with cooperation across the continent. As has often been said, 'Water is life'. How we manage this precious resource is critically important and yet the challenge continues to become more and more complex, especially in the case of shared international waters. This book provides new insights and invites and inspires continued research in this field. As we seek to address the world's transboundary water problems, we must continue to strive to sustain the higher education and graduate studies of students from around the world, who together will be the Lights of our Future.

Professor Patricia Wouters
Founding Director, UNESCO IHP-HELP Centre for Water Law, Policy and Science, University of Dundee, Scotland; Founding Director, International and National Water Law Programme, University of Xiamen, China under the Chinese Government Thousand Talents Programme.
Dundee, Scotland
1 November 2012

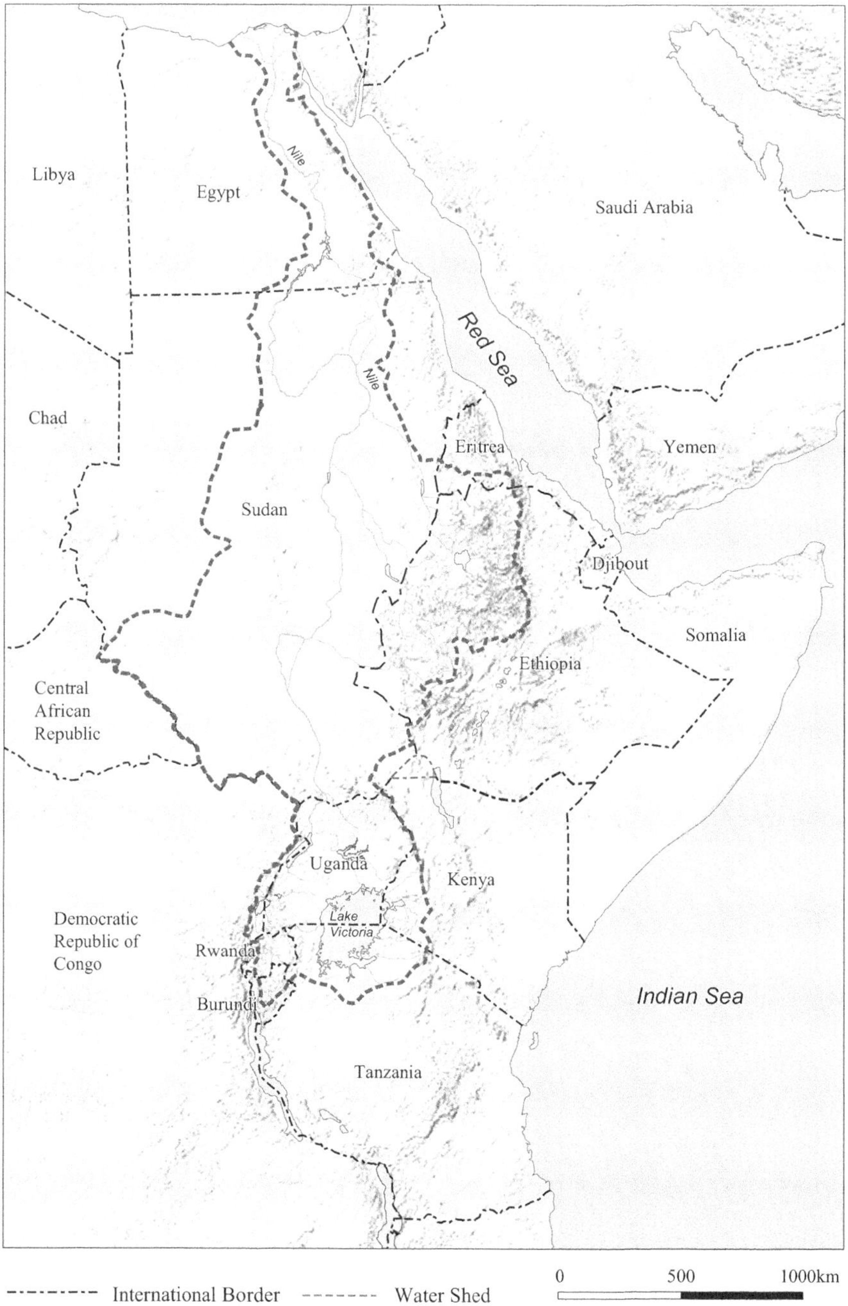

The boundaries and names shown and the designations used on this map do not imply official recognition acceptance by the Nile Basin Research Programme

Figure 0.1 The Nile River Basin (courtesy of the NBRP)

1 Book organization

Introducing the contemporary context

Riparian disputes involving rights of access to fresh water resources, their non-navigational uses and collective management have progressively occupied prominence in interstate relations. Water scarcity, variations in spatial and seasonal distribution of precipitation and, most notably, rising variability in climatic patterns have only exacerbated the competition between basin states for *physical* and *juridical* control of transboundary water endowments.

Indeed, concerns over scarcity of fresh water resources are not merely illusory. In the past, investigations had confirmed that while the planet earth is endowed with an enormous mass of water body, a trival proportion, less than 3 percent to be precise, makes up *fresh water*, a fraction only of which is derived as *surface water* from rivers, lakes and wetlands. Saline oceans make up a disproportionately larger block, about 97 percent, in the distribution of the planet's water reserves.[1] Among fresh water reserves too, river courses provide only negligible volumes, preceded by contributions from icecaps, glaciers, underground waters, lakes and swamps.[2]

The essence of this revelation is self-evident: while water may have been presented constantly in the natural hydrological cycle, the availability of fresh water resources is extremely limited in many jurisdictions, often displaying considerable gaps between supplies and perpetually growing demands.

Commonly, this has also been attended by a complex set of impediments involving the absence of joint institutional and legal frameworks, and hence engendering contentions both with regard to rights of utilization, comprehensive planning and the sustainable management of shared watercourses. The Nile River basin, the most imposing geophysical feature across the east, central and north Africa, is a case in point.

The Nile River and its basin, a home to an estimated population of 238 million, ensconces over a distinctive geophysical cord connecting eleven sovereign

1 P.H. Gleick (1996) 'Water resources', *Encyclopedia of Climate and Weather*, New York, Oxford University Press, pp 817–23.

2 Combined, rivers, swamps and lakes contribute 0.9 percent of the earth's total freshwater resources (which stands at 3 percent); 30.1 percent of this volume is locked in ground waters, and 68.7 per cent in glaciers and icecaps. See Gleick (1996), note 1, pp 817–23.

states: Egypt, Sudan, South Sudan, Eritrea, Ethiopia, Kenya, Uganda, Rwanda, Burundi, Tanzania and Congo.[3]

The core legal regime regulating rights of utilization and management of the Nile waters has been constituted through an intricate web of treaties and incompatible set of national legal conceptions organized in the first half of the twentieth century. For the most part, the legal schemes projected to address colonial-epoch strategic, economic and political considerations.

Although a shared transboundary resource, the Nile River had barely had analogous impact on the lives of its basin communities. In fact, in Egypt, the most-downstream riparian endowed with meagre water resources, the Nile floods have since the ancient epochs presented the foundation of one of the most stable and structured social, economic and political realms in human history. Likewise, in Sudan, the grandiose Gezira irrigational scheme constituted one of the single-largest agricultural projects in the world. A mix of historical, political and economic considerations coincided to spur the planning and commissioning of water resource development ventures, nearly entirely, along the lower reaches of the basin. Against a steadily rising discontent over riparian entitlements, irrigational and industrial developments in Egypt and Sudan persevered to consume the biggest proportions of the Nile waters to date.

Conversely, both during colonial and the post-independence periods, the upper-course of the basin witnessed trifling Nile resources development initiatives; for long, the institution of appropriate policies, regulatory frameworks and hydraulic infrastructures remained an utterly underconsidered commission.

Officially and in public opinion, this enduring misfortune was generally conceived as a direct upshot of sheer failure of the riparian states to capitalize on the potential of the Nile River water resources. Beneath mere conjectures of political, fiscal and technical limitations, however, upstream underutilization has been attributed to the complex juridical hurdles engendered by treaty regimes mainly organized in the past century.

Hence, despite the slight regression in traditional downstream positions that ostensibly exhibited a scale of resilience in user-right approaches, in the opening decade of the twenty-first century, upstream onslaught against existing use-regimes remained exceptionally strong.

In recent years, changes in the political, economic and demographic landscape of the Nile basin region and a strong psychological momentum induced through the gradual evolution of international watercourses law precipitated concentrated involvement of the riparian states in the Nile waters and Nile-related developmental discourses. In the past decade alone, a growing number of upper basin states defied the status quo now prevailing, and pushed forward schemes for a

3 The respective population figures have been accounted as follows. Eritrea 5.2, Burundi 8.5, Rwanda 10.2, Uganda 33.7, Kenya 40.8, Sudan 43.1(of which 8.26 millions are South Sudanese), Tanzania 45.0, DR Congo 67.8, Egypt 84.4, and Ethiopia 84.9. United Nations Department of Economic and Social Affairs, Population Division (2008) 'World Population Prospects', <http://esa.un.org/unpp>, last accessed December 2010.

unilateral implementation of multifaceted projects; indeed, in upstream Nile, the size of population depending on the river's flows – both for domestic stipulations, industrial and agricultural uses as well as the generation of hydro-electric powers has been steadily growing.

Inevitably, in Egypt and Sudan, such development manoeuvres have been received with a measure of apprehension. Admittedly, both downstream polities continued to engage in current negotiations of the Transitional Institutional Mechanism of the Nile Basin Initiative (TIM-NBI); the cooperative design has been mandated to set in place a Commission and endorse an Agreement on the Nile River Basin Cooperative Framework based on a vision to achieve sustainable socio-economic development through equitable utilization of, and benefit from, the common Nile Basin water resources.[4]

Yet, while the basin-wide diplomatic exercise may have driven user-right dialogues to unprecedented heights, the origin and substance of sovereign rights of utilization of the Nile waters have still been perceived incongruously.

As the result, the slight shifts in user-right perspectives and the high-profile political pledges to work on the attainment of equitable utilization of the Nile waters notwithstanding, the winding phases of negotiations on the Nile River Basin Cooperative Framework were held back by serious impediments. This was particularly evident in the course of 2008–2012. In contrast to the position held by upstream states, Egypt and Sudan reverberated *water security* concerns; the states persisted to qualify the endorsement of pending negotiations only subject to specific guarantees recognizing *prior uses* sustained through colonial treaties and the natural-historical rights arguments.[5] Along the downstream Nile, the equitable and reasonable uses doctrine introduced in the proposed regional platform has been embraced merely in a context that upholds the integrity of *established* riparian rights.

Broader structure of the book

This volume comprises of eleven chapters. Preceded by a comprehensive presentation on the physical and hydrological specifics of the Nile River system, the normative expositions in this book commence by submitting a case study of just one aspect of a multifaceted legal organization that regulated the utilization of Nile waters in the basin; hence, the first part shall examine the origin, composition and

4 Meeting of the Council of Ministers of the Nile Basin States held in Dar-es-Salaam, Tanzania, on 22 February 1999 established a 'Transitional Institutional Mechanism of the Nile Basin Initiative (TIM-NBI)' pending the conclusion of the 'Agreement on Nile River Basin Cooperative Framework'.

5 Mohamed El-sayed (2010) 'Dangers on the Nile', *Al-Ahram Weekly Online*, April Issue 995. <http://weekly.ahram.org.eg/2010/995/eg3.htm>, last accessed December 2010.
Nile Basin Initiative (2010) 'Ministers of Water Affairs End Extraordinary Meeting over the Cooperative Framework Agreement', Press Release, 14 April.
<http://www.nilebasin.org/index.php?option=com_content&task=view&id=161&Itemid=102>, last accessed April 2010.

construction of the Anglo-Ethiopian Treaty of May 1902, and its legal implications on contemporary riparian discourses involving the states of Ethiopia and Sudan.[6]

This is followed by an investigation of the *non-treaty*-based claims of rights of the basin states to the Nile waters, propounding, in effect, the applicable rules of customary international law that set out riparian rights in the utilization of shared watercourses. Presented in a context that is relevant to the Nile River basin's legal discourse, the theoretical exposition will be attended by a complete outline and assessment of riparian policies and perspectives in the states of Egypt, Sudan and Ethiopia.

Within the broader frame of this part, the study will also strive to understand why, in spite of the concentrated engagements of the basin states in negotiations on the Transitional Institutional Mechanism of the Nile Basin Initiative (TIM-NBI) in the course of the 1990s and the early decade of the twenty-first century, the origin and substance of water uses rights continued to be perceived diversely. The legal impediments that held back progress in negotiations on the 'Nile Basin Cooperative Framework' shall be presented.

Inevitably, the quintessence of riparian entitlements hinges on how profoundly the standard embedded in the equitable and reasonable utilization principle has been entrenched in current legal discourses to define and constrain the discretion of states sharing the Nile River water resources.

This would presume an extensive delving into the subject of what the equitable uses principle entails as a means of reconciling competing riparian interests, and most importantly, how its functioning affects contemporary legal settings, perceptions and practices in the basin to accommodate subsequent claims of the upstream Nile.

Constitution of the principal and subsidiary themes

In understanding the hydrological, physical and developmental specifics of the Nile basin, the initial undertaking in this volume will concentrate on accounting the early surveys, description of river drainages and seasonal flood regimes; this is followed by a discussion of key historical events involving water resources development patterns and projections across the Nile basin region.

Within the confines of an elaborate outline stated below, the substantive presentation in this volume anticipates to proffer clarification to two general but imperative themes.

For a little more than a century now, Ethiopia, Sudan and Egypt have continued to harbour a perturbed Nile diplomacy; in international relations, political

6 The Treaty Between Ethiopia and the United Kingdom Relative to the Frontiers between the Soudan, Ethiopia and Eritrea, Addis Ababa, 15 May 1902. Although several authors claimed the Treaty had never been ratified, the accord was indeed presented to both Houses of the Parliament in the United Kingdom in December 1902 by commands of 'His Majesty' and a letter of ratification submitted to Ethiopia on the 28 October 1902.

Printed for His Majesty's Stationery Office, Harrison and Sons, St Martin's Lane, London.

niceties inclined to highlight the positive prospects of contemporary cooperative initiatives. Hence, the incidence of deep-seated disparities in core national values that manoeuvre water resources development policies has generally been played down. In reality, however, riparian rights of utilizing the Nile River waters have been *perceived* and *defined* in disparate languages.

Preceded by a conscientious account of fitting diplomatic history, riparian claims and limited treaty engagements, the thematic discussions will concentrate on a vital issue of discord between the three named basin states, and draw conclusions on the status of the trilateral juridical relationship. In specifics, it will aim at elucidating the substance of rights vesting in the states by virtue of operation of existing *treaty* frameworks.

On the other hand, the United Nations Convention on the Law of the Non-navigational Uses of International Watercourses (1997) has incorporated two fundamental principles of international law regulating the use and management of shared watercourses. A first rule stipulated that basin states should exploit shared watercourses in an equitable and reasonable manner; a second principle obliged watercourses states to take appropriate measures to prevent causing significant harm against other states in the utilization of a transboundary river.[7]

The two basic principles have generally been regarded as restatements of customary international law on the subject, and constitute cornerstones of the legal regime regulating the uses and management of international watercourses.[8] Indeed, the explicit reference to the rules, both under the Agreed Minutes of the Transitional Institutional Mechanism of the Nile Basin Initiative (TIM-NBI) and the Agreement on the Nile River Basin Cooperative Framework[9] represents one patent demonstration of this verity.

7 United Nations Convention on the Law of the Non-navigational Uses of International Watercourses (1997), Adopted by the General Assembly of the United Nations on 21 May 1997, General Assembly Resolution 51/229, annex, *Official Records of the General Assembly, Fifty-first Session, Supplement No. 49* (A/51/49). Not yet in force.

8 In fact, during the early commissioning of its undertakings on the progressive development and codification of the international water courses law regime, the International Law Commission (ILC) had itself admitted that the chief issue with respect to some of the basic principles had barely been one of whether 'they existed as such', but rather how they should be formulated under the Convention to regulate future conduct effectively.

International Law Commission (1983) *Yearbook of International Law Commission*, vol 2, no 1, p 157.

The Commission reflected the introduction of the basic principle under the UN Convention on the Non-Navigational Uses of International Watercourses had widely been regarded as 'codification of prevailing principles of international law following from customary international law, and evidenced by general state practice and general principles of law'. International Law Commission (1983), pp 170, 75.

9 The Agreement on the Nile River Basin Cooperative Framework was opened for signature at Lake Victoria Hotel, Uganda, on 14 May 2010 for a period of one year, until 13 May 2011. The decision formally initiated the transformation of the Nile Basin Initiative into a permanent Nile River Basin Commission. Ethiopia, Rwanda, Tanzania and Uganda signed the Framework Agreement immediately after its opening; Kenya followed suit on 19 May 2010 and Burundi on 28 February 2011.

However, uncertainties lingered both with regard to the substantive scope of and the correlation between the two norms of international watercourses law. Their contents remained exceedingly indistinct, and their application contentious.

Since, in practice, the true essence of riparian rights hinges on how these principles would actually be interpreted or applied in specific circumstances involving their uses, one of the issues of elemental interest this book will discuss is how significantly the equitable and reasonable uses principle has been entrenched in contemporary international legal relations to define and constrain the discretion of basin states in the uses of the Nile River resources. An attempt will be exerted to characterize in detail the substance of the equitable and reasonable uses expression and to enlighten its connotations in light of the specific factors and circumstances that prevail in selected constituencies of the Nile basin region.

In particular, this volume also covers numerous themes and contentious legal issues.

A wholesome observation of the Nile River and its position in the region's developmental history entails a sufficient command of the minutiae that depict its past and envision its future impacts on the lives of the basin's inhabitants. In this regard, hydrological information has constantly played crucial functions.

For centuries, a systemic synthesis of hydrological explorations, investigations and specifics, proffering enhanced scientific information with regard to basin drainages, water discharges, and flows lost in swamps, evaporation and transpiration formed the essential foundation of one of the most complex civilizations along the lower-reaches of the Nile River – in Egypt. Hydrological facts steered the choice and placement of vital water control works that enhanced the river's utility over time. What is more, in the late nineteenth and first half of the twentieth century, such details impelled the colonial conquest of nearly all the Nile River basin region, *ipso facto* shaping the nature of treaty relationships among European and indigenous powers of the time.

In contemporary contexts too, hydrologic details constituted themes of exacting concern, and assumed significant roles not only in gearing developmental discourses, but also in qualifying the relative eminence of riparian states within the complex framework of the region's hydro-political make-up.

No comprehensive study covering the entire Nile basin region had been undertaken to date. Still, certain fragments of national reports composed in the states of Egypt, Ethiopia and Sudan will be pulled together to provide an in-depth introduction of a subject that had been the focus of numerous expeditions and scientific investigations by men of all ranks in philosophical and geographic circles. This involves the basic hydrologic and physical features of the Nile River basin, its sources, discharges, meteorology and the relative import of its potent tributaries across various parts of the region (Chapter 2).

The great potentials of the river notwithstanding, the Nile basin's water resources had hardly affected the lives of the riparian population in comparable ways. While agriculture continued to compose a vital constituent of the socio-economic setting, the institutional organization, water-control infrastructures as well as the scales of resource development and projections persisted to exhibit conspicuous gaps. For the most part, they concentrated in Sudan and Egypt, attended by a trifling transformation of patterns in a few upper-course states. National tribulations, mainly engendered by a complex web of colonial, historical and legal accounts, stalled growth and prompted an uneven level of development in the territories of the Nile basin states.

In an attempt to tender a comprehensive perspective of the contemporary state of utilization in the basin, therefore, the historical milieu in which major water-control works had been framed and implemented in selected constituencies of the basin will first be presented (Chapter 3). Far from a purely legalistic enquiry, such description of the ever-rising imbalance in resource utilization aims at affording explicit set of facts that shall be employed in the juridical assessment of the equitability of uses under Chapters 10 and 11.

In the immediate aftermath of the scramble for the African continent in the 1880s, the British Colonial Empire expanded its African acquisitions in fierce competition with the French. At the zenith of its imperial power, its dominion extended over large territorial stretches across the East and North African regions situated in the Nile basin. By 1890, Great Britain had already declared the whole Nile valley as its exclusive sphere of influence,[10] and the British Foreign Office had transformed itself into protector of the Nile and heir of anxieties over the Nile's sources.[11] In the negotiations relating to east and north-eastern Africa which Lord Salisbury conducted with a series of his European counterparts in 1890–91, the desire to safeguard waters of the upper and middle Nile occupied a predominant position.[12]

With the occupation of Egypt (1882) and the Sudanese conquest (1896/98), Great Britain grasped in no time that in order to safeguard its regional geopolitical interests and sustain the economic affluence of both states in which the Lancashire and Manchester textile interests had then developed profound stakes, it had to set out a fitting stratagem. British foreign policy aspired to secure an *unqualified monopoly* or comparable *legal warranties* establishing a regime of non-interference with the hydraulic integrity of the Nile River system.

The Anglo-Ethiopian Treaty, signed on 18 May 1902[13] constituted part of this broader imperial objective for a legal and political domination. Article III of the ensuing arrangement regulated the utilization of the Lake Tana, Abay (Blue Nile) and Sobat (Baro-Akobo) rivers, which ostensibly set far-reaching limitations on the sovereign rights of the state of Ethiopia.

Throughout its tenure as overseer of Egyptian and Sudanese interests, Great Britain deduced from the treaty and pursued a Nile policy which presumed that

10 Terje Tvedt (2004) *The River Nile in the Age of the British, Political Ecology and the Quest for Economic Power*, London/New York, I.B. Tauris, p 40.

11 J. McCann (1981) 'Ethiopia, Britain and Negotiations for the Lake Tana Dam 1922–1935', *The International Journal of African Historical Studies*, vol 14, no 4, p 670.

12 G.N. Sanderson (1964) 'England, Italy, the Nile Valley and the European Balance, 1890–91', *The Historical Journal*, vol 7, p 94.

13 The Treaty Between Ethiopia and the United Kingdom, note 6.

Ethiopia was bound to refrain, nearly completely, from laying any water-control works on the Blue Nile and its tributaries. Ethiopia's views largely deviated; time and again, Ethiopia espoused a national perspective that disfavoured the established British, and later, Sudanese and Egyptian conceptions and anticipations.

Organized in four closely interrelated units under Chapters 4 through 7, the book shall re-construct and analyse the legal and historical origin and functioning of the British Nile policies in Ethiopia, and particularly, the Anglo-Ethiopian Treaty of May 1902. The objective sought would be straightforward: to fully grasp the convoluted legal dilemmas that involved the interpretation, application and continued validity of the treaty scheme.

Hence, first, a brief prelude of the origin and functioning of the British Nile policies in Ethiopia, as well as the plain composition of the Anglo-Ethiopian Treaty will be submitted (Chapter 4). This shall be followed by an analytical endeavour that dwells on elucidating the geographical (physical) scope of obligation assumed under the same treaty scheme (Chapter 5).

In this context, the presentation will briefly address contemporary legal debates under international law with regard to the definition of the concept of an international river course. The scrutiny proceeds with the treatment of whether the Anglo-Ethiopian Treaty, purportedly forbidding the construction of any work on or across the Blue Nile, Lake Tana or the Sobat, can be conceived as covering flows not only of the named principal rivers as such, but also the consequences of major uses of secondary river courses in the natural drainage basins of these rivers. How states perceive the close physical interdependence of various components of river systems in concluding accords regulating the utilization of shared river courses will be the subject of consideration.

Likewise, specific legal issues flowing from national statements of the parties to the treaty in connection with textual and connotational interpretation of the bilateral scheme, as well as variations exhibited between the Amharic and English texts of Article III will be addressed (Chapter 6).

In this context, the first theme will involve the issue of whether a textual discrepancy worthy of legal interpretation truly subsists, and where it does, how, a treaty version that can be reasonably supposed as constituting a joint volition of the parties can be discerned. This objective presumes an extensive employ of interpretative techniques provided under the pertinent rules and principles of international law, and most notably, the Vienna Convention on the Law of Treaties of 1969.[14]

Ethiopia's challenges against the uses-regime instituted through Article III of the Anglo-Ethiopian Treaty have not been exclusively premised on rules of treaty interpretation under international law. The eventual findings relating to the interpretative dilemmas of the Anglo-Ethiopian Treaty notwithstanding, therefore, the continued legal authority of the treaty will further be scrutinized on the basis of three auxiliary juridical theories (Chapter 7).

14 United Nations Vienna Convention on the Law of Treaties (1969), Vienna 23 May 1969. UN Treaty Series Vol 1155, p 331 (entered into force 27 January 1980).

First, the Anglo-Ethiopian Treaty has widely been labelled as representing one category of treaties so described in international custom as *pactus leonine* – wherein one party reserves for itself rights or privileges without a reciprocal undertaking or compensation. Accordingly, this part of the reflection will concentrate on the issue of whether the treaty can be proposed as falling under a class of unequal treaties, imposed by Great Britain in its fiduciary capacity as guardian of the interests of the Sudanese co-domini, and where it does, on revealing the specific juridical consequences that follow under international law in virtue of such a designation.

Within the international legal order, a no-less formidable defiance of unequal treaties has also been procured by a series of United Nations General Assembly resolutions adopted in the 1950s and 1960s.[15] Several of the General Assembly resolutions instituted a systematic framework of conceptual correlation between the principles of sovereign equality, self-determination and permanent sovereignty of states over natural resources. Hence, the second investigation will attempt to expose whether the sweeping languages of the UN resolutions had contemplated transboundary rivers as proper subjects of their treatment, and if so, the nature and scope of rights inferred from such declarations as affecting substantive stipulations under the Anglo-Ethiopian Treaty regime.

The last major issue under the same heading will consider the doctrine of *rebus sic stantibus*. Generally, this canon confers disenfranchised states a measure of cause to withdraw from binding treaties on account of fundamental change of circumstances which occurred with regard to those existing at the time of the conclusion of a treaty, and which was not foreseen by the parties.[16] If the rule of fundamental change of circumstances can also translate in the particular context of the Anglo-Ethiopian Treaty, concluded more than a century ago, it will be another object of legal enquiry.

Inevitably, these discussions will heavily draw on a rich pile of diplomatic communications exchanged between the partaking states shortly before and subsequent to the conclusion of the treaty. The main objective is to resolve the question of whether the treaty scheme has indeed continued to instruct a legal order today. By design, though, the study has also dwelled at length on reconstructing the intricate historical milieu in which the pertinent legal issues had arisen; the opportunity of legal analysis so availed will be exploited to incidentally account and structure the pertinent historical events in a juridically relevant context.

In international juridical relations, not every legal regime bearing impact on the rights of utilization of shared watercourses derives from specific treaty frameworks. Indeed, the structure of legal relations in the Nile Basin transcends far

15 To list a few: United Nations General Assembly Resolution 523 (VI) on 'Integrated Economic Development and Commercial Agreements' (12 January 1952); UNGA Resolution 626 (VIII) 21 December 1952; UNGA Resolution 1314 (XIII) 12 December 1958; UNGA Resolution 1515 (XV) 15 December 1960; UNGA Resolution 1803 (XVII) Permanent Sovereignty Over Natural Resources, 14 December 1962; UNGA Resolution 3281 Charter of Economic Rights and Duties of States 12 December 1974.

16 United Nations Vienna Convention on the Law of Treaties (1969), note 14, Article 62.

beyond stipulations of the Anglo-Ethiopian Treaty just discussed in the preceding paragraphs or the complex legal order organized through a chain of contentious colonial pacts in the course of the late nineteenth and the twentieth centuries. State practice bears extensive evidence as to the existence also of customary rules and generally accepted principles of international law regulating riparian relationships, and particularly so in cases where all-inclusive treaties are not in place. In fact, from time to time, states have asserted claims and defended user-right positions based on diverse principles enunciated under the system of international watercourses law. Chapters 8 through 11 of this work will be devoted to analysing the non-treaty-based rights and duties of riparian states in the Nile Basin, and most notably Egypt, Sudan and Ethiopia.

This presentation is unavoidable because of several rationales. The legal authority of many of the Nile water treaties has been habitually questioned for want of valid consent to be bound on the part of upstream states. The continuity of such regime was challenged under rules governing state succession to treaties, not to mention also that in a few cases, no treaty exists at all connecting some of the riparian states. Besides, in defence of rights of utilization, several basin states have from time to time resorted to regional customs, self-conceived notions or historical perceptions, as well as principles of customary international law regulating the use, development and management of shared watercourses.

Hence, in order to thwart a possible legal vacuity and evaluate the legality of riparian claims as are not based on particular treaty regimes, the entitlements of the basin states shall be examined on the basis of the pertinent rules of the international watercourses law, most of which have also been incorporated under the United Nations Watercourses Convention. In this context, customary rules offer crucial functions not only in spelling riparian rights and obligations, but also in setting out the specific legal standards against which claims of rights premised on non-treaty sources will be eventually appraised.

In spite of the normative dictates embedded in the principle of sovereign equality and a right in equity, the Nile basin states, and most particularly, the lower-most basin states holding a foremost stake in the subject – Egypt, Sudan and Ethiopia – persevered to espouse incompatible water uses policies. Both existing patterns of use as well as future rights of resource development have been defended through the employ of divergent principles and perceptions.

In national policies and basin-wide cooperative initiatives, an upstream defence of riparian rights had originally endeavoured to proclaim and preserve both present and prospective rights of use particularly but not exclusively accentuating the respective hydrographic contributions of each watercourse state to the basin system. Over a course, this approach has been progressively moulded to highlight sovereign rights of use of water resources as enunciated under the principle of equitable and reasonable uses.

On the other hand, with a favourably protected hegemonic claim, traditionally, Egypt and Sudan espoused a few legal hypotheses that ventured to sustain and rationalize the continued downstream appropriation of the Nile waters. In the wake of the twenty-first century, Tvedt's depiction of the pre-1960 Egypt which regarded 'the whole Nile . . . as an Egyptian river' and a national discourse which 'conceived it [the river] as a property of Egypt' still lingered.[17] Modern setting of the psychological momentum tended to champion strategic thoughts moulded along historical lines, defining rights of utilization in entirely downstream perspective.

In ostensibly legal idiom, the *natural* and *historical* rights (or prior use) expressions constituted central pillars of the claims of downstream rights; they formed the doctrinal platform on which the water-sharing schemes and institutional arrangements constituted through two successive Nile agreements – concluded in 1929 and 1959,[18] had been premised.

Against the backdrop of a précis review of stated national positions, actual use patterns and conventional stipulates under the Nile waters agreements (of 1929 and 1959), therefore, the origin and essence of the two central concepts – the natural rights and historical/acquired rights – will be scrutinized in Chapter 8. The legal authority of the notions shall be assessed on the basis of certain normative dictates of contemporary international watercourses law.

On the other hand, to the extent that riparian discourse relies on the utility of customary rules and general principles of international law in articulating rights, the next challenge is largely one of expounding their substantive contents. The early development of the international legal regime had witnessed several incompatible and vaguely defined theories regulating the utilization of transboundary waters.

In contemporary institutional and state practices, two doctrines will appear to have attained supremacy: a first canon cautions riparian states to exploit an international watercourse in an equitable and reasonable manner; and a second rule obliges basin states to take appropriate measures in developing transboundary rivers such that significant harm is averted against the stakes of other watercourse states.[19]

Chapter 9 engages in a comprehensive construction and presentation of the evolution of claims and counter-claims espoused in selected constituencies of the Nile basin in relation to the equitable uses and the no significant harm principles. Likewise, the reflection presents on the exceedingly incompatible positions of the basin states reverberated in current discourses of the Nile Basin Initiative.

Eventually, this recital shall be followed by and would be linked with the analysis of the essence and bearing of the two named principles of international watercourses law; the objective is to establish the specific standing of the basin states with regard to rights of utilizing the Nile River water resources (Chapters 10 and 11).

17 Tvedt (2004), note 10, p 100, 136.

18 Exchange of Notes between his Majesty's Government in the United Kingdom and the Egyptian Government in regard to the use of the waters of the River Nile for irrigation purposes, 7 May 1929, Cairo;
United Arab Republic and Sudan Agreement for the full utilization of the Nile waters, 8 November 1959, Cairo.

19 United Nations Convention on the Law of the Non-navigational Uses of International Watercourses (1997), note 7, Articles 5 and 7.

In revealing the deep-seated rift in contemporary legal approaches, Chapter 9 lays emphasis on presenting the impacts of the evolution of international watercourses law on national policies relating to the use and management of the Nile basin water resources. More importantly, however, the discussion will direct attention to a vital question of why, in spite of concentrated diplomatic actions and a fragile gesture of regime change in the past decade, ambiguities that characterized early developments of international watercourses law itself sustained to still influence riparian dispositions, and hence elude a homogeneous reading of the pertinent rules and principles.

The empirical investigations in Chapters 10 and 11 proceed on a well-considered inference that, if in some form, international watercourses law has indeed influenced national policies and perceptions in the Nile basin with regard to the rights of use of transboundary rivers. Admittedly, at the domestic levels, political and socio-economic considerations have continued to hamper concrete cooperative initiatives; yet, water diplomacy in the Nile basin has slowly but securely evolved from archaic approaches of flat rejection to a reciprocal acknowledgement of at least some common principles prescribing rights of riparian use.

Hence, the fundamental right of each watercourse state to engage in the utilization of a transboundary river in an equitable and reasonable manner has seldom been disputed.

In the first instance, though, and before engaging in discussions of the right to equitable utilization of the Nile basin states, a fitting exposition of a certain hydrological conception of legal significance would be imperative: does the Nile River present an adequate water-flows regime such as to circumvent riparian competition in the beneficial uses of the watercourse?

The examination of this issue is simply vital, for in the last two decades, the Nile basin region has progressively witnessed concretely competing interests, aspirations and incompatible development strategies involving the river. The gloomy repercussions of a conflicting course over a scarce natural resource is self-evident: any enthusiastic implementation of self-claimed rights in one of the late-coming upstream states, withdrawing certain volumes of the Nile floods, can eventually prejudice established uses along the downstream Nile.

Concerns associated with the potential effects of conflicting patterns in the utilization of the scarce water resources are not merely speculative; indeed, such agitations have been recited in national policies of certain riparian states. This explains why, in the context of determining each basin state's equitable entitlements, hydrological facts particularly relating to the flow-regime of the Nile River basin would constitute important physical considerations.

In general, should it be held that the flow regime of the Nile River is *limited*, it follows that not all reasonable uses outlined as part of the water resources development strategies of the individual riparian states or implemented in pursuance of the stated right to equitable utilization can be realized to their full extent, without involving some conflicts of uses between riparian states. Due to the insufficiency of the total river discharge, some needs in certain basin states, although critical, will remain unmet. This calls for a complex task involving the balancing and re-drawing of riparian entitlements on the basis of the principle of equitable utilization.

On the other hand, should it be submitted, and this was contended in a few circumstances, that the Nile River has been endowed with ample waters to satisfy both existing and future requirements of the basin states, a conflict of uses scenario will barely arise, obviating the need for engaging in the definition of the equitable entitlement of each riparian state, at least in the immediate future.

The crux of this matter lies in a venerable debate under international law that involves the issue of how the concept of *international watercourse* has been perceived as a physical unit of regulation, and by inference, which particular components of the entire water balance of river basins constitute, legally, the objects of common riparian appropriation.

Under the UN watercourses convention, it will be noted that hydrological and hydrographic factors have been listed as crucial factual considerations.[20] Legal arguments pertaining to the right to equitable apportionment and whether a conflict between various beneficial uses actually arises are *ipso facto* affected by the overall quantity of the floods availed in each basin state and the river course in entirety.

And depending on the conceptual perspective adopted in any given juridical discourse, the total volume obtainable for riparian appropriation may refer to meagre water mass presented by a *river channel* or else to the water endowments of the whole *riverine basin*. With exacting specificity, various sections in Chapter 10 will endeavour to address the theoretical dilemmas of international law and the practical implications thereof.

Where it could be established that the Nile river presents a limited resource base such that not all beneficial uses can be realized to their full extent without involving conflicts of uses, the next obvious question in articulating the scope of riparian rights in Ethiopia, Egypt and Sudan will be the analysis of what the equitable uses principle as such entails as a means of reconciling competing riparian uses. This cannot be settled merely by reiterating that the doctrine constitutes a settled rule of customary international law. Its contents must be elucidated and the particular attributes of its application will need to be brought to light.

Hence, a brief overview of the essence and status of the legal standard embedded in the concept of equitable utilization shall also be provided, followed by empirical assessments of contending riparian interests of basin states on the basis of factors and circumstances listed under Article 6 of the UN Watercourses Convention. In effect, this undertaking, which also addresses a series of distinct questions aimed at refining the contents and application of the factors and circumstances lined under Article 6, will involve the unwieldy task of transposing the broad and vaguely framed principle of international law in to the concrete developmental settings prevailing in the three Nile basin states (Chapter 11).

20 United Nations Convention on the Law of the Non-navigational Uses of International Watercourses (1997), note 7, Article 6.1.

In this regard, of course, a selective approach will be applied; among the protracted list of factors depicted under the UN Watercourses Convention, only geography, hydrology, climate, existing/future utilizations, and economic/social needs will be highlighted to provide guidelines that would help states work out the allocation of waters or beneficial uses of a river course in which they all have interest.

The weight accorded to any given factor is decided by its importance in comparison with that of other relevant factors, which must be considered *together* and a conclusion reached on the basis of the *whole*.[21] While this implies that not all factors and circumstances will be attributed absolutely equal standing, and hence, unique circumstances of each particular basin must be taken into account, the actual application of factors and circumstances as such prompts a series of challenging dilemmas which shall all be discussed in sufficient details.

On the other hand, it would be noted that even within the framework of the equitable uses doctrine, the utilization of an international watercourse in one's jurisdiction presumably involves a duty to take appropriate measures to thwart the imposition of significant harm against co-basin states.

In a juridical reading of the circumstances prevailing in the Nile basin, the right to equitable utilization and the scale of water security invested in the states of Egypt, Sudan and Ethiopia would fatefully depend on the essence of the relationship of between the principle of equity and the no significant harm doctrine, and on how *significant harm* is conceived, defined and applied. The final sections of Chapter 11 shall also consider this contentious theme in a relevant context.

In presenting a systematic account and investigation of the factors and circumstances affecting the equitability of uses, the ultimate objective has been to determine the basic question of whether contemporary uses along downstream Nile have encroached upon the equitable utilizations threshold under international law, and if so, how subsequent claims of the upstream Nile could be accommodated and adjustments effected to address the pursuit of equity across the basin.

More significantly, however, the substantive exposition establishes a conceptual underpinning that can be utilized to influence future legal discourses in the Nile basin, particularly in relation to pending negotiations on the issues of water security, equitable uses and allocation of the Nile waters. While negotiated settlements tender the most ideal solutions, divergences in legal opinions and perceptions are inevitable; hence, a judicious illumination of the respective riparian rights under the applicable regime of public international law would play a critical function in setting out specifics of the legal high ground on the basis of which claims of rights may be legally framed and put forward.

21 United Nations Convention on the Law of the Non-navigational Uses of International Watercourses, note 7, Article 6.3; International Law Association (1966), The Helsinki Rules on the Uses of the Waters of International Rivers (Revised under the Berlin Rules), Article 5.3. (Text in International Law Association, Report of the 52nd Conference, Helsinki, 14–20 August 1966, pp 484–32).

Book objectives

Although user-right perceptions are essentially social and political in construction, the discussions in this volume take particular note of, and are induced by the obvious trend in international legal relations that states have constantly endeavoured to camouflage national positions within the embrace of the normative dictates of international law. Admittedly, water disputes will not be resolved exclusively through the application of legal doctrines alone; yet, international law has continued to play crucial functions in interstate relations. While the means for achieving cooperation may originate from a number of sources – with politics playing an important role – water law, whether national or international, is relevant at all stages of water resource development and management.[22] Hence, states cannot ignore the legal dimensions of disputes, even where such arguments have not played a decisive or even a large part in the solution of the disputes.[23]

For more than a century now, the search for *legitimacy* of user perceptions and water-uses practices in the Nile basin has been an unending exercise, hence meriting an elucidiation of the contemporary state of international legal norms.

This Book would aim at tendering a comprehensive and contextual examination of each of the specific legal problems highlighted in the preceding paragraphs. Of course, it is admitted that the legal issues so identified are not wholly inclusive, nor liable to irrefutable explanations. Unlike investigations in methodical sciences, legal presentations can be swayed by subjective interpretations; conclusions drawn in the end, whether on points of law or fact, are essentially coefficients of the strength and consistency of legal arguments and corroborations presented to buttress any side of a given issue.

Such methodological challenges notwithstanding, a scholarly deliberation on contentious themes of water rights could serve certain imperative objectives. For decades, the hydropolitical and developmental discourse in the Nile basin has characterstically exhibited policies of intense distrust, dodging and unyieldy diplomatic confrontations. In particular, Egypt, Sudan and Ethiopia have continuously harboured perturbed riparian relationships. The rhetorical myth that prescribed an eternal monopolistic holding of the resource for beneficial uses in the lower-reaches of the river has been firmly grounded. In consequence, since the turn of the twentieth century, Ethiopia has been bogged down in hostile political and legal bickering on cooperative initiatives, joined by the rest of the upper-course states in the later part of the past century. A mix of factors, including ecological distresses, population growth and increasingly pressing developmental requirements engendered discernible drives in contemporary challenges against the existing state of water utilization in the basin.

22 Patricia Wouters, Salman M. A. Salman, and Patricia Jones, 'The legal response to the world's water crisis: What legacy from the Hague? What future in Kyoto?', p 5 <http://www.africanwater.org/Documents/colorado_draft_4.doc>, last accessed in December 2010.

23 Charles B. Bourne (1965) 'The Right to the Waters of International Rivers', *Can YB Int'l L* vol 3, pp 187–8.

By conversing in specifics on the legal regime that regulates utilization of the Nile River water resources, the basis of riprian claims of rights, the appropriate standards under international custom and eventually, the state of contemporary cooperative initiatives, the book anticipates to present a comprehensive legal perspective of the subject on an academic platform and to surge scholastic dialogues involving the themes.

More significantly, however, this presentation targets a wide range of policy makers and executives engaged in the framing and implemention of regulations that bear impact on riparian rights of utilizing shared watercourses. The conflicting accounts of national conceptions of rights notwithstanding, the book aims to contribute to a lucid understanding of the substance and implication of rights conferred by virtue of the operation of existing treaties and the appropriate rules of international watercourses law.

Moreover, picking on a steadily unfolding momentum of cooperation in the Nile basin region, the book will attempt to reveal certain shortcomings of the proposed legal arrangement, and hence help inform on the essence of legal modalities that should steer prospective cooperative enterprises.

Methodological issues, sources of international law and data

An assessment of the scale contemplated in this book will call for a scrutiny of mundane events that crossed the threshholds of water politics over extensive historical epoch and geographical locations across the Nile basin. While the expositions would esssentially remain legal constructs, a meaningful presentation of the status quo in a juridical context obliges a scrupulous orientation to related historical, political and developmental events impacting on the utilization of the Nile River water resources.

Admittedly, a partial employ of such a multidisciplinary model risks inflating the volume of issues rupturing with every presentation of facts, and complicates the charge of framing and explaining the main and subsidiary research questions.

While a fitting caution has been exerted to restrictively define the methodological scope and overstress the primarily legal nature of the undertaking, it will be noted, and quite often so, that issues of water rights are multifaceted. In some contexts, legal themes may not be grasped properly without a glimpse of the social, economic and political perspectives as well as national policies and actions that characterized the colonial and post-independence epochs in the basin. The extensive reference in the book to diplomatic and historical recitals has been justified on this account.

The method of enquiry in the book employs international legal concepts and standards to test the footing and juridical sustainability of specific claims of rights reiterated in old and contemporary Nile basin legal discourses. For the most part, this procedure involves a personal investigation, interpretation and analysis of the relevant historical archieves, declassified diplomatic correspondences, government memos, legal texts, conventions and local customs. Naturally, such assessment will be attended by a careful assemblage of various sources of international law, and is corroborated by observations of international law scholars, both in printed and unpublished literature, adressing varied themes of international law.

An empirical input has also been drawn from open-ended interviews carried out on a limited scale with key officials at the ministries responsible for Foreign Affairs and water resources development in Ethiopia. Temporal limitations obliged that on-site observations and inquiries had not been conducted in the rest of the basin states. To mollify the negative effects, therefore, an extensive use has been made of the master plan studies on the Nile River, statements of national policies and water-linked prognosis both in Egypt and Sudan, reported in official lines, independent channels and academic literature.

The primary formal sources of the legal analysis are produced under Article 38 of the Statute of International Court of Justice: international conventions, international custom, general principles of law and judicial decisions, and as a subsidiary means, teachings of the most highly qualified publicists. While due note has been taken of the relative *normative* values of various sources of international law, riparian claims relating to the utilization of the shared watercourses – whether based on international custom or texts of the pertinent treaty frameworks will be appraised by reference to the standards and understandings of law set out under the principal and subsidiary sources of international watercourses law.

With regard to international conventions, two sources have been expansively utilized in the research: the Vienna Convention on the Law of Treaties (1969) and the UN Convention on the Non-navigational Uses of International Watercourses (1997).[24] As demonstrated earlier, the Nile River user-right disputes encompass a complex and wide range of themes. However the legal issues may have been framed or espoused, selected provisions of the conventions will proffer the essential formal basis of the legal analysis; several of the conventions' stipulates reiterate custom, and hence apply even under circumstances where the instruments may not have been duly ratified.

Drawing the relevant rules of custom in any particular setting is an exigent undertaking. Legal literatures have extensively propounded on the theoretical framework of 'custom', and endeavoured to elaborate how state practice and a perception of an obligation to behave in a particular way engenders certain normative dictates of international law. Yet, the divergent opinions which have been exhibited in state practice and the views of learned publicists will tend to uphold that any classification of a certain pattern of states' conduct as creating a rule of custom will simply be susceptible to dispute.

In many ways, the voluminous literatures of the International Law Commission – a UN body responsible for the progressive development and codification of international law, the annual reports of the Sixth Committee sessions of the United Nations General Assembly, as well as key resolutions of the International Law Association (ILA) and the Institute of International Law (IIL) have been

24 United Nations Vienna Convention on the Law of Treaties (1969), note 14; United Nations Convention on the Law of the Non-navigational Uses of International Watercourses (1997), note 7.

exceedingly relieving.[25] They presented piercing details with regard to the evolution of the pertinent laws and facts of state practice, acuity, national reports and comments submitted in connection with the drafting of the UN watercourses convention.

Of course, the normative authority of each of these sources varies, and has been subjected to a scrupulous scrutiny on each particular occasion. With regard to works of the ILC, Birnie et al. have established in their seminal work on International Law and the Environment in 2008 that many of the ILC's codifications have become widely regarded as authoritative statements of the law and are relied upon by international courts, international organizations and governments. This consideration justifies the extensive employ of the specifics provided by the ILC's literatures both to the material fabric and as sources of legal authority in the analyses. Still, the ILC is not a law-making institution and hence, in some parts, certain of its conclusions or reports of the ILA and IIL as reciting the state of the law have been subjected to further inspection.

The analytical endeavour cannot be complete without a corresponding illustration of the effects of judicial/arbitral decisions on the issues clutched in various parts of the book. A limited jurisprudence of national, regional and international bodies, and most notably, the Permanent Court of International Justice, and later, the International Court of Justice shall be drawn in quite regularly.

Several proceedings had adjudicated on contentious cases involving the doctrinal foundation and interpretation of the laws of treaties and rules governing the use and management of international watercourses. Of course, the recurring incidence of strong dissenting opinions challenging core legal theories espoused in majority rulings, and even more, the absence of a system of binding precedent in international law can represent limitation with regard to judicial decisions as sources of international law. Yet, authoritative interpretations proffered in relation to certain provisions of the conventions as well as various stipulates of customary rules are presented to draw on another, albeit supplemental source of law germane to the study.

On the other hand, it should be noted that the frequent reference to judicial decisions, adjudications or arbitral awards of the US Supreme Court and various tribunals in India and Europe has been induced so much by the opportunity they

25 By resolution 2669 (XXV) of 8 December 1970, the General Assembly recommended that the Commission should take up the study of the law of the non-navigational uses of international watercourses with a view to its progressive development and codification, and in the light of its scheduled programme of work, to consider the practicability of taking the necessary action as soon as the Commission deemed it appropriate.

At its 26th session in 1974, the Commission, pursuant to the recommendation contained in General Assembly resolution 3071 (XXVIII) of 30 November 1973, set up a subcommittee to consider the question. The Commission proceeded with its work on the topic in a series of sessions lasting from 1976 to 1994.

International Law Commission 'Law of Non-navigational Uses of International Watercourse', <http://untreaty.un.org/ilc/summaries/8_3.htm>, last accessed in December 2010.

avail in elaborating various rules and principles of international law *than* by their status as principal sources of international law.

Sequential presentations of the ILC on the historical anthology of the relevant laws and state practice, the periodic resolutions of the ILA and IIL and national jurisprudence are not the exclusive sources. A bulk of the material employed in this book expounding on the development patterns, perceptions and interpretations of rights-claims has also been drawn from the extensive diplomatic correspondences swopped between Ethiopia, Great Britain and its colonial offices (in Egypt and Sudan) in the last decade of the nineteenth and first half of the twentieth centuries.[26] True, the essay would merely concentrate on a few of the most crucial Foreign Office materials held in reserve at the British Public Records Office in London – sources whose existence was apprised through courtesy of Terje Tvedt; evidently, such reference would be impertaive considering the sheer size influence British policies of the time have had in shaping both colonial-epoch and contemporary user-right perceptions across the Nile basin.

Yet, certain methodlogical challenges have been posed in the use of diplomatic correspondences. This emanates from facts of broader inconsistency in their contents and the multiplicity of actors that had manoeuvred water rights conceptions and development policies in the past. The challenge would particularly be evident in *translating* official dialogues, interdepartmental memos and letters exchanged between diplomatic missions of the states involved in to a unified national policy perception to which substantial credence could be attached in the context of factual and legal interpretations in the Book.

Finally, it is important to underscore that since the earliest periods when the 'sources' mystery had enthused a succession of explorers and expeditions, the Nile River has been a subject of investigation by writers of all ranks. Connecting epic scholastic presentations by the likes of Herodotus and Ptolemy several centuries back to Tvedt's magnum-opus publication in the twenty-first century, voluminous literatures parading its history, hydrology and hydro-politics have been published. A limited study had also been undertaken on the international aspects of the legal wrangling in the basin.

Inopportunely, though, no academic work this author knows of has approached the legal issues on a scale so comprehensive as has been embarked in this book, yet, on the limited editions available, the scholarly opinions and findings of legal theorists, historians and political scientists relating to points of facts or laws have been duly consulted as secondary sources to confirm or refute streaks of propositions encased in the book.

26 These materials have been reserved at The National Archives, Kew, Richmond, in the United Kingdom.

2 Understanding the Nile

Surveys, physical and hydrologic specifics

The Nile River and its basin, a home to diversely contrasting ecology, political creeds and economic order, the unfailing spectacle that yielded precious waters since the dawn of human history, entrenches between 4°S in the equatorial region and 31°N in the Mediterranean. It constitutes a territorial contiguity of varying sizes in eleven north, north-eastern and central African countries – Egypt, Sudan, South Sudan, Eritrea, Ethiopia, Kenya, Uganda, Rwanda, Burundi, Tanzania and Congo. Across several districts, no clearly marked water shade exists, and surveys of its outer-most reach remain varied, but generally, the drainage ensconces over an estimated catchment area of 2.9–3.5 million sq.km. In a unique blend of topography, the Nile basin exhibits stretches of land covered by vegetation widely ranging from dense equatorial and tropical rainforests to rain-flooded grasslands, woodlands, papyrus and the scanty arid desert scrubs. A great deal of provinces along the equator and the high plateaus receive continual rainfall for several months of the year; the precipitation and density of the vegetation drastically trifles toward the north.

This part presents an account of the early surveys, explorations, hydrologic features and seasonal flood regimes of the White and Blue Nile river systems.

The Nile River, composed of three major sub-basins, the White Nile, the Blue Nile and the Tekeze-Atbara, and a string of other streams lying within the drainage basin, is, the issue of its furthest source still outstanding, the longest river in the world.[1]

A correct description of the length of any river presumes a settled understanding of its source and mouth, a complex undertaking particularly when a head river receives discharges from numerous distant tributaries. Over the years, a handful of geographers had computed the distance of the White Nile from one of the few tributaries draining the central lakes region, selected on the basis of not only

1 The Amazon River, at 6387km long, is (was) the second longest river. In 2007, a scientific expedition in South America claimed 'to have discovered for fact a new starting point of the Amazon in the South of Peru', putting the river at 6,800km long, and consequently naming it as 'the longest river in the world' (BBC News, 16/06/2007) <http://news.bbc.co.uk/2/hi/6759291.stm>, last accessed in December 2010.

its farthest location – but also the volume of its flows, so that remotely situated but sporadic effluents are excluded. Consensus on the location of the most distant headwater from among the many effluents still lacks in literatures. A widely diverging statistics had accounted that the White Nile River traverses for 6,058km from a source in Tanzania – the Luvionza River, for 6,000km from a remotely situated spring of the Kagera River in the mountains of Burundi, or for 6,671km from another of its distant stream in Burundi – the Ruvyironza (Lavironza) River, itself a tributary of the Ruvubu River. The measure from the northern shores of Lake Victoria, near Jinja, to the Mediterranean Sea is a mere 5,584km.

The second, albeit more significant wing of the Nile, the Blue Nile, originates from the Lake Tana area in Ethiopia, and flows for about 4,588km before it drains to the Sea, joined by the White Nile in the vicinity of Khartoum.

The White Nile: early surveys and the sources mystique

For centuries, the sources of the Nile River system, its topography and meteorology had been the subject of copious expeditions, investigations and speculations by people of all ranks in the spiritual, philosophical and geographic circles. Countless personalities had sought to resolve the secrecy that underlies not only the volume and nature of the irregular yearly cycles of inundation from the high plateaus to the most-arid deserts, but also the causes and location of the springs that gave rise to such floods.

The legendary Egyptian kings Sesostris, Alexander and Ptolemy Philadelphus conceived of glaring glories in reaching at the head of the Nile, but only commanded

Table 2.1 Nile basin: areas and rainfall by country (adapted, courtesy of FAO)

Country	*Total area of the country*	*Area within basin*	*Percentage of total area of basin*	*Percentage of total area of country*	*Average annual rainfall in the basin area (mm)*		
	(sq.km)	*(sq.km)*	*(%)*	*(%)*	*Min.*	*Max.*	*Mean*
Burundi	27,834	13,260	0.4	47.6	895	1 570	1 110
Rwanda	26,340	19,876	0.6	75.5	840	1 935	1 105
Tanzania	945,090	84,200	2.7	8.9	625	1 630	1 015
Kenya	580,370	46,229	1.5	8.0	505	1 790	1 260
Congo	2,344,860	22,143	0,7	0.9	875	1 915	1 245
Uganda	235,880	231,366	7.4	98.1	395	2 060	1 140
Ethiopia	1,100,010	365,117	11.7	33.2	205	2 010	1 125
Eritrea	121,890	24,921	0.8	20.4	240	665	520
Sudan*	2,505,810	1,978,506	63.6	79.0	0	1 610	500
South Sudan	619,745	—	—	—	—	—	—
Egypt	1,001,450	326,751	10.5	32.6	0	120	15
Nile Basin		3,112,369	100.0		0	2 060	615

* The figures relating to the *Sudan* refer to facts existing before the separation of South Sudan in 2010.

failed expeditions one after the other, generally directed en route to Ethiopia. In The Histories,[2] Herodotus (484-ca.425BC), an extensive traveller and author of the popular idiom – Egypt is the gift of the Nile – submitted that he was told by 'the recorder of the sacred treasures of Athena in the Egyptian city of Saïs' that the springs of the Nile rise 'between two hills with sharp peaks at Thebaid and Elephantine', with two separate branches, the right bank running to Egypt and the other to 'Æthiopia'. However, his description confined the source and mouth of the Nile River within Egypt, and failed to match geographical indications since identified.

In perfect harmony with the contemporaneous culture of intellectual effort and confrontation, successive philosophers, including Strabo (63/64BC–AD24), Gaius Plinius Secundus (23–79AD)[3] and Ptolemy Claudius Ptolemaeus (ca 100–170AD) theorized extensively on coordinates, maps and marked details concerning provinces flooded by the river course, tributaries, tide velocity and designation of the physical landscapes. Although only in a vague construct, several of the illustrations represented the contemporary state.

The classical scholarly conjectures of the Greco-Roman writers offered expedient guides to a wave of major cartographic and theoretical presentations by Arabs and the Portuguese at the turn of the fourteenth century, and to the great occupations of Captain John H. Speke, Samuel Baker, Richard Burton, Henry M. Stanley and Dr David Livingstone in the nineteenth century. In fact, some of the earliest perceptions characterizing the hydrologic and physical phenomena of the Nile remained dominant Nile theories for centuries. A great deal of the ensuing developments had put up new ideas largely based on the early records.

In the wake of the nineteenth century, prying on the subject fascinated not only travellers pursuing pleasure and recognition, but also society and privately commissioned scholars engaged in geographical, geological and anthropological explorations, and missionaries pursuing a blend of religious and political calls. Most wedged by the theme had also been major European colonial and trading powers. Several governments encouraged, and indeed funded expeditions across the basin with a view to compiling hydraulic information and enhancing the river's utility through advanced management and control works in designated areas of strategic and economic interest. In fact, in the late nineteenth and early twentieth centuries, colonial aspirations and conquests pursued by European powers in Africa had been invariably facilitated by explorers who offered substantiated intelligence on human settlement and physical resources of the region.[4]

2 Herodotus (1920) *The Histories,* A.D. Godley trans, Cambridge, MA: Harvard University Press, *Book 2 Chapter 28 Section 1.*

3 Pliny the Elder (1855) *The Natural History*, ed John Bostock and H.T. Riley, London, Taylor and Francis, Book V.

4 A closer investigation of the exploring and missionary operations of the time and the subsequent developments corroborates the long-standing adage that 'the explorer is the precursor of the colonizer'. In fact, in his detailed review on penetrations to interior Africa over a period of fifty years, William Garstin stressed that 'England's acquisition of the large territory (in East and Central Africa in 1894) was the direct consequence of Speke's discovery, nearly forty years before.' William Garstin (1909) 'Fifty Years of Exploration and Some of its Results', *The Geographical Journal*, vol 33 no 2, p 134.

The latest expeditions refuted some of the ages-old misconceptions of the Greco-Roman cartography and confusing accounts of early writers about the upper-reaches and attributes of the Nile river system. Today, the near-conventional perspective which claimed that the White Nile sub-basin originates in the northern tip of Lake Victoria, at the Ripon Falls in Jinja, Uganda, is based on Captain Speke's discovery.[5]

Captain Speke's elaborate description of the travels and findings had squirted illumination on the broader knowledge base of the geography and hydrography of the Lakes Region and the White Nile River basin.

Over the years, his conclusions had been supplemented by accounts of other explorers in Bahr el Ghazal, upper Nile below Khartoum, the Sobat River, the Ruwenzori heights and other parts of the Nile basin. These ventures tiled smoother avenues for further expeditions, scientific investigations and precise map plotting,[6] and particularly so by the likes of Lyons, MacDonald, Dupuis and William Garstin since the partitioning of Africa. This historical incidence influenced the institutional organization and transformation of the Egyptian, and later, Sudanese Irrigation Departments adopting elaborate techniques of hydrologic surveys, analysis and Nile control schemes in the lower-reaches of the river.

Today, it is established that Lake Victoria, the fourth largest lake in the world and source of the Nile,[7] receives its net water supplies from feeder streams to the west and south-west, with a few sporadic rivulets in the south, east and north-east.[8] Direct surface precipitation remains the main contributor. Reiterating William Garstin's views as early as in the 1920's, H.E. Hurst explained that among the scores of swamp-bordered watercourses gushing to Lake Victoria, the Kagera River, a stream of less hefty discharge with effluents rising from the Congo, is the most important of the runoffs in the catchment area.[9] Its

5 J.H. Speke and J.A. Grant (1862–63) 'The Nile and its Sources', *Proceedings of the Royal Geographical Society of London*, vol 7, no 5, pp 217–18.

6 Concrete water planning, control and development required more than a mere hydrological and topographic descriptions offered by explorers – a subject treated at length in the next sub-topics. For now, it would suffice to present some of the later investigations of the nineteenth century along various segments of the White Nile and which facilitated better understanding of the river system (summarised by Garstin (1909) and Tvedt (2004)). Hence, between 1853 and 1864, Patherick and Tinne explored Bahr el Ghazal several times; between 1868 and1871, professor George Schweinfurth investigated the same basin; in the same period, Gordon Pasha and his staffs surveyed and mapped much of upper-Nile between Khartoum and Lake Albert; in 1874, colonel Chaille Long explored Victoria Nile; between 1875 and 1886, Wilhelm Junker researched the Sobat and Bahr el Ghazal rivers; in 1885, Hungarian Count Samuel Teleki discovered the last of the Great African Lakes – Rudolf; in 1885 Joseph Chavanne compiled surveys on Bahr al Jebel and Victoria Nile, Alfred J. Chelu dealt with the Blue and White Nile systems south of the Nile (1891), and De Martonne investigated the Upper-Nile (1897); and between 1890 and 1897, the British East Africa Company undertook several surveys of the region.

7 With a total area of 69,485sq.km, the Lake is next only to the Caspian Sea, Michigan and Superior lakes.

8 Apart from the Kagera River, important streams include the Simuyu and Ruwand joining the Lake in the south-western shores, the Mara (Tanzania), and the Kuja, Awach (Kiboun), Mirin, Nzoya and Sio in the north-eastern shores.

9 H.E. Hurst (1936) 'A Study of the Upper Nile', *Discover*, vol 17, p 173.

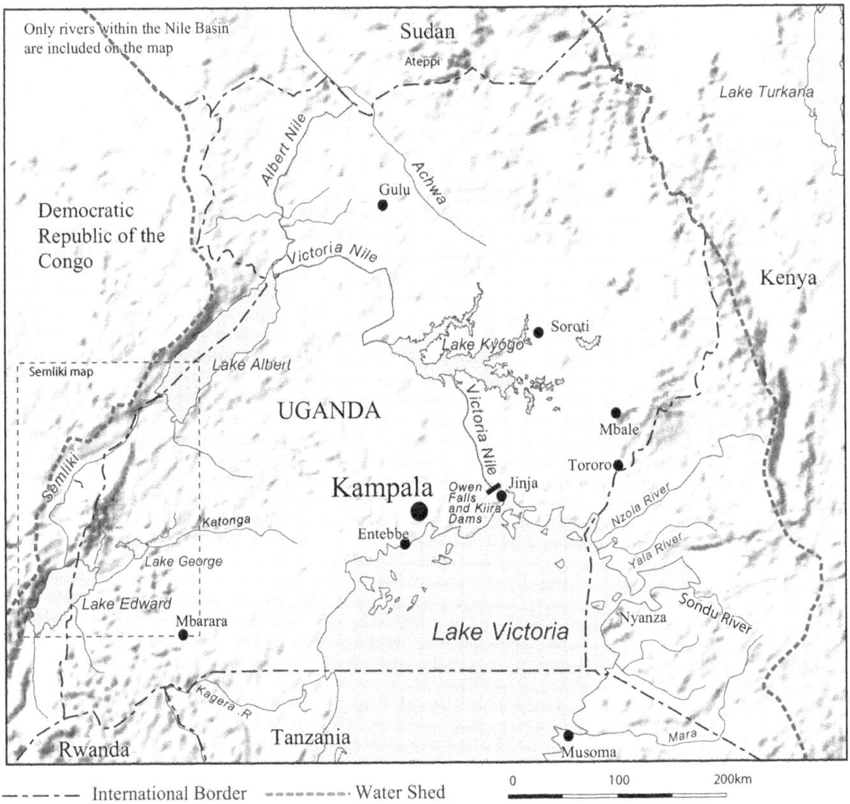

The boundaries and names shown and the designations used on this map do not imply official recognition or acceptance by the Nile Basin Research Programme

Figure 2.1 The Nile in the Great Lakes Region (Courtesy of the NBRP)

main course starts in Rwanda, and drains patches of territories in Burundi and Uganda. In fact, some authorities had alluded that the Kagera River, formed of three streams – the Nyavarongo drawing supplies from the high-ground rivulets adjoining the Lake Kivu, the Akanyaru, and the Ruvuvu in Burundi (with a still another most-southern tributary-the Lavironza at about 3° 45'S,) – is, should any of such rivers be so identified, the true remote source of the White Nile River system. Hurst furthermore remarked that if the principal source of a river is defined by reference to the quantity of its discharges, the Nyavarongo River should be regarded as the source of the river.[10] In contrast, however, William Garstin, a foremost authority on Nile hydrology and a long-time master of Egyptian irrigation had always maintained that the lake reservoir of the Victoria Nyanza is the true source of the White Nile.

10 H.E. Hurst (1927) 'The Lake Plateau Basin of the Nile', Ministry of Public Works, 2nd Part, Physical Department Paper No 23, Cairo, Government Press, p 15.

Hydrologic and physical features

The White Nile River chiefly draws its waters from Lake Victoria. In a series of falls and rapids, the river flows further west-north to the shallow swamps of Lake Kyoga forming no regular course, and passes through the Murchison Falls in central Uganda, ultimately draining in to the marshy area in the north-eastern end of Lake Albert. The river re-issues from a north-western spot of the Lake Albert, and proceeds northerly to the Bahr el Jebel in Southern Sudan. Although Lake Albert receives sizeable waters that make up the White Nile from Lake Victoria, nearly a third of its water is derived from a multitude of other direct and indirect streams, western and southerly effluents, most importantly from the Semilinki River, but also from streams (Mpologoma and Seziwa) flowing from Mount Elgon and the marshy Kyoga environs. The Semilinki River, collecting waters from rainfall and Lake Edward on the Uganda–Congo border (itself connected to Lake George by the Kazinga channel), traverses to the west of the Ruwenzori ranges and discharges to the southern tip of Lake Albert.

Consistent surveys and records had not been availed to gauge the relative contributions, but it is evident that in the upper-reaches of the Great Lakes region in central Africa, the White Nile River receives waters from more than just one source: the Lakes George–Edward–Albert and Semilinki River systems and adjacent runoffs to the left, and the Victoria–Kyoga basin. And as such, to draw on a catching expression by Samuel Baker, 'the Nile as it issues from the Albert Nyanza is the entire Nile, and prior to its birth from the Albert Lake, it is not the entire Nile.'[11]

Continuing a 225km journey from the northern ends of Lake Albert up to the Nimule town in the southern border of Sudan as Albert Nile, the broad swamp-framed river flows on a generally gentle slope. Beyond Nimule, it assumes the name Baher Al Jebel (Mountain River) and fast-flows to the south Sudanese plains, receiving additional discharges from tributary torrents on its way, the Asua, Kaia and Kit Rivers. The river empties its water to a marshland in the impassable Sudd region of southern Sudan. The Sudd constitutes a vast expanse of an over-flooded low-lying land, generally covering large tracts between Bor and Lake No, where the river is maintained to lose as much as half of the waters received when it crosses Mongalla in the far-south. A project to eliminate the losses by digging the Jonglei Diversion Canal across the eastern bank of Sudd region by joining the Bahr el Jebel at Jonglei with the Bahr el Zaraf, an upper right-bank tributary of the White Nile, near the confluence with the Sobat River had to be halted after two-thirds of the work was undertaken because of threats and attacks during the Sudanese civil war. At Lake No, where the marshes end, the Bahr El Jebel is joined by Bahr el Ghazal, another stream which derives its waters from a different but outsized catchment area along the south-western Congo–Sudan borders. Now called as the White Nile (Bahr el Abiad), it takes a sharp turn to the east, (re)joined first by Bahr el Zaraf, and a few miles downstream, by the Sobat River,[12] which draws its

11 Samuel W. Baker (1866) *The Albert Nyanza, Great Basin of the Nile and Explorations of the Nile Sources*, London, Macmillan, Chapter XVIII.

12 Jongei Investigation Team (1953) 'The Equatorial Nile Project and its Effects in the Sudan', *The Geographical Journal*, vol 119, no 1, p 34.

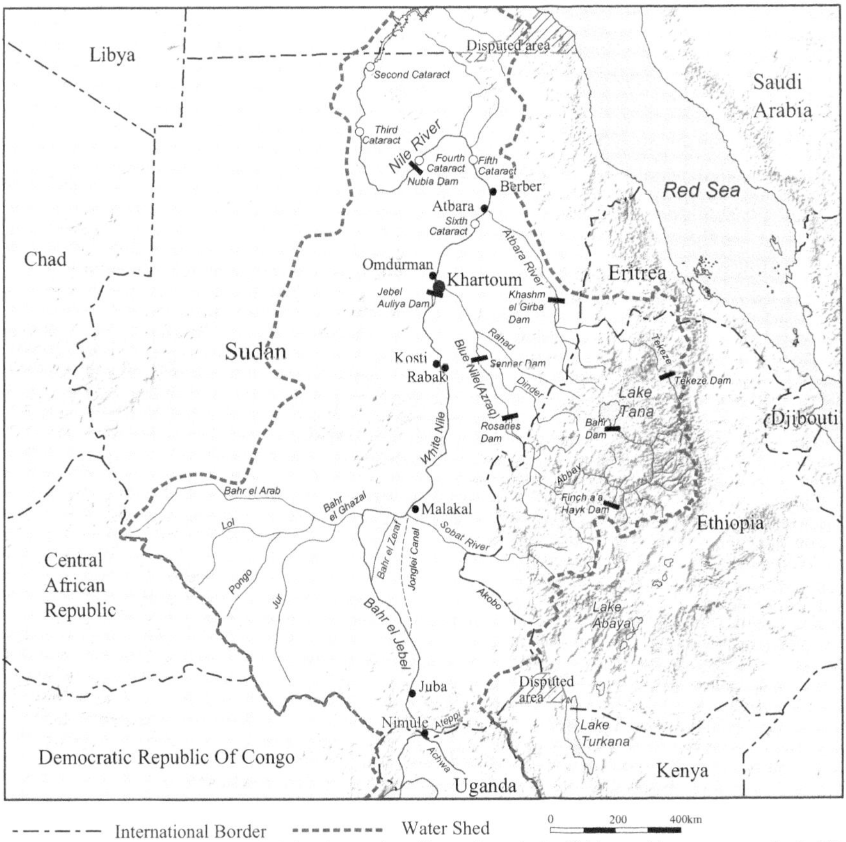

The boundaries and names shown and the designations used on this map do not imply official recognition or acceptance by the Nile Basin Research Programme

Figure 2.2 The Nile River system in the Sudan (courtesy of the NBRP)

stream from Pibor-Akobo and Baro rivers.[13] The White Nile derives its supply in about equal parts from the Sobat and from the Lake Plateau.[14]

Running just from the north-eastern edges of the huge swamps surrounded by the Bahr Al Gazal River (at Lake No), and joined further downstream by the river Sobat from Ethiopia, the White Nile proceeds to Khartoum, crossing the Jebel

13 The Sobat River, an important tributary of the White Nile, essentially receives its waters from the Baro River originating in south-western Ethiopia. Whereas the total annual discharge of the Pibor is 2.8 billion cubic meters per year (bcm/yr), the Baro branch discharges as much as 13bcm/yr at Gambella, but loses close to 4bcm/yr in the adjacent swamps, before it reaches the Sobat. Indeed, the Baro is one of the three Ethiopian head-streams that feed enormous waters to the White Nile and hence, the Nile proper.

A.B. Abalhoda (1993) 'Nile Basin General Information and Statistics', ICOLD 61st Executive Meeting, Cairo, p 13.

14 H.E. Hurst (1927) 'Progress in the Study of the Hydrology of the Nile in the Last Twenty Years', *The Geographical Journal*, vol 70, no 5, p 448.

Aulia Dam. Except for small portions of its course south of the Sobat mouth which run through a broad flat swamp and forest-boarded riverbank, the river navigates largely through well-defined channels.

The Blue Nile (Abay)-Tekeze/Atbara River systems: early and contemporary explorations

The second major sub-basin of the Nile River is the Blue Nile (Abay) River, also referred to as Bahr Al Arzak in Sudan. The source of this potent river had been shrouded by no lesser mysteries and ill-assorted accounts than its counterpart originating in the Lakes Region. However, in contrast to the interior Africa, Ethiopia's relative geographical proximity had permitted traces of European understanding of the river's sources long antedating the grand explorations along the Victoria Basin. A few thorough studies completed since the turn of the twentieth century had also been published.

The first extensively accounted expedition by a Scottish traveller James Bruce (1768–1773), which was pursued with a view to removing 'the opprobrium of travellers and geographers by discovering the sources of the Nile', established Gilgel Abay as the head stream of the Nile.[15] On 28 October 1770, Bruce marched to the northern shores of Lake Tana and passed to the Geeth, an eastern-most territory of the Agew in Gojjam. Instinctively, he discerned, the constituency on which he stood was the spot that lingered in perpetual concealment and identified through 'the protection of providence and . . . own intrepidity [he] had gained all over that were powerful, and all that were learned, since the remotest antiquity'.[16]

Yet, European penetration and understanding of the Lake Tana shores and Abay (Blue Nile) River long predated Bruce's advent at Gondar and Gojjam. Ethiopia's close relations with Portugal setting off at the height of the Portuguese colonial and trading empire had already resulted in a dispatch of a mission as early as in 1490. The intrusion was further bolstered by the subsequent arrival, in 1520, of a Portuguese embassy consisting of Don Rodriguez de Lima, Francisco Alvarez and Joao Bermudez. Several publications were printed shortly afterwards tendering an account of the Portuguese Father Francis Paez[17] as the first (European) to sight the most-remote sources of the Blue Nile River.[18]

15 James Bruce (1790) *Travels to Discover the Source of the Nile, in the Years 1768, 1769, 1770, 1771, 1772 and 1773*, London/Edinburgh, J Ruthven, vol I, p LXII.

Of course, Bruce's journey had been preceded by little valued adventures of the French Jacques Charles Poncet and Danish Fredrick Lewis Norden through segments of the Blue Nile.

16 James Bruce, *Travels to Discover the Source of the Nile, in the Years 1768, 1769, 1770, 1771, 1772 and 1773*, printed for P Wogan et al, vol IV, pp 270–1.

Bruce failed in the eyes of conformist Nile intellectuals of the time, who for no plausible hydraulic reasons perceived of Herodotus' and Ptolemy's conjectures of the *Nile sources* as merely referring to the sources of the White Nile in the equatorial region, and hence asserted Lake Victoria as the *true source* of the river.

17 Father Paez was perhaps the ablest Jesuit, excessively courted by the Ethiopian royals (1604–1622), he was able to convince Emperors Ze Dingil and Susenyos and many of their subjects to hold on to the Roman Catholic faith.

18 In sighting springs of the Abay River at Geeth, Kircher wrote that Pedro Paez transcribed :'together

Indeed, the most outlying fountainhead of the Abay (Blue Nile) River rises at an elevation of 1,850 meters above sea level, springing from the Gish Abay stream,[19] in the Sakela district, which, joined by a handful of other intermittent rivulets, makes up the Gilgel Abay River. Gilgel Abay enters to and its torrent distinguishably surges *over* the surface of Lake Tana, a 3,042sq.km wide fresh water lake in north-western Ethiopia, and ultimately issues in the marshy south-eastern shores of the Lake in Bahar Dar town as River Abay. Gilgel Abay is but only one of the multitude of feeder streams draining the Lake Tana.[20]

Despite a minuscule wave of early travels and explorations, a complete investigation of the Ethiopian Nile, its topography and tributaries had been conspicuously missing in the succeeding centuries and well in the twentieth century. In 1928, Major Cheesman, an eminent traveller along the Blue Nile courses of Ethiopia wrote: 'it seemed strange that one of the most famous of the rivers of the world, and one whose name was well-known to the ancients, should so long have been neglected in its upper waters'.[21]

Within a broader framework of British colonial strategies in Egypt and Sudan which first sought to assemble meteorological and hydrological specifics of the Nile River, and later, to secure concessions for constructing the Lake Tana Barrage in Ethiopia, a series of engineers had been sent to the district since as early as in 1906.[22]

Yet, a systemic synthesis of hydraulic information and firmer plans relating to the Blue Nile River crossed the threshold of the Ethiopian hydro-political discourse only belatedly, with the ascent to power of Ras Teferi both as Crown Prince and Regent of the Ethiopian Empire. Hence, only two decades since Emperor Menelik assented to a Nile accord with the British–Sudan in May 1902, the scale of hydrologic perceptions had gone through dramatic transformation in Ethiopia. The Blue Nile River and Lake Tana did not only constitute the mainstays of the government's endeavours for overall development, but the resources had also been crooked into vital tools of diplomatic manoeuvres in foreign policies and relationships. As early as in 1924–25, Ras Tefrei (later crowned as Emperor Haileselassie) had already started setting the development stage by employing, 'a Swiss hydrologist to survey the Lake Tana.'[23]

Yet, progresses remained fragmented; in the early years of the twentieth century, individual explorations remained the chief sources of information. While

with the king, I ascended the place . . . discovered first two round of mountains . . . and saw, with the greatest delight what neither Cyrus king of Persians, nor Cambyses, not Alexander the Great, nor the Great Julius Caesar could ever discover. J. Lobo (1789) *A Voyage of Father Jerome Lobo – A Portuguese Missionary*, S. Johnson translation, London p 209.

19 Federal Democratic Republic of Ethiopia (2006) 'Ethiopian Nile Irrigation and Drainage Project, Consultancy Service for Identification of Irrigation and Drainage Projects in the Nile Basin in Ethiopia', Final Report, Ministry of Water Resources, Addis Ababa, p 10.

20 Other important streams draining to Lake Tana include the Ribb, Megech and Gumara rivers.

21 Major R.E. Cheesman (1928) 'The Upper Waters of the Blue Nile', *The Geographical Journal*, vol 71, no 4, p 358.

22 Edward Ullendorf (1976) *The Autobiography of Emperor Haile Selassie I, My Life and Ethiopia's Progress 1892–1937*, Oxford, Oxford University Press, p 125.

23 Harold Marcus (1987) *Haileselassie I: The Formative Years 1892–1936*, Berkeley, University of California Press, p 72.

attempts by a chain of such navigators to trail the Blue Nile's whole course had met with limited degrees of success, the private enterprises proffered an unprecedented measure of geographical and hydrologic minutiae with regard to the sub-basin. On the main river, notable explorations included by Oscar T. Crosby (1901), Colonel Lewis (1903), H. Weld Blundell (1906), the W. N. Macmillan Expedition of B. H. Jensen (1902, 1906), R.E. Cheesman (1926), Herbert Rittingler (1962) and Arne Rubin (1965); Samuel Baker (1861) studied the Atbara-Tekeze-Angereb rivers and effluents draining to Tekeze River.

However, complete scientific mapping with respect of some of the major tributaries has continued to date.

River drainage

The Blue Nile River issues from the Lake Tana area. Only a small portion of its waters, 3.5 billion cubic meters per year (bcm/yr) to be precise, leaves the Lake's

The boundaries and names shown and the designations used on this map do not imply official recognition or acceptance by the Nile Basin Research Programme

Figure 2.3 The Nile River system in Ethiopia (courtesy of the NBRP)

narrow strip outlet in its south-eastern shore. A greater part of the 49.5bcm annual average that arrives at the Rosaries, near the Ethio-Sudanese border, is derived from its major left and right bank, and largely perennial tributaries in north and south western Ethiopia (including the Diddessa, Dabus, Fincha, Mugher and Beles) in the same vicinity.

Shortly after leaving Lake Tana on the shores of the town of Bahar Dar, the Blue Nile thrusts in to a steep gradient to a magnificent 45 meters long Tis Isat (Fire-Smoke) Falls, and its thunderous inundation passes through a narrow confine of an old bridge, probably built with the ingenuity of the Paez during the years of active Portuguese missionary activity in region. The river continues its south and north-westerly precipitous descent in the Ethiopian highland plateau through gradually increasing cleft thousands of meters deep, unravelling high-rising peaks on its sides. Through the gigantic deep gorge (the Abay Gorge), the Blue Nile eventually proceeds to the low-lying terrain along the Ethio-Sudanese border, covering roughly 992km. On its course north of the Rosaries in Sudan across the border, the river is joined by highly seasonal runoffs from two small tributaries of considerable volume, the Dinder and Rahad, whose headwaters are also located in Ethiopia.[24]

Crossing the Sudanese border, and now called Bahr Al Arzak, the clear (and when in flood, the sand-loaded red-brownish) river flows north; shortly north of Khartoum, it flows together with the greenish White Nile River from the equatorial region, enclosing just below the junction the grandiose Gezira schemes of irrigation. The two combined river systems constitute the main Nile.

The Nile River proper

Leaving Khartoum, 310km down the stream, the Nile is joined by the third and last powerful tributary from another major sub-basin originating in Ethiopia – the Tekeze-Atbara river system, which collects most of its waters from the Ethiopian highlands in Gondar and Lasta regions to the north and north-west of the Lake Tana area. The Atbara and Tekeze flow in rapid velocity westward to Sudan, confluence at Tomat, shortly past the Ethio-Sudanese border and head north-westward to north of Khartoum as river 'Atbara' to join the main Nile at Atbarah City. The Tekeze (also called Setit in Eritrea) makes up a small section of the Ethio-Eritrean border across the peripheral districts of Humera and Teseney. In terms of yearly flow to the main Nile in Sudan, the Tekeze River is among the most-potent rivers in the basin, although seasonal fluctuations affect its input significantly.[25]

From the Sudanese capital, the river pours through narrow valleys, cliffs, barren lands and about six cataracts northwards in Sudan and Egypt, without receiving

24 The two rivers add up 4bcm/yr of water to the yields of the Blue Nile in Sudan so that the Blue Nile's total annual discharge between Sennar and Khartoum reaches 54bcm/yr, while the measure remains 48bcm/yr at Aswan. Abalhoda (1993), note 13, p 14.

25 The average total discharge of the Tekeze-Atbara river systems is computed at 12bcm/yr at Aswan.

floods from any tributary. In fact, the Nile joins Egypt as Lake Nasser, a huge non-natural lake extending over a ravine of about 480km wide between the Nubia region in North Sudan and the High Aswan Dam. It flows through the Aswan Dam; north of Cairo, the river splits in to two of the remaining distributaries: the Rosetta and Damietta, adjoining a vast triangular land coated by fertile river sediments over the centuries, called Delta, according to Strabo, on account of the similarity of their shapes. The *little* water left from regulated storages at the dams, domestic and industrial consumptions and perennial agriculture eventually drains to the Mediterranean Sea.

Seasonal flood regimes of the White and Blue Nile river systems

That the Nile traverses colossal lengths from its headwaters in the Equatorial Plateau and Ethiopian Highlands down the Delta region in Egypt connotes that the river advances through hugely varied landscapes, accommodating a cross-section of weather conditions and affected by variations in climate, recurring droughts, warming and evaporation. Each phenomenon has bearings on the availability and variability of the annual and seasonal flood regimes in the basin.

To date, no comprehensive investigation has been undertaken covering the whole Nile basin. For centuries, the annual inundation of the Nile sustained thriving civilizations and development only in the lower-most courses, explaining why conjectures with regard to the nature and origins of the river have been of exacting concern to the Egyptian society since the earliest centuries. While the Nilometer was put to utility since antiquity and moderately finer records of the river's attributes had been maintained from time to time,[26] thorough studies were availed only at the turn of the twentieth century. Largely commissioned by the British colonial administration in Egypt and Sudan, the latest investigations revealed enhanced scientific information regarding drainage of the basin, including water discharges at different spots and volumes lost in swamps, evaporation and transpiration.

Bearing for variations in seasons, the flood and drought years as well as the series of years picked for computation, the average discharge of the Nile River course has generally been recorded about 84bcm/yr. During the period extending over 1869–1945, the lowest and highest flows had ranged between 45 and 137bcm/yr; between 1908 and 1945, the mean annual inundation was 81bcm; and during 1963–1991, it had varied between 32 and 140bcm/yr measured at Aswan.

The subject of the relative significance of the White Nile, Blue Nile, Baro-Akobo-Sobat and the Tekeze-Atbara river systems was initially settled when, in 1902–1903, Sir Henry Lyons sent a team with current meters to measure the

26 Some of the earliest records dating back to three millennia had been recorded on rocks of cataracts, notably at Semma, south of the Wadi Halfa, where the river has eaten through a rock barrier on which about 1800BC a number of high watermarks were cut. Nilometers were established in various places along the river . . . and the Roda Nilometer in Cairo, first erected about 620AD, still exists and has been in continuous use . . . until the last century when readings on the a modern gauge began; Hurst (1936), note 9.

discharge of the rivers.[27] The findings, by William Garstin, of the most scrupulous investigation on the precise hydrologic association of the White and Blue Nile flood systems had been published in 1909.

The most widely established account holds that the White Nile, including its Sobat River tributary mostly gushing from Ethiopia, provides for two-sevenths of the total waters received at Aswan, while the Blue Nile and the Tekeze-Atbara river systems cover four-sevenths and one-seventh respectively.

The Blue Nile sub-basin is responsible for significant proportions of the mean annual floods of the Nile arriving in Egypt. The river collects about 49.5bcm/yr of waters from its own drainage in the highland plateaus and its tributaries in Ethiopia, and from the Lake Tana; the greater part joins the Blue Nile just between Lake Tana and the Ethio-Sudanese border. Its mean annual yield at Aswan is however 48bcm/yr, losing certain volumes along its trail.

Ethiopia's contribution through the three head streams, the Baro-Akobo-Sobat, the Blue Nile, and the Atbara-Tekeze basins stands at 68.7bcm/yr of waters at Aswan, or 82 percent of the entire mean annual flow of the Nile arriving in Egypt.[28]

The White Nile, the Blue Nile and the Tekeze-Atbara river systems display a great deal of seasonal interdependence; their annual floods not only rise and fall at different seasons of the year, they also fluctuate at different paces. This verity affects their relative *seasonal* contributions at any given period of the year.

There is no a necessary correlation between meteorological events that present crucial rains to the White Nile on the one hand, and the Blue Nile-Atbara-Tekeze river systems on the other. The Nile floods are affected by climatic conditions in two important regions of the basin: the Northern and north-western Ethiopian highlands and the Equatorial Lakes Plateau.

While deviations remain between the recorded outflows of individual years in both the Lakes Region and Ethiopian sources, the Blue Nile and Tekeze-Atbara river systems receive considerable rainfall from the south-west tropical monsoons in the summer and trivial north-east monsoon precipitations during the winter. Comparatively, they also feature a higher seasonal flood regime. Hence, they swell to torrents, discharging sizeable proportions of their waters just during the peak season – the Ethiopian *kiremt* (rainy) months, generally lasting between July and October, but starting to receive rain as early as in May, and gradually declining after November. While the two river systems supply an average annual flood of some 60bcm of Nile waters, hence accounting for about 71.4 percent of the total

27 Hurst (1936), note 9.

28 Ethiopian Government studies put the annual runoff of the Blue Nile (Abay) River at 49bcm/yr; average downstream contributions by Dinder, Galegu and Rahad rivers in Sudan, whose headwaters are located in Ethiopia, was computed 5bcm/yr. The Blue Nile basin in Ethiopia contributes 62 percent of the Nile total at Aswan, and together with Baro-Akobo and Tekeze river systems, Ethiopia accounts for 86 percent of the annual runoff at Aswan. The study did not address the hydrologic features of the White Nile.

Federal Democratic Republic of Ethiopia (1999) 'Abay River Integrated Development Master Plan Project', Ministry of Water Resources, Addis Ababa, Phase 3, vol 1, p11.

mean annual discharge of the 84 bcm arriving at Aswan in any normal flood year, much of the inundation, about 80 percent of the annual downpour to be precise, comes in just a few months. The flow dwindles significantly during the low- or no-rain months. In fact, in April when the flood volume is the lowest, the Blue Nile discharges as little as 1/45th of the deluge it carries in peak season,[29] accounting for a minimal volume of the water reaching at Aswan during this time of year. The White Nile provides almost all the season's waters, whereas the Tekeze-Atbara diminishes to oblivion, turning in to a mere pond of water in certain spots of the riverbed.

Before the construction of the Aswan High Dam providing for an over-year storage facility holding the floods until required for irrigation, the kiremt downpour from the Ethiopian highlands provided more than sufficient waters for basin agriculture downstream. Hence, excluding for the meagre proportions retained through small-scale control works along the lower reaches of the basin, a good deal of the surplus had to pour to the sea every year.

On the other hand, the rain pattern within 3° North and South of the Equator is extended well over much of the year. This explains why, apart from the regulating roles of the lakes and the seasonal swamps along the river's banks, the White Nile presents a steady supply in the upper and middle-reaches of the river throughout the year. It receives rain between January and June, but the peak and lowest flows come in March and August. Hurst explained the variability in the White Nile river system by illustrating that the White Nile at the tail of the swamps, before it receives the Sobat, fluctuates only by about one-sixth throughout the year, and along with Sobat, contributes during its peak seasons slightly more than twice as much as the Blue Nile and Atbara together.[30]

Indeed, a great deal of the variation in the White Nile flows has been caused by the Baro-Akobo-Sobat River system, which receives its highest floods in August and the lowest in March. The natural phenomenon that causes this seasonal swapping of water supplies is indescribably stunning.

The seasonal attribute and quantum of discharge of the two Niles would appear to validate one important postulate: whereas the Blue Nile and Tekeze-Atbara rivers continue to deliver about 71.4 percent of the total average yearly Nile flow, conversely, the White Nile, including the Sobat River, makes available about 70 percent of the hitherto crucial supply between January and July.[31]

29 Conversely, Ethiopian Government studies revealed that of the total annual discharge of 49.4bcm crossing Sudan, the *lowest* flow registered in April is 2.5 percent of the *highest* flow in August, with a 1/40th variability.

Federal Democratic Republic of Ethiopia (1999), note 28, p 11.

30 H.E. Hurst (1948) 'Major Irrigation Projects on the Nile', *Civil Engineering and Public Works Review*, vol 43, no 507, p 451.

31 Hurst, who had once been Director General of the Physical Department of Egypt and a traveller along sectors of the Nile Basin, presented a different account. His Nile chart explained that two-thirds of the total discharge of the Nile passes in August–October and two-thirds (66 percent) of this portion comes from the Blue Nile, while the remainder is divided approximately equally between the White Nile and Tekeze-Atbara.

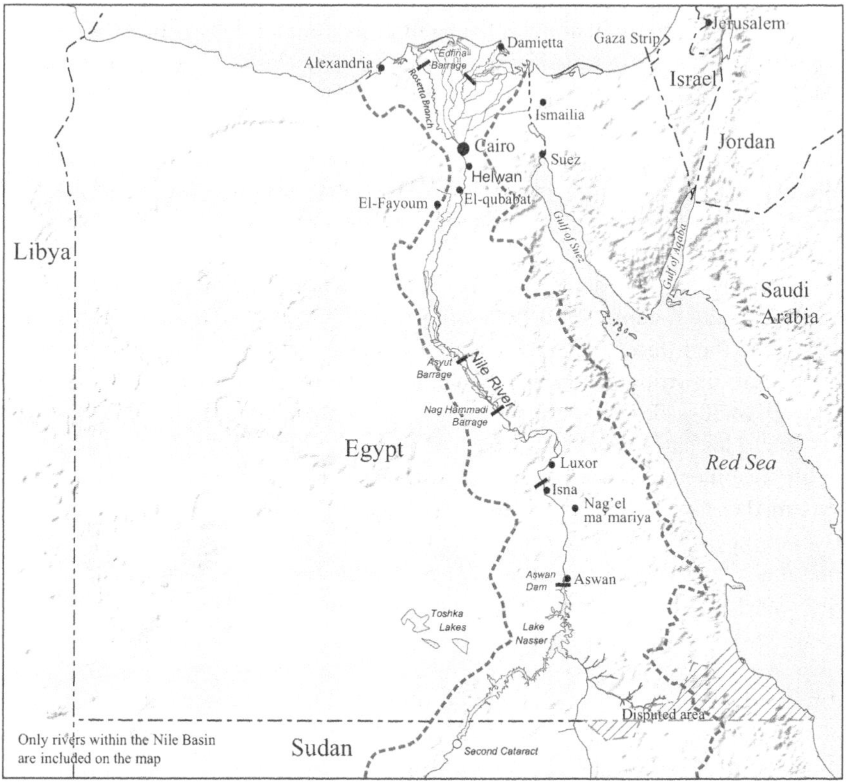

The boundaries and names shown and the designations used on this map do not imply official recognition or acceptance by the Nile Basin Research Programme

Figure 2.4 The Nile River Basin in Egypt (courtesy of the NBRP)

Yet, since the construction of the Aswan High Dam, it would appear, this *seasonality* of the flow regimes has ceased to affect meaningfully the relative significance of the two river systems. The institution of the new water control edifice, with a capacity of holding more than twice the average annual floods of the Nile, did not only put an end to dependence on traditional flood irrigation practised for

On the other hand, in April and May when the Nile is at its lowest, the White Nile (of course, including the Baro-Akobo-Sobat river system) contributes about 85 percent of the total discharge, and the Blue Nile the remainder.

Tvedt's account presented an entirely different picture of the relative discharges of the two river systems. His statements relied mostly on investigations undertaken by British engineers of the colonial periods. Hence, the White Nile's contribution to the total flow regime was computed as standing between 10 and 20 percent but between January and June/July, the mean total discharge of the main river at Aswan was about 13.8bcm/yr. of which the White Nile contributed 10bcm/yr. and the Blue Nile (referring to Abay and the Atbara-Tekeze) 3.8bcm/yr; Terje Tvedt (2004) *The River Nile in the Age of the British, Political Ecology and the Quest for Economic Power*, London/New York, I.B. Tauris, p 69.

centuries, it also embanked the whole waters of both the White Nile and the Blue Nile-Tekeze-Atbara river systems.

The increased quantity and securely regulated supplies enabled intensive expansion of cultivable lands regardless of the rain patterns or the seasonality of flows in the upper-reaches of the rivers.

Most importantly, however, this development led to the conclusion that today, the relative hydrological import of the White and Blue Nile rivers is essentially a coefficient of the aggregate volumes each river system provisions in the course of the year, hence setting Ethiopia's sources on a grander scale of hydrologic prominence.

3 The Nile Basin

Development patterns and projections

Introduction

The Nile River had never had comparable impacts on the lives of its diverse communities. True, agriculture continues to compose a vital constituent of the social and economic setting of all the basin states. Yet, institutional and hydrologic infrastructures in Sudan and Egypt, on the one hand, and the rest of the upstream Nile persisted to display conspicuous gaps in terms of organization and development. A mix of historical, diplomatic and economic factors coalesced to direct the commissioning of water resources utilization initiatives solely along the downstream reaches of the basin, leaving important legal consequences.

This part would *reconstruct* and *reflect* on the history of major water resources development patterns and projections in selected constituencies of the Nile basin region. The objective of this presentation is to depict a glowing perspective of the imbalance in the levels of resource utilization and to afford explicit set of facts eventually employed in the juridical analyses of Chapters 10 and 11.

River resource developments: the background

Several factors could be recited as accounting for the lopsided pattern of water resources development in the Nile basin. Foremost among others is Egypt's inimitable civilization, which, coupled with its vulnerable dependence on Nile waters in catering for domestic, agricultural and industrial stipulations, has given way to vital innovations in irrigation and water management techniques that over time intensified the yields of the river.

More importantly, though, British colonial policies and the legal snag it orchestrated may be considered as the most swaying rationales for the virtual underdevelopment of water control works in the upper-reaches of the river. Great Britain carried out river development policies that accorded loftier strategic significance to the economic interests and wellbeing of two downstream constituencies: Egypt and Sudan. Stirred by imperial visions that served geopolitical considerations of the time and the economic stakes of the British cotton concerns, a string of hydraulic infrastructures were initiated and instituted in the lower-reaches of the basin with a faintly corresponding contemplation for the prospective requirements of Ethiopia, and indeed, the upper basin states.

From the outset, the colonial administration viewed the interests of the Nile basin states as entirely distinct. Congo's stakes were assessed as confined to the amount of compensation ensuing from a possible realization of Nile control works potentially flooding parts of its territory; Uganda's interest had been limited to 'the development of hydro-electric power without affecting the flow of the Nile'. Likewise, Ethiopia's only takings in the resource was generally forecasted as the 'development of hydro-power for which there is no market in the near future', hence directing British water diplomacy to 'the amount of money it [Ethiopia] can secure from Egypt and Sudan in return for the permission to construct the Lake Tana Dam'.[1]

The specific economic logic behind British policies of the time had been premised on safeguarding the cotton trade which then constituted 'the largest manufacturing industry in the world', the spine of its trading enterprise, with 'about 10 million of its population directly dependent . . . for their daily bread'.[2] The sector needed to diversify its supply base for the raw material, and hence looked for productive openings in the irrigational fields of Egypt and Sudan. In course of time, a mammoth stream of British capital, technology and irrigational investments had not only instituted a highly organized physical infrastructure, in the subsequent decades, but it also set in motion a psychosomatic momentum for increased control and management of the river's resources.[3]

Since the collapse of colonial empires in Africa and until the late 1990's, the upper Nile region had barely witnessed significant developments in water resources schemes. A complex web of legal, financial and political tribulation persisted to stall growth.

Yet, recent changes in the political, economic and demographic landscapes of the region had tended to precipitate a greater degree of involvement of the stakeholders in resources of the Nile, increasingly eying on the resource's development potentials.

Hydraulic works: Egypt and Uganda

As noted previously, the Nile flows had fluctuated over the years and seasons, responding to weather cycles both in the Ethiopian highland plateaus and the Great Lakes region. During peak seasons, the surface water flow of the river had for years surpassed the claimed, if not acknowledged needs of Egypt and Sudan, with about 32bcm of Nile floods pouring to the Sea every year. During the low seasons, however, the two states had always faced water deficits.

1 Cairo to Foreign Office, 16 July 1949, FO 371:73619.

2 FBOR File 1, London.

3 On one particular occasion, British Secretary of State for Colonies remarked that Great Britain deserved better credit and needed to portray its light of achievement over the bushel for 'it was British brains, British Engineering skill, British products, and British organization and management that had made it possible to harness the Nile'. Minutes on conversation with the Secretary of State, 31 September 1949, FO 141/1414.

To overcome the negative effects of seasonal fluctuations and secure a steady provision of water throughout the year, several hydraulic structures had been contemplated during the past century, mostly commissioned by and in Egypt.

A parched land with a mean annual rainfall barely passing 18mm,[4] Egyptian preoccupation has resolutely focused on the optimal utilization of the Nile waters since the days of King Menes about 3200BC. Indeed, the Egyptian socio-political establishment has been fixated with the defence of two vital columns of the national water security strategy – a perpetual possession of the Nile floods historically withdrawn and the institution of water conservation works in the upper and lower-reaches of the river with a view to securing stable flows during all seasons.

In Egypt, the ancient system of irrigation had relied on the *basin* system where large areas of land had been enclosed by embankments and canals dug taking waters at points far south of the areas they were intended to serve, and where the water level in the river would naturally be higher than *ex-adverso* of their banks.[5] This traditional practice continued until the 1820s when the cultivation of cotton and sugar cane was first introduced, obliging the conversion of some basin lands into *perennial* irrigation.[6] In the same century, the Egyptian Viceroy of Albanian decent, Mohamed Ali Pasha introduced the perennial system and initiated a pioneering hydraulic structure on the Nile: the Delta Barrage. It was built to raise the level of water behind the barrages during the low period.[7] Thus, when the river subsided during the summer season, gate after gate was closed to keep a more constant supply in the channels that cut across the Delta area.[8]

Great Britain occupied Egypt in 1882; in tune with the local and imperial exigencies of the time, the British exerted substantial efforts to transform and expand the water infrastructure and narrow down the gap between water supply and demand. To suit a rolling local economy and sustain pressing demands of the growing population as well as the agricultural community, Great Britain undertook successive investments in the water sector. Institutions primarily entrusted with irrigational, hydrological and meteorological services had been set up, and meteorological stations and river gauges were installed across several spots of the basin.

Yet, at the turn of the twentieth century, it was evident that 'despite the great effort put in to it, [the water control system] was simply not enough to meet growing demands, with grave economic consequences'.[9] The shortfall distressed agricultural, industrial, and domestic requirements.

4 The total annual rainfall in Egypt is a mere 1bcm/yr and can only withdraw up to 7.5bcm/yr of ground waters.

5 H. Weld (1928) 'The Blue Nile and Irrigation', *Journal of Royal African Society*, vol 27, no 106, pp 97–103.

6 W. K. Shenouda (1993) 'The High Aswan Dam – A Vital Achievement, Fully Controlled Symposium', ICOLD, 61st Executive Meeting, Cairo.

7 Dante A. Caponera (1993) 'Legal Aspects of Transboundary River Basins in the Middle East, the Al Asi (Orentes), the Jordan and the Nile', *Natural Resources Journal*, vol 33, p 652.

8 Terje Tvedt (2004) *The River Nile in the Age of the British, Political Ecology and the Quest for Economic Power*, London/New York, I.B.Tauris, p 20.

9 Tvedt (2004), note 8, p 23.

In consequence, a provisional solution was implemented based on investigations initiated by Collin Scott Moncrieff, the first colonial head of the Egyptian Irrigation Service.[10] The old Aswan Reservoir was built on the first cataract of the Nile between 1898 and 1902 to hoard 1bcm/yr of water for dry season irrigation.[11] Pictured 'as a victory of British political, economic, and technological might', the dam was purported as 'the biggest reservoir of its kind in the world and one of the soundest projects in the history of water control, [but] failed to store sufficient water demanded in the summer.'[12]

This development was attended by the strengthening of the Delta Barrage and the building of other barrages at Asyut in 1902, feeding the Ibrahimia canal in summer – one of the biggest canals in the world, and the Esna in 1908, which raised the river level and thus provided command of other canals. The old Aswan Dam, no longer operated as a reservoir, had been successively heightened between the years 1907–1912 and 1929–1933 to increase its capacity to 2.5[13] and 5bcm/yr respectively.

Over the years, though, Egyptian agricultural development and water consumption grew steadily. In 1920, the total yearly requirement for Egypt was 30bcm/yr at Aswan, or 50bcm/yr at Khartoum.[14] In 1995, the figure surged to 62bcm/yr of Nile floods, watering more than three million hectares of irrigation land and increased to almost 70bcm/yr today.[15]

As the need for more water increased, between the 1930s and 1950s, a series of plans were floated and the construction of over-year and annual reservoirs was either initiated or implemented.[16] While solely in pursuit of its compelling stakes in downstream irrigation, in the 1940s, Great Britain also considered a whole set of Nile water conservation and storage schemes on a grandiose scale, projecting to achieve full development of the river in various parts of the region. Lake Victoria, Lake Albert and Lake Tana were identified as keystone sites of hydraulic works that would assure all foreseeable requirements of the lower basin states.

As a result, in 1945, the colonial administration in Egypt, under the technical counsel of Hurst, proposed the *Century Storage Scheme*, very much in harmony with an earlier scientific presentation assembled by Black, Samaiko and Hurst himself on future conservation works affecting the Nile and Great Lakes region.[17]

10 Weld (1928), note 5, pp 97–103.
11 Caponera (1993), note 7, p 652.
12 Tvedt (2004), note 8, p 102.
13 Caponera (1993), note 7, p 652.
14 Caponera (1993), note 7.
15 See discussions in Chapter 11.
16 Including the Nag Hammadi Barrage in 1930, (replaced in 2006 with a new structure that combines higher storage and hydropower generation and a water diverting canal, hence enabling massive cropping of land round the year); the heightening of the Aswan Dam in 1933 (5.3 bcm); new strengthening of the Assuit Dam in 1938; the construction of the new Delta Barrage in 1940; the strengthening of the Esna Barrage in 1947; and erection of the Edifna Barrage in 1951; Caponera (1993), note 7.
17 In Volume VII of the Nile Basin, Hurst, Black and Samaiko, then working under the Egyptian Physical Department, published an ambitious scheme for the control of the Nile. The Annual Storage was hence designed to hold back water for part of the year in order to release more during the timely period when it is required in Egypt, where as the Century Storage had been planned to give a very large reserve in order to overcome the difficulties caused by a series of abnormally dry or wet years.

Among others, the new development chart projected to raise a dam at Nimule in Sudan, increase the level of Lake Albert to a maximum of 25 meters, regulate its mean annual discharges, store main Nile waters and prevent occasional floods.[18] Attended by adjunct conservatory works in the Sudd swamps (through the Jonglei Canal), an over-year storage at Lake Tana in Ethiopia and seasonal storages along the Tekeze-Atbara River, the plan also aimed to store up to 155bcm/yr of waters at Lake Albert, lying over a total of 8750sq.km of space – a volume only slightly less than the capacity storage of the High Aswan Dam today.

In essence, the grand design merely safeguarded entrenched downstream interests. Operationally, the tail of the Blue Nile flood would have been captured by the then existing Low Aswan Dam; storage in Lake Albert would be used to supplement the low summer flows in the main Nile, after the majority of the Blue Nile waters had flowed into the Mediterranean.[19]

This development on the White Nile river course, along with a parallel enterprise proposed for the Lake Tana in Ethiopia, hoped to capture surplus waters in years of good supply and hence permit a steady discharge from year to year. This would compensate deficits during seasons of low supply and satisfy all prospective water requirements of Egypt.

Nevertheless, ecological implications, financial considerations and intricate rivalries within the colonial establishment itself mired effective realization of the sketch. Unlike its post-independence beleaguered posture, Uganda had then been at the centre of the hydropolitical row, occuring in the forefront of the diplomatic hassle.

Long before it attained a self-governing status, the British Colonial Government in Uganda under Sir John Hall had consistently portrayed unsympathetic consideration to schemes that inclined to shore-up downstream interests without corresponding gains for the Great Lakes region. Hence, when the Egyptian request for the grandeur scheme was introduced, requiring closer collaboration with the states of Ethiopia and Sudan, its repercussion was subjected to wide-ranging censor and eventually rejected by Uganda. In official lines, Uganda explained the unrevised implementation of the proposal would cause inundation of large tracts of land used for the maintenance of its fast increasing population and compromising the power-generating potentials of its various waterfalls.[20] In reality, though, the concerns were but reiterations of a bitter complaint addressed by the Governor to the British Secretary of Colonies only a year earlier over the lopsided British policies across its African possessions.[21]

18 Memorandum on future conservation works, October 1945, CO 537/1521.

19 The Governor of Uganda to the Secretary of State for Colonies, Egyptian Proposals for Water Storage in Lake Albert, 15 April 1947, FO141/1191.

20 Dale Whittington (2004) 'Visions of Nile Basin Development', *Water Policy*, vol 6, p 4.

21 The Governor of Uganda to the Secretary of State for Colonies, Egyptian Proposals for Water Storage in Lake Albert, 15 April 1947, FO141/1191, p 2.

In his telegraphic mail, Governor Hall warned the British Government not 'to take up a *non possums* attitude' advocating Egyptian interests and should he be forced to accept the Albert Dam scheme, he insisted that the British Government must seek 'to relax clause II of the 1928 Agreement to allow some water to be withdrawn for irrigation etc. purposes by the East African Territories'.

However, the Governor of Uganda realized the limits of his resistance within the complex structure of the British colonial authority in the Basin. Hence, 'constant with the safeguarding of the rights of the population of Uganda', he counter-proposed a new scheme, a blue print of an early sketch of the 'Equatorial Nile Project'[22] that he judged would aid Egypt achieve analogous objectives with a much lesser outlay, while causing negligible nuisance to Ugandan interests.[23]

His new development chart, which placed all works within the Ugandan territory, hence affording Uganda greater hydropolitical prominence, outlined the establishment of 'a hydro electric power on the Victoria Nile at the Owen Falls, about 3 kms downstream of the Rippon Falls'. Likewise, it permitted Egypt 'to make use of Lake Victoria (not Albert) to store 120 *milliard* (billion) cubic meters for the purpose of the Century Storage.'[24] The counter-offer permitted the use of Lake Albert simply as a balancing reservoir, with a limited storage capacity not exceeding 16bcm/yr of waters. Likewise, it provided for the stationing of an Egyptian resident engineer near control works on the Albert Nile and the Owen Falls Dam to supervise the release of waters through the installations, subject to the water discharge requirements of the Ugandan power development scheme. As the prime beneficiary, Egypt ought to cover the entire engineering costs of the dam at Owen Falls and all incidental expenses related to the institution of the huge storage, while Uganda shall bear expenses associated with the powerhouse, including the turbine dam and hydro-electrical equipment.

Following a series of diplomatic discourses between Great Britain and Egypt, the parties eventually sanctioned the Lake Victoria storage scheme and the plan for dam construction and power production at the Owen Falls, subject to conditions and with certain adaptations. The Egyptian Parliament set aside £E4.5 million as cost of the dam and buildings at Owen Falls and compensation for consequential damages necessitated by the use of Lake Victoria as storage; expenses relating to the remaining elements of the scheme were estimated at £E7.5, payable by the Ugandan Government.[25]

As a result of this arrangement, water facilities that preserved the long-term water security concern of the states of Egypt and Sudan, the accord foresaw, would have entirely depended on reservoirs situated in remote territories and, indeed, quite beyond their jurisdictions.

Sir John Hathorn Hall to Secretary of the State of Colonies, Lake Albert Dam 12 May 1946, CO 536/217.

22 The Equatorial Nile Project contemplated to make possible 'the storage and conservation of the waters of the Equatorial Nile for the purpose of irrigation and hydro electric power'. The objective was meant to be realized through the construction of combined regulating dams, hydropower stations and canal systems across the Victoria Nile, Albert Nile, Lake Kyoga and the swamps in the Sudd. Outline of the Equatorial Nile Project, 4 December 1948, FO 371/69233.

23 Sir John Hathorn Hall to Secretary of the State of Colonies, Lake Albert Dam 12 May 1946, CO 536/217.

24 The Governor of Uganda to the Secretary of State for Colonies (1947), note 20.

25 Draft of a Note to Be addressed by His Majesty's Ambassador to the Egyptian Minister for Foreign Affairs, April 1949, FO 371/73616.

An impressive but thorny undertaking, several of the project's essentials never saw the light of the day, with the exception of the Owen Falls Power House scheme[26] and meagre water conservatory works undertaken along the Jonglei Canal in the Sudd. Since then, Uganda's Nile water resources development enterprise had remained far from impressive.

Naturally, the imposing scale of the venture would have called for a stable and dependable diplomatic relationship between the parties affected, an enormous fiscal facility and detailed technical investigations. Moreover, although its interests were modestly accommodated, Sudan's increased propensity to integrate the Lake Tana Project with the impending proposals for the Lakes Region, and Great Britain's colonial strategy that held the plan as a pawn in its perturbed political relations with Egypt contributed to the eventual stalling of the venture.

In any event, Egypt, the principal beneficiary and close associate in the management, financing and execution of the schemes had had legitimate fears not to be easily swayed by political wrangling with Great Britain regarding the execution of the Lake Tana and the equatorial area projects. Considering the long years of troubled Anglo-Egyptian colonial bond, the construction of strategically vital reservoirs in remote regions where Egypt had neither political nor physical control, it could be reasoned, would only have afforded Great Britain greater leverages over Egyptian economy and domestic governance. As a result, sincere Egyptian commitment in executing the technical accords had always been less forthcoming.

Because of these intricacies, a milestone plan which could have transformed the nature and intensity of basin-wide strategic associations and indeed the water politics of the Nile as we know it today was aborted. In contrast to British imperial ideas of the 1940s, the subsequent decades witnessed a growing Egyptian nationalism that sought to formulate growth strategies on a more secure water resources base and hence place its water policy on an entirely distinct platform.

In this spirit, in 1955, the Egyptian government undertook the study and construction of the engineering masterpiece, the 'Sadd el Aali Dam' (Aswan High Dam), with the finance and technological assistance of Soviet Russia. The landmark edifice not only replaced the contemplations for over-year storage under the Century Storage Scheme,[27] but it also changed quite fundamentally the legal and hydropolitical configuration in the region, reinvigorating Egypt's age-old proprietary perceptions. The dam laid a keystone for new water resources development perspectives that portrayed a stronger downstream orientation.

26 After a series of failing diplomacy for a joint implementation of the projects, Uganda had no option but to proceed with its own hydro-electric scheme, without prejudicing the future execution of the remaining elements of the equatorial projects. The final agreement for the construction of the Owen Falls Dam between Great Britain and Egypt was effected through Notes Exchanged in May 1949; the text of the treaty was presented before the House of Commons on 19 May1949.

27 Today, Whittington argued, the Century Storage Scheme remains the only explicit basin-wide plan for the development of the Nile, and as such, exerts a powerful influence on the collective consciousness of the Nile development planners. Whittington (2004), note 19, p 6.

When the construction was completed in 1970, the dam was measured 4.5km long across the river's path, and rose over 100 meters off the ground. It created the second biggest artificial lake in the world, the Lake Nasser.[28] It stretched between the northern tip of Sudan previously inhabited by the Nubians and southern Egypt, with a reservoir capacity of 168.9bcm/yr of waters.

While alluvial soil from Ethiopia continued to pile up in the lake increasing soil salinity, the dam averted the annual cycle of damage caused by the overflowing summer deluge; but, more importantly, the dam embanked enough waters to permit transformation from flood irrigation as Egypt had practised for centuries to a modern perennial irrigation. Using canals branching from the lake that provides stable supplies, crops have now been cultivated more than once in any given year and agricultural development expanded beyond the narrow strips of the Nile valley through the reclamation of barren lands. Recurrent droughts upstream ceased to pose as a huge a threat as in the pre-dam decades. In fact, when the dam had registered its record low level as the result of successive low rain-yielding seasons in the Ethiopian highlands (1980–87) with dreading famine in the aftermath, the reservoir forestalled analogous dangers in Egypt; the drought's effect was hardly felt in the irrigational fields.

Apart from irrigation agriculture, the dam also provided half of Egypt's hydro-electric power supply using a powerhouse with an initial capacity of 2100MW/yr.[29]

In 1991, Egypt and Ethiopia, potential woes in prospective Nile water development works, signed a cooperative accord. The two states agreed to define their rights in accordance with the fundamental principles of international watercourses law. The bilateral convent notwithstanding, though, Egypt foresaw that the ultimate security of its entitlements lay in the volume of waters it withdraws from time to time and the facts of dependency created on the ground.

Hence, in the last decades of the twentieth century, Egypt embarked on the implementation of contentious development works on a *unilateral* basis. Protected by reserves of the Aswan High Dam, a policy of horizontal expansion had been put in place since 1982 where new, large-scale agricultural schemes were initiated by reclaiming tracts of desert lands beyond the fertile Nile valley. Analogous plans were also instituted in 1997 which aimed at developing about 1.4 million hectares (3.4–3.5 million feddans) of land up to the year 2017.[30] Two landmark projects dragged for years in the Sinai and along the Toshka depression.

28 So impressed, Soviet Russia's Nikita Khrushchev marked the first stages of construction of the Dam in 1964, in company of Egypt's Gamal Abdul Nasser; Khrushchev remarked 'the dam should be called the eighth wonder of the world.' BBC 14 May 1964:
<http://news.bbc.co.uk/onthisday/hi/dates/stories/may/14/newsid_2511000/2511423.stm>, last accessed December 2010.

29 The old Aswan, the Esna Barrage and the Nag Hammadi produce 615MW, 90MW and 5MW of hydropower respectively. Arab Republic of Egypt (2005) 'National Water Resources Plan for Egypt 2017', Cairo, Ministry of Water Resources and Irrigation, Planning Sector, pp 2–6.

30 Arab Republic of Egypt (2005), note 29, p 3.

The development in Northern Egypt concentrated on eastern Delta and the Sinai areas where the reclamation of 92,400 and 273,000 hectares (220,000 and 650,000 feddans) had been anticipated, respectively.[31]

Under the El Salam Canal/Northern Sinai Agricultural Development Project, construction of the Al-Salam Canal began in 1976 to bring water from the Damietta branch of the Nile, crossing under the Suez Canal south of Port Said by means of a siphon. It was designed to provide water to irrigation lands both in Eastern Nile Delta and the Sinai. The water for the project, estimated at 4.45bcm/yr, would be derived from agricultural drainage water and from the Damietta branch of the Nile River.[32]

On the other hand, new reclamation projects and developments in southern Egypt basically depended on the South Valley Development Project, commissioned in 1997 as part of the 25-year national land reclamation plan. The scheme had featured three important components along the Toshka, East Oweinat and the New Valley Oases situated west of Lake Nasser. The projects contemplated the institution of a new productive valley and human settlements outside the natural drainage of the Nile River. A significant proportion of the Egyptian population, it is noted, lives on just 4 percent of its land; a spatial expansion has traditionally been justified by the government to mitigate the needless consummation of fertile agricultural lands along the valley through increased urbanization and industrial expansion.

The Toshka scheme required the interlinking of four canals from pumping stations on the north-western shores of Lake Nasser with the western deserts, ultimately allowing Egypt to divert as much as 4–5bcm of overflowing water from the Aswan reservoir annually. It was designed to settle new communities of a large number of people far from the Nile valley on 226,800 hectares (540,000 feddans) of agricultural land.[33]

The East Oweinat project started in 1998 and would reclaim 107,100 hectares (255,000 feddans) using renewable underground water.[34] The expansion of the oases projected to irrigate up to 187,740 hectares (447,000 feddans) similarly using groundwaters.[35]

The strings of schemes are part of the national plan that had hoped to reclaim as much as 15,000sq.km of land by 2017, transforming up to 3200sq.km of central-western desert in to agricultural land, and accommodating about six million people.[36] Upon completion of the 25-year planning period, therefore, Egypt would

31 Arab Republic of Egypt (2005), p 3.

32 Arab Republic of Egypt (2005), pp 4–7, 8.

33 Arab Republic of Egypt (2005), pp 4–7, 8.

34 Egypt State Information Center, <http://www.sis.gov.eg/En/Story.aspx?sid=835> last accessed December 2010

35 Arab Republic of Egypt (2005), note 29, p 3.

36 Egypt State Information Center, <http://www.sis.gov.eg/En/Story.aspx?sid=835> last accessed December 2010.

gain between 300,000–500,000 additional hectares of irrigated lands,[37] withdrawing 5–10bcm/yr of waters.[38]

On the whole, the plans reinvigorated the pattern of prior uses and generated new development facts potentially distressing prospects of a comprehensive accord on the Nile. Egypt's current desert reclamations, Caponera argued, would make it extremely difficult to reduce its water allocation in order to adjust to new upstream uses.[39]

Over the years, though, Egypt had emphasized and in fact tabled a series of measures to streamline current practices in water uses, adopting new techniques to guarantee stable production by using less quantity of waters. Waterbury et al lauded Egyptian policy makers' increased willingness in such initiatives, but expressed deep suspicion on the costs and time consumed to achieve savings of such magnitude.[40]

On the other hand, braced by unfathomable domestic pressures for accelerated development, riparian states in the upper-reaches of the Nile basin defied Egyptian positions without fail, and commenced to lay concrete plans for utilization the resource in their jurisdictions. For the most part, the national perceptions and development strategies adopted by basin states remained incompatible. Indeed, this explains why contemporary enterprises laboring on the optimal and equitable utilization of the Nile River water resources, both within and outside the framework of the Nile Basin Initiative, continued to endure an uphill diplomatic exertion.

Developments in Sudan

Experimentation on the huge potentials of Sudanese agriculture dates back to 1910. Sudan has for long had an elaborate system of irrigation covering a vast area of about 2 million hectares using dams and diesel pumps. On independence in 1956, the Republic of Sudan had already developed approximately 840,000 hectares (two million feddans) under the command of irrigation canals.[41] Nearly exclusively, the Nile River and its tributaries supply the waters. Sudan's colonial status under the Anglo-Egyptian condominium, its rich alluvial fields, the possibility of growing cotton in the winter seasons and most importantly, dire concerns of the British cotton industry associated with the supply of the raw material accelerated the gradual transformation of the 'empty barrel' as it had once been named in to a vast commercial estate.

37 John Waterbury and Dale Whittington (1998) 'Playing Chicken on the Nile, Implications of micro-dam development in Ethiopian highlands and Egypt's New Valley project', *Middle Eastern Natural Environment Bulletin*, vol 103, p 150.
38 Waterbury and Whittington (1998), p 157.
39 Caponera (1993), note 7, p 656.
40 Waterbury and Whittington (1998), note 37, p 158.
41 Bret Wallach (1988) 'Irrigation in Sudan since Independence', *Geographical Review*, vol 78, no 4, p 417.

Throughout its pre-independence history, Sudanese development concerns and juridical perspectives had been thoroughly intertwined with its neighbour to the north, Egypt. In bilateral and regional diplomacy, it concentrated on the preservation of its shares in the Nile waters.

As in Egypt, Great Britain had been the principal actor in ushering modern water control infrastructures and in organizing the early administrative machinery that routinely oversaw their functioning. Yet, as colonies, Egypt and Sudan had enjoyed contrasting autonomies in managing their national affairs, including in the fields of hydrology and irrigation. Egypt's special co-domini status over Sudanese administration had sanctioned greater space for manoeuvring the water diplomacy in its favour.

In the first half of the twentieth century, Egypt recognized the great potentials of conservation works upstream, particularly the Great Lakes region, so as to meet its annual and over-year water requirements. While Egyptian water policy was conceived in such a context, Sudan grappled for the adoption of a comprehensive approach of Nile water resources development that also encompasses the construction of dams on the Baro-Akobo and Lake Tana in Ethiopia.[42] Among others, it anticipated that such a scheme would have regulated the flow of the Blue Nile and secured immediate and sufficient supplies to its massive irrigation along the Blue Nile fields in the Gezira.

Throughout the 1940s, a purely downstream water resources development perspective had been espoused to settle the issue of whether the two projects on White and Blue Niles should be linked jointly or treated separately, dragging Ethiopia and Uganda to the centre stage of basin-wide discourse. Negotiations lingered since the 1920s, but in 1949, after years of enterprise, the Egyptian Government appeared to have 'come in to line'[43] when it expressed intention to participate in both schemes, including the plan for Lake Tana Dam.

However, the reclusive dialogue between Great Britain, Egypt and Sudan erroneously took Ethiopia's compliance for granted, and hence failed. In spite of the potential benefits in Egypt and Ethiopia, the political and strategic objections had been strong and intricate. The fate of the Equatorial Nile projects was barely any different.

As a result, Sudan had but to resort to substitute arrangements to satisfy its present and prospective water requirements.

Still, it should be noted that the major hydraulic infrastructures instituted as the result in the course of the 1950s and 1960s had been preceded by pioneering developments in the early twentieth century. Completed a little more than a decade since its first launch in 1913, the Sennar Dam, originally sketched by Sir M. Macdonald had been built on the Blue Nile in Sudan to provide water for the Gezira

42 The plan goes very much along the lines of the Century Storage scheme addressed earlier, attended, among others, by proposals for power and irrigation dams across different locations in Sudan (Sabolaka, Fifth Cataract, Merowe, Roseires and Khashim el Girba).

43 Addis Ababa to Foreign Office, 17 February 1949, FO 371/73613.

scheme, a vast, gentle-sloped fertile land lying between the White and Blue Nile rivers. Its construction was undertaken to supply regulated waters for the biggest cotton plantation on earth, competing with Egyptian cotton on the world market of the time.[44] The project involved the storage of 600 million tonnes of waters at Sennar so as to allow water flowing in autumn and winter over a considerable area of the Gezira; at the same time, the scheme made possible the storing of water that could be made available in early spring when the natural supply must be passed to Egypt without loss or diminution.[45] Before the Nile treaties established the relative shares of the two basin states in unequivocal terms, agricultural expansion in the Sudan had constantly aroused sombre discord with Egypt. Sudanese irrigation could not have extended without some detrimental consequences on the summer water requirements of Egypt.

Today, the Gezira fields, along with the subsequent expansions undertaken in the 1960's on the Manaqil, comprised a total irrigated area of 860,000 hectares, nearly half of the country's total land under irrigation.[46]

On the Tekeze-Atbara river system, construction of the Khashim al Qirbah Dam (1.2bcm/yr) situated just across the north-western border of Ethiopia and Sudan began in 1959 and was carried out until 1964. The design projected to cultivate about 165,000 hectares of land. Originally intended to resettle Nubians and certain nomadic families affected by the southward extension of the Aswan Dam in northern Sudan, the reservoir lost as much as 40 percent of its storage capacity due to heavy siltation and suffered salinity and drainage problems; hence, the New Halfa irrigation project established for the purpose failed.[47] Today, the system irrigates less than half of the 168,000 hectares (400,000 feddans) of land under command.[48]

Located further upstream near the border with Ethiopia, the multipurpose Rosaries Dam and Reservoir (3bcm) was completed in 1966 to increase the storage of the Blue Nile, provide hydropower and intensify agricultural production in the Gezira region. The reservoir, 80km long and 50 meters deep, provided the electrical power required to lift and pump Nile waters to the Rahad River and the Rahad Irrigational Project I some 80km away, extending over 63,000 hectares of arable land. It was completed in 1983.[49] The Rosaries had then accounted for a substantial proportion of Sudan's total power output.

On the White Nile in Sudan, the Jebel Aulia Dam (3bcm) just north of the Sudd was commissioned in 1937 by the Anglo-Egyptian condominium to hold back part of the White Nile for summer cultivation in Egypt.[50] The project guaranteed that

44 Tvedt (2004), note 8, p 112.

45 Weld (1928), note 5, p 102.

46 Irrigated agriculture, *Control device for switching water flow to one of the many canals used for irrigation in Al Jazirah, Khartoum*, <http://www.country-data.com/cgi-bin/query/r-13379.html> last accessed December 2010.

47 World Facts Index, Sudan, Irrigated agriculture, on <http://countrystudies.us/sudan/55.htm> last accessed December 2010.

48 Wallach (1988), note 41, p 424.

49 Wallach (1988), p 425.

50 Wallach (1988), p 425.

flows of the White Nile River remained steady during the Egyptian summer when the Blue Nile subsides. No longer operated as a reservoir, this edifice was handed over to Sudan in the 1970s, following the operation of the Aswan High Dam.

Concurrently, Sudan had also ventured to compose greater gains from the Nile waters resources by undertaking a series of small-scale pump irrigated projects where the placement of large-scale irrigation and infrastructures appeared unfeasible. As late as in the 1990s, plantations watered through pumps both on the White and Blue Niles had accounted for as much as 275,000 hectares of arable land.

In the 1970's, construction of a controversial structure had also been initiated in South Sudan, across the extensive swamps of the Sudd region – a rare ecological setting responsible for the loss of some 42bcm of Nile waters every year. A 267km-long diversion duct, so called the Jonglei Canal, was designed to take away water from the swampy area of Bahr el Jebel to the White Nile system; but construction had to be halted in 1983 just 100km short of completion during the Sudanese civil war. Despite interest by the north Sudanese Government to proceed with the project, unbefitting political and ecological considerations made completion of the scheme a difficult undertaking.

Sudan's latest venture on the Nile River had been the 67 meters high Merowe hydropower facility; the Dams Implementation Unit in Sudan unveiled that the scheme, just completed in 2009 produces up to 1250MW of energy. Hence, it constituted one of the biggest hydropower projects in Africa, trailing the Grand Ethiopian Renaissance Dam, the Inga III Dam in the DR Congo and the Ingula Scheme in South Africa – which are all under construction, and the Aswan Power Station in Egypt.

Ethiopia: a belated awakening?

The legal and historical dynamics that stage-managed an uneven pattern of water resources development in each of the Nile basin states vary greatly. Since Great Britain set foot on Egyptian soil in the early 1880's, the colonial administration had been absorbed by enormous eco-political stakes that induced the initiation, planning and execution of a series of basin-wide projects serving, nearly exclusively, interests in the lower-reaches of the river.

Across the upstream Nile region, no other state had grappled against the Anglo-Egyptian dominion for control of the Nile as robustly and consistently as Ethiopia, both in public opinion and diplomatic courses. Ethiopia's embedded perception of a leading stake in the subject had been enthused by a range of geopolitical and simple physical facts that as provider of the largest proportions of the Nile deluge, it should be entitled to a corresponding reward in the utilization of the shared resource.

In the 1890's, the British colonial enterprise in the Nile region reached its zenith, stretching its political control and influence over the entire span of the basin. Although Ethiopia remained a self-governing polity and indeed successive British governments had decreed allegiance to the territorial integrity of the Ethiopian Empire, the Nile River and the Lake Tana Dam project essentially defined the nature of the diplomatic intercourse between the two states.

Of course, Ethiopia's sovereignty did little to guard it from the knotty British pressures and manipulations. In May 1902, Emperor Menelik had already concluded a treaty that ostensibly restricted Ethiopia's sovereignty with respect to the utilization of the Tana, Baro-Akobo and the Blue Nile rivers.

Up until its exit from African possessions in the 1950s, the fundamentals of British policy remained unchanged: Ethiopia had no pressing uses for the Nile, and 'its benefit from the Nile is apparently limited to the development of power for which . . . there is no immediate market . . .'; the country was '. . . only interested in the amount of money it can secure from Egypt and Sudan in return for permission to construct the Lake Tana Dam'.[51]

This unconstructive diplomatic outline wholeheartedly inherited by Egypt and Sudan and coupled with Ethiopia's cynical approaches against British motives on the subject had depressed opportunities for earlier development of hydraulic infrastructures across Ethiopia's Nile basin region. Noteworthy utilization of the Nile water resources was further hampered by fiscal and technological limitations, inert visionary acumen, political vacillation and quiescent water diplomacy of Ethiopia's leadership.

Hence, with a notable exception of the wave of private explorations pursued in the nineteenth and early twentieth centuries, complete hydraulic and meteorological investigation of the Ethiopian Nile, its tributaries and topography – crucial ingredients for proper utilization of water resources, had been lacking until the last few decades. Virtually, Ethiopia remained a rain-fed agriculture economy; the potential provision of its hydropower endowments had been able to influence the national economy only inconsequentially.

In May 1991, the civil war that devoured the nation's lacking resources for nearly two decades concluded. The new government's increasing orientation to market economy and developmental state ideologies revived valuable partnerships with political orders and fiscal establishments both in the east and the west alike. Hence, master plans of major national river basins were worked out or reorganized; and since, a chain of prefeasibility and feasibility studies had been completed.

Likewise, a broader strategic thinking was put in place to direct future utilization of the resources and a few capital-intensive investments, mostly involving the hydropower sector, had been implemented. This relative renaissance in water resources development represented a greater leap since the conclusion, in 1964, of a fairly comprehensive, but poorly perceived investigation of the Blue Nile Basin by the US Bureau of Reclamation.[52]

51 Sir Ronald Campbell, From Cairo to Foreign Office, 16 July 1949, FO 371/73619.

52 The scheme, which had been part of a broader and long-term 'military and economic assistance' contemplated to 'survey . . . the Ethiopian portion of the blue Nile'. United States, BFOR No 4 and 5.

4 Legal regimes regulating utilization of the Nile waters

A case study of the Anglo-Ethiopian Treaty of 1902

Introduction

During the immediate aftermath of the scramble for the African continent, the British colonial empire expanded its African acquisitions in fierce competition with the French. At the zenith of its imperial power, its dominion had extended over large territorial stretches across the East and North African regions situated in the Nile basin. By 1890, Great Britain had already declared the whole Nile valley as its exclusive sphere of influence,[1] and the British Foreign Office had transformed itself into protector of the Nile and heir of anxieties over the Nile's sources.[2] In the negotiations relating to east and north-eastern Africa, which Lord Salisbury had conducted with a series of European counterparts in 1890–91, the desire to safeguard waters of the upper and middle Nile occupied a predominant position.[3]

With the occupation of Egypt (1882) and Sudan (1896/98), Great Britain grasped in no time that in order to defend its regional geopolitical interests and sustain the economic affluence of both states in whom the Lancashire–Manchester textile interests had developed profound stakes, it had to work out on a fitting stratagem. British foreign policy aspired to secure a complete monopoly and/or unqualified warranties of non-interference with respect to the hydraulic integrity of the Nile River system across the whole basin. By concluding vital accords with the sovereign states of Italy, Ethiopia, France, Germany and Belgium, Great Britain toiled to further augment its hegemonic bliss in the colonies of Egypt, Sudan, Kenya, Uganda, and later Tanzania.

Hence, on the 21st of March 1899 France agreed to cease active manoeuvres in the Nile basin aspiring to establish political spheres of influence. An Anglo-German arrangement concluded on 1 July 1890 urged Germany to withdraw claims to several regions of influence across or adjacent to the Nile basin.[4] In 1894 and

1 Terje Tvedt (2004) *The River Nile in the Age of the British, Political Ecology and the Quest for Economic Power*, London/New York, I.B. Tauris, p 40.

2 J. McCann (1981) 'Ethiopia, Britain and Negotiations for the Lake Tana Dam 1922–1935', *The International Journal of African Historical Studies*, vol 14, no 4, p 670.

3 G.N. Sanderson (1964) 'England, Italy, the Nile Valley and the European Balance, 1890–91', *The Historical Journal*, vol 7, p 94.

4 Agreement between the British and German Governments Respecting Africa and the Helgoland, Berlin, 1 July 1890, reprinted in Sir Edward Hertslet (1984) *The Map of Africa by Treaty*, London, Harrison and Sons, vol II, no 103–208, p 642.

on 9 May 1906 accords reached with King Leopold of Belgium, a colonial power in the 'independent state of Congo', obliged the latter not 'to construct or allow to be constructed any work over or near the Semliki or Isango rivers which would diminish the volume of water entering Lake Albert, except in agreement with the Sudanese Government'.[5] In a related engagement, a tripartite 'Agreement between Great Britain, France, and Italy respecting Abyssinia' signed on the 13th of December 1906 affirmed the 'prior hydraulic rights' of Egypt in the Nile waters. In 1934, another arrangement regarding water rights on the boundary between Tanganyika, Rwanda and Burundi required Belgium to return waters of streams originating in areas of its control without substantial reduction of the natural bed before they form a common boundary with British controlled regions.[6]

In a parallel adjust, under two clandestine protocols signed in Rome on 24 March and 15 April 1891, Italian encroachment potentially jeopardizing the security of headwaters of the Nile in two particular directions, Eritrea and the Kassala in Sudan, had been dealt with.[7] Italy was permitted the possibility of operational occupation of the Kassala district and adjoining lands and as far as the Atbara in situations of military necessity, subject to certain reservations, but most importantly, Italy undertook 'not to construct on the Atbara River, in view of irrigation, any works which might sensibly modify its flow in to the Nile'. In consequence, Italy was cornered to abandon all previous aspirations of political foothold in the Nile basin.[8]

The legal regime constituted through the Anglo-Ethiopian Treaty signed on 18 May 1902[9] was just one other outcome of Great Britain's pursuit of such a broader strategy.

Parts 4–7 of the Book will endeavour to reconstruct and analyse the legal and historical origin and functioning of the British Nile policies in Ethiopia, and particularly, the Anglo-Ethiopian Treaty concluded in Addis Ababa in May 1902.

In this context, the diplomatic genesis of the bilateral scheme will be presented methodically; the contents of the treaty shall be elaborated, interpreted and corroborated by contemporaneous understandings and subsequently evolving perceptions of the parties with regard to the pertinent matters addressed in the treaty.

5 Treaty Between the United Kingdom and the Independent State of Congo to Redefine their Respective Spheres of Influence in Eastern and Central Africa, London, 9 May 1906.

6 Agreement between the Belgian Government and the Government of the United Kingdom of Great Britain and Northern Ireland regarding water rights on the boundary between Tanganyika and Ruanda-Urundi, London, 22 November 1934.

7 The Protocol between the British and Italian Governments for the Demarcation of their Respective Spheres of Influence in East Africa, From Ras Kasar to the Blue Nile, Rome, 15 April 1891..

8 Protocol between the British and Italian Governments for the demarcation of their respective spheres of influence in Eastern Africa, from the river Juba to the Blue Nile, 24 March 1891;

Protocol between the British and Italian Governments for the demarcation of their respective spheres of influence in East Africa, From Ras Kasar to the Blue Nile, 15April 1891

Reprinted in Sir Edward Hertslet (1984) *The Map of Africa by Treaty*, London, Harrison and Sons, vol. II, no 103–208, pp 665–9; also confirmed in: Sanderson to Harrington, 28 August I902, FO 1/47

9 The Treaty Between Ethiopia and the United Kingdom Relative to the Frontiers between the Soudan, Ethiopia and Eritrea, Addis Ababa, 15 May 1902.

The legal analyses will be based on diverse principles of international law, but most notably, rules regulating the interpretation of treaties.

The presentation shall blend a wide range of legal, historical and diplomatic accounts involving the states of Great Britain, Sudan and Ethiopia – with a view to exposing long-standing juridical dilemmas that persisted with regard to the essence, application and continued validity of the Anglo-Ethiopian treaty.

One can barely doubt that Great Britain's old river uses policies and legal manoeuvres have endured to generate far-reaching impacts on the basin's economic, hydro-legal and political configurations today. The main justification for engaging in the analysis of the Anglo-Ethiopian Treaty has been premised on this vital assumption.

In the post-treaty periods, the arrangement constituted through the Anglo-Ethiopian agreement intertwined riparian relationships between the states of Ethiopia and Sudan. Since Sudanese independence, the treaty remained the *only* authoritative instrument defining water rights and duties of the state parties involved. The treaty also represented a standing symbol of categorical scepticism and sense of disregard ingrained in Ethiopia's legal discourse; this perception has been evident in Ethiopia's defiant engagements in the developmental politics of the Nile basin and the deleterious state of facts presented in the immediate aftermath of the treaty's conclusion.

Today, while Sudanese position with regard to the continued legitimacy of the treaty has been incoherent or incomprehensible, at least in Ethiopia, the Anglo-Ethiopian Treaty has barely been mentioned in formal communications; it is more appreciated in a historical context than as a legal convention that spells riparian rights and obligations.[10] Contemporary, ultra-vocal postures of Ethiopian governments have time after time declared the status quo as unacceptable, admitting limitations on the utilization of the Nile River system as stemming only from the country's lacking resources and principles of international watercourses law rather than the dictates of any specific treaty regime as such.[11]

Yet, technically, the accord remained a binding bilateral instrument; in international legal relations, Ethiopia's deportment of disregard, alone, cannot constitute a controlling factor in obviating treaty responsibilities. The treaty's effects can be rescinded only in accordance with the basic stipulates of public international law.

This fact had presented the rational for conversing at length about the Anglo-Ethiopian Treaty regime. But it has not been the sole consideration.

10 During the VIIIth Nile-2002 Conference held in Addis Ababa (June 2000), for instance, the Government of Ethiopia reasserted its long-stated position that *no international agreements* on water and allocation exist between itself and neighboring countries and hence that it would work on legal and institutional frameworks regulating uses in the Nile basin on the basis of equitable sharing of the resource among the basin states.

Nile 2002 Conference (1996), Proceedings of the IVth Nile 2002 Conference, Country Paper: Ethiopia, 26–29 February, Kampala, p C-24.

11 Cases in point are Prime Minister Meles Zenawi's interviews aired on TV-2 (Norway Documentary, Sunday 28 October 2007, 'Reise til vannets fremtid'), Aljazeera TV (Qatar) and ETV (Ethiopia) in the course of 2007–2011 and the Government of Ethiopia's formal positions reiterated within the framework of negotiations of the Nile Basin Initiative.

The comprehensive discussion was also spurred by the need for *reconstructing* landmark legal relationships and presenting the same as *historical anthologies*, the outcome of the bilateral legal wrangling notwithstanding.

Besides, separate from mere issues of the continued validity of the treaty as such, the incidental function of such analyses involving multifarious legal themes of contemporary significance cannot be underrated and had factored in the decision for discussing on the Anglo-Ethiopia treaty of 1902.

Hence, under Chapter 4, a brief prelude to the origin and functioning of the British Nile policies in Ethiopia and a presentation on the plain composition of the Anglo-Ethiopian Treaty will be tendered.

Chapter 5 elucidates the geographical scope of the obligation assumed under Article III of the treaty. This would start by addressing the concept of transboundary watercourse under international law. More specifically, it investigates the issue of whether the Anglo-Ethiopian treaty, purportedly forbidding the construction of any work on or across the Blue Nile, Lake Tana or the Sobat could be conceived as having contemplated to cover the flows not only of the named principal rivers as such, but also the consequences of major uses on secondary river courses in the natural drainage basins of these rivers.

On the other hand, within a broader framework of Part 6, various sections would address specific legal issues and arguments espoused by the parties in connection with textual and connotational variations disclosed in the wordings of Article III of the treaty. In essence, the discussions would attempt to determine if a textual discrepancy worthy of legal interpretation truly subsists, and where it does, to elucidate an interpretation of the treaty that most reasonably constitutes the joint volition of the parties. For this purpose, interpretative techniques provided for under international law, and most notably, the Vienna Convention on the Law of Treaties of 1969 would be extensively employed.

In Chapter 7, the continued legal authority of the Anglo-Ethiopian Treaty is further tested on the basis of three supplementary juridical premises.

The first reflection would concentrate on the issue of whether the treaty can be proposed as falling under a class of unequal treaties, imposed by Great Britain in a fiduciary capacity as guardian of the interests of the Sudanese co-domini, and where it does, on revealing the juridical consequences that ensue under international law in virtue of such a designation.

Within the international legal order, a no-less formidable defiance of unequal treaties had also been procured by a series of United Nations General Assembly (UNGA) resolutions adopted in the 1950's and 1960's. Several of the General Assembly resolutions had instituted a systematic framework of conceptual correlation between the principles of sovereign equality, self-determination and permanent sovereignty of states over natural resources. Hence, the second investigation would focus on revealing whether the sweeping languages of the UN resolutions had in fact contemplated transboundary rivers as proper subjects of treatment, and if so, the nature and scope of rights inferred from such declarations as affecting substantive stipulations under the Anglo-Ethiopian Treaty of 1902.

The last section considers the doctrine of *rebus sic stantibus*; generally, this canon of international law confers states a measure of cause for withdrawing from binding treaty regimes on account of 'fundamental change of circumstances which has occurred with regard to those existing at the time of the conclusion of a treaty, and which was not foreseen by the parties'.[12] If indeed the rule of fundamental change of circumstances translates in relation to the Anglo-Ethiopian treaty, concluded a little more than a century ago, would be the core object of the analysis.

Inevitably, the parts shall work on a rich pile of the pre- and post-treaty diplomatic communication of the stake-holding parties and reconstruct the historical milieu in which pertinent legal issues had arisen.

The origin and functioning of the British Nile policies in Ethiopia

From the onset, British water development planners had been under constant pressure to cope with the necessities of superior control and enhanced utilization of the Nile in Egypt, which, Tvedt noted, could not have been achieved without 'looking upstream beyond Egypt's borders'.[13] In justifying the occupation of Uganda and Sudan, both the British Government and its colonial office in Egypt had accentuated that 'the effective control of the waters of the Nile from the Equatorial Lakes to the Sea is essential to the existence of Egypt.'[14] Without a firm rule over the entire Nile stretch, at least, the economic logic for setting up political control over Egypt and Sudan could have been neither secure nor sustained.

In diplomatic deportments that evolved ad infinitum, Great Britain's strategic consideration had persistently renounced direct territorial ambitions in Ethiopia;[15] instead, Great Britain strove to institute a special sphere of political and economic influence by concluding a conventional pledge that prescribed a regime of non-interference with the hydraulic integrity of the Blue Nile River and its tributaries.

This undertaking was simply vital before an archrival European power, France, sets foot in the Nile basin. Following the defeat of Italian forces by Ethiopia at the Battle of Adwa (1896), Italy's exit had already provoked a chain of events that among others compelled a provisional halt of its colonial ambitions in the region. Great Britain had to guardedly watch increased French manoeuvres in the basin and move with resolve to slam the vacuum created following Italy's exit.

In fact, the same years also witnessed that long-standing French aspiration for control of some parts of the White Nile appeared highly probable when its mission proceeded along the Upper Nile in the Sudan by taking advantage of Egyptian evacuations.

12 United Nations Vienna Convention on the Law of Treaties (1969), Vienna 23 May 1969. UN Treaty Series Vol 1155, p. 331 (entered into force 27 January 1980), Article 62.

13 Tvedt (2004), note 1, p 25.

14 Tvedt (2004), pp 25, 29.

15 William Garstin (1905) 'Report upon the basin of the Upper Nile, with proposals for the improvement of that river', *The Geographical Journal*, vol 25, no 1, p7 6.

British diplomatic moves to conclude the treaty had also been triggered by developments within Ethiopia itself. Spurred by the French and capitalizing on the principle of effective occupation in establishing new territorial dominions, Emperor Menelik's nation-building enterprise had penetrated deep in the equatorial regions of Sudan, along the White Nile; the measures intended to obviate British encroachments from the west.

Hence, where French conspiracy on the one hand and a sustained vigour of the expanding Ethiopian Empire on the other posed a threat to the Victorian hegemony in the Nile valley, Great Britain had to deal with the uncertainties by pre-emptively occupying Sudan, and by engaging in rigorous diplomatic ventures that hoped to craft an accord with the state of Ethiopia.

In the ensuing communications that covered multifaceted themes, Great Britain put into service its long-conceived riverine policy, one that endured to date to generate far-reaching impacts on the region's economic, hydro-legal and political configurations.

With respect to Ethiopia, its rejuvenated approach identified great potentials of both the Blue Nile River and the Lake Tana. Throughout the last decade of the nineteenth century, the prime occupation of British foreign policy in the region had particularly whirled on the subject of obtaining two vital concessions: an Ethiopian treaty undertaking guaranteeing the unimpeded flow of the Blue Nile River (and its tributaries) to Sudan and Egypt, and a consent for the construction and operation of a dam on the head sources of the river at Lake Tana, including the leasing of its waters. The dam scheme had been intended to meet the rapid expansion of irrigational water requirements in Egypt, and later, in the Sudan.

The Anglo-Ethiopian accord, signed in Addis Ababa in May 1902 satisfied only part of this long-standing aspiration; still, it constituted a relieving development sealing Great Britain's objectives for unquestioned legal and political domination over the Nile River and its tributaries across the basin.

The treaty was initiated after Emperor Menelik sent, in April 1891 a circular letter to European powers defining what he considered the Ethiopian borders to be.[16] In the same epoch, Emperor Menelik had been engaged in the occupation and expansion of the Ethiopian empire on an unprecedented scale, incorporating vast adjoining territories to the south, east and the west. His communication had primarily intended to soothe the uncertainty produced in Europe by virtue of operation of the Italian version of the Wuchiale Treaty;[17] it also served to dodge

16 Harold G. Marcus (1963) 'Ethio-British Negotiations Concerning the Western Border with Sudan, 1896–1902', *The Journal of African History*, vol 4, no 1, p 82.

Also accounted in FO 403/155, Circular Letter, April 1891; and FO 1/32, Menelik to Rodd, 13 May 1897.

17 The Treaty of Wuchiale was concluded in May 1889 between Ethiopia and Italy. Among other issues, the accord recognized continued Italian occupation of Eritrea and regulated delineation of the boundary between the occupied territories north of the Mereb River and the rest of Ethiopia. Shortly after the deal had been struck, Italy claimed a controversial Italian version of Article XVII of the treaty gave it a *protectorate power* over Ethiopia, hence *obliging* Menelik to avail himself of the Italian government for all negotiation of affairs with the outside world.

a probable conflict of interest with the European states which had then encircled Ethiopia in all directions.

Judging by the contents, the Anglo-Ethiopian arrangement had been crafted to essentially address border delimitation issues between Ethiopia and the Anglo-Egyptian Sudan.

The immediate substantive genesis of the Anglo-Ethiopian Treaty of May 1902 dates back to diplomatic notes exchanged in March of the same year between Alfred Ilg, Emperor Menelik's foreign affairs councillor, and Lt Colonel John Harrington, the British emissary in Addis Ababa.[18]

Under the notes, Ethiopia undertook an oral commission to the effect that 'there is to be no interference with the flow of the Blue Nile or Lake Tana except with the consultation of His Majesty's Government', and should there be any interference, 'all conditions being equal, preference will be given to the proposals of His Britannic Majesty's Government; and that His Majesty the Emperor Menelik has no intention of giving any concessions with regard to the Blue Nile and Lake Tana except to His Britannic Majesty's Government, the Government of Sudan or one of their subjects.'[19]

Composition of the Anglo-Ethiopian Treaty

Constituted in notes exchanged between the respective governments, the Anglo-Ethiopian Treaty represented a key chapter in the winding phases of London's imperial quest for juridical protection and control of the Nile basin.

The English version of Article III of the resulting agreement pertaining to the regulation of use of the Nile River in Ethiopia read:

> His Majesty Emperor Menelik, king of kings of Ethiopia, engages himself towards the Government of His Britannic Majesty not to construct or allow to be constructed any works across the Blue Nile, Lake Tana or the Sobat, which would *arrest the flow* of their waters in to the Nile, except with His Britannic Majesty's agreement and the Government of the Sudan. [Emphasis added]

In the ensuing communication between agents of the two states, the word *arrest* surfaced as the most contentious expression of the treaty undertaking. Like scores of other accords that suffered from composition, the Amharic and English versions

Several European powers followed suit, duly recognizing the proclaimed status. It required the 'Battle of Adwa' (1896) before the Treaty was rescinded formally and Italy was obliged to recognize full sovereignty of the Ethiopian state, obliterating its claims of protectorate.

18 A technocrat in engineering and diplomacy, since 1879, Ilg rendered three decades of services to Emperor Menelik. In recognition of his contributions, he was appointed as 'Councillor of State, together with the many honours and commercial concessions' in 1896. Harold G. Marcus (1995) *The Life and Times of Menelik II, Ethiopia 1844–1913*, Lawrenceville, NJ, The Red Sea Press Inc, p 59.

19 Ilg to Harrington, 18 March 1902, FO 403/322; Abyssinia, Record of meetings to discuss the method of negotiation with Abyssinian Government for the Lake Tana Concession, 4 August 1926, FO 371/13099; Lake Tana, Record of Conversation between Dr Martin and Murray, 11 November 1927, FO 371/12343.

of the treaty appeared to display a notable discrepancy and had been comprehended as entailing disparate obligations. The original Amharic script conveyed:

፫ተኛ፡ ክፍል ።

ጃንሆይ፡ ዳግማዊ፡ ምኒልክ፡ ንጉሠ፡ ነገሥት፡ ዘኢትዮጵያ፡
ከጥቁር፡ ዓባይና፡ ከበሕረ፡ ፀና፡ ከሶባት፡ ወንዝ፡ ወደ
ነጭ፡ ዓባይ፡ የሚወርደውን፡ ውሀ፡ ከእንግሊዝ፡ መንግሥት፡
ጋራ፡ አስቀድሞ፡ ሳይስማሙ፡ ወንዝ፡ ተዳር፡ አዳር፡የሚደ
ፍን፡ ሥራ፡ እንዳይሰሩ። ወይም፡ ወንዝ፡ የሚደፍን፡ሥራ፡
ለማሠራት፡ ለማንም፡ ፈቃድ፡ እንዳይሰጡ፡ በዚህ፡ ውል፡
አድርገዋል ።

A literal translation of the Amharic text more or less read:[20]

> His Majesty Menelik II, King of Kings, Ethiopia, has agreed in this treaty not to construct, nor authorize anyone to construct a work that blocks up/stops up from river bank to river bank the water descending from the Black Abbay, from the Tana Sea, and from the Sobat River towards the White Abbay without previously agreeing with the English Government.

The puzzling phrase in the Amharic version, and employed as controlling text of Article III of the treaty‘ወንዝ፡ ተዳር፡ አዳር፡የሚደፍን፡ ሥራ፡ እንዳይሰሩ’ is a derivative of an Amharic root word ‘dafanna’, which, according to volume I of Thomas Kane’s dictionary denotes ‘to stop up, to fill, plug or close tightly, or to block passage’.

In the immediately ensuing years and the subsequent decades, successive governments, both in Great Britain (and later the Sudan) and in Ethiopia construed Article III of the bilateral accord as prescribing contrasting scales of obligation. With shifting scales of enthusiasm and perspective, the states endeavoured to define, design and carry out Nile River resources development schemes along lines that projected their respective interpretations and that suited national strategies and interests.

Hence, throughout its tenure as overseer of Egyptian and Sudanese concerns, London deduced from the treaty and pursued its policies on the assumption that

20 In the course of the diplomatic controversies that resurfaced in the 1920’s, Bentinck, the British representative in Addis Ababa, submitted his government’s view of a literal translation of the Article 3 of the Amharic text as follows.

‘His Majesty Menelik II, King of the Kings of Ethiopia, has agreed in the treaty not to construct a work to block up from river bank to river bank, without previously agreeing with the English Government, the water descending from the Black (ie Blue) Abbai (ie Nile) and from the Tsana Sea, from the Sobat River towards the White Abbai (ie Nile) nor to give permission to anyone (whomsoever) to construct a river blocking up work.’ Bentinck to Austen Chamberlain, 9 January 1928, enclosure 2.1, FO 371/13099.

Ethiopia had been bound to *completely refrain* from laying any water control work on the Nile and its tributaries, the scale of the construction or its impact on the sustained flow of the watercourse notwithstanding. Shortly afterwards, the perception of rigid monopoly was tenderly moderated to accommodate utilization of the River for minor cultivation schemes serving the immediate needs of local consumption.

Ethiopia's views largely deviated. For the most part, it espoused an external relations policy that tendered a downright disservice to long-standing British, and later, Sudanese interests. Ethiopia inferred that Emperor Menelik's pledge, more unequivocally conveyed in the Amharic text, only stipulated a duty not to *wholly stop up* the flow of the river without British consent, leaving other, less detrimental uses for irrigational, industrial or domestic purposes to its own discretion.

5 Geographical scope of the Anglo-Ethiopian Treaty undertaking

The physical unity of river courses and international law dilemmas

Noticeably, the physical scope of the framing under Article III would be limited. The Nile in the Sudan receives waters streaming from three potent headwaters in Ethiopia: the Baro-Akobo-Sobat basin, the Blue Nile (Abay) basin and the Tekeze-Atbara basin. In what appears to constitute an inadvertent composition, the Tekeze river system, a powerful tributary of the Nile proper had been exempted under the Anglo-Ethiopian Treaty regime.

The treaty allegedly restricted constructions on or across the Blue Nile, Lake Tana or the Sobat which would arrest the flow of their waters in to the main Nile. The Baro-Akobo-Sobat River system flows directly to the White Nile from south-western Ethiopia; the Blue Nile spills over Lake Tana, issues from the Lake's narrow south-east outlet and proceeds to the Sudan. Along the course, a crowd of tributaries join both river systems.

In fact, only a small portion of the Blue Nile's waters, 3.5bcm per annum to be precise, leaves the Lake's vent in the south-eastern shoreline. A significant percentage of the 49.5bcm mean annual outflow of the Blue Nile waters arriving at the Rosaries is derived from the River's major, largely perennial, tributaries in north and north-western Ethiopia. This verity raises interesting issues with respect to the physical scope of the treaty undertaking and the juridical fate of tributaries under the Anglo-Ethiopian Treaty.

From a strictly geographical point of view, river systems have been treated as physical unities, and this does make a perfect sense. River basins, occasionally referred to as river drainages, embrace not only waters of a channel through which the main course traverses, but also the whole complex of water body originating in tributaries, sub-tributaries, streams, lakes, glaciers, canals and underground waters situated in the adjoining regions. The main stem of a river course, i.e. the waterway through which a sizeable proportion of the drainage eventually flows – supplied by a string of tributaries and brooks – is simply one petite constituent of the entire riverine hydrology.

For this reason, any blend of interaction between human activity, the drainage, climatic conditions and the vegetation in any part of the basin can ultimately affect the quality and volume of water transported in the riverbed of each river. Hydrologically, this close physical unity of the system implies that any interference with or withdrawal of water from tributaries in the drainage basin is capable of manifesting corollary effects in the overall volume, velocity and quality of flow of the floods in the eventual terminus – the head course.

The Nile system is not an exception. The connection between various units of the river system is so strong that hefty hydraulic installations on the feeding streams of the Blue Nile and the Sobat rivers will, without doubt *diminish*, if not arrest, the quantity of water received by the head courses, and ultimately, by the Nile River proper in far distant locations.

Hence, how states forging new legal regimes for regulation of the utilization of shared river courses appreciate the *interdependence* of river systems and couch the specific terms of treaty undertakings is critically important. The geographical bound of the Anglo-Ethiopian Treaty must be considered in this context.

The issue is whether the treaty can be interpreted as inflating the dimension of Ethiopia's obligations to a point where it would be disallowed to utilize sequences of tributaries and rivulets spread across the western half of its landscape and contributing to the eventual flood of the Blue Nile and Sobat river basins.

Framed in a different way, can the treaty, in forbidding the construction of any work on or across the Blue Nile, Lake Tana or the Sobat be conceived as having contemplated to cover the flows not only of the named principal rivers as such, but also the consequences of major uses of secondary river courses in the natural drainage basins of these rivers? An approach that adopts the unity of river systems naturally promotes strategic interests of downstream states.

How the concept of a *river* is depicted legally constitutes the core essence of the matter. The international legal order has for long had trouble forging the correct expression and characterization of rivers in laying conceptual frameworks for a global regulation of transboundary watercourses. Regional river organizations and bilateral treaty arrangements too have approached the term with prudence and unceasing reservations. Nearly all initiatives have underscored the distinction between legal formations that constituted obligation in respect merely of the water that flows along a specified channel, on the one hand, and other regimes whose spatial scope transcended to an entire geographic basin.

Surely, rising knowledge with regard to the physical attributes of river systems has influenced contemporary juridical discourses in several river basins. In many instances, modern planning conceptions dealing with the management and conservation of river courses seem to have embraced *comprehensive* approaches, proceeding on the basis of the totality of waters presented in a basin. This naturally makes sense. A wider basin constitutes the most ideal unit for investigating meteorological, hydrological and climatic facts of a particular region; it provides the essential factual basis for organizing and executing contending water resources development projects more optimally and comprehensively.

However, such a predisposition in conservation approaches notwithstanding, it would remain erroneous to propose, merely on the basis of such accounts and limited state practice, that international watercourses law has similarly considered the whole physical feature of a *basin* and *basin-flows* as proper units of international legal regulation.

Instead, it would be noted that since the turn of the twentieth century, there had been an impression among jurists, treaty practice of states and certain institutional initiatives that the basin conception did not constitute a basis for the application of legal rules of international law. This contentious character of the legal expression has constantly lingered during the codification and progressive development of the UN Watercourses Convention itself in the 1990s, the proceedings of the International Law Commission, in various academic publications and institutional initiatives as well as the practice of states.

The possible divergence in opinion notwithstanding, one fact had appeared sufficiently evident: that an *international water course* is not a practical or notional equivalent of *international drainage basin*. In fact, during the commissioning stages of the 1997 UN Watercourse Convention, the General Assembly had rejected Finland's request to cross-refer to the Helsinki Rules that endorsed the basin conception. The International Law Commission chose to 'accept the ambiguity of the term international watercourse and determine to what extent the Commission and states are prepared to resolve the problems that arise from the physical aspects of the hydrographic process in dealing with specific uses of fresh water'.[1]

Hence, for the moment, it can be submitted that customary international law has barely evolved to a scale where a basin hydrology will *ipso facto* be treated as a unit of international legal regulation. Despite a broader support for the drainage basin concept in modern treaty practice and works of international bodies, Birnie et al concluded, the evidence of disagreement in the ILC suggests that it is premature to attribute customary status to this concept as a definition of the geographical scope of international water resources law.[2] Consequently, riparian obligations which are implicit in a wider depiction of the physical scope of a river course cannot be readily admitted, except in circumstances where bilateral or regional treaties have expressly provided to that effect.

In understanding the ordinary meaning of Article III, a question then remains how this brief analysis of the pertinent rules of international law translates in the particular context of the arguments that involved the Anglo-Ethiopian Treaty.

Physical scope of the Anglo-Ethiopian Treaty undertaking

Great Britain's strategic design for control of the Nile could have hardly succeeded without a legal regime that offers complete guarantee of non-interference both with respect to the head courses and feeding streams of the White and Blue Nile river systems. Indeed, qualitative and quantitative considerations had been at the heart of its downstream-oriented river development policy.

1 International Law Commission (1979) *Yearbook of International Law Commission*, vol 2 no 1, p 158.

2 Patricia Birnie, Alan Boyle and Catherine Redgwell (2009) *International Law and the Environment*, New York, Oxford University Press, p 539.

In spite of the underlying policy objectives, literally, neither the Amharic nor the English versions of the 1902 treaty would appear to provide a room for extended application of the accord internationalizing tributaries and streams of the Blue Nile and the Sobat rivers wholly situated within the Ethiopian territory.

Still, in bilateral dealings, Great Britain espoused a position that advocated the prohibition of nearly all scales of interference with the hydraulic integrity of the river basin. The stated reflection of the respective parties can be grasped clearly through a comprehensive recital of historical and diplomatic facts of the time.

Shortly after the conclusion of the Anglo-Ethiopian Treaty, the prime preoccupation of London's viceroy in Egypt, Lord Cromer, focused on reinforcing the diplomatic gains in the field of water security. The idea of pecuniary reward to Emperor Menelik, in consideration for his undertakings under the treaty, started to float in all circles following a statement by J. Harrington, the British emissary in Addis Ababa, that his government had 'no desire to demand from the Emperor that he should deprive himself of a valuable asset without equivalent compensation'.[3] Apparently, the UK was convinced that the pact had validated a permanent renunciation of Ethiopian rights in respect of the use of the Nile.

With a view to executing the payment scheme, in 1904, Cromer authorised Harrington to enter into negotiations with and formally extend to Emperor Menelik a British offer of fiscal subsidy. Under the proposed subsidy agreement, the Anglo-Sudan government undertook 'to pay to the Emperor or his successors a sum of £10,000 sterling annually so long as the friendly relations of the two governments continue'.[4]

For an Emperor who emerged from the unpleasant ordeals of European conspiracy and particularly the interpretative hullabaloo of the Wuchiale Treaty with Italy only a decade earlier, the espousal of an apprehensive approach to proposed treaties had always been a standing policy. Hence, in spite of the protracted efforts by the British to get him on board, and some progresses in 1907, he neither refused to accept the grant formally, nor approved contents of the subsidy enclosure.

It proves difficult to establish with certainty the specific raison d'être that prompted Menelik to overlook the British offer. In February 1907, Clark, London's representative in Addis Ababa requested Cromer 'if there is any objection to my giving Emperor Menelik written assurance on behalf of the Anglo-Sudanese Government that Article III of the 15 May 1902 Treaty is in no way meant to interfere with local irrigation rights of natives of districts watered by Lake Tana, Blue Nile and the Sobat'.[5] He did not say what 'local irrigational rights' as such involve, nor did his query involve the tributaries. A month later, he reported that Menelik had made it difficult to sign the negotiated note without an unequivocal extension of the assurances contained above and revealed that the real cause that prompted him to put the signature on hold was that 'he wants to sell cotton

3 Memorandum, History of the Lake Tana Negotiation, Foreign Office, 23 January 1923, FO 371/8403.

4 Memorandum (1923), note 3.

5 Draft Telegram to Cromer, Addis Ababa 16 February 1907, FO 371/14591.

concessions in the low country and fears that we may object to making canals for irrigation'.[6]

Lord Cromer weighed on the impact of the events, incidentally demonstrating his construction of the privileges accorded under the 1902 Treaty. On the advice of his irrigation experts whose sole concern had been the steady flow of the river downstream, he ordered Clark to give a guardedly framed surety to Menelik that 'the terms of Article III of the Treaty of May 15, 1902 do not imply any intention of interfering with local native rights, provided that no attempt is made to arrest or interfere in any way with the flow of these rivers by placing obstructions of any sort in their channels or by constructing regulators or dams of any kind across their channels or beds'.[7]

By subscribing to the claim for insertion of a clause in the subsidy note, in effect, Cromer submitted not only to Menelik's *calculated* request but also to a probable contour of understanding of his treaty commitments. Two decades later, and in retrospect Foreign Office officials construed Menelik's enterprise as an attempt to 'get something in note watering down or interpreting [the existing treaty] in the sense which he wishes it'[8] to imply.

It is possible to infer that the insistent claims by the Emperor could have been stimulated by one of three things. Probably, he was striving to trim down the harm supposedly inflicted by concluding the treaty with the British; or that the Emperor had merely tried to exploit the occasion to convey a line of responsibility which his undertaking under Article III should be read as entailing; or it could simply be an economic and political ploy brought forward to safeguard prospective interests in irrigational concessions.

Whatever the motives, it appeared in the letters that Cromer's lucid instructions fell short of clearly suggesting that his strategic concern for control of the Nile did, by virtue of the treaty, extend to tributaries of the Blue Nile and Sobat river systems.

Two decades after the treaty had been concluded, though, British reading was increasingly refined to imply that the treaty did in fact entail a qualified obligation in respect of the supplying streams of the two river basins.

In 1922, in the course of the Lake Tana Dam Concessions negotiations, Major Dodds, the British delegate in Ethiopia approached the Abyssinian authorities with a draft Tana Dam Agreement, which reminded Ethiopia of its obligation not to construct nor authorize the construction of any work 'which would diminish the volume of the waters flowing in to the Nile.' A circumspectly couched proposal recognized the 'existing native rights and those of the Abyssinian Government to use the Lake Tana, the Blue Nile and its tributaries', subject to the condition that any contemplated use shall not involve 'the arrest or diverting in anyway whatsoever of the flows of the waters . . . by placing constructions of any sort . . . or by constructing regulators or dams of any kind, or by any other means which would

6 Draft Telegram to Cromer (1907), note 5.

7 Telegram from Cromer, Cairo, 7–9 March 1907, FO 371/14591.

8 Sir Barton, Lake Tana Negotiations, Addis Ababa, 18 August 1930, FO 371/14591.

diminish the waters of the Lake Tana, the Blue Nile or its tributaries in any manner whatsoever'.[9]

Cromer's assurance of limited rights with regard to the Blue Nile and its tributaries was replicated with enhanced lucidity and alteration in another draft treaty proposed in 1927 in connection with a Tana Dam concession. In his projected framework, Bentinck, the British emissary in Addis Ababa acknowledged that 'the riparian rights of the inhabitants dwelling on both sides of the Blue Nile throughout its length in the Ethiopian territory to use this water for domestic purposes as well as for the cultivation of food crops necessary for their own subsistence will not be questioned, but it is understood that no attempt will be made to arrest, divert or obstruct in any way the flow of the Blue Nile or any of its tributaries . . .'[10]

In all subsequent communications, the Foreign Office endorsed this official view unceasingly.

If late-arriving post-facto interpretations could also be presumed as clutching legal credence, in 1929, the Foreign Office likewise held the view that 'the principle is accepted that the waters of the Nile, that is to say the combined flow of the White and Blue Niles and their tributaries must be considered as a single unit, designed for the use of the peoples inhabiting their banks according to their needs and their capacity to benefit therefrom; and in conformity with this principle, it is recognized that Egypt has a prior right to the maintenance of her present supplies of water for the areas now under cultivation . . .'[11]

In 1935, the British colonial office in Cairo suggested, in view of a similar pledge delivered to Italy under the Anglo-Italian Notes of Exchange of 1925, that some lines should be inserted in the Draft Anglo-Ethiopian Agreement on Lake Tana Dam. This, it was proposed, should define the duty not to arrest the flow of the Blue Nile as not precluding 'a reasonable use of the waters in question by the inhabitants of the region, *even to the extent of constructing* dams for hydro-electric power or small reservoirs in minor effluents to store water for domestic purposes, as well as for the cultivation of food crops necessary to their subsistence.'[12] [Emphasis added]

Admittedly, a British concession of such a scale had never been proposed in any of the preceding communications. Progressive as it may have appeared, Great Britain conceived that such formulation of local interests would needlessly involve a continuous description of what does or does not include reasonable use in any given circumstance; hence the proposition was not officially endorsed and the draft had to employ the exact phrases previously suggested by Bentinck. Simply, the Foreign Office establishment took the view that the treaty had a wider scope than revealed by its express wording.

Evidences of the scale of obligation involved under the Anglo-Ethiopian Treaty are not inferred solely from the illuminations afforded in diplomatic and historical

9 Huge Dodds to Viscount Allenby, Draft Agreement, Addis Ababa, 26 December 1922, FO 371/8403.

10 Bentinck to Sir Austen Chamberlain, Suggestions for a Treaty, Addis Ababa, 10 May 1927, Enc2.1, FO 371/12341.

11 International Law Commission (1986) *Yearbook of International Law Commission*, vol 2, no 1, p 110.

12 Sir M Lampson, Lake Tana Dam Project, Draft Agreement or Treaty, Cairo 22 June 1935, Minutes, FO 371/19186.

recitals. It must be noted in like order that the Anglo-Ethiopian agreement was tied in an epoch that witnessed the expansion of myriads of bilateral and multilateral treaty frameworks regulating the utilization of shared water resources, mostly engaging European powers. Each of the agreements portrayed a set of unique features depending on the 'balance of power' of the parties involved; some had established reciprocal benefits, while others had merely instituted incongruous servitudes with regard to the beneficial uses of international watercourses.

The international legal regime governing the non-navigational uses of transboundary rivers had also been just evolving. In spite of the great variations in state practice, at least in the earliest decades of the twentieth century, the most predominant line of thinking had adopted a narrower perception of the river concept.

Overall, the early developments and experiences afforded states increasingly refined understandings of not only some of the rudimentary principles of international watercourses law as such, but also the conceptual and physical relationships between various elements of hydrologic phenomena in river basins. Most importantly, the distinction and interdependence between *rivers* and *river systems* had been highlighted.

Hence, if, in their dealings states willingly choose to apply one concept and not the other, or couch the phrasing of their agreements in a particular way, it would be reasonably presumed that such a course had been adopted simply because the states had cautiously wished-for the consequences.

The conflicting British diplomatic deportments of the post-treaty decades notwithstanding, on its face, the Anglo-Ethiopian Treaty appears too plain to call for sophisticated elaboration.

Consequently, in tying the eventual accord, if Great Britain had solely employed the phrase 'on or across the Blue Nile, Tsana and Sobat rivers' without explicit or implicit reference to the source-components of these two head streams, one can deduce that the phrases were framed as such either because J. Harrington could not have mustered a better deal or probably because he felt content with the treaty's present formulation. At least, several of Lord Cromer's diplomatic correspondences exchanged in the immediate aftermath would tend to corroborate this contention.

Besides, looking at the contents of contemporaneous treaty engagements and its repute in contriving intricate accords, it would be naïve to presume that Great Britain's stipulation under Article III had been funnelled by lack of proper forethought about the impending implication of obvious exclusion of parts of a river system from the purview of the treaty regime. A wealth of water uses treaties involving the same country and concluded over the same epoch sufficiently demonstrate that in fact it was not.

A few such treaties can be presented here. A tripartite agreement concluded in 1906 between itself, France and Italy secured British objectives by laying down a provision that safeguarded its hydraulic interests in 'the Nile basin, and more specifically as regards the regulation of the waters of that river and its tributaries'.[13] Under

13 Agreement Between Great Britain, France, and Italy respecting Abyssinia, London, 13 December 1906.

Article III of the Anglo-Italian Notes exchanged in 1925, Great Britain promised Italy an exclusive sphere of economic influence in west Ethiopia provided that the Italian government 'recognizing the prior hydraulic rights of Egypt and Sudan, will not engage to construct on the head waters of the Blue or White Niles or their tributaries or effluents any work which might sensibly modify their flow in to the Nile'.[14]

In a similar development involving Great Britain and Belgium, London dealt with its rights as relating not only to the use of the head course but also the streams which form part of the boundary between the territories or which flow from one of those territories into the other.[15] Likewise, Article VI of the 1909 Treaty signed between the USA and Great Britain (representing Canada) with a view to regulating the use of transboundary waters plainly stipulated that 'the Saint Mary and Milk Rivers and their tributaries are to be treated as one stream for purposes of irrigation and power . . .'[16]

Of course, it could be admitted that each of the treaty schemes had been concluded against a backdrop of unique political and historical circumstances that dictated the particular composition of the terms. A few had tended to set a fairly reciprocal rights-regime while others did quite the inverse.

Without losing sight of this fact, in the specific context of the case under consideration, there appears little or no conceivable reason to suppose why Great Britain, then at the height of its imperial powers and hence in an imposing position, could not have framed Article III along the *same model* reiterated above, if indeed such objective had been contemplated.

After all, the physical characteristics as well as the pattern of lives sustained by the Blue Nile and Baro-Akobo river basins had been such that any consideration of a broader construction of the treaty, transforming minor streams and tributaries into international rivers could in effect turn the country in to a state of permanent servitude as regards its key resources. Such a view would prove politically objectionable to any independent state and legally the subject of intensive scrutiny. A limitation of such a scale distresses sovereign prerogatives and cannot be upheld unless it has found an *unequivocal expression* in a treaty undertaking.

Conclusions

From a geographic point of view, the absolute hydrological interdependence of tributaries and head courses of a river system cannot be refuted. Yet, the plain composition of the Anglo-Ethiopian Treaty can hardly warrant a line of interpretation that implies the extension of the non-interference obligation to a range of tributaries and rivulets supplying floods to the Blue Nile and Baro-Akobo-Sobat rivers.

14 The Exchange of Notes between the UK and Italy Respecting Concessions for a Barrage at Lake Tana and a Railway Across Abyssinia from Eritrea to Italian Somaliland, Rome, 14/20 December 1925.

15 Treaty Between the United Kingdom and the Independent State of Congo to Redefine their Respective Spheres of Influence in Eastern and Central Africa, London, 9 May 1906.

16 Treaty between the USA and Great Britain Relating to the Boundary Waters, and Questions Arising Between the USA and Canada, Washington, 11 January 1909.

In consequence, should Ethiopia's institution of major water control works on the feeding streams entail appreciable levels of effect against the interests of Sudan – a succeeding state, or that its actions are assessed as transcending the equitable uses threshold, its accountability would be called for but only as a corollary of a breach of contemporary rules of customary international law, and not a violation of Article III of the Anglo-Ethiopian Treaty.

It is true that in substantiating the respective positions of the states propounded in connection with the treaty, discussions in this Part had made extensive references to the subsequent practices of the parties. Potentially, this can raise some legal and methodological concerns.

Still, while the Vienna Convention on the Law of Treaties has provided for a clear hierarchical order, the use of historical and diplomatic correspondences and other supplementary means of interpretation is neither novel nor unwarranted.[17] In fact, it will be demonstrated in Chapter 6 that there had been many instances where, in resolving disputes relating to interpretation, various international courts and tribunals had resorted post-facto to historical and diplomatic manuscripts detailing diverse aspects of sovereign conducts.

Of course, neither *preparatory works* nor the *subsequent communications* of states parties to a treaty could be introduced enthusiastically to counter the meaning of an unambiguous treaty text. No interpretative enterprise can concern itself with the unrestricted exposition of extrinsic materials, but endeavour to identify and apply the objective meaning as conveyed in treaty texts as such. In its disposition on the Interpretation of the Statute of the Memel Territory, the Permanent Court of International Justice rightly opined:[18]

> As regards argument based on the history of the text, the Court must first of all point out that, as it has constantly held, the preparatory works cannot be adduced to interpret a text which is, in itself, sufficiently clear.

On the other hand, in its views on the Advisory Opinion on the Interpretation of the Greco-Turkish Agreement of 1 December 1926, the same Court pronounced:[19]

> In the Court's opinions, this view is well founded; it considers that the attitude adopted by the British and Turkish Governments after the signature of the Treaty . . . is only valuable in the present respect as an indication of their views regarding the clauses in question', and not as a means of authoritatively establishing their meaning.

17 United Nations Vienna Convention on the Law of Treaties (1969), Vienna 23 May 1969. UN Treaty Series Vol 1155, p 331, Articles 31.3 and 32.

18 *Interpretation of Statute of Memel Territory (UK vs. Lith)*, Judgment, August 11, 1932 PCIJ (Ser A/B) No 49, p 10.

19 *Interpretation of Greco-Turkish Agreement of Dec. 1st, 1926*, Advisory Opinion, August 28, 1928 PCIJ (Ser B) No 16, p 24.

6 Construing the substantive scope of the Anglo-Ethiopian Treaty of May 1902

The import and suitability of international rules of treaty interpretation

Establishing interpretation of a treaty that prevails in the relations of the two states and in the process, trying to ascertain the nature of obligations depicted under the Anglo-Ethiopian Treaty presumes a cautious employ of the appropriate rules of international law not only to the treaty regime as such, but also to events that preceded and followed its conclusion.

In this section, two vital issues would need to be addressed beforehand: on what basis would contemporary rules of international law codified under the Vienna Convention on the Law of Treaties (1969) be applied *retroactively* to regulate the interpretation of the Anglo-Ethiopian Treaty of 1902, and acts and facts associated with the conclusion of the treaty? In addition, what suitability dilemmas does the employ of the Convention's rules prompt?

These questions shall be dealt with first, before engaging in the discussion of multifaceted issues involving the interpretation of the ordinary meaning of certain controlling phrases under Article III the Anglo-Ethiopian treaty, given in their context and in the light of its object and purpose.

The contemporary rules of international law that proffer an essential framework for the juridical analysis of interpretative dilemmas are largely but not exclusively composed in the Vienna Convention on the Law of Treaties of 1969.[1] The Convention's provisions had codified several of the pertinent rules defining the competence of state officials and regulating the formation, interpretation, application and termination of treaties.

The Vienna Convention had instituted a legal regime structured to govern only such contracts as are concluded between states who are parties to it.[2] Ethiopia signed the treaty on 30 April 1970, a year after it was opened for signature by the United Nations Conference on the Law of Treaties on 23 May 1969, but stopped short of ratifying the instrument. Sudan, on the other hand, signed and ratified

1 United Nations Vienna Convention on the Law of Treaties (1969), Vienna 23 May 1969. UN Treaty Series Vol 1155, p 331, Article 4, Article 7.

2 United Nations Vienna Convention on the Law of Treaties (1969), Article 4, Article 7.

the instrument respectively on 23 May 1969 and 18 April 1990, and has since remained a party.[3]

Without prejudice to the independent application of any of its rules by virtue of the operation of customary international law, the Convention has expressly interdicted the retroactive use of its provisions to all treaties, including the Anglo-Ethiopian accord of May 1902, and all acts, facts or situations which took place before its entry in to force. At first glimpse, the circumstance may appear to pose an insoluble hitch and hence diminish the practical merit of conversing on the contents of the Convention.

Quite conversely, the Convention's vitality lay in the fact that several of its provisions had attempted to merely codify the customary law relating to treaties, although there are other provisions that represent progressive development rather than codification.[4]

In fact, in numerous contentious proceedings, the International Court of Justice (ICJ) had the occasion to affirm that the Convention's rules on interpretation reproduced custom. In the Territorial Dispute case between Libyan Arab Jamahiriya and Chad, for instance, the Court pronounced that 'in accordance with customary international law, reflected in Article 31 of the Vienna Convention, a treaty must be interpreted in good faith, in accordance with the ordinary meaning to be given to its terms in their context, and in the light of its object and purpose'.[5] In delivering its judgment involving the interpretation of treaties associated with boundary regimes, the Court made an effective use of all the principles featured in Article 31 of the Vienna Convention, although neither Chad nor Libya had been parties to the Convention.

In like tune, in the *Oil Platforms* case, the International Court re-established the view that general rules of treaty interpretation are incorporated under the 1969 Vienna Convention on the Law of Treaties; in its disposition, the Court utilized several of such principles constituted under Article 31 although Iran had not ratified the instrument.[6]

In consequence, neither the operation of Article 4 of the Vienna Convention forbidding retroactive application nor the fact that Ethiopia had opted not to ratify the instrument can preclude analysis of the Anglo-Ethiopian Treaty on the basis of rules of interpretation incorporated under the Vienna Convention. The Convention's rules on interpretation of treaties had merely reiterated international custom. Indeed, it will be shown later that several tribunals and judicial institutions had routinely declared the instrument as a primary source of international rules on treaty interpretation, even with respect to treaty relations between states who are not parties to the Convention. The discussions in the forthcoming units are enlightened by such considerations.

3 United Nations, *Treaty Series*, Vol 1155, p 331.

4 Peter Malanczuc (1997) *Akehurst's Modern Introduction to International Law*, New York, Routledge, p 130.

5 *Territorial Dispute (Libyan Arab Jamahiriya/Chad)*, Judgement, ICJ Reports, 1994, p 19.

6 *Oil Platforms (Islamic Republic of Iran/United States of America)*, Judgement, ICJ Reports 2003, p 25.

Inevitably, the application of the provisions embraced under the Vienna Convention is not called for in all cases. To address cases of inconsistencies or ambiguities, bilateral or multilateral agreements may themselves insert a final clause proclaiming particular treaty version as the authoritative edition. A provision in such accords may stipulate that all authentic texts or only one of such as is drawn in a particular language shall be endowed a status of an authoritative treaty version, hence ascribing different languages varying scales of eminence for purposes of interpretation. The point is that treaties may themselves address problems associated with interpretative dilemmas and discrepancies in meaning.

Article 5 of both the English and Amharic editions of the Anglo-Ethiopian Treaty has particularly provided that 'the treaty equally drawn in Amharic and English languages, was signed and sealed by Emperor Menelik, on behalf of his kingdom, and Colonel Harrington, Her Britannic Majesty's Agent in Ethiopia'.

Disputes over the interpretation of authentic texts of validly concluded accords are not uncommon. This reality largely emanates from the obvious imperfection of human language that employs words and phrases susceptible to multiple explanations. In part, the cause could also be attributed to the international legal order itself which bestows states a degree of discretion in interpreting treaty commitments. Of course, the support which any unilateral reading of a treaty commands would naturally vary and while only independent umpires would possess the eventual say, the international system also permits states to appreciate (in good faith) their treaty pledges in manners they particularly deduce as appropriate.

However, the discretion of states is not without bounds. In particular, when an objective elucidation of the contents and connotation of treaty provisions is at issue, which is the very purpose of interpretation, the liberty of states is aptly circumscribed by the dictates of rules and principles of interpretation of international law, and especially, the cannons instituted under the Vienna Convention on the Law of Treaties.

Unfortunately, rules of interpretation developed over the years are, as Brownlie observed, general in content, question begging and contradictory. Whereas there is sufficient evidence of their use in international adjudications, several authorities, including the first two Special Raporteurs of the International Law Commission on the Law of Treaties, had expressed doubts as to the very existence in international law of any 'general rules for the interpretation of treaties'.[7] Other jurists uttered reservation as to their 'obligatory nature', but admitted the existence of some canons to which they affixed unequal levels of credence.[8]

Even under circumstances where recourse to such rules may be presumed as obliging in constructing the intended meaning of any particular text, neither states nor adjudicating bodies are bound to pick any specific rule of interpretation; their choice of the applicable principle hinges on a number of considerations and subjective appreciation of the circumstances. In reality, this abundance and imprecision of rules of interpretation has unwrapped some contour for egocentric selection and application of any meaning which an interpreter may wish to form in any

7 International Law Commission (1966) *Yearbook of International Law Commission*, vol 2, p 218.

8 International Law Commission (1966), note 7.

given situation. To a degree, this would seem to affect the relative value of rules of interpretation as objective tools for resolving disputes.

What is more, a scanty inspection of the pertinent legal regime applied during the conclusion of the Anglo-Ethiopian Treaty of 1902 reveals certain evolution of the rules of treaty interpretation, possibly differing from stipulations of the Vienna Convention. If the generally recognized principle that facts need be appraised by reference to rules existing at the time of their incidence sways current wisdom, a sequence of dilemmas would also surface instantaneously: what unique features do the rules of international law applicable at the time of the conclusion of the treaty exhibit? How considerably have they evolved over the decades to disparage current dialogues on contemporary laws governing the theme? Moreover, what import, if any, have the parties attached to the temporal element?

The issues could simply be unending and versatile. In the forthcoming sections, therefore, the pertinent provisions of the Vienna Convention on the law of treaties would be investigated bearing in mind some of these associated challenges and 'appropriateness' dilemmas.

Applying rules of treaty interpretation to the Anglo-Ethiopian Treaty

Article 33 of the Vienna Convention on the Law of Treaties sets forth the relevant rules. Hence, when a Treaty has been authenticated in two or more languages, the text would be regarded as equally authoritative in each language unless the parties agree or the treaty provides otherwise that in case of divergence, a particular text shall prevail. Both the English and Amharic texts of the Anglo-Ethiopian Treaty have provided for the parity of the two languages.

Yet, authentic texts may carry provisions that bear out different connotations and as in the Anglo-Ethiopian treaty, the parties may well fail to set beforehand the version that shall prevail in cases of variance. In such eventuality, the Convention institutes a fundamental general assumption: that the terms of a treaty are presumed to have the same meaning in each authentic text. The rule absolves one of the necessities of engaging in routine comparison of multiple texts with a view to carrying out their application.

The presumption is, however, nothing more than a mere theoretical implement and indeed rebuttable as soon as a plausible claim of difference surfaces. As noted above, while the legal basis constituting the freedom of choice of states is hardly definitive, in the face of discrepancy, contracting parties generally tend to rely on a version of a treaty that suits their stated positions. In practice, the ingenuity and organization of human language has been such that in all probability, hard-to-reconcile variations of facts or allegations of different understandings crop up as soon as agreements are inked in multiple languages.[9]

9 In contrast, Hardy argued that in theory and as a general rule, the existence of more than one text gives a clearer indication of the intention of the contracting parties and even if it does not facilitate interpretation, makes the same more accurate and thorough. Jean Hardy (1961) 'The Interpretation of plurilingual Treaties by International Courts and Tribunals', *BYIL*, p 139.

Contradictory perceptions arising from a multilingual make-up of treaties notwithstanding, interpretative endeavours must in any event emphasize the unity of agreements. True, bilateral or multilateral accords may be drawn authentically in several languages, with each language text authoritatively expressing the contents, which potentially exacerbates the risk of deviation. Yet, as the International Law Commission had noted, 'in law, there is only one treaty – one set of terms accepted by the parties and one common intention with respect to those terms – even when authentic texts appear to diverge';[10] the judge 'gives effect to all the texts by adopting a single interpretation to which they all lend themselves'.[11]

In this Chapter, what prompted the interpretative debate under the Anglo-Ethiopian Treaty, if at all a variation that warrants interpretation can be displayed beyond any shade of doubt, and whether the ambiguity of the crucial phrases under Article III had been occasioned solely in the English edition or in both authentic texts of the treaty shall be the object of meticulous investigation.

In either case, any enterprise that seeks to elucidate the terms of a treaty and construct a meaning which can be reasonably presumed as constituting the joint volition of the parties at the time of the agreement should highlight the equal authority of both the Amharic and English texts, and must utilize tools recognized under the Convention and the rules of custom.

The multilingual constitution of a treaty as such hardly ordains the utility of a special set of interpretative rules. In fact, with respect to the interpretation of treaties drawn in two or more languages, the Vienna Convention merely foresaw the application of the ordinary rules of interpretation stipulated under Articles 31 and 32.

In some instances, the task of constructing the true meaning and harmonizing conflicting languages may complicate where the texts not only lend themselves to multiple readings, but also that the discrepancy is, as in Article III of the 1902 agreement, manifestly huge, at least in the eyes of the parties involved.

In such cases, an unpretentious effort to forge the parties' common intention would probably not be achieved except through preferring the readings of one text over the other.

In the case in point, Great Britain had naturally advocated the wider view that obliges Ethiopia not to arrest the flow of the rivers in anyway whatsoever, whereas Ethiopia's observation deviated. The latter made a case under Article III of the treaty that it was merely bound not to block up, stop up its flow from banks to banks, and nothing further. If ambiguously, the first edition would further Great Britain's monopolistic holding of the resource for downstream uses, whereas the latter version, at least on its face, afforded Ethiopia substantial discretion in terms of a right of future uses of the river resource.

Yet, an objective umpire had to legally construct the version that best conforms to the texts and expresses the underlying intent of the parties.

The discrepancies in the connotation of the two texts cannot be resolved except through the combined employ of technical tools of interpretation: the standard

10 International Law Commission (1966), note 7, p 225.
11 Hardy (1961), note 9, p 82.

rules contained in Articles 31–32 of the Convention. Article 33(4) stipulated that when comparison of the authentic texts discloses a difference, which the application of Articles 31–32 does not remove, the meaning that best reconciles the texts, having regard to the object and purpose of the treaty, shall be adopted.

Consequently, in resolving the mystery, the first commission would evidently involve the application of the spirit of Articles 31–32 of the Convention.

The Convention obliges the parties to interpret the treaty in question 'in good faith in accordance with the ordinary meaning to be given to the terms of the treaty in their context and in light of its object and purpose' (Article 31.1). The context may include not only the text itself, but also the preamble, its annexes, other agreements and accepted instruments between the parties to the treaty (Article 31.2). Subsequent agreements of the parties regarding interpretation and application of the treaty and subsequent practice in the application of the treaty shall likewise be taken in to account (Article 31.3).

Where such means prove unable to ascertain the meaning or leaves it ambiguous, or their application leads to a result that is manifestly absurd or unreasonable, the Convention authorizes, as a supplementary means of interpretation, recourse to the preparatory works of the treaty and the circumstances of its conclusion.

As depicted in the careful display of tools under Article 31, the Convention had not pronounced the principle that should be particularly emphasized in any given interpretative situation. International law does not recognize the existence of a rigid system or hierarchy that invariably applies in all contexts; nor does it offer perfect solution to every inscrutability caused by language variations in treaties. Several tribunals and judicial bodies had constantly applied one or another of these rules in different circumstances.

Over the years, the emphasis on each of the tools thus employed had evolved; some attached greater weight to the underlying intent while others gave preference to the objective contents of the text as such. In light of such practices, it is not impossible to perceive of a kaleidoscope of interpretations of the same treaty text if any given rule is accorded unwarranted credence, erroneous precedence or is employed in isolation. The greatest heed to the underlying spirit of Article 31 of the Convention is only obliging.

Yet, any enterprise that seeks to blend the principles proposed under Article 31 would by no means constitute an easy undertaking.

In one of its reports to the United Nations General Assembly, the International Law Commission tendered only part of the solution when it highlighted that the successive paragraphs of the Convention do not by any means 'lay down a hierarchical order of the various elements of interpretation'.[12] The Commission recognized the concerns stated in the preceding paragraphs and confirmed that the arrangement of Article 31, in its present form, has been prompted solely by 'considerations of logic, not any obligatory legal hierarchy'.[13]

12 International Law Commission (1966), note 7, p 219.
13 International Law Commission (1966), note 7, p 220.

Textual interpretation of Article III

Texts as objective proofs of the parties' intentions

Repeatedly, the Permanent Court of International Justice had the occasion to employ the tools depicted under Article 31 of the Convention. In several dispositions, the Court applied the *ordinary* and *contextual* meaning approaches, and had tended to favour the general rule of *restrictive interpretation* adopting a more limited meaning in harmonizing contradictory versions. Similarly, the jurisprudence of the International Court of Justice followed suit of 'the majority of international tribunals' in favouring the *textual* approach;[14] the Court attached primacy to the ordinary meaning of the text of a treaty.[15] Cases adjudicated over the years corroborate this account.

Hence, in the proceedings of the Ethio-Eritrean Boundary Commission arbitrating on boundary disputes, the Boundary Commission reiterated the stances of the PCIJ, ICJ and the ILC. In ascertaining what the parties had intended under the pertinent treaty, the Commission asserted, it would apply the general rule that a treaty is to be interpreted in good faith, in accordance with the ordinary meaning to be given to the terms of the treaty in their context, and in the light of its object and purpose.[16]

While the Convention's tools proffer an organized set of techniques crucial in establishing a common intention, their application is not necessarily called in every circumstance. The particular framing of the treaty itself, the special features of the case and development of the disagreement must be such that there certainly is a need for interpretation.

Where such necessity is established, common sense and the order of arrangement of the interpretative tools under Article 31 would dictate that the initial phase in any investigation must focus on the treaty texts as such, and aim at ascertaining the ordinary meaning of the terms at issue. The International Court of Justice had already declared that 'the textual approach to treaty interpretation is regarded by it as established law'.[17] Textual formalism had been highlighted in several of the Court's jurisprudences.

Texts are objective proofs of the parties' intentions, and normally, the search for common volition should not endeavour to read the treaty as denoting a line contrary to the express stipulations. This reference constitutes an implied warning to any undertaking that places undue emphasis on the intention of the parties as an independent tool where the text exhibits plain and simple content. In the words of the International Law Commission, the parties would simply be presumed to have that intention which appears from the ordinary meaning of the terms used by them,[18] and that must be championed within reasonable confines. An excessively

14 International Law Commission (1966), note 7, p 218.

15 Ian Brawnlie (2003) *Principles of International Law*, New York/Oxford, Oxford University Press, p 612.

16 *Eritrea-Ethiopia Boundary Commission Decision Regarding the Delimitation of the Border between the State of Eritrea and the Federal Democratic Republic of Ethiopia*, The Hague, 13 April 2002.

17 International Law Commission (1966), note 7, p 220.

18 International Law Commission (1966), note 7, p 220.

liberal approach under any other guise could defeat the very object of a treaty regime.

Hence, the declared policies and conflicting observations of the parties to the Anglo-Ethiopian Treaty notwithstanding, at this particular juncture, the theme that merits deliberation shall be what precisely an elucidation of the ordinary meaning of Article III unveils.

The English edition of the treaty obliged Ethiopia 'not to construct or allow to be constructed any work across the Blue Nile, Lake Tana or the Sobat, which would arrest the flow of their waters in to the Nile', except with a previous agreement of the Anglo-Sudanese government.

Under the Amharic equivalent of the treaty text, Ethiopia's undertaking, composed in 'ወንዝ ፡ ተዳር ፡ እዳር ፡ የሚደፍን ፡ ሥራ ፡ እንዳይሰራ' stipulated that Ethiopia shall not construct, nor authorize anyone to construct a work that blocks up/stops up from river bank to river bank the water descending from the Black Abbay, from the Tana Sea, and from the Sobat River towards the White Abbay without a previous authorization. The root verb of the same text in the Amharic parlance – *daffana* – denotes the equivalent meaning of 'to stop up, to fill, plug or close tightly, or to block a passage'.

Shortly after the conclusion of the Anglo-Ethiopian treaty, the bilateral relations between the contracting parties tended to expose that if on anything, the scale of pledge assumed by Ethiopia rested on the interpretation and potential implication of the phrases *arrest* and *block up from bank to bank* both under the English and Amharic texts of Article III, respectively.

In colloquial lexicon and a context emphasizing its particular use in the English version of the treaty, arrest was employed as conveying a counterpart meaning of 'to stop, check, brake automatically a motion; to cease, cause something cease from, or discontinue' or as 'a device for stopping motion'.[19]

Both parties held different perceptions with regard to the substantive scope of obligation assumed under the treaty.

In conversational dictionary and in the context emphasizing its particular use under Article III, neither the expression arrest nor its Amharic equivalent appear to insinuate a controversial language. In fact, the description of the English text has been intimately congruent with the corresponding Amharic text which had been constituted as 'ወንዝ ፡ ተዳር ፡ እዳር ፡ የሚደፍን ፡ ሥራ ፡ እንዳይሰራ'; literally, the latter translates to denote the meaning 'not to block up/stop up from river bank to river bank'.

If Article III is interpreted in light of a literal use of both phrases, the treaty can be construed as instituting an Ethiopian commitment not to engage in the development of any hydraulic installations on the aforementioned headwaters that shall have the effect of 'blocking up/stuffing up the inundation from river bank to river bank'. In effect, this involves a prohibition against storing the entire floods behind dams or analogous hydraulic structures without a fortiori obtaining

19 Refer to various explanations proffered under the Cambridge Online Dictionary, Merriam Webster's Dictionary, Wikipedia, *Encyclopaedia Britannica* and Dictionary Thesaurus.

Anglo-Sudanese authorisation. Advancing the proper spirit of the treaty would likewise presume the extension of such prohibition to cases of complete diversion or appropriation of the river courses and all other obstructions factually producing similar effects.

Should such interpretation be pressed to the next logical stratum, an a contrario reading of this exposition would appear to uphold that the treaty does not bar Ethiopia from engaging in the assembly of hydraulic edifices that propose to merely cause a diminished flow of the headwaters, and not their arrest/blocking up. There exists a material distinction between arrest, which denotes a state of complete grip, and other ventures reducing or diminishing the course, which merely presume conditions of partial interference or control. On its face, at least, the ordinary meaning of terms of the accord had hardly anticipated to exclude all forms of interference with the flow of the rivers, and hence did not appear to accommodate long-advocated British or Sudanese monopolistic perceptions.

In as much as the foregoing approach is adopted, therefore, no connotational qualms can be expected to arise. And the established tenet that treaty terms drawn in multiple languages are presumed to embody the same meaning in each authentic text naturally holds ground. To extract other objectives beyond the clear expression of terms and venture to ascribe the letters a countering meaning could potentially constitute an act of treaty revision, and not interpretation.

To conclude, in so far as the treaty has been conceived as the product of the free acts of two sovereign states, concluded with a view to settling long-standing boundary issues and ancillary matters, both Great Britain and Ethiopia shall be presumed to subscribe to that intention which is implicit in the simple expression of the words used in their agreement. If Great Britain had intended to enlarge the scope and read the Article differently, it should have striven to have such a position find expression in the treaty itself. As it stands, the wording of Article III is neither obscure nor ambiguous.

Conflict between textual interpretation and 'perceived' treaty objectives

However convincing the ordinary interpretation of the treaty presented above may sound, common sense promptly poses the obvious question: why would Great Britain engage in a treaty scheme that apparently has no merit in shielding its monopolistic designs?

From a purely physical point of view, the scale of understanding that had then prevailed in relation to the essential features of river basins, water control works and competences had been such that in the early decades of the twentieth century, it would be extremely unfeasible to block floods of a river course as huge as the Blue Nile in *entirety*. This practical consideration derides the proximity of potential threats and hence weakens the interpretation of Article III in its aforesaid form.

In fact, in the 1900s, Sir Murdoch MacDonald, an able engineer then working as technical counsel of the Egyptian Ministry of Public Works had summarized the core essence of the contemporaneous perception. 'Egypt has nothing to fear over its water . . . [for] no human power exists that could prevent the winter floods from passing through their course from the Blue Nile in Ethiopia to Sudan, and from there to Egypt.'[20]

While challenges associated with the clarity of the treaty's specific objectives could be admitted, certain extraneous evidences can be adduced indicating in some form that the parties, or perhaps one of them, could not be presumed to have intended the particular formulation implicit in the ordinary reading presented above. This assertion may not be substantiated without recourse to the post-treaty historical accounts of the state parties to the treaty, re-constituted in a legally relevant context below.

Arguably, Ethiopia's phrasing of the Amharic version which prohibits only the complete arrest of the Nile floods could have been triggered by a conscious defence of its sovereign interests.

In 1907, i.e. a few years after the conclusion of the treaty, Emperor Menelik was engaged in negotiations for the insertion of an interpretative note into the Anglo-Ethiopian treaty, which he computed would water down its downbeating implication. In the same year, the Emperor succeeded in retaining Lord Cromer's guarantee that 'the terms of Article III of the Treaty of May 1902 do not imply any intention of interfering with local rights',[21] so long as 'no attempt is to be made to arrest or interfere in any way with the flow of these rivers by placing obstructions of any sort in their channels or by constructing regulators or dams of any kind across their channels or beds'.[22]

In one of his regular telegrams to Cromer, Clark, London's representative at Emperor Menelik's Court communicated that the Ethiopian king had 'most earnestly assured [me] that he has no intention of in any way breaking his pledge given in Article III of the Treaty of May 15, 1902'.[23] The correspondence did not say whether such a proclamation had intended to admit a narrower obligation implicit in the above interpretation, or a broader scenario forbearing all forms of interference.

If only incidentally, however, Lord Cromer's formulation of Ethiopia's rights highlighted the distinction between arrest and other forms of interference. In fact, in reading the treaty as implying the prohibition of all other forms of interference with the exception of those required for native uses, Cromer appeared to introduce clauses which were not present in the treaty text, and hence, broadened its scope. As noted above, Article III had merely barred river uses that arrest the flow, leaving other scales of intervention outside its purview.

What prompted Menelik to call for the insertion of an interpretative clause in to the treaty accommodating a line of understanding that the accord should not bar Ethiopia's utilization of the rivers, and why he declined the offer when Lord

20 Yunan Labib Rizk (2004) 'Chronicles, War Games', *Al-Ahram Weekly Online*, Issue 711 <http://weekly.ahram.org.eg/2004/711/chrncls.htm>, last accessed December 2010.

21 Telegram from Cromer, Cairo, 7–9 March 1907, FO 371/14591.

22 Telegram from Cromer (1907), note 21.

23 Telegram from Cromer (1907), note 21.

Cromer proffered a guarded surety remained vital pieces of detail which cannot be established indisputably.

A few hypotheses may however be presented in this regard. In view of his qualified leverage in a decentralized administrative structure, the Emperor might have grasped that politically, it would be suicidal to engage in private-like treaties that could have been readily interpreted as trading out sovereign interests. On one occasion, the Emperor reportedly justified his insist for insertion of an interpretative clause since without such enclosure, the subsidy arrangement in return for which he would have received some fiscal recompense might be identified as a price for the purchase of Nile waters for which 'he will be accused of selling his country'.[24]

In the same year, Clark, the British representative in Addis Ababa speculated that the probable explanation had been that the Emperor 'wants to sell cotton concessions' to certain big powers and assumed that the British may 'object to irrigation canals'[25] on the basis of the treaty.

Most probably, though, Great Britain would not have opposed such schemes, for such developments could have withdrawn only meagre volumes of waters. A sizeable proportion of the Nile floods had then poured to the sea without use; any pattern of utilization on such scales would not have posed serious prejudice to downstream interests.

This reading of British position could be inferred from the Foreign Office's subsequent reportage which adopted the procedures that should be followed in order to obtain Italian political support for British dam concessions in Ethiopia. In the report, it was conceded that the British Government could not insist (against Italy) 'on a rigid monopoly in every drop of water as would prevent even small local schemes . . . a position which could hardly be maintained against the Abyssinians themselves'.[26]

Whatever the factors that engendered Emperor Menelik's moves, the early negotiations under the subsidy arrangement alluded to the Emperor's restrictive reading of how Article III should be perceived; if in a limited form (applying to local irrigational rights), the British interpretation tended to fortify the Emperor's position under the treaty.

Nevertheless, this British construction would still fall far from admitting an absolute discretion on the part of Ethiopia with respect to rights of utilization; nor did it imply that Ethiopia could engage on any scale of development of the resources short of fully arresting the river flows.

Quite on the contrary, in view of its huge economic and geo-political stakes in Egypt and Sudan, it would be bewildering to observe how Great Britain could have intended to profiteer from a legal arrangement that merely forbids Ethiopia from damming up the whole flow of the rivers while permitting other scales of

24 Sir Barton, Lake Tana Negotiations, Addis Ababa, 18 August 1930, FO 371/14591.

25 G. Schuster, Note on Italian Negotiations for Concessions in Abyssinia, 6 June 1925, FO 371/10872.

26 G. Schuster (1925), note 25.

utilization that shrink the deluges and hence cause as much an injury. If anything else, five decades of British water diplomacy in the Tana dam negotiations (1900–1950) had copiously demonstrated that Great Britain had craved ad infinitum to secure increased volumes and steady flows of waters of the rivers.

Of course, the deep gorges and inaccessible geographical formation of the Blue Nile basin region had prompted Great Britain to rule out, from the onset, any grave threats related to significant irrigational developments in Ethiopia. Any engineering works, whether for complete diversion or for irrigational use of the waters would have largely constituted, in Dupuis's words 'an enormously costly and perfectly futile proceeding'.[27]

Indeed, a 1925 Foreign Office Report had post-facto confirmed Dupuis' observation. The report stated that one of the factual considerations that influenced London's early hydraulic policies with regard to the Blue Nile, and which had probably shaped the particular framing of Article III had presumed that 'the configuration of the land in Abyssinia and agricultural and other conditions are such that there is nothing which could usefully be done in the way of irrigation schemes in Abyssinia which would bring damage to the Sudan and Egypt . . .'.[28] The document concluded 'that cultivation in Abyssinia must be mainly rain cultivation'.[29]

On the part of the British, this line of geographical perception which ruled out the possibility of any scale of potential utilization of the Nile in Ethiopia could have prompted the framing of Article III in *more* than its ordinary context proposed earlier.

This would be particularly evident when one also notes that traditionally British water policies had pursued a firm downstream-oriented approach; it would appear naïve to presume that Great Britain would discount prospective threats of small scale interferences with the flow of the river that could have emerged within the range of practical economics, technology and politics.

True, this insinuation had not been clearly conveyed under Article III of the treaty. Yet, it can be reasonably submitted that London's disposition in the matter was but a cautiously thought-out retort in preserving its entrenched stakes in the basin. This can be explained as follows.

First, since the early expeditions of Dupuis, then acting under the instructions of Sir William Garstin, an Advisor of Egypt's Ministry of Public Works, the climatic

27 C.E. Dupuis (1936) 'Lake Tana and the Nile', *Journal of the Royal African Society*, vol 35, no 138, p 21.

After his expeditions in the Lake Tana environs and the Blue Nile Basin (1902–03), Dupuis suggested three possibilities of interference with the flows of the Blue Nile. One of his theories involved a complete diversion of its waters into some adjacent valley outside the Nile system. He noted the complete diversion of the river, even if possible, would be an enormously costly and apparently futile proceeding. From the point where it leaves the lake, the Blue Nile plunges down a great trench valley which forms one of the outstanding physical features of central Abyssinia. The sides of the valley rise thousands of feet to the plateau level on either hand; there would not seem to be any point within a great distance to which the water could be diverted and any idea of such diversion may be dismissed as *a practical impossibility*.

28 G. Schuster (1925), note 25.

29 G. Schuster (1925), note 25.

and physical conditions of the Blue Nile River and the Lake Tana areas had been constantly investigated with a view to optimizing their utility.

Besides, by 1902, British engineering had successfully completed construction of the first Aswan Dam which held 1bcm/yr of Nile waters.

And in the course of the 1930s and 40s, Great Britain's colonial administration had already mustered considerable hydrologic data that eventually prompted the floating of a whole set of grand Nile waters conservation schemes, projecting to achieve complete development of the resources across the basin. Two such plans – the Century Storage Scheme and the Equatorial Nile Projects, attended by adjunct works, proposed to undertake construction of a series of reservoirs that would have embanked unprecedented volume of Nile waters – ranging between 120 and 150bcm/yr.

The fundamental point of this presentation is that at the time when the treaty had been concluded, the *depth* of hydraulic information and engineering knowledge was not really too shallow to prompt Great Britain dismiss the incidence of future threats of water resources development in Ethiopia affecting downstream interests.

To this may also be supplemented concerns associated with the bitter competition of the British Empire with a no-less potent colonial power – France, and in some measures, Italy. Since the inception of the treaty, Great Britain had had genuine reasons to fear potential complicity between France or Italy and Ethiopia in prospective irrigational concessions. In fact, Italy's colonial manoeuvres in the same region that could have threatened long-recognized British stakes along the downstream Nile were forestalled only at about the same epoch.[30]

For all these reasons, to construe Article III of the Anglo-Ethiopian Treaty in a manner depicted above [as merely forbidding complete arrest of the flows] would potentially lead to a manifestly unreasonable conclusion. In engaging in the treaty, Great Britain had anticipated to gain greater privilege than is implicit in the ordinary reading of the terms of Article III.

If, while craving for some corroboration, a slight departure from the particular wordings of the treaty could be justified, one cannot help but note a solid sequence of post-accord diplomatic exchanges effected between the two states and demonstrating that in fact, Great Britain had advocated Article III as implying a near-absolute prohibition.

This proscription extended to the headwaters and tributaries alike and applied virtually to all proposed schemes, whether such had involved a complete

30 Since long before the conclusion of the Anglo-Ethiopian treaty, Italy had harboured the idea of a colonial possession in Ethiopia; a tripartite accord involving Great Britain and France (1906) had already acknowledged Italy's sphere of economic influence in western Ethiopia.

When Italy controversially interpreted its interests under the trilateral arrangement as *also* including a reservation of hydraulic rights on the Blue Nile and the Lake Tana waters, the British defended what they called 'unending Italian nuisances' in multiple diplomatic forums.

Great Britain's position reiterated the *inviolability* of the Nile flows in Ethiopia and projected to forestall any development initiative on the Blue Nile and Sobat rivers, whoever proposes any such enterprise.

damming or the organization of engineering works that merely proposed less detrimental uses.[31]

The state parties' understanding of Article III

In addition to Emperor Menelik's early efforts for a post-facto insertion of an interpretative clause under Article III, the state parties to the treaty had also had the occasion to bring forward their positions on the literal quintessence of their respective undertakings.

One of the earliest incidences took place three decades since the conclusion of the treaty, in 1927, when Crown Regent of the Ethiopian Empire, Ras Teferi referred the British Government's attention to the particular phraseology of Article III. He argued that the stipulation should be read correctly so that 'Emperor Menelik has made a Treaty not to construct a work which will block up the river completely . . . (and) that it does not forbid a construction in the interests of the natives'.[32]

Shortly after taking audience with the Crown Regent, Bentinck, the British ambassador in Addis Ababa, dispatched a letter addressed to Chamberlain along with reportage of his stormy meeting with Ras Teferi. Among other issues, his memo inscribed that Ras Teferi read him Article III of the treaty where he 'appeared to stress the words arrest the flow of their waters as though implying that so long as the work did not arrest the flow of the water [in entirety], it would not be contrary to the Treaty'.[33]

Caught by the new revelation, Great Britain spared no moment investigating the composition of Article III both in the Amharic and English versions with the aid of translators. Confident, the British envoy in Addis Ababa in the agent of Bentinck branded Teferi's paraphrase, which he claimed had introduced *completely* and *Bacharach* right before the term *arrest* in both versions, as erroneous quotation

31 In addition to Lord Cromer's demonstration submitted above, this approach had similarly been revealed in a series of communications of the time. Hence, in the early 1920s, Major Dodd, the British representative in Addis Ababa, approached the Abyssinian authorities with a draft Tana Dam agreement. His proposal recognized 'existing native rights and those of the Abyssinian Government to use the Lake Tana, the Blue Nile and its tributaries', subject to the condition that any contemplated use shall not involve 'the arrest or diverting in anyway whatsoever of the flows of the waters . . . by placing constructions of any sort . . . or by constructing regulators or dams of any kind, or by any other means which would diminish the waters of the Lake Tana, the Blue Nile or its tributaries in any manner whatsoever'.

Huge Dodds to Viscount Allenby, Draft Agreement, Addis Ababa, 26 December 1922, FO 371/8403.

Later, an analogous script by Bentinck reiterated British resolve which underlined that 'no attempt will be made to arrest, divert or obstruct in any way the flow of the Blue Nile or any of its tributaries . . .'

Bentinck to Sir Austen Chamberlain, Suggestions for a Treaty, Addis Ababa, 10 May 1927, Enclosure 2.1, FO 371/12341.

32 Teferi to Austen Chamberlain, Enclosure in Addis Ababa Dispatch 363, Bentinck to Chamberlain, Addis Ababa, 14 December 1927, FO 371/13099.

33 Bentinck to Sir Austen Chamberlain, Addis Ababa, 14 December 1927, FO 371/13099.

of the treaty. In a memo sent in the instant, Bentinck drew the attention of the Ethiopian Government to the 'serious clerical error'[34] committed.

Very oddly, though, his translation of the Amharic version annexed in the same memo, inscribed the phrase 'block up from river bank to river bank' (*daffana*) as the Amharic equivalent of the term arrest in the English edition.

On receiving the communication, Ras Teferi moved swiftly to challenge and dispel any allusion of misunderstanding on the part of the British. In reply, the Ras disparaged Bentinck's conception, retorting that 'he may have difficulty assuring himself of the Amharic' language and confirmed him that in any event the words 'from bank to bank are the correct and unmistakable Amharic expression meaning completely.'[35] The emissary reported Ethiopia's reaction to the Foreign Office. Only that with an added impetus, he pushed forward the previous argument, particularly emphasizing that 'any interference with the flow of the waters, even if this were *geographically possible*, would be a breach of the treaty, and the Abyssinian Government has no intention of acting in any way contrary to its letter or spirit'[36] (Emphasis added).

Concluding textual interpretation

Inopportunely, the formulation of the term arrest did not enjoy a wide-ranging precedent in other treaty regimes; this precludes an opening for elucidation of the Anglo-Ethiopian Treaty on the basis of common technical benchmarks utilized elsewhere.

Of course, in pursuing comparable objectives contemplated under Article III of the Anglo-Ethiopian Treaty (i.e. forestalling prejudicial interferences), a wealth of bilateral treaties and regulations proposed by the ILC, the ILA and the IIL had adopted quite different courses and employed different expressions.

Some of the most commonly employed phrases instituting duties of non-interference included prohibition against 'prejudicial uses', 'appropriation', 'partial/complete diversion' or 'withdrawal' or restricting conduct which may otherwise 'diminish', 'obstruct' or 'sensibly modify' the flow of river channels.

In this regard, it might even be possible to refer to two relatable treaties which involved Great Britain itself. Under the Anglo-Italian Protocol of 1891, for instance, Italy undertook 'not to construct on the Atbara, for irrigation purposes, any works which might sensibly modify its flow to the Nile'.[37] On the other hand, Article III of the Anglo-Belgian Treaty obliged the Congo not to undertake construction of any work 'on or near the Semliki (Isango) River which would diminish the volume of water entering Lake Albert . . .'.[38]

34 Bentinck to Ras Teferi, Addis Ababa, 20 December 1920, FO 371/13099.

35 Ras Teferi to Bentinck, Addis Ababa, 26 December 1927, FO 371/13099.

36 Bentinck to Sir Austen Chamberlain, Addis Ababa, 30 January 1928, FO 371/13099.

37 Protocol between the British and Italian Governments for the demarcation of their respective spheres of influence in East Africa, From Ras Kasar to the Blue Nile, 15April 1891.

38 Agreement between Great Britain and the Independent State of Congo modifying the 1894 Agreement relating to their respective spheres of influence in East and Central Africa, 9 May 1906.

To recapitulate the analyses on textual interpretation, it can be proposed that in espousing the proper spirit of the treaty regime, it would appear sensible to maintain that latitude of reflection implied in the simple reading of Article III which squeezes Ethiopia's obligations merely to cases of complete blocking of the Nile waters. Under international law, textual interpretation places significant authority on the plain text of the treaties as such.

Given such a rule of interpretation, therefore, it would prove difficult to deduce from the languages that Great Britain had indeed considered a broader reading of the term arrest so as to proscribe Ethiopia, nearly completely, from interfering with the hydraulic regimes of the Blue Nile and the Sobat rivers. Even worse, the Amharic translation offered no opening to allusions of a wider construction.

Although only implicitly, this position had been corroborated through Great Britain's early treaty practice in Africa; on the basis of the various engagements, one can convincingly submit that British employment of specific, hardly interchangeable languages in its treaty relations was but an outcome of a conscious choice in legal framing. Indeed, several communications of its governments had utilized 'arrest, obstruction and non-interference' just side by side, which bears out that each of these expressions had been instilled to connote entirely distinct meanings; this implies that, after all, the term arrest under Article III was not applied to proscribe *all* forms of interference.

The point remains that although the textual interpretation presented above had barely matched with the practical approaches or treaty objectives espoused by the British in subsequent diplomatic discourses, as a tool, treaty interpretation could not involve in an excessively liberal process so as to defy the clear spirit of expressions. Instead, it needs to be geared towards giving treaties a proper effect which conforms to the context and the intended objectives.

On the other extreme, however, to restrict the Anglo-Ethiopian treaty's obligations solely to cases of complete arrest may defy both reality and logic. At the turn of the twentieth century, or in the immediately ensuing decades for that matter, the stage of development of national economies in the Nile basin, the level of hydraulic understanding and engineering had not yet advanced to a heightened scale as to prompt Great Britain entertain a perceived apprehension of Ethiopia's interferences only on a measure anticipated in the ordinary reading of the treaty (i.e. complete damming).

Indeed, geographically, blocking the whole Blue Nile torrent behind barriers in Ethiopia could not have been undertaken without the attendance of an array of compelling preconditions which had not existed at the time. These important facts weaken the logic of interpreting the Anglo-Ethiopian Treaty in the ordinary form depicted above.

Hence, in concluding the accord, Great Britain had most probably foreseen an enlarged Ethiopian responsibility which included forbearing threats emanating from lesser scales of interference with the flows of the river courses.

Of course, the true spirit of the treaty cannot be grasped properly except through a complete recital of *all* tools of interpretation. This is particularly important where the use of terms engenders divergent connotations in the eyes of the parties.

In elucidating Article III of the Anglo-Ethiopian treaty, this state provokes the employ of other procedures: interpreting the ordinary meaning in the context of its application in the whole treaty and in light of the object and purpose of the treaty.

In a closely analogous incidence where a party to the International Court of Justice's advisory-opinion proceeding had attempted to attribute a text a meaning different from its natural connotation, the Court had the occasion to summarise the procedures that should be followed and the structural relationship that exists between textual and contextual interpretations. The Court held:[39]

> . . . the first duty of a tribunal which is called upon to interpret and apply the provisions of a treaty, is to endeavour to give effect to them in their natural and ordinary meaning in the context in which they occur. If the relevant words in their natural and ordinary meaning make sense in their context, that is an end of the matter. If, on the other hand, the words in their natural and ordinary meaning are ambiguous or lead to an unreasonable result, then, and then only, must the Court, by resort to other methods of interpretation, seek to ascertain what the parties really did mean when they used these words.

Contextual interpretation of the Anglo-Ethiopian Agreement

Shaping the context

The international legal order does not forbid states from holding divergent positions with respect to treaty responsibilities. If anything, the foregoing analysis has exhibited one occasion of interpretative predicament prompted by incompatible readings of Article III of the Anglo-Ethiopian treaty.

It was noted earlier that from the very inception and when an occasion for interpretative dialogues had arisen, Great Britain had steadfastly defended a position that countered both the plain reading of the treaty and Ethiopia's deportment on the subject.

With evidence of two versions radiating from their practice and arguably discerned from the objective reading of the treaty texts, further implement of interpretative tools embraced under the Vienna Convention is only indispensable.

The Convention enlightens that in interpreting such arrangements, the ordinary meaning of words and phrases shall not be sought in the abstract or in isolation, but in their context and in light of the object and purpose of the treaty of which they are only a part. The employment of these tools of interpretation could aid in closing the gaps apparently exhibited in the two interpretative versions and in establishing a common design of Article III.

Contextual interpretation presumes the reading of a treaty as a whole, attributing terms that may be understood in several ways the particular meaning which best fits the whole context.

39 *Competence of the Assembly regarding Admission to the United Nations*, Advisory Opinion, ICJ Reports, (1950), p 8.

In this regard, investigating the context and more particularly, the structural organization of the Anglo-Ethiopian Treaty could have become an ideal tool if all provisions of the treaty had dealt with an intertwined theme or were to reflect some logical pattern in substantive flow.

Quite on the contrary, the treaty was composed in five separate articles, with each stipulation addressing virtually distinct matters. Articles I and II covered border and delimitation issues, Article IV regulated the grant of lease rights in south-western Ethiopia, and Article V awarded the UK a right of constructing a railway passing through Ethiopia and touched upon other ancillary matters. The phrases now the source controversy are neither employed nor referred to in any other part of the treaty. And as such, the particular arrangement of the treaty's provisions can barely aid in elucidating the ordinary meaning of the texts.

Yet, contextual interpretation involves more than a simple analysis of the structural relationship between various components of a treaty regime. In fact, it engages the reading and construction of the preamble, annexes, subsequent practices and agreements co-related with the treaty in issue.

Of course, it has been noted with forethought that the Vienna Convention on the Law of Treaties does not provide for an outright inclusion of all preceding and subsequent manuscripts associated with a treaty as forming part of the context. Article 31 has plainly specified that in shaping the context, recourse can be had only to:

i. agreements, relating to the treaty, and made between the parties in connection with the conclusion of the treaty;
ii. instruments made by one of the parties in connection with the conclusion of the treaty and accepted by the other party as related to the treaty;
iii. subsequent agreements between the parties regarding the interpretation of the treaty or the application of its provisions;
iv. subsequent practices in the application of the treaty which establishes the agreement of the parties regarding its interpretation, and;
v. any relevant rules of international law applicable in the relations between the parties.

Some of the communications listed above such as agreements or instruments composed in protocols, declarations, memos or formal pacts would generally cause less trouble. The joint interpretative will of the parties can be inferred from such materials without much equivocation.

In the context of the discussions at hand, only one source indicated under Article 31 would appear relevant: 'the subsequent practices in the application of the treaty which establishes the agreement of the parties regarding its interpretation'. While not part of the original accord, the reference to subsequent practices would cover views expressed by the parties on different occasions and in diverse contexts. It constitutes a crucial tool, which, if exploited prudently can help form a proper conclusion as to the intent and meaning of phrases used in treaties.

In reality, however, it would usually prove difficult to ascribe certain patterns of conduct of the parties as intended to constitute a definitive interpretative process.

Subsequent practice involves a wide range of express or implied positions depicted by states in the conduct of treaty affairs; the task of identifying, with reasonable certainty, which of such acts makes up the agreement or consensus of the parties regarding its interpretation can constitute a demanding enterprise. Facts of state practice not embodied in a clearly ascertainable agreement or written instrument are susceptible to multiple explanations.

Yet, in spite of the implicit limitation laid under the Vienna Convention, both the PCIJ, the ICJ and several tribunals had generously admitted extrinsic communications of disputing parties on various occasions. They had been employed as material evidences in establishing broader intentions with respect to treaty undertakings and in a few cases, with a view to ascertaining the meaning and effect of dubious terms and phrases in treaties.[40] In the Interpretation of the Greco-Turkish Agreement of 1 December 1926, for instance, the PCIJ held:

> The facts subsequent to the conclusion of the Treaty . . . can only concern the Court in so far as they are calculated to throw light on the intention of the parties at the time of the conclusion of that Treaty . . . In this connection, the exchange of views which took place between the parties at the meetings held by the Council . . . is of special importance.[41]

In an earlier Advisory Opinion on the competence of the ILO with respect to the international regulation of the conditions of agricultural labour, the PCIJ refuted the existence of any ambiguity in the framing of the pertinent ILO Convention. It added:

> if there were any ambiguity, the Court might, for the purpose of arriving at the true meaning, consider the action which has been taken under the Treaty.[42]

The Court made no distinction whether such actions are expressed in agreements, instruments or any other medium of state behaviour.

Moreover, a similar view had been reproduced quite recently involving interpretation of Part II of the same treaty now under investigation. The Eritrea-Ethiopia Boundary Commission (EEBC), constituted of among others Sir Elihu Lauterpacht and Stephen Schwebel, ruled that the resolution of the interpretative problems encountered in the boundary dispute depends initially on the proper construction of the Treaty. This, the Commission explained, in turn depends 'upon the text of Article I, read in light of its object and purpose, its context and negotiating history, and the subsequent course of conduct of the Parties in its application'.[43]

In consequence, in examining the principal items evidencing subsequent conduct or practice of the Parties, the Boundary Commission authoritatively employed

40 A case in point could be the *Kasikili/Sedudu Island (Botswana/Namibia), Judgement, ICJ Reports 1999.*

41 *Interpretation of Greco-Turkish Agreement of Dec. 1st, 1926*, Advisory Opinion, August 28, 1928 PCIJ (Ser B) No 16, pp 24–5.

42 *Competence of the ILO to regulate Agricultural Labor,* Advisory Opinion 2, PCIJ (1922) Ser B, No 2 pp 39–40.

43 *Eritrea-Ethiopia Boundary Commission Decision Regarding the Delimitation of the Border between the State of Eritrea and the Federal Democratic Republic of Ethiopia*, The Hague, 13 April 2002, p 61.

a sequence of materials held in reserve. The references, utilized as demonstrating proof of acquiescence, admissions or assertions of the Parties' understanding of the Treaty at issue included diplomatic exchanges, internal memos, decrees, declarations, reports, protests, complaints, formal and informal reactions, counter-reactions, unilateral/bilateral interpretations and even the Parties' own constructions of events. Under a strict application of Article 31 of the Vienna Convention, several of such items could not have been readily admitted.

In fact, the Boundary Commission had itself noted this particular departure; yet, drawing precedent from the jurisprudence of the PCIJ, the ICJ and other international tribunals, the Commission emphasized the import of subsequent conduct or practice of the parties whose purpose, it noted, would not be limited to issues of 'the interpretation of treaties' as such. It held 'it is quite possible that practice or conduct may affect the legal relations of the Parties even though it cannot be said to be practice in the application of the Treaty or to constitute an agreement between them'.[44]

Comprehensive review of extrinsic communications of the parties

Against the background of the theoretical exposition, this section of the Book will engage in a contextual interpretation of the Anglo-Ethiopian treaty. This obliges a comprehensive review of history and bilateral diplomacy involving relationships between Great Britain and Ethiopia. Several of the pertinent diplomatic manuscripts had already been highlighted in the preceding parts in connection with elucidation of the ordinary meaning of Article III of the treaty. Hence, they shall not be wholly restated in this part.

In the immediate aftermath of the Anglo-Ethiopian treaty, Great Britain geared its diplomatic efforts on obtaining Ethiopia's approval of a fiscal subsidy in exchange for certain commitments under a treaty. In virtually all occasions of bilateral encounter, the British reiterated that no hydraulic structures of any feature could be installed on or across the headwaters of the two river courses arresting or diminishing their flows. Concurrently, Great Britain acknowledged very limited rights with regard to irrigational uses essentially targeting domestic requirements of the local population.

Lord Cromer, master-architect of the Anglo-Ethiopian Treaty and Great Britain's viceroy in Egypt tendered the first formal recognition of such right. In 1907, his instruction to Clark acknowledged that the Anglo-Ethiopian Treaty did not imply any intention of interfering with local natives' rights, provided that no attempt is to be made to arrest or interfere in any way with the flow of these rivers by placing obstructions of any sort in their channels or by constructing regulators or dams of any kind across their channels or beds.[45]

44 *Eritrea-Ethiopia Boundary Commission Decision* (2002), note 43, p 22.
45 Telegram from Cromer, Cairo, 7–9 March 1907, FO 371/14591.

In 1927, Lord Cromer's assurance was replicated with improved lucidity in Bentinck's proposed treaty framework for a dam concession. The British envoy's script read that 'the riparian rights of the inhabitants dwelling on both sides of the Blue Nile throughout its length in Ethiopia to use this water for domestic purposes as well as for the cultivation of crops necessary for their own subsistence will not be questioned, but it is understood that no attempt will be made to arrest, divert or obstruct in any way the flow of the Blue Nile or any of its tributaries . . .'.[46]

What scale of native utilization could have been pursued without building water-control works, and whether such rights had also anticipated 'reasonable uses' for agricultural and industrial developments remains uncertain. Most probably, the tautly conditioned admissions were projected to merely instil British monopolistic perceptions with regard to rights of use of the rivers, and hence to construe the expression of Article III as prohibiting all forms of interference arresting or materially diminishing the flows of the Blue Nile, Lake Tana and the Sobat.

On the other hand, Ethiopia's post-treaty position and diplomatic reflection contradicted any such conclusion. Since Emperor Menelik's rejection of the subsidy arrangement in 1907, the matter remained in abeyance for some years but resurfaced in 1914 in a broader context of the Lake Tana Dam negotiations. In 1930, Sir Barton, the British representative in Addis Ababa chronicled the events in his diplomatic despatch. He reported that during the negotiations in 1914, one of the claims the Ethiopian Government put forward in response to a draft agreement submitted had been that 'they wished to safeguard not only their existing but future rights to the use of the water for their own irrigation purposes'.[47]

Of course, Ethiopia had had no concrete irrigational schemes at this particular epoch in history; the declaration had merely hoped to preserve a prescriptive right to a share of the Nile waters. While British reactions to such request was not accounted in the narrative, Sir Barton deduced that Ethiopia's move had been induced by 'rights to Abyssinian irrigation which might be very valuable' even though they 'concerned petty irrigation'.[48]

Admittedly, since the earliest decades, Ethiopia's successive governments had failed to unveil tangible plans for water resources development, nor score on a string of opportunities that emerged from time to time. Still, in the Ethiopian corners, there was a clear discernment that London's unvarying diplomatic enterprise in the Nile basin region had been triggered by no other consideration than its egocentric interests in Egypt and Sudan. In part, this explains Ethiopia's aloofness to the chain of the Anglo-Egyptian and Sudanese proposals submitted in the course of the succeeding decades.

Specifics of Great Britain's professed policies with regard to the Anglo-Ethiopian Treaty were further paraphrased in multiple diplomatic encounters in the 1920's

46 Bentinck to Sir Austen Chamberlain, Suggestions for a Treaty, Addis Ababa, 10 May 1927, Enclosure 2.1, FO 371/12341.

47 Sir Barton to Hon. Arthur Henderson, Addis Ababa, 29June 1931 FO 371/15388.

48 Sir Barton to Hon. Arthur Henderson, Addis Ababa, 29June 1931 FO 371/15388.

proposing to cement the gains under the treaty itself that 'purportedly' preserved the inviolability of the hydraulic integrity of the Blue Nile basin in Ethiopia.

On one such occasion in 1924, Prime Minister MacDonald's letter to Ras Teferi stated a view that advocated construction of a reservoir with Anglo-Sudanese finance and British possession of full operational control of the facility.[49] This development had been preceded by a countering Ethiopian reaction; since the reopening of the Tana dam negotiations in 1922, Ethiopia had increasingly leaned towards pursuing the technical investigation and construction of the project as a purely Ethiopian undertaking. In blatant disregard of British understanding of the treaty's stipulations, Ras Teferi wrote P.M McDonald that 'the Ethiopian Government, in its own interest and for all other purposes, is willing to build the dam . . . and to rent to the Sudan Government the surplus waters . . .'.[50] The letter did not anticipate Sudanese involvement in the costs and clearly dispelled allusions of operational control of the dam by the Anglo-Sudan Government.

The legal significance of this unparalleled diplomatic incidence lay in one essentially figurative gesticulation: it touched deeply upon the core theme of dispute involving interpretation of the Anglo-Ethiopian treaty; indeed, the move constituted a complete upset to take for granted conjectures harboured in the psych of successive British administrations with regard to the non-interference proviso of the Anglo-Ethiopian treaty.

In his reply to Ras Teferi's statement of right, Prime Minister MacDonald pretended undisturbed by Ethiopia's actions, and even more, confessed that he was happy 'to note that the course you (Teferi) suggest appears to offer a chance of an arrangement being reached which would be beneficial both to the Abyssinian Government and to the Sudan'.[51] He did not draw any reference to the 1902 treaty to obstruct Ethiopia's declared intent. What is more, despite McDonald's plea to be informed of the engineers to whom the Ethiopian Government wished 'to entrust the preparation of the plans and the eventual supervision of construction of the (Ethiopian) dam',[52] the technical competence as such, not the right of commissioning the work considered as more vital, Ras Teferi simply ignored the request.

Two years on, in August 1926, an interdepartmental meeting was summoned at the Foreign Office where the British Government endeavoured to design and approve a strategy that should be followed in its dealings with the Ethiopian Government.[53] The effort had aimed at correcting the diplomatic slip-ups and reinstating the old paradigm. The assembly endorsed a point of departure for future negotiations, and held the view that the proposal by the Abyssinian Government to

49 Ramsay Macdonald to Teferi, Foreign Office, 19 July 1924, FO 371/10872.

50 Also in: Edward Ullendorf (1976) *The Autobiography of Emperor Haile Selassie I, My Life and Ethiopia's Progress 1892–1937*, Oxford, Oxford University Press, p 125.
Teferi to Ramsay McDonald, Paris, 26 July 1924, FO 371/10872.

51 Ramsay MacDonald to Teferi, Foreign Office, 14 August 1924, FO 371/10872.

52 Ullendorf (1976) *The Autobiography of Emperor Haile Selassie I*, note 52, p 125.

53 Lake Tana, Record of Conversation between Dr Martin and Murray, 11 November 1927, FO 371/12343.

build the dam by itself is hardly in accordance with the notes exchanged between Harington and Alfred Ilg in March 1902.[54]

In spite of the British reservations and Ethiopia's countering diplomatic enterprise, London pledged to go a long way to meet the wishes of the Abyssinian Government 'to have an interest' in a reservoir which might be met by constituting an Anglo-Abyssinian company – a concessionaire who shall construct the reservoir and lease the water stored to the Sudan. Obviously, this proposal disclosed that Great Britain had fine-tuned its position on the subject.

Yet, it remained dubious whether Great Britain had acted as such acknowledging Ethiopia's rights under the Anglo-Ethiopia treaty, or had merely embarked on a policy decision that projected to accommodate new realities ensuing long since the conclusion of the treaty. Either way, Great Britain's declaration produced a vital legal momentum confirming, and in a sense, altering certain preconceived juridical relations affecting the rights of the two states under the Anglo-Ethiopian treaty, and enlightening on the broader context of their respective undertakings.

In 1927, Bentinck developed the Foreign Office's theory further, branding MacDonald's position as a 'face-saving device which may commend itself to the Abyssinian Government'.[55] No doubt, Bentinck had sensed the chilly implication of his prime minister's earlier communication in defining the essence of Ethio-Sudanese water uses rights. Hence, he adhered to a strict interpretation of the Anglo-Ethiopian Treaty espoused previously which highlighted the significance of operational control. He advocated 'a mere undertaking by the Abyssinian Government or by a company not under effective British control . . . would be insufficient'.[56] And his superior's appeasing statement notwithstanding, Bentinck reflected 'the tone of Ras Teferi (enclosed in a note of 22nd September, and addressing an identical theme) cannot be regarded at all as satisfactory'.[57]

Consequently, in his memo produced in chorus and communicated a month later, he strove to slacken the damage by soliciting his government to endorse his own observations that the British Government should remind Ethiopia 'that they are obliged by treaty not to construct or allow to be constructed any work across the Blue Nile or Lake Tana . . .', and that Sudan is entitled to 'complete operational control' of the dam.

The response articulated by the British colonial administration in Sudan was certainly prompted by bad temper. As though Ethiopia had no stake whatsoever in a resource that pours from its territory, the Sudanese representative in London labelled the Emperor's description of right as 'offensive and impertinent' deserving a reply and defended an arrangement that adopts 'a lease of the dam and not merely of the waters'. Moreover, the representative argued there had been nothing in his view that may be construed as 'inconsistent with Ramsay MacDonald's letter'.[58]

54 Lake Tana (1927), note 53.
55 Bentinck, Addis Ababa, October 1927, FO 371/12341.
56 Bentinck (1927), note 55.
57 Bentinck (1927), note 55.
58 Sudan Government London Office to John Murray, London, 11 October 1927, FO 371/12341.

Holding against a scarcely steady British position on the theme, Ethiopia pushed forward its negotiations on the Tana Dam, this time with an American construction firm – the J. G. White Engineering Company. When major press reports covered the new development, the Foreign Office veiled itself as un alarmed but accelerated its diplomatic wrestle carrying out protests to all media organizations and press attaches in the US and European states as well as in Egypt, Sudan and Ethiopia. The core precept of its remonstration questioned the right of the Ethiopian Government to pursue a dam scheme without getting hold of British consent purportedly required under the Anglo-Ethiopian treaty.

Inopportunely, an array of multifaceted factors turned the J. G. White company's involvement in Ethiopia into a failing business proposition. Espousing a fresh approach in 1931, Ethiopia opted to undertake the project as a joint venture with the Sudan and flaunted offers to that effect. Hence, it was contemplated that the scheme shall constitute a 'system of irrigation for the two countries' whereby 'engineers of the two governments will regulate the flow of the water according to the needs of the countries'.[59] Despite this extraordinary inducement, the inconvenient economic situation in which Sudan found itself prevented it from taking a definite stand on the subject. However, the point remained that the move represented a further way from the strict positions maintained earlier.

Concluding contextual interpretation

Each of the diplomatic communications effected by diverse functionaries of Great Britain may command distinct legal authority, this being contingent on the relative position of the issuing authority, the formal sanctioning afforded and most importantly, the extent to which they represent, expressly or by implication, the joint volition of the parties involved.

Assuming that the manuscripts, chronicling diplomatic events that took place between 1902 and 1935 can well fall under Article 31 of the Vienna Convention as subsequent practices of the parties in the application of the treaty which establishes their agreement regarding its interpretation, the systematic presentation of these documents bears out one important conclusion. With modest digressions from time to time, both parties reiterated contrasting observations in relation to the scope of water uses rights radiating from Article III of the Anglo-Ethiopian treaty.

As far as objective stipulation of the ordinary meaning of the terms at issue, construed in their context is concerned, the historical narration merely substantiates an inconclusive pattern of facts, conceptions and national perceptions that cannot be easily reconciled.

The divergence was even more so manifest in the aggressive water resources development policies and practices espoused both in Sudan and Ethiopia in the 1980s, 90s and early twenty-first century, although in some cases, water resource developments in either of the states had been attended by relative acquiescence.

59 Sir P. Loraine, Cairo, 26 March 1931, FO 371/15388.

Reflecting on the object/purpose of the Treaty

Contextual presentation of the treaty, largely premised on varying post-treaty practices of the two parties, had demonstrated two conflicting readings of Article III. A broader interpretation of arrest was advocated by Great Britain as imposing an obligation of non-interference with the use of the Blue Nile, the Sobat and Lake Tana waters which may cause a diminished flow or complete arrest of their inundations (except in the context of local irrigational uses). A second line Ethiopia pursued conceived the country's legal undertaking as solely involving restraint against complete embankment or diversion of the watercourses.

Based on the foregoing facts and relatable discussions and bearing in mind the broader objectives of the treaty, a few observations and concluding remarks can be drawn.

In sanctioning the contents of Article III within a wider treaty framework that regulated assorted themes, what both parties might have anticipated to realize remains too complex to discern with certainty. The intentions of the parties or their functionaries are mere subjective abstractions; and when there is little structural relationship between various provisions making up the treaty, or where its preamble fails to proffer a clear communication,[60] it so happens that the underlying objectives of the treaty could not be detected readily from a simple reading of the scripts as such.

Based on a limited exposition of provisions of the Anglo-Ethiopian Treaty and relatable legal-historical chronicles above, one can gather that the most important object and purpose of the accord, that design which prompted the parties to conclude the treaty had been to 'settle and delineate' long-standing boundary issues between Sudan and Ethiopia.

Indeed, the border squabble along the western corridors had constituted a high profile mission of Colonel J. Harrington, when, in 1897, he assumed office as the British representative in Ethiopia. This is evident in the treaty's preamble, which read that the parties 'being animated with the desire to confirm the friendly relations between the two powers and to settle the frontier between the Soudan and Ethiopia . . .' had agreed to conclude the bilateral accord.

The provision requiring Ethiopian guarantee of non-interference with the flow regimes of the named river systems was supplemented as one component of his diplomatic undertaking only in due course and upon express instructions from his overlords in Cairo and London. Therefore, it is not surprising that up until 1900, both Harrington and Menelik had been engaged in winding up their negotiations which covered no other theme but the regularization of territorial gains along the western corridors.[61]

In September 1900, i.e. when the two countries appeared through with much of the painstaking boundary negotiation, though, the Foreign Office redefined

60 The only essential reference in the Preamble states that the parties 'being animated with the desire to confirm the friendly relations between the two powers and to settle the frontier between the Soudan and Ethiopia . . .' '. . . have agreed up on and do conclude the following articles, which shall be binding on themselves, their heirs and successors'.

61 Harrington to Salisbury, 14 May 1900, FO 403/299.

Harington's tasks in Addis Ababa. Hence, the envoy was instructed to approach the Ethiopian government with a view to getting hold of, among others, an Ethiopian guarantee for unimpeded flow of the Blue Nile and the Sobat rivers and a right to construct a railway traversing through the Ethiopian territory.

Of course, Great Britain's treaty engagement with the state of Ethiopia was not an isolated legal incident. Its scheme under the Anglo-Ethiopian Treaty was but only one facet of a prudently coordinated initiative for absolute control of the Nile River water resources throughout the whole basin. On different occasions, London had already secured similar assurances from Belgian Congo and Italy – who controlled petite constituencies in the Nile basin and from France and Germany. Its overwhelming interest in the subject, from the early years of Lord Cromer at the tail of the nineteenth century to the 1950s, was essentially dictated by the strategic, economic and political necessities of its colonial and capitalist enterprises in Egypt, Sudan and the near east.

On the other hand, for Emperor Menelik, the negotiations presented a formal legal forum for soliciting recognition of Ethiopia's sovereignty over the vast territories subjugated during his decade-long empire building enterprise. Likewise, the treaty was utilized as a diplomatic invent to preserve Ethiopia's territorial integrity by remaining neutral in his dealings with three European states – France, Great Britain and Italy who pursued conflicting interests in the basin hovering around his independent empire. Along with other minor compromises, the controversial pledge under Article III of the treaty was slotted in to meet such compelling objectives.

Indisputably, Great Britain had sought from the onset to bar Ethiopia or other European powers for that matter of any rights of use of the rivers. The earliest communication by Colonel Harrington setting out the terms of compensation payable to Emperor Menelik in consideration for his treaty undertaking and Lord Cromer's guarded notes that forbade nearly all forms of constructions across the named watercourses plainly allude to this fact.[62] Identical perceptions had also been restated quite constantly forming the mainstay of Great Britain's water diplomacy for well over five decades. On a handful of occasions too, both Emperor Menelik and Emperor Haileselassie had assured the British governments that Ethiopia would respect the terms of the treaty without explaining what such guarantees in fact entail.

The diplomatic records presented above are too sparse to discern with certainty the factors that prompted Menelik to undertake the obligation under Article III within a broader treaty framework which intended to regularize boundary issues. Similarly, it is evident that in the early decades of the twentieth century, Ethiopia had hardly had any irrigational schemes to speak of. It is not totally inconceivable that the impenetrable geographical landscape through which the rivers traverse could have convinced the Emperor to underrate the significance of the rivers for prospective agricultural uses in Ethiopia.

62 Memorandum, History of the Lake Tana Negotiation, Foreign Office, 23 January 1923, FO 371/8403.

On the other hand, it remained that the crucial provision of non-interference under the Anglo-Ethiopian accord was endorsed after intensive negotiations involving, among others, the Emperor's Swiss advisor, Alfred Ilg. The agreement was concluded in the same epoch when the Emperor had been engaging in massive nation-building enterprise advancing territorial claims as far as Khartoum and regions of the Blue and White Nile in the Sudan. These key facts tend to refute assumptions that the Emperor would display a grave act of imprudence by conceding under the Anglo-Ethiopian Treaty Ethiopia's sovereign prerogatives in resources of the Nile River system.

Moreover, it can be noted that the treaty was concluded only less than a decade since the colonial force of a major European power – Italy was utterly defeated at the 'battle of Adwa' – in North Ethiopia in 1896. This reinforces the conjecture that the accord had been signed in a cordial milieu when the Emperor commanded economic and political buoyancy in local and regional affairs.

One can also consider detailed accounts of the diplomatic letters swapped during the border negotiations which corroborate that Ethiopia had largely engaged in the treaty as a co-equal, from an angle of strength and not submission. In contrast to the immediately preceding decade, clearly discernible threats to Ethiopia's sovereignty had not been in attendance during the conclusion of the treaty.

Closing observations

Along with the earlier discussions involving the ordinary meaning and contextual interpretation of the treaty, the historical anecdotes validate that whatever obligation the terms of the treaty stipulated, Ethiopia had deduced that they did not imply the wider construction to which the Great Britain had adhered in the ensuing decades.

Besides, it could be that the broader interpretation espoused by the British might have been enthused by the augmented pressures of the rapidly expanding irrigational agriculture which had then required enhanced provision and secure control of the rivers' flows, than by a genuine interpretation of the texts as such.

Over the years, Great Britain's ingrained fixation with the Tana Dam Concession had influenced the conceptual framing and eventual construction of its privileges under the Anglo-Ethiopian treaty. This could have prompted it to conjure, in defence of its economic and strategic interests, a broader right than was legally warranted by the plain wordings of the text of Article III.

By way of summing up the whole discussions, the following key observations and conclusions can be drawn.

First, in spite of the rigorous negotiations on the subsidy accord involving Emperor Menelik and Clark, the fact that the Emperor declined the negotiated note even when Lord Cromer went to great lengths assuring him of the protection of native irrigational rights can potentially imply that Menelik had in any event harboured a constricted contour of reading of his treaty obligations.[63] For some

63 On advice of his irrigation experts whose sole concern had been the steady flow of the river downstream, Cromer ordered Clark to give a guardedly framed surety to Menelik that 'the terms of Article III of the Treaty of May 15, 1902 do not imply any intention of interfering with local native rights, provided that no attempt is made to *arrest or interfere* in any way with the flow of these

reason, the Emperor had not been moved by the pecuniary reward proposed and had never accepted the arrangement formally; whatever the facts that might have prompted such a resolution, the occasion presented one of the earliest opportunities that tested British interpretation and perceptions on the subject. The British legation had full knowledge that Ethiopia was contemplating to sell European powers certain irrigational concessions in the low country which would employ some waters and canals.[64] Against the background of such a setting, Cromer's subscription to Emperor Menelik's request for an explicit assurance and insertion of interpretative note that safeguarded Ethiopia's prospective interests would seem hardly consonant with the monopolistic mind-set hitherto advocated.

Moreover, as noted earlier, the preservation of Great Britain's economic and strategic interests had presupposed a wider construal of the treaty scheme under Article III which, with the exception of native irrigational rights forbade all other scales of utilization. With the increasing congregation of hydraulic data and engineering know-how, it would be naïve to presume that the UK would discount prospective threats of interference by Ethiopia, acting alone or in concert with Italy or the French. Indeed, elsewhere in the basin, Great Britain had successfully forestalled such contingencies by entering into various agreements. Unlike under Article III of the Anglo-Ethiopia treaty, the specific wordings in each of these juridical arrangements had been framed with substantial caution and clarity so as to fulfil the stated objectives.

In consequence, one may strongly infer that the fact that the relevant text under Article III of the Anglo-Ethiopian Treaty had been phrased differently could not have resulted from a mere inadvertent drafting. Its implications could have been intended. It would be hardly defensible for Great Britain (and by succession, for Sudan) to pull broader privileges from the treaty simply because its subsequent practice had persistently manoeuvred a wider interpretation. Its acts alone cannot destabilize the sanctity of the treaty as such or its plain expressions.

This disputation is reinforced by Great Britain's earliest proposal of a draft agreement on the Tana Dam scheme which projected to institute a servitude in the Ethiopian territory with full financing and operational autonomy of the Anglo-Sudan government.

The negotiations had been premised on the theory that while the 1902 treaty had barred Ethiopia from constructing any dam or system of regulators across the Nile and Sobat rivers, Ethiopia may still charge 'water-rental profits' by permitting the Sudanese government undertake the venture.[65]

rivers by placing obstructions of any sort in their channels or by constructing regulators or dams of any kind across their channels or beds'.

Telegram from Cromer, Cairo, 7–9 March 1907, FO 371/14591.

64 Telegram from Cromer (1907), note 63.

65 Within the framework of broader colonial developmental contemplations, Ethiopia's only takings in the Nile resources was considered as the 'development of hydropower for which there is no market in the near future'; this directed the concentration of British water diplomacy to 'the amount of money it [Ethiopia] can secure from Egypt and Sudan in return for the permission to construct the Lake Tana Dam'.

Cairo to Foreign Office, 16 July 1949, FO 371/73619.

All along, Ethiopia renounced such conceptions which it argued had been based on a misconceived reading of the treaty's text. As noted earlier,[66] in a letter addressed to Prime Minister R. McDonald, Ras Teferi expressed his country's resolve to install the dam project as a purely 'Ethiopian' enterprise and 'rent surplus waters' to the Sudan. At one point, he even entered into negotiations to employ the capital and technical services of an American construction firm, the J. G. White Engineering Co.

This deportment constituted one of the few occasions where, scraping diplomatic niceties to the side, Ethiopia clearly declared what it regarded is its legitimate rights. The high-profile diplomatic incident marked a vital juridical stature underpinning Ethiopia's narrower reading of the treaty texts.

These incidences, coupled with London's subsequent inclination to consider offers of pursuing the dam project as an 'Anglo-Ethiopian Company' and the high-level negotiations between Ethiopia and Sudan (in the late 1920s and early 1930s) proposing to undertake the scheme as a 'system of irrigation of the two countries' constitute further proofs of Great Britain's propensity to accommodate a narrower version of rights under the treaty.[67]

To capitulate, while the early positions cannot claim to be unwavering and that Great Britain had advocated Article III as outlawing nearly all forms of interference, unfortunately, in framing the treaty text in its present form, the British had simply failed to substantiate this position by reference to a clear stipulation to that effect.

66 Teferi to Ramsay McDonald, Paris, 26 July 1924, FO 371/10872.

67 In 1931, Ethiopia was poised to take measures with a view to executing the project. It abandoned its original design that proposed to surrender a concession in favour of an American company with a power to construct a reservoir and possibly rent its waters. Instead, it offered to carry out the venture as a joint Ethio-Sudanese undertaking.

Unfortunately, the new opening coincided with worldwide collapse of the prices of cotton, Sudan's chief export commodity. Consequently, economic factors rendered Sudan unable to fully engage in the scheme and denied it of a chance to exploit the prospect thus availed. Against 'the risk that Sudan may permanently lose ground on the Lake Tana Question', its Governor General Sir Maffey admitted that its government's 'own circumstances would preclude it from making any move' by way of committing resources for construction of works.

Sir J. Maffey to Sir P. Lorraine, Khartoum, 26 April 1931, FO 371/15388.

In 1954, a 'British memorandum on International Aspects of the Waters of the Blue Nile' prepared for presentation to Emperor Haileselassie was constituted on the assumption that Article III of the Treaty would continue to instruct identical obligations as before.

Under the memorandum, though, for the first time, Great Britain recognized publicly that apart from fetching mere *water-rent prices* under the Tana scheme where operational control had always been stipulated as resting in the hands of the Anglo-Sudan government, there is 'the possibility of working out an arrangement that would satisfy the legitimate requirements of Ethiopia [if only in the provision of hydro power], Egypt and the Sudan'.

E.B. Boothby to D.L. Busk, London, 5 February 1954, Enclosure FO 371/108264.

A few months on, the Foreign Office instructed its representation in Addis Ababa to point out to the Emperor that 'both Egypt and Sudan fully appreciate that his main interest is in hydro electric power and that they will undoubtedly be prepared to pay generously for as much of the project as will contribute towards their needs'.

T. E. Bromley to Busk, London, 29 July 1954, FO 371/108264.

However inconclusive, the parties' subsequent conduct would seem to have put an authoritative interpretation of the treaty which presented a constricted construction of Article III stated above.

One intrinsic element of sovereignty of states universally recognized under international law has been the freedom of command over natural resources situated in their jurisdiction. While states may willingly relinquish certain aspects of their autonomy through treaties, an arrangement requiring a permanent surrender of rights of utilizing a river course cannot be presumed from an indistinct state of facts.[68]

By way of a final note, Arbitrator Borel's fitting observation in the Kronpris Gustaf Adolf *vs.* Pacific case shall be recounted to wind up the present discussions. The Arbitrator held that 'considering the natural state and liberty of independence which is inherent in sovereign states, they are not to be presumed to have *abandoned any part* thereof, the consequence being that the high contracting parties to a treaty are to be considered as bound only within the limits of what can be clearly and unequivocally found in the provisions agreed to, and that those provisions, in case of doubt, are to be interpreted in favour of the *natural liberty* and independence of the party concerned'[69] (Emphasis added).

The foregoing parts had expansively laboured on exposing if a textual discrepancy worthy of legal interpretation truly subsists under Article III of the Anglo-Ethiopian Treaty of 1902 and where there is, on elucidating interpretation of the treaty that reasonably presumes as constituting the joint volition of the parties. Interpretative techniques presented under the pertinent rules and principles of international law and most notably the Vienna Convention on the Law of Treaties of 1969 have been employed for the purpose.

Yet, independently of issues involving treaty interpretation as such, the continued legal authority of the Anglo-Ethiopian Treaty can also be examined on the basis of three distinct juridical premises under customary international law.

Hence, the first reflection would examine the issue of whether the treaty can be proposed as falling under a class of unequal treaties imposed by Great Britain in a fiduciary capacity as guardian of the interests of the Sudanese co-domini. And where it does, the analysis would reveal the legal implications that ensue by virtue of such a designation.

The second investigation would examine if the language of the United Nations General Assembly resolutions adopted in the 1950s and 1960s and instituting a systematic framework of conceptual correlation between the principles of sovereign equality, self-determination and permanent sovereignty of states over natural

68 Besides, the steady transformation of the post-independence relations between the Sudan, a succeeding state, and Ethiopia cannot be underrated, further influencing the legal foundation of the Anglo-Ethiopian treaty.

69 *Arbitral Decision, Rendered in Conformity with the Special Agreement Concluded on December 17, 1930, Between the Kingdom of Sweden and the United States of America Relating to the Arbitration of a Difference Concerning the Swedish Motor Ships Kronpris Gustaf Adolf and Pacific.*

(Reported in): *The American Journal of International Law* (1932), vol 26, no 4, p 834.

resources could engender certain normative rights affecting the substantive stipulation under the Anglo-Ethiopian treaty.

The last theme would consider the doctrine of *rebus sic stantibus*; this canon confers states a measure of cause for withdrawing from binding treaty regimes on account of 'a fundamental change of circumstances which has occurred with regard to those existing at the time of the conclusion of a treaty, and which was not foreseen by the parties'. The core object of the examination is to analyse how the rule of fundamental change of circumstances translates in relation to the Anglo-Ethiopian Treaty concluded a little more than a century ago.

The three themes shall be addressed in Chapter 7.

7 The Anglo-Ethiopian Treaty and selected principles of public international law

The Anglo-Ethiopian Treaty: a *pactus leoninus* haggle?

Traditionally, both in international law and diplomatic discourses, the concept of sovereignty has presumed that states shall, in the pursuit of their foreign and internal affairs, maintain full autonomy and equality, fettered only by such restrictions as specific rules of international law place.

On top of impositions of the international legal order, though, states commanding diverse economies and political authority had also undertaken in treaties certain commitments inflicting a degree of limitation on the exercise of sovereignty in relation to persons, properties or natural resources. Several of such obligations had been assumed without reciprocal compensation or commensurate undertakings on the part of the partaking parties. Not so few had also been instituted through military conquests, threats of force or economic and political pressures.

What legal effect such accords, variedly designated as imposed treaties, unequal treaties or *pactus leoninus* produce remains far from comprehensible. International law has yet to contend with elucidation of the specific circumstances under which alleged encroachments on sovereignty may still be held as legitimate without at the same time jeopardizing the desire to preserve the greatest possible liberty of states.

On the basis of the contents and circumstances attending its conclusion, if the Anglo-Ethiopian Treaty could be proposed as falling under a class of unequal treaties imposed by Great Britain and where it does, the consequences such a designation entails under international law shall be the subject of investigation.

The bargaining milieu

The Anglo-Ethiopian Treaty had been concluded in exceptionally apprehensive political setting at a time when European colonialism reached its zenith in Africa. As stated earlier, in the decades preceding the conclusion of the treaty, Emperor Menelik's prime occupation had concentrated on the expansion and consolidation of the Ethiopian empire in the south, southeast and western boundaries adjoining present day Kenya, Somalia and the Sudan. With the fall of the latter regions to European powers, encircling Ethiopia and its new acquisitions in nearly all directions, it was only inevitable that the Anglo-Ethiopian border negotiations had to follow with the object of regularizing the respective domains of the parties.

In fact, during the last legs of the 1890s, the pressing objective of Colonel Harrington's mission in Ethiopia was to settle outstanding frontier issues between Sudan and Ethiopia, and thereby dodge an impending conflict of interests between the neighbouring states. Article III of the accord regulating the use of Lake Tana, the Blue Nile and Sobat Rivers was merely inserted at a later stage in a chain of communications that lasted for more than three years.[1]

The boundary negotiation was attended by noticeable perceptions of threat to Ethiopian sovereignty. In spite of the overwhelming defeat of the Italian forces in 1896, which measurably boosted Ethiopia's standing in regional affairs, Great Britain, Italy and France had coalesced to execute conflicting expansionist policies in the horn of Africa, bitterly competing for territories and spheres of influence in Ethiopia.

However, a broader strategic design that advanced British interests in Ethiopia had urged Great Britain to renounce, 'any intention of adopting an aggressive policy towards any portion of His Majesty's [Menelik's] Dominions',[2] to employ Lord Cromer's expression.

Hence, since the earliest periods, Great Britain pursued a general strategic course that endeavoured to preserve the territorial integrity of Ethiopia. At the same time, Great Britain predicted a possible disintegration of the Ethiopian empire and hence engaged in a string of elaborate conventions with France and Italy in the courses of 1891, 1894, 1906 and 1925. Essentially, the accords intended to safeguard its hydraulic stakes in the Blue Nile and Sobat river basins in Ethiopia.

Evidently, Emperor Menelik had always been conscious of the European manipulation and of the threats posed by their presence in the immediately adjoining regions. Hence, in his relations with European powers, the central feature of his foreign policy had generally lacked dedication to any particular approach. In his associations, he ventured to maintain the equilibrium between Khalifa's Sudan (shortly before its re-occupation), France, Italy and the United Kingdom without engaging in the risks attendant in alienating or excessively courting anyone of the powers. Through the non-committal schemes he put in place industriously, historian Marcus recited, 'Menelik had once again protected himself against all foreseeable eventualities', secretly extending his good will to French ambitions along the White Nile before the Fashoda Crisis with which 'he would doubtless have found ways of turning their success to his advantage'. At the same time, he 'avoided placing himself in a potentially awkward strategic and political position in his relations with Great Britain'.[3]

The border negotiations that led to the conclusion of the Anglo-Ethiopian Treaty of May 1902 had been accounted in several historical manuscripts in great

1 Harrington to Salisbury, 14 May 1900, FO 403/299.

2 Mr Ronald, FO Memorandum, Lake Tana, 31 May 1927, FO 371/12341.

3 Harold G. Marcus (1966) 'The Foreign Policy of the Emperor Menelik 1896–1898: A Rejoinder', *The Journal of African History*, vol 7, no 1, p 20.

detail. Sir Rennell Rodd initiated the bargain in 1897, shortly before the re-conquest of the Anglo-Egyptian Sudan; although the accord was concluded with a dominant European power commanding a hugely disproportionate leverage, the border settlement was generally conducted in cordial diplomatic milieu and dexterity with a few exceptions where intense altercations were displayed.[4] Hence, during the negotiations, John Lane Harrington acting on the specific instructions of Lord Salisbury and Lord Cromer, on the one hand, and Emperor Menelik, accompanied by his councillor Alfred Ilg presented and countered claims which each contended belonged to their respective domains on the basis of history, effective occupation, the balance of power and comity.

True, Emperor Menelik's extraordinary claims to a 'sphere of influence including all the territory that had at any time in the past been tributary to Abyssinia, and which it was his avowed intention to bring once more within the area of his dominions',[5] were not accepted. The claims had advanced rights to territorial stretches extending as far as 'Khartoum and Lake Victoria'. It is equally correct that at a late stage in the negotiations, the Emperor's last-minute enterprise to introduce revisions that 'knocked the whole negotiation upside down' had been labelled as unreasonable and hence dismissed out of hand by J. Harrington.

However, in spite of the edgy ambience that over-clouded the process, both parties ceded uneasy concessions in the diplomatic exercise. On the whole, the circumstances tended to impress that Ethiopia had not engaged in the frontier haggle with so manifestly impotent a stature as to deduce that it had been subjected to measures of coercion, and that the terms of the treaty were imposed against its will. In sharp contrast to the lopsided agreements saddled on the rest of Africa's tribal kingdoms in the same epoch or the old capitulation accords *concluded* with China and the Asian countries, the treaty, although favouring British views on certain matters, was nonetheless constructed on the basis of recognition of rudiments of sovereign equality.

This notwithstanding, the system of international law still lacks a theoretical frame applied across the board which could be utilized to adjudge the juridical fate

4 On two occasions, the negotiation was charged with tense emotions that the parties had to resort to threats of force. Hence, during the bargaining where Emperor Menelik's 'grievance' over British encroachments in to his territories had been addressed improperly, Menelik warned Harrington, through his advisor Ilg that 'if the British did not cease their activities', he 'would do the same with us as he did with the Italians, i.e. draw us on into the country and then hammer us, or wait his chance till we have had complications elsewhere'. The British representative replied 'we . . . [are] not Italians.' Harold G. Marcus (1966), note 3, p 83.

Again, when Emperor Menelik wished to demand *new* terms taking advantage of British preoccupation in Southern Africa, Harrington had to tender Menelik an implicit warning against Great Britain's stated policy not to be involved in a colonial war with Ethiopia. He proclaimed Great Britain's long-standing policy had been to 'to keep Abyssinia independent, as it was our interest to do so, we did not want to *take* his country. . . . [nor do we] want Abyssinia to fall into the hands of any hostile power, which would be extremely undesirable from our point of view'. Harrington to Boyle, 27 March 1902, FO 1/40.

5 Harold G. Marcus (1963) 'Ethio-British Negotiations concerning the Western Border with Sudan, 1896–1902', *The Journal of African History*, vol 4, no 1, p 83.

of unequal treaties as such, and in any event, if the emphasis should be placed on the objective contents of treaties or the circumstances of their creation.

Although immunities and privileges extended, surrendered to or forced on one state by another state can be effected under seemingly questionable guises, in general, the weight of legal literatures would appear to hold that pacts concluded between states could not be appraised as unequal merely on account of the 'circumstances' under which they had been negotiated. A great many smaller states may, even in the absence of any direct compulsion, willingly engage in conventional pledges that capitulate sovereign interests. The inequalities in such undertakings can simply be discerned from the particular features of the commitments assumed.

In qualifying treaties as unequal, Putney, Buell and Detter investigated the classical prototypes of such a regime including the Treaty of Versailles, the infamous Chinese Capitulation accords on extra-territorial jurisdictions and agreements entered with the Ottoman Empire.[6]

The authors acknowledged that the named treaties exhibited distinct attributes; in common, however, the inequality in the agreements had been prompted by the fact that the commitments had been undertaken without quid pro quo, reflecting a great deal the standpoint of a stronger party and imposed under some form of pressure.

In general, purely formal but unrealistic expressions where the interests of a weaker party are accommodated only nominally, or in contrast, compromises graciously tendered by a smaller sovereign without involving any subordination will generally merit cautious considerations for they can infringe the sovereignty of states.

Still, the foregoing arguments cannot impress that every imbalance in the measure of favour accorded shall *ipso facto* render treaty regimes susceptible to challenge. The particular context in which a treaty is concluded and its contents need to be scrutinized on a case-by-case basis.

The Anglo-Ethiopian Treaty: an unequal convention?

Should Article III of the Anglo-Ethiopian Treaty be read as implying obligations advocated in the British line of interpretation, the treaty would feature the essential elements of unequal treaties illustrated in the preceding paragraphs. Article III would then require Ethiopia to refrain in perpetuity from engaging in the construction of any works on or across the Blue Nile, Lake Tana or the Sobat rivers which arrest the flow of their waters in to the Nile, except with the previous authorisation of Great Britain and the Government of the Sudan. The treaty would bar any development of the resources in Ethiopia apart from meagre waters withdrawn to satisfy domestic requirements and small-scale irrigations. Neither Great Britain, nor its successor – the Sudan – had undertaken fiscal obligations to recompense the losses.

6 Albert H. Putney (1927) 'The Termination of unequal treaties', *Am Soc'y Int'l L Proc*, vol 21, p 89.

The Anglo-Ethiopian Treaty constituted a central theme within a broader British colonial scheme that projected to integrate the entire Nile valley under its exclusive domain. Throughout its tenure as colonial overseer of Sudanese and Egyptian interests, Great Britain framed and consistently defended a diplomatic deportment that required Ethiopia to refrain from interfering with the hydraulic integrity of the Sobat and Blue Nile River systems.

Indeed, from the onset, Great Britain had perceived the unfair composition of the treaty. Its admissions can be discerned from the earliest reports of Colonel John Harrington, where he presented that 'his Majesty's [British] Government had no desire to demand from the Emperor [Menelik] that he should deprive himself of a valuable asset without equivalent compensation'.[7] In a bid to remedy the damage, Lord Cromer authorized Harrington to formally offer a British undertaking 'to pay to Emperor Menelik or his successors the sum of £10,000 Sterling annually . . .' in consideration for 'Menelik having agreed by Article III of the Treaty . . . not to construct . . . any work across the Blue Nile, Lake Tana, or the Sobat . . .'.[8] Intensive negotiations ensued in the course of 1904–1907, but for a blend of reasons the subsidy arrangement was never pushed through.

In retrospect and reconsidering its long advocated river policy in the Nile basin, Great Britain dispensed its most assuaging confession five decades after the treaty had been struck. Hence, in 1956, it openly acknowledged that in discharging its responsibility of protecting downstream user rights, it had in the past 'leaned heavily towards the Sudan, and in consequence away from Ethiopia . . .'.[9] It was further noted that 'there is without doubt some justice in criticism of us voiced in certain Ethiopian quarters that we have dealt unfairly with her . . . by imposing servitudes such as that in Article III of the 1902 Treaty . . .'.[10]

During his reign, Emperor Haileselassie grasped the implication of British designs and the impression of rights it had endeavoured to craft out of the treaty. As a Crown Regent in the 1920s and Emperor since the 1930's, he engaged in a convoluted political wrestle with a swaying colonial neighbour. A considerable scale of royal diplomacy had been invested in attempting to discredit not only what he perceived was an erroneous interpretation of Ethiopia's obligations under the treaty, but also to positively assert his country's right to carry out developments which defied the plain spirit of Anglo-Sudanese reflections.

Yet, while the state of affairs established through the treaty had been the cause of formal resentment in the Ethiopian quarters, the basic tenet of Ethiopia's early retractions, it can be noted, had barely questioned the treaty's legitimacy on the basis of the dictates of international law governing unequal treaties as such,[11] rules

7 Memorandum, History of the Lake Tana Negotiation, Foreign Office, 23 January 1923, FO 371/8403.

8 Memorandum (1923), note 7.

9 J.E. Killick to J.H.A Watson, British Embassy, Addis Ababa, 26 September 1956, FO 371/119063.

10 J.E. Killick to J.H.A Watson (1956), note 9.

11 While Albert Garretson argued that Ethiopia appeared to hold the provision in the treaty as likened to a *pactus leoninus* where in one party reserves for itself the rights and privileges, leaving the other

governing the uses of transboundary watercourses,[12] or the doctrinal guidelines regulating the fundamental change of circumstances.

Because of a dearth of empirical details, it could prove difficult to establish a coherent link between fundamentals of Ethiopia's imperial-epoch hydropolitical discourses and the strategies advocated by the succeeding governments in the 1970s and through the 1990s. On the whole, however, it is evident that five decades of Emperor Haileselassie's spirited engagement in the developmental politics of the Nile River resources and the deleterious facts presented in the immediate aftermath had left a vivid mark of scepticism and sense of disregard ingrained in the Ethiopian psyche with regard to rights of utilization.

Today, one direct upshot of this influence has been that the Anglo-Ethiopian Treaty is hardly referred to in formal communications, more appreciated in a historical context than as a legal instrument spelling international obligations. Of course, earlier, it has been submitted that in international relations, Ethiopia's deportment of disregard, alone, would not be a controlling factor in obviating treaty responsibilities.

Hence, whereas British acknowledgement of the unfair composition of the pact had been recited and its unequal attribute confirmed by reference to its contents (on the basis of accounts depicted in British Nile diplomacy), the next charge would involve investigating the concept of unequal treaties under the pertinent rules of international law.

The issue is, apart from alternative solutions proffered in diplomacy, can Ethiopia proclaim, as a matter of legal right, that Article III of the Anglo-Ethiopian Treaty supposedly restricting its rights of use no longer commands juridical order on the account of its unequal composition?

International law and the validity of unequal treaties

The doctrinal discourse on the subject of unequal treaties has hardly displayed identical orientation. The dearth of firm guidelines in international law that establish parameters for appraising the inequality and legal effect of such treaties had prompted states and legal authorities to uphold varied stances.

Long before codification of the regime of international treaty law in Vienna, Putney summarized the applicable law, the doctrinal instruction that existed prior to the Covenant of the League of Nations. He submitted that whatever the category of treaty referred to and regardless of the circumstances of its making, there is no 'principle of international law . . . that on account of the inequality of the treaty,

party without reciprocal undertaking or compensation, Ethiopia's arguments had been channelled along entirely different legal premises.

Albert Garretson (1960) 'The Nile River system', *American Society International Law Proceedings*, vol 54, p 143.

Also cited in: Bonaya Adhi Godana (1985) *Africa's Shared Water Resources: Legal and Institutional Aspects of the Nile, Niger and Senegal River Systems*, p 156.

12 Except in the later twentieth century, and particularly since the 1990s.

the party suffering under the inequality has a right to abrogate it for this reason alone . . .'.[13] Other essential elements, and most notably, that 'there was marked injustice at the time of the conclusion of the treaty' or that the right to end the treaty had been sought 'on account of changed conditions',[14] should as well be in attendance. Similarly, it was held that the validity of a treaty would not be affected by the mere fact that it had been brought about by a threat or use of force.[15]

In contrast, adherents of the Soviet doctrine spearheaded by the USSR (Soviet Russia) had generally condemned what they called leonine arrangements advocating a position shared by a multitude of developing countries.[16] Hence, 'all agreements under international law forced up on a state, or agreements that are of an enslaving nature, and those that disregard the principle of equality', (arguably including accords which do not correspond to the real will of one of the parties) are rendered 'without any legal effect under international law'.[17] Others espoused a narrower deportment, permitting denouncement only under circumstances where proof could be adduced that they had been imposed by force or threat of force.

Indeed, a sequence of classical literatures of international law dating from the times of Grotius and Vattel to Fauchille and Oppenheim approached the subject matter indirectly and nearly unanimously had held the view that the rule of duress applies only in a limited mode, with respect to constraints, serious physical menace or intimidation, employed against 'treaty-making representatives' of states.[18] The traditional authorities did not question that a genuine freedom of consent of states makes up an essential condition of a binding treaty but refused to admit pleas of coercion practised by one state against the other, whether that be a defeat in war or threat of a strong state against a weak one as a ground for vitiating consent.[19] No distinction was proffered between conventions solicited through the application of legitimate or illegitimate use of force.

Certainly, modern international law has long evolved to tender a broader thinking. In fact, the *lex lata* has inclined to debase nearly all accords obtained through the employment of grave pressures exercised against states as such or their representatives. The present formulation of Articles 51 and 52 of the Vienna Convention on the Law of Treaties reflecting on the spirit enshrined in Article 2(4) of the UN Charter expressly propounds this view.

Hence, without prejudice to the principle of *ratione temporis*, the Vienna Convention provided that a treaty whose conclusion has been procured by the coercion of its representative through acts or threats directed at him or through the coercion of

13 Putney (1927), note 6.
14 Putney (1927), note 6, p 89.
15 International Law Commission (1966) *Yearbook of International Law Commission*, vol 2, p 246.
16 International Law Commission (1966), note 15, p 16.
17 Ingrid Detter (1966) 'The Problem of Unequal Treaties', *Int'l and Comp LQ*, vol 15, p 1082.
18 An extensive summary of the pertinent literatures has been provided in Concord *Am J Int'l L Sup* (1935), vol 29, pp 1150–51.
19 Concord, N.H. (American Society of International Law) (1935) 'Supplement to the American Journal of International Law', *Am J Int'l L Sup*, vol 29, p 1151.

a state by the threat or use of force in violation of the principles of international law embodied in the Charter of the United Nations shall be rendered void *ab initio*.[20]

Of course, Articles 51–52 of the Convention addressed only cases of consent obtained through 'duress', and not the theme of incongruent treaties as such. During the drafting deliberations of the ILC on the Law of Treaties, observations held out by several government delegates had been swayed by the conviction that the Convention's provisions would eventually confirm a legal rule that pronounces the invalidity of unequal treaty regimes concluded between states situated in incongruent positions.[21] The spirited expectation was triggered by the fact that in most accounts several of the treaties designated as unequal were consequences of some form of unpreventable pressure exerted by one state against the other.

Yet, while ordinarily states exercising a genuinely free will could not be expected to surrender their interests without a quid pro quo gain, it is evident that not every regime of inequality in treaties fits in the category of pacts procured through the coercion of a state by threat or use of force. This explains why the Vienna Convention failed short of regulating the subject matter of unequal treaties directly and distinctly.

Hence, unequal treaties would be regulated by the Convention's provisions not merely on account of the lopsided regime they may have procured in any given scenario, but only in limited circumstances where proof could be adduced that they had been instituted through means particularly depicted under Articles 51 and 52.

To contextualize this regime of international law to the issues at hand, it was noted above that in the early decades of the twentieth century, the particular vulnerability of Ethiopia's sovereignty required Emperor Menelik to construct a circumspectly scaled diplomatic relationship with the British, Italian and French powers in the horn region. The pertinent records tended to verify that although Great Britain's power of political manipulate of the time had been compelling, in the context of the phrases' use in international law and practice, Emperor Menelik was hardly threatened with force or actually forced into accepting the eventual treaty version.

Indeed, apart from a few occasional outbursts, there was no plain evidence demonstrating that the treaty negotiations had been accompanied by direct economic or military threats or an ultimatum of potential occupation of the Blue Nile basin if, for instance, the Emperor had failed to ink the proposed accord. Nor had there been manifestation of other levels or forms of duress recognized under the pre- or post-Vienna Convention international legal order that provide ground for causing nullity of the Anglo-Ethiopian Treaty. International law seems to proffer little help in this regard.

20 United Nations Vienna Convention on the Law of Treaties (1969), Vienna 23 May 1969. UN Treaty Series Vol 1155, p 331, Article 51.

21 International Law Commission (1966), note 15, p 16.

Even so, this conclusion may take a converse course if Judge Padilla Nervo's reproving opinion in the *Fisheries Jurisdiction* proceedings can be regarded as propounding the normative yardstick for appraising the admissible levels of pressure in interstate relations.[22] Yet, it remains evident that the pertinent legal regime essentially constituted under the Vienna Convention on the Law of Treaties does not accommodate such an approach.

The principle of permanent sovereignty over natural resources (PSNR): the interplay

Within the international legal order, a more formidable defiance of unequal treaties had been procured by a series of United Nations General Assembly (UNGA) resolutions adopted in the 1950s and 1960s. Among others, General Assembly Resolution Nos 523, 626, 1314, 1515, 1803 and 3281 instituted a systematic framework of conceptual correlation between the principles of sovereign equality, self-determination and permanent sovereignty of states over natural resources.[23]

The question is whether the sweeping languages of the UNGA resolutions had contemplated transboundary rivers as proper subjects of treatment and if so, what the nature and scope of rights tendered by virtue of such stipulations would be as affecting the continued validity of existing treaties.

Transboundary rivers: covered themes?

Much of the fuss during the UNGA's preparatory deliberations and successive sessions of its committees essentially highlighted the anti-colonial movement. Principally, the movement was stirred by the desire to confer some degree of protection to foreign investments and concessions and by the need for setting procedures that regulate expropriation and compensation. In limited contexts, the resolutions and soft-law regime they instituted had also been employed to slacken the disproportionate economic gain major powers had fetched through treaties concluded during and in the aftermath of the colonial epochs both in Africa and Asia.

The operative and substantive parts of the UN resolutions and particularly UNGA Resolution No1803 had been framed broadly enough to encompass

22 *Fisheries Jurisdiction (United Kingdom/Iceland)*, Dissenting Opinion of Judge Padila Nervo, ICJ Reports 1974, p 47; he submitted that certain detrimental conditions prompted by the exercise of duress are not brought about by mere threats or uses of force and presented the view 'well known by professors, jurists and diplomats acquainted with international relations and foreign policies that certain Notes delivered by the government of a strong power to the government of a small nation may have the same purpose and the same effect as the use or threat of force'.

23 United Nations General Assembly Resolution 523(VI), Integrated Economic Development and Commercial Agreements, 12 January 1952; UNGA Resolution 626 (VIII), 21 December 1952; UNGA Resolution 1314 (XIII), 12 December, 1958; UNGA Resolution 1515 (XV), 15 December, 1960; UNGA Resolution 1803 (XVII), Permanent Sovereignty Over Natural Resources, 14 December 1962; UNGA Resolution 3281, Charter of Economic Rights and Duties of States, 12 December 1974.

themes associated with the use of transboundary watercourses. In fact, the adoption of Resolution No1803 was preceded by comprehensive studies on the status of the principle of permanent sovereignty over natural wealth and resources (PSNR), submitted to the Commission on Permanent Sovereignty over Natural Resources.[24] The final report tendered a compilation of the relevant laws, observations and practice of states. Although subordinated to other contested sub-topics, views submitted by some states had expressly outlined riparian rights as a proper subject of investigation within the broader premises of the concept of PSNR.[25]

More specifically, Article 3 of the UNGA Resolution No3281, pursuing a correlated agenda and establishing the UN Charter of Economic Rights and Duties of States (UNCERD) had made specific reference to the duties of states in respect of the exploitation of natural resources shared between two or more countries. Such a reference encompasses the collective management and use of fisheries, oil and gas deposits as well as transboundary river courses.

That the principle of PSNR applies to international watercourses had been the subject of deliberation by the International Law Commission during codification the UN Convention on the Non-navigational Uses of International Watercourses. In spite of the early conceptual controversies involving the unique characteristic of water, it was subsequently reiterated that 'water could be said to be the one natural resource over which states truly exercised permanent sovereignty'[26] and that as a shared resource, it constituted one of the objects covered by the UN resolutions on PSNR.[27]

Rights inferred from UNGA resolutions

The UNGA resolutions on PSNR had essentially laid one facet of the doctrinal and legal regimes that govern the use of natural resources, and the measure of discretion afforded to states in exercising such rights.

Inter alia, the above-stated resolutions declared the permanent and sovereign right of every state to freely dispose of its wealth and resources in accordance with national interests and in the spirit of economic collaboration. Furthermore, it was affirmed that any violation of such rights constitutes an infringement of the principles of the Charter of the United Nations, hindering the development

24 The Commission on Permanent Sovereignty over Natural Resources was established by UNGA Resolution 1314(XIII), 12 December 1958.

25 Report of the Commission on Permanent Sovereignty over Natural Resources, Resolution II, UN Doc A/AC 97/13, 23 May 1961.

26 International Law Commission (1976) *Yearbook of International Law Commission*, vol 2, no 2, p 160.

Yet, this raised the question of to what extent, if at all, the concept PSNR would be applicable to its cases. Water can be said to be in perpetual motion; this mobility of water as a natural resource meant that permanent sovereignty would have to be exercised differently than in the cases of resources that were not naturally mobile. The task of the Commission had been to propose how sovereignty situated in a particular river basin should be exercised over the natural resource which, because of its physical qualities, was common to several states.

27 International Law Commission (1982) *Yearbook of International Law Commission*, vol 2, no 1, p 72.

of international cooperation and the maintenance of peace. Similar provisions highlighting the principle's eminence had also been incorporated under the UN human rights conventions adopted in 1966 on civil, political, economic, social and cultural rights, and the UN Convention on the Law of the Sea (1982).

Generally, of course, mere declarations of the United Nations General Assembly as such, however fashioned and even when endorsed within its recognized spheres of competence, could not clutch concrete legal credence. However, it is evident that in specific circumstances, the General Assembly's actions can potentially engender certain operative designs.

A great anthology of literatures had been inked propounding on the legal status and significance of the concept of permanent sovereignty over natural resources, and particularly, its ramification on contested issues such as the nationalization of alien economic entities and the right of governments to disregard treaty commitments assumed by preceding regimes. Developing states and some international law publicists exerted efforts to form a principle (and perhaps a legal authority) that secures 'emancipation' from the injurious effects of treaties engaged in unequal economic and political power setting and to direct their execution in the attainment of equitable gains.

Based on the vigour, consistency and near-unanimity of the views of states in some of the resolutions, a few authors had even been impelled to attribute PSNR a status of a *jus cogens* norm of international law.[28]

Of course, an observant assessment of the deliberations in the General Assembly or its various committees does not bear out such a proposition. In fact, in the *Texaco Overseas Petroleum et al vs. Libyan Arab Republic* arbitration, Arbiter Rene-Jean Dupuy had had the occasion to investigate the chronological development of the various resolutions wherein he concluded that 'on the basis of the circumstances of adoption mentioned above and by expressing an opinio juris communis, Resolution 1803 (XVII) [alone] seems to this Tribunal to reflect the state of customary law existing in this field'.[29]

A thorough review of the UN declarations tendered by Karol Gess observed 'most members held that the [original] resolution [No.626] was intended to express existing law'.[30]

On the other hand, some states approached the theme of PSNR with a degree of doubt generally emanating from the General Assembly's incompetence in pronouncing mandatory dictums of international regulation. A few argued the concept had been embodied in a mere declaration that commands no binding legal force. For instance, the United States expressed its view that 'General Assembly statements of policy could not affect the powers of a state or the principles of international law', but acknowledged this particular mechanism as setting forth the

28 See, for example: Kamal Hussain and Subrata Roy Chowdhury (1984) *Permanent Sovereignty over Natural Resources in International Law, Principle and Practice*, London, Francis Pinter.

29 American Society of International Law (1978) *International Legal Materials*, vol 17, no 1, pp 1–37.

30 Karol N. Gess (1964) 'Permanent Sovereignty over Natural Resources: Analytical review of the United Nations declaration and its genesis', *Int'l &Comp L Q*, vol 13, p 398.

'rights and duties of states, which affirms their sovereignty and the modalities of the exercise of that sovereignty'.[31] On the other hand, France submitted that while the principle of permanent sovereignty had its basis in international law, it has not yet become an element thereof.[32]

The divergence in the views of states was largely prompted by the fundamental interest both capital-exporting and capital-importing countries had hoped to preserve through the machinations of the declarations. The fundamental moral conviction of the community of states was hardly at variance on the issue of permanent sovereignty. The overwhelming support the last major declaration, UNGA Resolution 1803 had garnered was most likely as the result of the strong assumption that in many respects the principle had restated a prevailing regime proposing 'no substantial modification' to international law.[33]

Still, a distinct legal regime, the application of the principle of PSNR would in any given setting involve its synchronization with other rules of the international legal order regulating diverse themes of interstate relations. This will naturally constitute a convoluted commission and shall be revisited later.

PSNR, self-determination and shared river courses

The preceding section has considered the status of PSNR under general international law. A noteworthy boost to the juridical stature of the concept had also been endowed through its intrinsic organization under another specific theme of public international law – the right to self-determination.

Whether the permanent sovereignty of states over natural resources constitutes one basic constituent of the right to self-determination, hence engendering a far more concrete basis for claiming rights of use of international water courses, had been the subject of deliberation both in the early UN resolutions and literatures.

The decolonization process in Africa and Asia, now nearly over, had been espoused politically, legally and morally under the banner of the right of people to self-determination. The explicit recognition afforded to the right to self-determination under the two UN human rights covenants adopted in 1966 is generally employed to corroborate the view that the principle, whether in its political or economic context had been transformed into a hard dictate of public international law.

The significance of this discussion lays in the close association of the political and economic aspects of the right to self-determination. The political facets of the right cannot be considered in isolation, without a parallel regard to treaty arrangements gravely impinging on the right of states to economic self-determination, a right whose elements had been sanctioned, among others, under UNGA Resolution 1803. This intimate bond between the principle of PSNR and the right to

31 Karol N. Gess (1964), note 30, p 409.

32 Karol N. Gess (1964), note 30, p 410.

33 UNGA Resolution 1803(XVII) was adopted with 87 votes for, 2 votes against (France and South Africa), and 12 abstentions.

self-determination reiterated in many contemporary treatises is essentially premised on such a theory.

The International Court of Justice had a limited opportunity to reflect on the development and significance of the pertinent principle in the *East Timor* case.[34] During the proceedings, Portugal requested the Court to adjudge that Australia's initiatives, in contemplating to explore and exploit the sub-soil of the Sea in the Timor Gap on the basis of a plurilateral title which does not involve itself as the administering power, infringes the right of 'the people of East Timor to self determination . . . and permanent sovereignty over its natural wealth and resources'.[35]

The Court reasoned that the right of peoples to self-determination as evolving from the Charter and from United Nations practice has been recognized in the jurisprudence of the Court and constituted 'one of the essential principles of international law' that has long evolved to compose 'an *erga omnes* character'.[36] Nevertheless, lack of jurisdiction on the matter precluded the majority from decreeing on the merits, which, given the issues presented would have established the juridical standing and relationship between the right to self-determination and the principle of PSNR under the international legal order.

Somewhat, a dissenting opinion by ad hoc judge Skubizewski remedied the fracture. He presented that the right of the people of East Timor to self-determination, including its right to permanent sovereignty over natural wealth and resources which are recognized by the United Nations, 'require observance by all members of the United Nations'.[37]

Similarly, a dissenting view by Judge Warramantry reiterated the significance of the aforementioned General Assembly resolutions and confirmed that 'self-determination includes, by very definition, the right of permanent sovereignty over natural resources'[38] and that 'sovereignty over . . . economic resources is, for any people, an important component of the totality of their sovereignty'.[39]

True, these observations did not enlighten on the specific legal standing of the concept as such within the broader system of international law, which exhibits a complex interaction between manifold legal regimes, including the law of treaties. It is also difficult to speculate on the essence of the Court's potential verdict on the merits. Still, given the weight attached to the opinion of the dissenting judges as well as the impression created by the successive UNGA resolutions and subsequent political developments, it will be reasonable to assume that the Court's findings would hardly have varied substantially, at least, on the issue of the association between the principles of self-determination, sovereignty and rights over natural resources.

34 *East Timor (Portugal vs. Australia)*, Judgment, ICJ Reports 1995, p 93 para 10.

35 *East Timor* (1995), note 34, p 94.

36 *East Timor* (1995), note 34, p 102.

37 *East Timor (Portugal vs. Australia)*, Dissenting Opinion of Judge Skubizewski, ICJ Reports 1995, p 276.

38 *East Timor (Portugal vs. Australia)*, Dissenting Opinion of Judge Weeramantry, ICJ Reports 1995, p 200.

39 *East Timor* (1995), note 34, p 197.

One natural consequence of the prominence of PSNR as a principle of international law and even more, as a vital constituent of a superseding concept of international law – the right to self-determination, is that it *ipso facto* imposes certain obligations on the community of states.

Stated differently, the combined operation of the principles could afford states a substantial legal lee in seeking the nullification of such treaty undertakings as may for instance alienate or perpetually curtail the sovereign freedom of states to use their natural resources, including shared river courses.

Conclusions: correlating PSNR and the Anglo-Ethiopian Treaty

The call for the application of the principle of PSNR in a strictly legal configurement requires a cautious consideration of a wide range of contexts. In disputing the continued legality of treaties that are repugnant to the theory of PSNR, the interplay between various *pillars* of international law and most notably, the rules of state succession to treaties, principles governing the utilization of international watercourses and the canon of *pacta sunt servanda* must be pondered with the greatest prudence. After all, while the legal value of the concept of PSNR may not be contested, both UNGA resolutions 1515 and 1803 had references that could be interpreted as stipulating implicit conditions on the exercise of rights inherent in the concept of PSNR.

In the interpretative spirit contemplated by Great Britain, the Anglo-Ethiopian Treaty can essentially be regarded as artefact of British authoritative drafting of a bilateral convention. In that limited context, the agreement has structured a case of permanent inequality of user-rights over Ethiopia's natural endowments. Along with other factors, this glowing state of inequity instituted by the treaty gravely jeopardized Ethiopia's development prospects and hence could afford a legal ground for calling the nullity of the arrangement.

Most certainly, though, against the background of radical evolution of international norms governing human rights, the utilization of transboundary watercourses and the succession of states to treaties, an Anglo-Sudanese expectation of non-interference with the utilization of the Nile waters in Ethiopia would engender, to employ Judge Warramantry's expression 'a permanent deprivation to the owners of the resources which is rightfully theirs'. A literal implementation of the Anglo-Ethiopian Treaty in the context perpetuated by Great Britain would naturally deny Ethiopia of a vital means of its subsistence. This could hardly be in consonance with the precepts of modern international law and particularly, the dictates and conditions for the application of the principles of equality and permanent sovereignty over natural resources which are implicit in the above-stated covenants and resolutions.

True, the status of PSNR as an overriding rule of *jus cogens* is unconvincing. However, the fact that successive forums had confirmed the inalienability and full permanent sovereignty of states over natural resources would seem to afford a strapping basis for rescinding a perpetual arrangement that *purportedly* deprived

Ethiopia of a right to develop its share of the natural resources. The inconspicuous scale of free will under which Article III had been concluded notwithstanding, the moderation imposed by the treaty against the nation's economic sovereignty would be paramount. Given the eternal features of the accord itself and the relative scale of eminence of the concept of PSNR in international law, the Anglo-Ethiopian Treaty could not sustain to instruct a strong legal charge.

However, it must also be noted that the concept of PSNR does not sanction rights carte blanche. As depicted in a series of resolutions and specifically under Article III of the UN Charter of Economic and Social Rights and cognizant of the duties stated in other regimes of international law, Ethiopia would also be expected to adhere to corollary responsibilities. It is bound to collaborate 'on the basis of a system . . . . of prior consultations in order to achieve optimum use of such [shared] resources without causing damage to the legitimate interest of others'.[40]

Fundamental change of circumstances (*rebus sic stantibus*)

Introduction

If there is a theory of international law to which states had resorted frequently to rectify an unequal state of affairs instituted through treaty regimes, it is the doctrine of *rebus sic stantibus*. The canon, it was stated under the Vienna Convention on the Law of Treaties, confers disenfranchised states a measure of cause for withdrawing from a treaty on account of 'fundamental change of circumstances which has occurred with regard to those existing at the time of the conclusion of a treaty, and which was not foreseen by the parties'.[41]

The principal justification that provided states a loop of manoeuvre for disputing the continued implementation of treaty responsibilities has recognized that '. . . the sanctity of engagements made internationally must lead . . . to the conclusion that there is a weighty obligation on all states to be responsive to demands for changes, where circumstances have altered, and where any engagement heretofore made could not be said to bear inequitably up on the other party to the engagement.'[42] This assumption enthused a view that tended to regard the principle of *rebus sic stantibus* as a tacitly embedded element of all contractual undertakings between states.

In this section, the issue that would be conversed is: how does the rule of fundamental change of circumstances translate in relation to the Anglo-Ethiopian Treaty concluded a little more than a century ago?

40 United Nations GA Resolution 3281, Charter of Economic Rights and Duties of States, 12 December 1974.

41 United Nations Vienna Convention on the Law of Treaties (1969), note 20, Article 62.

42 Raymond L. Buell (1927) 'The Termination of unequal treaties', *Am Soc'y Int'l L Proc*, vol 21, p 95.

The meaning, standing and effect of the principle of *rebus sic stantibus*

The insist for the security and sanctity of treaty relationships, discerned from the entrenched status accorded to the *pacta sunt servanda* rule has been duly highlighted both under the international legal order and in bilateral and multilateral discourses that pacts voluntarily assumed must be honoured in good faith. Hence, and this has been signified by the negative formulation of Article 62 of the Vienna Convention on the Law of Treaties, the principle of *rebus sic stantibus* applies but only as exception.

The controversial nature of the principle of *rebus sic stantibus* and particularly its standing in the complex system of public international law had been the subject of intensive discussions during the drafting stages of the Convention on the Law of Treaties. Views restated by participating governments and members of the International Law Commission diverged considerably on the issue of whether the principle shall be recognized as a rule of customary international law as such, or whether the ILC had to merely propose its inclusion as progressive development of international law on the subject.[43]

The relevant stipulation was eventually framed in a manner stated above, but more importantly, uncertainties involving its status were subsequently elucidated by the ICJ's ruling in 1997. Hence, in the *Gabcikovo-Nagymaros Project* case, the Court reiterated its position that 'in many respects, with Articles 60–62 of the Vienna Convention relating to the termination or suspension of the operation of a treaty', the Convention's rules are declaratory of customary law.[44]

At least based on the rules of the Vienna Convention, therefore, international law would seem to provide a sphere for accommodating the unconsidered effects of subsequent development of circumstances which tend to make existing duties more onerous or otherwise require the execution of pacts in an entirely unanticipated setting.

Of course, it can be inferred from the framing of Article 62 of the Vienna Convention that not every allegation of consequent change can *ipso facto* upset the application of treaty regimes as such. The change must be unforeseen, fundamental in nature and the facts existing at the time of the conclusion of the treaty must have constituted the essential basis of the consent of the parties.

The charge of labelling factual developments as essential or fundamental constitutes a knotty undertaking and largely involves a subjective exercise. It will be noted below that neither state practice invoking the principle in defence of national positions, nor opinions of international law publicists had been entirely congruent on the subject.

A broader illustration of cases of fundamental change of circumstances proffered by Woolsey embraced, among others, those which 'threaten or cause the sacrifice of a state's development or its vital requirements for political or economic

43 International Law Commission (1979) *Yearbook of International Law Commission*, vol 1, no 1, pp 77, 79, 85.

44 *GabCikovo-Nagymaros Project (Hungary/Slovakia)*, Judgment, ICJ Reports 1997, p 62.

existence to the execution of the treaty, that is, make performance impracticable except at an unreasonable sacrifice; [and those which] are inconsistent with the right of self-preservation, or incompatible with the independence of a state . . .'.[45]

The dictum in the *Lepeschkin vs. Gosweiler et Cie* case disposed by the Swiss Federal Tribunal (1923) and involving France and Russia further introduced a ground for terminating treaty relations on account of changed circumstances. Largely drawing on the political and ideological contrasts of the pre-1917 Tsarist Regime and the Soviet Socialist Republic, the Tribunal held '. . . the change in the form of government of Russia has carried a profound alteration of all the internal juridical organization and of the relations of individuals among themselves and with the state, the fact that from all this has resulted a situation contrasting fundamentally with the order prevailing in all other European states may have given the other Contracting States the right to withdraw eventually from the agreement by virtue of the principle of . . . *clausula rebus sic stantibus* . . .'.[46]

The fundamental attribute of any alleged state of fact is contextual. As distinguished from other less fundamental circumstances, such a distinction would have to be considered by reference to the scale of influence it had originally instructed in framing the consent of the contracting parties. In the *Fisheries Jurisdiction*, the International Court elaborated that the changed circumstance 'should have resulted in a radical transformation of the extent of the obligations still to be performed . . . the burden of obligations to be executed to the extent of rendering the performance of something essentially different from that originally undertaken'.[47]

Rebus sic stantibus and the Anglo-Ethiopian Treaty

It is evident from the theoretical expositions as well as the framing of the Vienna Convention on the Law of Treaties that permanent servitudes purportedly instituted through the Anglo-Ethiopian Treaty could not be abrogated merely because they tended to be cumbersome to one of the parties. Without prejudice to other legal regimes that afford sanctuary, the treaty may continue to encumber Ethiopia unless it can be demonstrated that there had been a *significant alteration* of those circumstances which then formed a tacit requirement of its existence in the understandings of both Emperor Menelik and the Anglo-Sudanese administration.

In light of the particular framing of the concept under Article 62 of the Vienna Convention, the themes that oblige examination are depicted as follows. What were the principal objectives and essential facts of the treaty undertaking whose continued existence had constituted, for the parties engaging in the scheme, fundamental conditions of the treaty? What assumptions and restrictions formed an integral part of the original arrangement, which, in contrast to the changed circumstances, the parties had anticipated as present when they committed themselves under Article III of the treaty?

45 Concord, N.H. (American Society of International Law) (1935), note 19, p 1101.
46 Concord, N.H. (American Society of International Law) (1935), note 19, pp 1103–4.
47 *Fisheries Jurisdiction (Federal Republic of Germany vs. Iceland), Judgment, .CJ Reports 1973*, p 21.

The preceding parts have illustrated that the interpretation of certain issues and factual settings involving the conclusion of the Anglo-Ethiopian Treaty cannot be established conclusively. In this book, the construction of intentions and objectives that prompted the parties into negotiating the treaty would be chiefly premised on the parties' own reflections as manifested in a series of diplomatic exchanges of the time.

The central objective of British manoeuvres in the Nile basin had always projected to preserve the rights of utilizing of the Nile and its tributaries. Within such a broader framework, Article III of the Anglo-Ethiopian accord had chiefly anticipated to shelter British hydraulic interests on the Baro-Akobo and Blue-Nile segments of the Nile River in Ethiopia. In fact, Great Britain's engagement with Ethiopia constituted only one facet of coordinated initiatives launched across the basin.

From the early years of Lord Cromer in the 1890s to the late 1950s, Great Britain's concentration on the subject was prompted by the overwhelming economic and geopolitical necessities of its imperial and capitalist enterprises in Egypt, Sudan and the near east. The insistence on the preservation of its stakes in the basin required that non-interference regimes and concessions for the construction of dams had to be installed through various pacts.

Evidently, Great Britain's dynamic involvement, prudent designs and implementation of water resources development schemes across various parts of the Nile basin were hardly altruistic, triggered by the long-term requirements of the colonies as such. Its own imperial ego, strategic concerns and the quest for the control of natural resources and raw materials had always been vital considerations. Various communications of the Foreign Office functionaries depicted earlier attest the power of manipulate British water engineers and the Manchester-Lancashire cotton interests had then commanded in national colonial politics and water uses policies affecting the Nile basin region.

Hence, although Emperor Menelik pledged not to construct any works across the named rivers except with a previous agreement of the British and Sudanese governments, in strict juridical parlance, the government of Sudan – then constituting but a mere extension of London's Colonial Office – did not as such exist. Within the broader objectives of deterring any implementation of water resource developments potentially damaging British interests in Sudan and Egypt, the accord was in reality concluded between Great Britain, a colonial power administering Sudan, on the one hand and the sovereign state of Ethiopia.

For Emperor Menelik, the sweeping concessions, as conceived in British *perceptions* of the time, were most likely tendered to fend off pressures exerted by a commanding colonial neighbour just next door by addressing serious issues relating to the boundary delimitation. Over the long term, the treaty's machinery had also been employed to safeguard Ethiopia's sovereignty by maintaining a deviously balanced diplomatic relations with the major European powers. This colonial-epoch-setting of the contractual undertaking, composing the essential basis of the consent of the parties, is even more implicit in the specific contents of the agreement.

Hence, the preamble introduced that the contracting parties, 'animated with the desire to confirm the friendly relations between the two powers [Great Britain and Ethiopia] and to settle the frontier between the Soudan and Ethiopia', agreed to carry out obligations featuring a series of compromises. Articles I and II foresaw to delimit and mark the boundary through the employ of a joint commission. Article III endeavoured to regulate the use of the Tana, Nile and Sobat river resources. Article IV granted Great Britain a piece of land in the western peripheries of Ethiopia for commercial activities, whereas Article V extended Great Britain permission to construct a rail line transiting through the Ethiopian territory.

In tune with customary treaty-making practices of the time, an eternity clause was also slotted in to the preamble, binding 'the parties and their successors'; this gives the impression that Great Britain had probably projected that its administrative authority would reign for an indeterminate period in the Sudan.

Whatever the larger assumptions, the specific arrangement regulating rights of utilizing the Nile River water resources had been orchestrated in such a way as to meet Great Britain's colonial-epoch objectives in the lower-reaches of the basin. Emperor Menelik's dispensation of special privileges under Article III had taken such facts into consideration. With respect to the commercial station in Gambella, for instance, it was expressly stated the lease of land should last only 'in so long as Britain remains the administrative authority of the Soudan'. Given the development of the pertinent political and historical facts and the balance of power then prevailing, it would be only commonsensical to deduce that Emperor Menelik would have barely bestowed such far-reaching compromises, say, to Kellifa's Sudan, or for that matter to a less influential France or Italy.

In this context, therefore, the demise of the British colonial establishment and institution of Sudanese self-rule in the mid twentieth century had represented a radical transformation of the status quo fundamentally affecting the position of the parties to the original pact. This upshot of the political developments, it could be argued, had been such that the prime *raison d'être* of Article III of the treaty, i.e., 'upholding the welfare of the British colonial establishment in Sudan and Egypt and the friendly relations between Great Britain and Ethiopia', could no longer be fulfilled through the same treaty scheme. By operation of the rules of state succession, Ethiopia would now be required to discharge the obligation to an essentially different party, a fact which itself depicts fundamental changes from the original practical anticipations of Great Britain and Ethiopia within the framework of the 1902 treaty.

For this reason, the disappearance of such vital condition of the treaty on which its continued functioning depended and which the parties had not anticipated could afford Ethiopia a ground for calling the abrogation of the agreement on the basis of changed circumstances.

Given the fundamental alterations that took place in the intervening period and the scale of transformation of the conditions that prompted the parties into concluding the agreement, calling for a plain execution of the treaty today can be considered as imposing a more burdensome obligation which had not been foreseen by the parties and which would be essentially different in context from the original undertaking.

So far, Chapters 4–7 of the Book have displayed *limited* perspectives with regard to the status quo prevailing in the Nile basin, essentially concentrating on a regime constituted through the Anglo-Ethiopian Treaty of 1902. The academic enterprise focused on *re-defining* riparian legal relations between Ethiopia and Sudan on the basis *treaty laws* and selected *principles of customary international law* which have been found relevant in illuminating the contents and continued validity of the treaty as such.

Yet, not every legal regime impacting on the rights of utilization of shared watercourses derives from specific treaty frameworks. The practice of states presents evidence of the existence of *customary rules* and *generally accepted principles* of international law regulating riparian relations and particularly so in circumstances where specific treaties are either absent or disputed.

In fact, from time to time, states have asserted claims and defended conduct on the basis of varied principles enunciated under the regime of international watercourses law.

The structure of legal relations in the Nile Basin cannot be any different: it transcends far beyond stipulations of the Anglo-Ethiopian Treaty just discussed in the foregoing parts. Over the course of the late nineteenth and throughout the twentieth centuries, the Nile basin has witnessed a complex legal order organized through contentious pacts, regional customs and perceptions as well as specific principles of customary international law regulating the use, development and management of shared watercourses.

Given the disputed context in which the Nile legal history has evolved, the virtual import of customary rules of international law, demonstrating evidence of a general practice accepted as law by the community of states, is exceptionally evident. The legitimacy of several of the Nile treaty regimes instituted during the colonial epochs had been subsequently contested. Moreover, to this very date, the basin has shunned comprehensive legal frameworks that could have addressed collective riparian concerns.

Contemporary rules of custom proffer crucial functions in filling the legal vacuity thus produced; they not only spell riparian rights and obligations but also provide the legal standards against which the basin states' claims as are founded on *non-treaty sources* are appraised and eventually determined.

No doubt, international custom has itself some limitations: often, its principles are broader in formulation, contentious on substance and occasionally argumentative. As Professor Charles Bourne noted, in the early 1950s the international lawyer faced with the question of 'what the law on the utilization of international water resources actually is' could not say with conviction that customary rules had indeed evolved sufficiently.[48] In defence of national water resources development policies, states had to select from a wide range of theoretical reserves: namely the doctrines advocating absolute territorial sovereignty, absolute territorial integrity,

48 Charles B. Bourne (1996) 'The International Law Association's Contribution to International Water Resources Law', *Natural Resources Journal*, vol 36, p 156.

the right to reasonable and equitable uses, prior utilization and the duty not to cause significant harm.

Modern international watercourses law has significantly developed since the 1950s. Several of its rules highlighted the sovereign equality of states and postulated a fundamental right of each watercourse state to equitably participate in the beneficial uses of international rivers. The right to equitable utilization, a keystone formulation reproduced under the 1997 UN Watercourses Convention has been endorsed as a universal theory that regulates the conduct of states sharing fresh watercourses.

In spite of the normative order embedded in the principle of sovereign equality and rights in equity, however, the Nile basin states and most notably, the three states holding leading stakes in the subject – Egypt, Sudan and Ethiopia persevered to espouse an incongruent water uses policies at the national levels. Existing uses and future rights of resource development were defended through the employ of conflicting principles.

Chapters 8–11 of the book would reconstruct the doctrinal foundation of the legal positions espoused in the states of Egypt, Sudan and Ethiopia, scrutinize their standing and eventually define riparian rights of utilization on the basis of various principles of international custom.

8 Rules and principles regulating the use of shared watercourses

Analysis of a non-treaty based claim of right to Nile waters

Downstream thesis of natural and historical rights: claims and legal challenges

In upstream Nile, the defence of riparian rights has progressively depended, both in national strategies and basin wide cooperative initiatives, on the principle of equitable and reasonable uses. The right-claims have also been attended by limited resource development manoeuvres endangering, in some measures, traditional assumptions of downstream entitlements.

On the other hand, with favourably protected hegemonic claims, Egypt and Sudan espoused certain legal hypotheses that ventured to sustain and rationalize the continued appropriation of the Nile waters. The modern setting of the psychological momentum tended to promote strategic thoughts moulded along historical lines, defining rights of utilization in an entirely downstream perspective.

In ostensibly legal idiom, the *natural* and *historical rights* (*prior use*) expressions constituted a central pillar of claims of downstream rights. The two notions formed the doctrinal platform on which the water-sharing schemes and institutional arrangements instituted through the two Nile agreements, concluded in 1929 and 1959, had been premised. The Nile treaties did not only compose explicit reference to the natural and acquired rights, they also formalized the historical water utilization patterns entrenched in the lower-reaches of the Nile basin.

In most regional discourses and bilateral diplomatic initiatives, Egypt and Sudan maintained a parallel pose, although in varying forms. In general, any scale of upstream development impacting on the natural and historical rights in the Nile waters, fixed at 55.5 and 18.5bcm/yr under the two bilateral accords, was held offensive of the rights so recognized. 'Historically only Egypt and the Sudan got shares in the water', and Egypt's claim of historical rights, 'confirmed by many agreements . . . are protected by international law', Mahmoud Abu Zeid – Egypt's former Minister of Water Resources and Irrigation had argued without fail.[1]

1 Mahmoud Abu Zied (1999) 'Managing Turbulent Waters', *Al-Ahram Weekly Online*, September Issue 447, <http://weekly.ahram.org.eg/1999/447/spec3.htm>, last accessed December 2010; Gamal Nkrumah (2004) 'Fresh water talks', *Al-Ahram Weekly Online*, June Issue 694, <http://weekly.ahram.org.eg/2004/694/eg4.htm>, last accessed December 2010.

In the course of the first decade of the twenty-first century, downstream riparian positions tended to exhibit a slight moderation, at least in appearance. Both Sudan and Egypt have been actively engaged in negotiations of the Transitional Institutional Mechanism of the Nile Basin Initiative (TIM-NBI) launched in Tanzania in February 1999. The transitional process has been mandated to set up a comprehensive Cooperative Framework Agreement (CFA) based on a vision 'to achieve sustainable socioeconomic development through equitable utilization of, and benefit from, the common Nile Basin water resources'.[2]

Yet, both in Egypt and the Sudan, equitable considerations espoused in the regional initiative have been embraced only in a context that upholds downstream water security concerns. The call for the absolute integrity of existing water use regimes has reverberated, emphasizing already *established* riparian rights. Fahmi argued 'existing uses . . . can hardly be disputed and equitable apportionment must be applied only to that portion of the water of the river not yet apportioned'.[3]

In upstream Nile, this proposition was regarded as another manifestation of a diplomatic exertion to uphold the status quo mantra and hence rejected.

Against such background, Part 8 of the Book will discuss the origin and essence of two central concepts employed in defence of continued downstream user rights – the natural rights and the historical/acquired rights hypotheses – and test their authority on the basis of normative stipulates provided in contemporary international water courses law.

The analytical deliberation would essentially scrutinize this issue: Can Egypt and the Sudan espouse under international law user rights of any scale on the basis of *long-established uses* and habitual references to the *natural rights* notions?

The fundamental argument, greatly drawing on interpretation of legal literatures and works of the ILA, IIL and the ILC, as well as some fitting discourses in state practice demonstrates that in the course of the second half of the twentieth century, customary international law has evolved to reject all extreme formulations of rights as objectionable juristic propositions.

While noting that user right perceptions are fundamentally social or political in construction, this presentation takes particular note of and is induced by the obvious trend in international relations that states have endeavoured to camouflage

Similarly, Ambassador Aziza Fahmi, former Deputy Assistant Minister for International Legal Affairs at the Egyptian Ministry of Water Resources submitted 'A nation that has built its economy, (and) indeed its very existence on the waters of a common river . . . will hardly accept reassessment of the waters of that river . . . the principle of safeguarding *existing rights* has been recognized by international treaties '.

Aziza M. Fahmi (1999) 'Water management in the Nile, opportunities and constraints', published in *Sustainable management and rational use of water resources*, Institute for Legal Studies on International Community, Rome, pp 140–41.

2 A Council of Ministers meeting of the Nile Basin States held in Dar-es-Salaam, Tanzania, on the 22nd of February 1999 formally established a 'Transitional Institutional Mechanism of the Nile Basin Initiative (NBI)', pending the conclusion of the 'Agreement on the Nile River Cooperative Framework'.

3 Fahmi (1999), note 1, p 140.

national aspirations within the broader embraces of international law. Indeed, international law has continued to play crucial functions in interstate relations. While disagreements over uses of international watercourses may not be resolved through a strict application of legal doctrines alone, in riparian discourses, the search for legitimacy of national expectations calls for elucidiation of the contemporary state of international legal norms.

The basin status quo: an overview of use patterns and legal stipulations

The pattern of utilization in Egypt and Sudan

The basic essence of claims of historical and natural rights of use over the Nile waters cannot be grasped without some reference to the context in which the conceptions had been produced and a brief account of the multiple platforms in which they found definite expressions.

As early as in 1965, Bourne observed the utilization of international rivers seldom proceeds at the same pace in the states through which it flows and such unequal development can cause great political, economic and legal difficulties.[4]

His conjecture had been right. As a resource, the Nile has never had analogous impact on the lives of its diverse communities. Tvedt reflected: the Nile had 'presented as it had for centuries and still does a kaleidoscopic procession of civilizations and cultures . . . an infinite range of political systems . . .'.[5] While agriculture remained the mainstay of the basin states' national economies, the organization of irrigational and water control infrastructures continued to flaunt a striking distinction in the lower-most and upper-reaches of the river. For a mix of historical, political and geographical reasons, Nile-related development initiatives had been oriented in a considerably downstream perspective.

Historically, Egypt's inimitable civilization, together with its vulnerable dependence on the Nile in catering domestic and agricultural requirements has paved the course to the earliest innovations in irrigation and water management techniques that over time intensified the yields of the river.

Egypt's geographic and climatic susceptibility has created a unique basin setting wherein the downstream polity could not exist without a secure provisioning of the Nile waters in its jurisdiction. On the national plane, therefore, its social, political and economic establishment has been engrossed with the defence of two vital columns of water security strategies: the perpetual protection of the Nile floods historically withdrawn and the institution of water conservation works that guarantee regulated flows during all flood seasons of the Nile.[6]

4 Charles B. Bourne (1965) 'The Right to the waters of International Rivers', *Can YB Int'l L*, vol 3, p 187.

5 Terje Tvedt (2004) *The River Nile in the Age of the British, Political Ecology and the Quest for Economic Power*, London/New York, I.B. Tauris, p 5.

6 Field-Marshall Viscount Allenby to Mr Austen Chamberlain, E 10986/192/16, Enclosure 3 in No. 1, Cairo, 29 November 1924.

Egyptian irrigational and water control infrastructure has undergone various stages of progress. By the turn of the nineteenth century, increased consideration was already afforded to the application of perennial system of agriculture whereby agricultural lands received irrigational waters throughout the year using a complex set of canal connections and barrages. Improved facilities were introduced from time to time to avail the Nile floods for uses during the low seasons. Yet, the old Aswan reservoir, the Gebel Aulia and other small control works failed to cope with the expanding needs of irrigation in Egypt. The limitations on further expansion of perennial agriculture could not have been curbed without storing larger volumes of Nile waters in reservoirs.

By the mid twentieth century, Egypt had fairly achieved both columns of its national aspirations, coalescing legal as well as physical schemes.

The completion, in the 1970s, of work on the Aswan High Dam, a huge water structure holding twice as much the total mean annual floods of the Nile, put an end to dependence on the traditional flood irrigation. The dam's increased quantity and securely regulated supply permitted large-scale expansion of cultivable lands. And using canals branching from Lake Nasser, today crops are cultivated more than once in any given year and agricultural developments expanded beyond the narrow strips of the Nile valley through reclamation of barren lands.

Over the years, Egyptian agricultural development and water consumption continued to grow steadily. By 1886, an important time-mark for computing downstream claims of historical rights, the area under perennial irrigation in Egypt was about 1.2 million hectares (3 million acres) consuming the entire *natural* outflow of the river during the low flow period and 800,000 hectares (two million acres) under basin irrigation.[7] By 2000, the United Nations Food and Agriculture Organization (UNFAO) estimated that 3.3 million hectares in the Nile valley and Delta rely almost exclusively upon irrigational waters from the Aswan High Dam.[8] Again, in 1920, the total yearly requirement for Egypt had been 30bcm per annum (at Aswan) or 50bcm/yr at Khartoum.[9] The UN Economic Commission for Africa (UNECA) assessed that by the 1990s, the figure had shot to as high as 62bcm/yr.

In official lines, unrelenting rumbles of the upstream Nile against the expanding pattern of utilization have been appeased by *justifying* all water requirements as withdrawn from *legitimate* shares under the 1959 Agreement, underground water reserves and agricultural water recycling.

On the other hand, developments in Sudan, grudgingly contending with a larger water requirement of its neighbour to the north, could be labelled as relatively impressive.

7 Dante A. Caponera (1993) 'Legal Aspects of Transboundary River Basins in the Middle East, the Al Asi (Orentes), the Jordan and the Nile', *Natural Resources Journal*, vol 33, p 652; also in: Albert Garretson (1960) 'The Nile River system', *American Society International Law Proceedings*, vol 54, p 137.

8 FAO (2000) 'Water and Agriculture in the Nile basin', Nile Basin Initiative Report to the ICCON, Rome, p 8.

9 Caponera (1993), note 7.

Today, Sudan can boast an elaborate system of irrigation covering a vast area of two million hectares using dams and diesel pumps[10] and principally stretching along the Gezira, Rahad and the New Halfa schemes. The Nile River supplies virtually all irrigational waters; its water requirements had been satisfied through the construction of a series of *facilities* inside its own territory: first the Sennar and later, the Rosaries dams on the Blue Nile and the Khashim al Qirbah Dam on the Tekeze-Atbara River.

The downstream-oriented juridical organization

By the mid 1970's, the complete *physical* and *juridical* control of Nile waters along the downstream course had been preceded by complex diplomatic negotiations. Two landmark legal episodes, concluded in 1929 and 1959, respectively between the colonial administration of Great Britain and a semi-autonomous government in Egypt,[11] and between Egypt and independent Sudan[12] formally sanctioned the use and allocation regimes of the Nile waters.

The ensuing juridical organization effected through both treaties institutionalized a century-old British legal enterprise that had labored on achieving an unqualified control of the Nile water resources. The treaties also laid a novel modus operandi for allocation of the natural flows as well as conserved waters of the Nile River just between Egypt and the Sudan.

The Anglo-Egyptian Treaty of 1929 was composed in notes exchanged between the United Kingdom, acting through the intermediary of its High Commissioner in Cairo – and representing the colonies of Sudan, Uganda, Kenya and Tanzania, on the one hand, and Egypt's president of the Council of Ministers – Mohamed Mahmoud Pasha. The notes composed the earliest formal expression of the natural and historical rights thesis.

The treaty set aside for exclusive uses in Egypt the waters conserved at the Aswan low Dam and the whole natural flow of the Nile River between January and July of each year. The Gezira in Sudan was allowed to withdraw water only outside of the stated seasons, subject to progressive scales, and in low periods, from water stored at the Sennar Reservoir.[13] In consequence, Egypt was guaranteed sufficient waters to irrigate the maximum acreage cultivable up to that time, five million feddans. Indeed, this quantitative estimate bestowed Egypt the acquired rights to a lion's share of the Nile waters.[14] The technical presentation in report

10 According to data assembled by a UN body, by 1995, Sudan had developed 1.26 million hectares of land drawing 16bcm/yr of Nile waters.

11 Exchange of Notes between his Majesty's Government in the United Kingdom and the Egyptian Government in regard to the use of the waters of the River Nile for irrigation purposes, 7 May 1929, Cairo.

12 United Arab Republic and Sudan Agreement for the Full Utilization of the Nile Waters, 8 November 1959, Cairo.

13 Abdul Hamid Soliman and R.M. MacGregor (1926) 'Reports of the Nile Commission', 21 March 1926, Cairo, para 88.

14 Tvedt (2004), note 5, p 145.

of the Nile Commission annexed to the treaty has been construed as respectively allotting Sudan and Egypt 4 and 48bcm of Nile waters annually.

Given the underlying eco-political considerations and venerable perceptions that inspired the negotiations, the ultimate framing of the treaty was barely startling. Sudanese interests were hugely discounted and the stakes of upstream states in the resource were ignored altogether.

Great Britain reasoned Ethiopia's rights had been attended to under the Anglo-Ethiopian Treaty of May 1902 which, although recognizing the 'riparian rights of inhabitants . . . to use . . . waters for domestic purposes as well as for the cultivation of food crops necessary for their own subsistence',[15] had proscribed the latter from arresting, diverting or otherwise obstructing the river's course in any form.

Under the 1929 treaty framing, a legal organization for absolute control of the Nile was cautiously orchestrated that if Egypt's historical claims should be shielded meaningfully, Great Britain had to work on a parallel order which also forbears threats of interference by states controlling the sources and tributaries of the White Nile upstream.

Hence, an infamous stipulation and indeed a provision that austerely impacted all subsequent developments of the resource in Tanzania, Kenya, Uganda and the Sudan itself completed the objective. Paragraph 4.b read that except with 'the previous agreement of the Egyptian Government, no irrigation or power works or measures are to be constructed or taken on the Nile river and its branches or on the lakes from which it flows, so far as all these are in the Sudan or in countries under British administration, which would in such a manner as to entail any prejudice to the interests of Egypt, either reduce the quantity of water arriving in Egypt or modify its date of arrival, or lower its level'.

While Sudan carved an improved allocation from a subsequently negotiated accord, the treaty remained a cause of bitter resentment in nearly all contemporary dialogues involving Ethiopia as well as the Great Lakes region's riparian states.

A novel initiative in the basin organizing a water allocations regime, the legal structure composed through the Anglo-Egyptian Treaty of 1929 appeared intrinsically unsustainable. It endured challenges from the outset, not least because it entailed serious limitations on the future expansion of irrigation in the Sudan wherein the largest swathe of the Nile basin is located, but also because it overlooked upstream stakes that supply virtually all floods of the Nile.

Political limitations arising from its constitutional status notwithstanding, Sudanese nationalism refused to consent to the perpetuation of the accord, dispelling the patterns of use and the classification of water rights as 'unjust'.[16] With Great

15 Charles Bentinck to Teferi Mekonnen, Suggestions for a Treaty, 25 July 1929, Addis Ababa Enclosure 1, FO 371/12341.

16 H.B Shepherd, Foreign Office Minute, 1929 Nile Water Agreements, 5 September 1956, FO 371/119063.

Britain's tacit encouragement,[17] Sudan adhered to the terms of the bilateral pact but tended to regard the agreement as not binding.

In the mid 1950s, deliberations for Sudanese independence, formally liquidating the Anglo-Egyptian co-domini coincided with the advent of the Aswan High Dam project in the ranks of Egyptian thinking. For decades, the future progress of both Egypt and Sudan had been conceived as contingent on the construction of integrated water-control works across the basin. On the basis of this proposition, and confronted by challenges of general economic decline, Egypt espoused the High Dam project which offered an opportunity for cultivating millions of hectares of new irrigation lands required to bring about stability and much hope of a better future.[18] Furthermore, the Aswan High Dam hypothesis projected to conserve and allocate about 32bcm/yr of the river's flood that normally drained to the Sea without being utilized.

The timing had been just compelling. With imposing signs of the collapse of colonial structures in Africa and fatigued by Great Britain's wily river politics across the basin, a self-governing Egypt could no longer anticipate, simply because of considerations of sovereignty, to enjoy similar scales of freedom in conniving upper-stream water-control schemes for its own exclusive uses. Hence, any thought of preserving the Nile waters otherwise than through the Aswan High Dam was not an open and politically dependable option.

In consequence, in November 1959, a new legal design for full utilization of the Nile waters was concluded between Sudan and Egypt addressing certain shortfalls of the previous arrangement and laying institutional and legal frameworks for the joint use and management of the resource. The new treaty underlined that full utilization of the yields of the Nile River required the construction of two water-control works, authorising the parties to commission the Sudd el Aali (Aswan High) and Rosaries dam projects in Egypt and Sudan respectively.

Most significantly, however, the treaty declared as acquired rights the shares of the two republics outlined under the 1929 arrangement (48 and 4bcm/yr of waters respectively). The treaty then divided the net additional gains of the new over-year storage, estimated about 22bcm/yr, in the ratio of 14.5bcm/yr for Sudan and 7.5bcm/yr of Nile waters to Egypt.[19] Hence, full operation of the Aswan High Dam bestowed on Sudan and Egypt an enhanced 18.5bcm and 55.5bcm of waters annually.

Unlike its precursor, though, the new deal foresaw potential upstream challenges, notably from Ethiopia, who had gradually held a radical deportment, and

17 Convinced, possibly for political reasons that the treaty is not binding on Sudan, Great Britain omitted this pact from a wide category of treaties communicated to the new republic on the grant of independence.
Shepherd (1956), note 16.

18 Ralph Stevenson to Harold Macmillan, British Embassy, Cairo, 16 May 1955, FO 371/113733.

19 United Arab Republic & Sudan Agreement for the Full Utilization of the Nile Waters (1959), note 12, Art II.

from Great Britain, who in the wake of its waning power of manipulate suddenly discovered the urge for staking the interests of its colonies of Kenya, Uganda and Tanzania. The accord stipulated that Sudan and Egypt shall take a united view 'if it becomes necessary to hold any negotiations with any riparian state', and to 'deduct from the shares of the two republics' if a joint consideration results in the acceptance of any such claims.[20]

Origin and essence of the natural/historical rights formulation

The natural-historical rights thesis constituted a central pillar of the Nile waters treaties concluded between the states of Great Britain, Egypt and the Sudan.

If the right in equity of other riparian states to co-utilize the same resource had not been highlighted in the bilateral negotiations nor expressed in the ultimate framing of the 1959 treaty, it was because as matter of strategic thinking, the accord had been wrought by identical perceptions that inspired the legal process three decades back. The Nile, folk idiom had relentlessly reverberated, is emblematically an Egyptian tenure; and without exclusive rights of access to the Nile waters, Egypt, barely endowed with analogous climatic settings as its upstream neighbours would remain but a ruined civilization.

As early as in August 1920, a Report of the Nile Projects Commission – a technical body constituted by the Egyptian Government with a view to determining, among others, the allocations regime of the increased supplies of Nile waters – recommended that Egypt and Sudan be considered as each having a vested right to all the *natural flow* (of 40 and 18bcm/yr of waters respectively).[21]

Again, in the 1920s, the growing economic import of the Sudanese territory prompted further perpetuation of Great Britain's long-standing policy that laboured on building a distinct Sudanese competence in the management of national affairs and water resources development. In December of the same year, the Milner Mission was released which firmly rejected the idea that any political nexus between the two countries should take the form of the subjection of the Sudan to Egypt.[22] The Report held relations between the two countries should be established for the future upon a basis which would secure the independence of the Sudan while safeguarding the vital interests of Egypt in the waters of the Nile; Egypt has an indefeasible right to an ample and assured supply of water for the land at present under cultivation and to a fair share of any increased supply which engineering skill may be able to provide.[23]

20 United Arab Republic & Sudan Agreement for the Full Utilization of the Nile Waters (1959), note 12, Art IV.

21 Report of the Nile Projects Commission (1920), Printed with the authority of the Egyptian Government, 25 August, London.

22 R. K. Batstone (1959) 'Utilization of the Nile Waters', *Int'l & Comp LQ*, vol 8, p 527.

23 Batstone (1959), note 22.

The same year also witnessed Great Britain's official reflection which held that 'the principle is accepted that the waters of the Nile . . . must be considered as a single unit, designed for the use of the peoples inhabiting their banks according to their needs and their capacity to benefit there-from; [and], in conformity with this principle, it is recognized that Egypt has a prior right to the maintenance of her present supplies of water for the areas now under cultivation, and to an equitable proportion of any additional supplies which engineering works may render available in the future'.[24]

Obviously, no other resource has emphatically shaped the evolution of economic and political structures in Egypt and the Sudan, as did the Nile.

While certain stages can be discerned in the progressive development of water control infrastructures, historically, the Egyptian order has been profoundly entwined with the Nile floods that as early as in 1910, virtually the whole of cultivable soil in Egypt was covered by cotton.[25] Further economic prospects of the lower basin induced British colonial authorities to propose plans for the construction of supplementary water storing facilities, and shortly afterwards, for enhancing the agricultural potentials of the Sudan. By 1913, the sketch for what was to be one of the world's single-largest irrigational fields along Sudan's triangular tract – flanked by the White and Blue Niles – was already set in motion.[26] The Nile floods have not only sustained Egyptian and Sudanese socio-economic orders, but the river has also defined their existence effectively.

Over the decades, such a pattern of vulnerable association between nature and civilization fostered an all-pervading stratum of values and beliefs that composed the mainstay of Egyptian and Sudanese economic and political thinking. At the heart of such system rests a deep-seated proprietary and possessory conception.[27]

Hence, the downstream insist for juridical preservation of the historical and/or natural rights of use could not be regarded as a sporadic phenomenon, abruptly manifesting under the 1929/1959 treaty arrangements. It evolved steadily and over a much longer span of time.

In more recent epochs, these values have been espoused in counts of discourses. In fact, throughout its extended tenure that lapsed in the late 1950s, British colonial objectives had agitated, both in diplomacy and legal avenues, for the preservation of prior downstream rights that implied complete monopoly,[28] and for the

24 International Law Commission (1986) *Yearbook of International Law Commission*, vol 2, no 1, p 110.

25 The British Cotton Growing Association, *Memorandum on the development of cotton in the Sudan*, November 1910.

26 Abdul Hamid Soliman and R.M. MacGregor (1926) note 13, para 9.

27 In fact, deep historical assumptions of the pre-Aswan High Dam Egypt wherein Egyptian public opinion and . . . the nationalist press not only viewed the Nile as 'Egyptian property' but also asserted 'again and again that the region of the upper White Nile and Equatorial Lakes was an unredeemed portion of the Egyptian Sudan' could not be expected to fade easily in the course of the next half of the twentieth century.

Tvedt (2004), note 5, pp 100, 136.

28 A Foreign Office's Memorandum, issued in 1927 summed up the basic tenets of British policy in the preceding forty years: '. . . in the interests of Egypt and the Sudan, no effort should be spared to

placement of water-control schemes that aimed at sustaining existing interests as well as future developments downstream. A strategic thinking formulated along such lines presented the psycho-momentum that subsequently moulded rights of utilization wholly in a downstream perspective.

Conceivably, the earliest formal expression of the natural-historical rights formulation had been depicted in the 1920s during tense diplomatic deliberations involving Egypt and Great Britain in relation to the allocation of Nile waters under the 1929 Nile Waters Agreement. Indeed, merely three decades since the inception of British colonial rule in Egypt, the downstream competition for Nile resources had become so intensely entrenched that Egypt and Sudan, natural allies against upstream threats, found themselves on a collision course with regard to the definition of the limits of unilateral development of the Nile waters.

The plan for future development of the Sudan had essentially focused on the Gezira, along the Blue Nile. It was based on reports of Murdoch MacDonald, then a British Advisor to the Ministry of Public Works in Egypt and endorsed, albeit with British support, by the Sudanese Plantations Syndicate in January 1913.[29]

For Sudan, the realization of its *full* potentials was contingent on Egypt's acquiescence to continued water withdrawals from the Nile, hence endangering one arch-column of Egypt's strategic philosophy: the unfettered custody of Nile waters.[30] Lord Allenby, the British High Commissioner in Cairo, wrote 'Egyptian nationalists described the Nile as an Egyptian river . . . (and) argued that Egypt had a right to a free hand in the use of its waters'.[31] In the interest of overriding stakes, Great Britain had to circumspectly balance the economic as well as political implications of enlargement of Sudanese irrigations on Egypt.

Yet, it was against a succession of historical events involving concerns over rising Egyptian nationalism, limited commissioning of the Gezira scheme, trailing negotiations over the Nile agreement and the assassination in Cairo of Lee Stack – Governor General of Sudan in 1924, that Lord Allenby, the British Commissioner in Egypt issued his infamous ultimatum on 22 November 1924. He declared the Sudanese Government should freely irrigate an unlimited extent of land along the Gezira, potentially withdrawing greater volumes of Nile waters.

prevent anything which could possibly interfere with the flow of the River Nile as this is a vital factor in the prosperity of these countries'. Foreign Office Memorandum, Lake Tana, 31 May 1927, FO 370/1234.

29 Tvedt (2004), note 5, p 93.

30 P.M. Tottenham, Under-Secretary of State for Ministry of Public Works in Egypt *ridiculed* Egypt's extremely possessive attitudes opposing all scales of development propositions in Sudan when he opined that 'in their ignorance, Egyptians will assume that when more than 300,000 feddans are irrigated, the water supply of Egypt will be reduced accordingly, that there is no limit to the reduction and that Egypt will, in due course, become a desert'; he noted experience has shown that much areas can be irrigated without detriment to Egypt.

Field-Marshall Viscount Allenby to Mr Austen Chamberlain, Cairo, 29 November 1924, E 10986/192/16, Enclosure 7 in No 1.

31 Tvedt (2004), note 5, p 95.

Shortly afterwards, the Egyptian government admitted the instruction had caused 'the most serious apprehension' in the country; Egypt maintained no agricultural expansion in the Sudan could be 'of such a nature as to be harmful to the irrigation of Egypt or to prejudice future projects, so necessary as to meet the needs of the rapidly increasing agricultural population of this country.'[32] Apparently, the deep-seated perceptions had translated into a definition of rights so framed that any upstream development maneouver, even in Sudan, was subjected to a strong resentment.

In a remarkable retractory reply issued on the same date, Lord Allenby wrote: '. . . the British Government, however solicitous for the prosperity of the Sudan, have no intention of trespassing upon the *natural and historic rights* of Egypt in the waters of the Nile, which they recognize today no less that in the past . . .'[33] (Emphasis added). Shortly after Lord Allenby's ultimatum had been rescinded, the Nile Commission was constituted. The Commission's report, published in 1926, succinctly presented the legal version of the perceptions that had hitherto evolved.

The Commission submitted that its conclusions had been based on the indubitable conjecture that Egypt and Sudan have established, through long use, acquired rights of varying measures to irrigation waters. In setting out the basis on which future agricultural developments may be founded and all existing rights may be perpetually safeguarded, the Nile Commission reasoned its proposals had been framed along the spirit of Great Britain's earlier recognition (in Lord Allenby's communiqué) that it had no intention of infringing upon the *natural* and *historic* rights of Egypt in the waters of the Nile.

Hence, the vulnerable political context in which Great Britain's declaration had been extended notwithstanding, British acknowledgement of historical and natural rights when the absolute territorial sovereignty principle could have been invoked to justify an unlimited growth of irrigation in upstream Sudan, constituted the formal foundation of the 1929 water allocations regime concluded in the immediate aftermath.

Under the 1929 Nile waters agreement, Great Britain and Egypt agreed to British proposals of increasing the quantity of Nile waters required for the development of Sudan 'as does not infringe Egypt's natural and historical rights in the waters of the Nile and its requirements of agricultural extension'.[34]

Egypt's reference to the natural and historical rights of use of the Nile waters did not articulate quantitative estimates at the beginning; instead, it was framed in

32 Ziwer Pasha, President of Council of Ministers to Lord Allenby, Cairo, 26 January 1925 (Nile Commission Report 1925, Appendix A).

33 Lord Allenby F.M, High Commissioner [Egypt] to Ziwer Pasha, Cairo 26 January 1925 (Nile Commission Report 1925, Appendix A).

Annexed also in: Abdul Hamid Soliman and R.M. MacGregor (1926), note 13.

34 Exchange of Notes between his Majesty's Government in the United Kingdom and the Egyptian Government in regard to the use of the waters of the River Nile for irrigation purposes, 7 May 1929, Cairo, Article II.

subtlety, proposing to safeguard both the integrity of current uses and pre-emptively secure prospective developments through the utilization of conserved floods.

What substance of right the natural/historical rights conceptions had projected to protect can be deduced from a closer reading of the Nile Commission reports, the states' bilateral communications as well as contents of the Nile treaties.

The treaty, and its annex, a technical presentation of the Nile Commission's findings, generally reserved the natural flow of the Nile between January–July for exclusive benefits of Egypt; the Gezira fields in the Sudan, operating since 1925, were allowed to abstract waters between late July–December, according to scales detailed in the annexes.[35] After February, the Gezira would only use water stored at the Sennar Reservoir. This total volume availed for Egyptian and Sudanese utilizations was construed as 48 and 4bcm/yr of waters respectively.

In November of 1959, a supplementary legal arrangement composed by Sudan and Egypt tailored the 1929 treaty to address new realities. Among others, the new pact underlined that full utilization of the yields of the Nile requires construction of two of a series of control works proposed and authorised the contracting parties to commission the Sudd el Aali (Aswan High) and Rosaries dam projects in Egypt and Sudan respectively.

As noted above, the treaty had already declared as acquired rights benefits of the two republics outlined under the old arrangement – before obtaining the increased yields of the Nile Control projects, and apportioned the net additional increases of the new over-year storage in the ratio of 14.5 and 7.5bcm/yr for Sudan and Egypt respectively.[36]

Consequently, the Aswan High Dam thesis mingled rights to natural floods cosseted under the acquired rights conception with rights to conserved waters availed for downstream uses through the construction of the new dam facilities.

The commissioning of the Dam fulfilled two core objectives of timeless downstream aspirations that dominated the basin's hydropolitical discourse in first half of the twentieth century and continued in the subsequent decades; the facility not only shielded existing downstream stakes but also secured the prospective water requirements of the states of Egypt and Sudan in the Nile waters.

An imperative theme of legal concern remained, though: how does a downstream oriented legal theory premised on considerations of such rights fit within the framework of the international legal order?

The legal status of natural/historical rights

However claims of natural and historical rights may have been framed, promoted or protected, in the context of basin-wide rights-relations, an indispensable under-

35 Abdul Hamid Soliman and R.M. MacGregor (1926), note 13, paras 21–22.

The effect was that without accounting for the yields of conserving Nile waters 'lost' through evaporation and extreme transpiration in the swampy basins of the Lakes Region, the Bahr el Jebel, Bahr el Zaraf and Bahr el Ghazal in south and central Sudan, and the Baro-Akobo-Sobat River systems along the Ethio-Sudanese corridors, the entire Nile floods were apportioned between the two most-downstream states.

36 Abdul Hamid Soliman and R.M. MacGregor (1926), note 13, paras 21–22.

taking involves assessment of the status of such formulations under international law. The question of what precisely rights so designated represent in international legal parlance requires a dutiful scrutiny.

The downstream legal pose

Over the last few decades, a range of constantly varying factors had influenced the legal and hydropolitical settings in the Nile basin. In contemporary legal relations, Egypt and Sudan maintained a parallel pose both with regard to the theoretical foundations of rights of use as well as in relation to future regional discourses impacting on the cooperative utilization of the Nile. The integrity of existing water allocation regimes essentially composed through the natural-historical rights and further articulated under the Nile waters agreements has been consistently called for.

A nation barely endowed with alternative means of subsistence, for Egypt, this rights thesis has been unamenable to any concessions. Any unilateral change of the historical rights and allocations scheme has been regarded as a breach of international law.[37] This restatement of a long-established position essentially composes the foundation of all contemporary water rights and policy rationalizations.

Of course, within the broader institutional framework of the Nile Basin Initiative, Egypt and Sudan recognized that the Nile is a shared resource of all riparian states and have admitted, at least in principle, the right of each state to equitable utilization and share; yet, in practice, both states persevered to condition such admissions on upstream requirements not to cause unnecessary or unprovoked harm.

In nearly all current initiatives on the cooperative management of resources of the Nile, the core assumptions mustered during the early colonial decades of the basin's development had been reinstated.

The climatic setting of upper riparian states receiving bounteous rainfall was routinely highlighted. Focus has also been diverted to less pressing schemes of technical cooperation and regional economic initiatives; on a few of occasions too, upstream user-rights grumbles had been pigeonholed as politically motivated.[38]

The historical pattern of use was moreover justified on the basis of wider geographical conceptions; recent policy papers endeavoured to re-establish a broader

37 Gamal Nkrumah (2004) 'Who runs the river?', *Al-Ahram Weekly Online*, Issue 685. <http://weekly.ahram.org.eg/2004/685/eg5.htm>, last accessed December 2010.

38 The user-rights framing had contentiously proceeded on the hypothesis that the Nile basin is endowed with immense water supplies of which significant proportions have been lost unused; it computes Egyptian-Sudanese shares as representing a mere 'six to eight percent of the total rainfall over the Nile basin'. This, it was submitted, affords all basin states a greater opening to increase supply and mitigate conflicts over waters.

This inveterate Egyptian perception had been concisely presented by Ahmed Abul-Wafa, professor of international law in 2009 in: Reem Leila (2009) 'Wading through the politics', *Al-Ahram Weekly Online*, June Issue 949, <http://weekly.ahram.org.eg/2009/955/eg2.htm>, last accessed December 2010.

definition of international watercourse – a legal concept of intense discord under international law, by computing the volume of Nile waters withdrawn for downstream developments as representing but 'a mere fraction of the overall basin precipitation'.[39]

In other, less politically bent regional discourses as well, downstream concerns of water security have resurfaced constantly. For more than three years now, the endorsement of pending negotiations on a comprehensive Nile framework agreement has been conditioned on a prior requirement of an upstream assurance that recognizes 'Egypt's rights to 55.5bcm of water annually'. In essence, this approach constructs on Egypt's declared position which admitted the right of each watercourse state to equitable utilization only in a context that causes no appreciable harm to its established interests.[40]

Examination of the 'right' claims: the state of international law

A circumspect delving into the mechanics of public international law obliges one to concur with an initial hypothesis that the argument for exclusive rights of use of the Nile waters premised on the natural-historical rights conception is unconvincingly linked to the essential dictates of international norms.

Under the constitution of modern international law, the defense of downstream percepts has to be inferred either from all-inclusive treaty regimes or plain dictates of customary international law governing the use of shared water courses.

It is true that at the turn of the twentieth century, the composition of international water courses law can best be depicted as laden with uncertainties. Its early evolution had influenced riparian discourse inconsequentially.

In spite of such limitations, however, the significance of limited reference to certain principles of international law has always been acknowledged.

Indeed, since the earliest decades of technocratic development of the Nile basin by the British, both Great Britain and later, Egypt had struggled to defend downstream rights not only on the basis of the historical-natural rights conceptions, but also through the employ of other notions as well. Such included the theory of absolute territorial integrity and most importantly, the principle prescribing duty not to cause significant harm.

Within the Nile basin's legal discourse, one can note that a broader doctrinal orientation of the sorts is quite compelling, given that persistent objections – both

39 Reem Leila (2009) 'Wading through the politics', *Al-Ahram Weekly Online*, June Issue 949, <http://weekly.ahram.org.eg/2009/955/eg2.htm>, last accessed December 2010.

Likewise, in a Country-Paper presented to a forum of basin states, the Government of Egypt submitted that 'in the case of the River Nile, the potentials are great and 95 percent of the water *is not yet* efficiently utilized'.

Nile 2002 Conference (1996), Country Paper Egypt, Proceedings of the IVth Nile 2002 Conf, Kampala, p C-10.

40 Nile 2002 Conference (1996) Country Paper Egypt, Proceedings of the IVth Nile 2002 Conf, Kampala, p C-10.

legal and political – have been mounted against the claims and water allocation regimes constituted through the 1929/1959 Nile waters agreements.

Of course, over the years, the coercive clout of the two Nile treaties has condensed considerably, primarily because of their bilateral constitution; they obligated only such states involved in their making, which refers to colonial dependencies on whose behalf Great Britain and Belgium had pledged duties of non-interference. This naturally leaves Ethiopia out of the treaties' scopes.

In highlighting the relevance of valid consent in treaties, the World Bank's policy paper concluded that one obvious indicator of the success of international water agreement is the number of countries affected, which are also parties to the agreement; the essay argued that the Nile treaties, negotiated just between two states, had in this sense been 'incomplete'.[41]

Today, while Caponera's observation that Egypt has not yet recognized generally accepted principles of customary international law does not seem to hold ground, he noted, and quite correctly so that a purely positivist approach to problems of water rights in international law would be prejudicial to Egypt since the legal validity of some of the Nile agreements is questionable, to say the least.[42]

These two annotations are based on a fundamental proposition of customary international law, restated under Article 34 of the Vienna Convention on the Law of Treaties (1969), which prescribed that a treaty cannot create obligations nor institute rights for a third state without its consent.[43] Ethiopia had not engaged, directly or through a proxy, as party to any of the above-stated treaty arrangements.

Hence, it is only commonsensical to submit that a mere entrenchment of the natural-historical rights clause in bilateral treaties would constitute a futile legal implement in defending downstream rights if the coercive utility of the accords themselves is challenged upstream, and particularly in Ethiopia, for want of consent to be bound.

In part, this potential legal hollow in the makeup of the treaties explains why downstream readings of natural-historical rights have also been perceived as *standing independently* of the treaties as such. The reflection provided in the succeeding sections has been justified by this vitality of the conceptions as separate sources of water use rights.

On its face, the downstream hypothesis of natural-historical rights impresses association with some doctrines of international watercourses law. Legal history offers plenty of testimonies where, under the guise of various theories, basin states have championed broader rights of use of international watercourses. In the following sections, the discussion will focus on revealing the status of the

41 Scott Barret (1994) 'Conflict and cooperation in managing international water resources', *Policy Research Working Paper 1303*, World Bank Research Department.

42 Caponera (1993), note 7, p 660.

43 The post-independence legal position of the east and central African riparian states on whose behalf Great Britain and Belgium undertook obligations fundamentally hinges on a contentious interpretation of international law principles governing state succession to treaties, an issue that has yet to settle.

natural-historical rights formulations under general international law, case law and the treaty practice of states.

Natural and historical rights: scrutiny under general international law

Traditionally, riparian states have defended rights of utilization of international watercourses on the basis of overlapping and at times inconsistent principles. In the functioning of international law, a state's perception of rights as linked to particular courses of conduct is very crucial in gauging its responsibility. Generally speaking, how riparian states venture to designate or justify a given pattern of water resources utilization would be less striking, for international law places greater emphasis on actual conducts manifested in appropriating, obstructing or otherwise diverting the flows of a shared watercourse.

In reality, however, states have persistently endeavoured to seek legitimacy to their actions. From time to time, basin states have espoused water resources development ventures under the banner of one or another of the formulations restated in international legal relations, including the natural rights, historical rights and a semblance of other theories proposing to invest special prerogatives that transcend the thresholds established under international law.

In most cases, the natural rights conception had been construed as embodying the natural flows doctrine, also referred to as the theory of absolute territorial integrity, generally vesting in lower riparian states exclusive rights to the natural, unhindered flow of shared watercourses.

However, there has been no conceptual precedence in contemporary international watercourses law or its application where a riparian state has maintained uninfringeable privileges of use by virtue only of natural rights as such. Even when Bangladesh resorted to the natural rights formulation as it endeavoured to preclude India's diversion of the Ganges River, both India and Bangladesh eventually justified their positions by referring to no other regime but the Helsinki Rules.

Among others, India argued, and quite in correct reading of the basic precepts, that in withdrawing parts of the Ganga waters at Farakka, India's sole obligation is limited to not adversely affecting Bangladesh's existing use of the flow (which had been so meagre). India held that according to the Helsinki Rules, there is absolutely no obligation for an upper riparian to leave intact the existing quantum of flow. In fact, to insist on the continuance of the historical or natural flows would constitute a total denial of the principle of equitable sharing enshrined in these rules; an assertion of 'natural flow amounts to exercising a veto on the rights of upper riparians to a reasonable and equitable shares of waters of common rivers.'[44]

Today, of course, extreme legal arguments premised on the theory of absolute territorial integrity had long been discredited, and hence, would not merit detailed consideration here.

44 International Law Commission (1979) *Yearbook of International Law Commission*, vol 2, no 1, p 164.

If, on the other hand, downstream arguments of natural rights had conceived to attend to a state's rights of utilizing resources nature has endowed its jurisdiction and thus generate the greatest good to its citizens, international law has already endorsed this view as one aspect of the exercise of territorial sovereignty of states. The right of each watercourse state to exercise certain powers within its jurisdiction has been acknowledged as a fundamental tenet of the system of international law.

From this hypothesis of the natural right of riparians follows that no state would be placed in a particularly singular position merely because of its first appropriation or an extended dependency on a shared watercourse, or its habitual marshalling of a natural-historical rights impression to validate exiting patterns of utilization.

A universally accepted rule of customary international law, restated both under the Helsinki Rules (1966) (as revised)[45] and the UN Watercourse Convention (1997),[46] has unequivocally confirmed the right of each watercourse state to a reasonable and equitable share in the uses of the waters of an international watercourse. The parity of rights of riparian states is acknowledged as 'a postulate of international law so basic that it is unchallengeable'.[47]

Indeed, in the course of the past century, a great dossier of international and regional resolutions, treaties and judicial/arbitral decisions have commonly endorsed the territorial sovereignty of states and the principles on which the right of utilizing shared watercourses shall be premised.

Just a few may be reproduced here. Principle 21 of the Declaration on the Human Environment, adopted in 1972 by the United Nations Conference on the Human Environment re-established 'the sovereign right (of states) to exploit their own resources pursuant to their own environmental policies . . .'.[48] In 1977, the Mar del Plata Action Plan adopted by the United Nations Water Conference recommended states to cooperate in cases of shared water resources 'in accordance with the Charter of the United Nations and principles of international law . . . exercised on the basis of the equality, sovereignty and territorial integrity of all States . . .'.[49] Earlier, an experts report constituted by the UN Secretary General pursuant to Economic and Social Council Resolution 599 (XXI) of 3 May 1956 had cross-referred to works of the ILA (1956) which emphasized that 'each state has sovereign control over international rivers within its own boundaries', exercised 'with due consideration for its effects upon other riparian States'. In 1968,

45 International Law Association (1966), The Helsinki Rules on the Uses of the Waters of International Rivers.

(Text in International Law Association, Report of the 52nd Conference, Helsinki, 14–20 August 1966, pp 484–532), Article IV.

46 United Nations Convention on the Law of the Non-navigational Uses of International Watercourses, Adopted by the General Assembly of the United Nations on 21 May 1997, Article 5.

47 International Law Commission (1980) *Yearbook of International Law Commission*, vol 2, no 1, p 163.

48 United Nations (1972) 'Report of the United Nations Conference on the Human Environment', Stockholm, Chapter 1.

49 United Nations (1977) 'Report of the United Nations Water Conference', Mar del Plata 14–25 March, Part 1.

a subsequent UN report on the 'Legal and Institutional Aspects of International Water Resources Development' reaffirmed that 'a basin state should recognize the legitimacy of the interest that its co-basin states have in the use of the waters of their international drainage basin or water resources system . . .'.[50] These and sequences of declarations adopted in the subsequent years basically restated the foundational resolutions produced by the ILA and the IIL in the course of the preceding century. A keystone principle articulated by the Institute of International Law in 1911 under the Madrid Declaration enunciated that 'the permanent physical dependence of riparian states precludes the idea of autonomy of each state in the section of the natural watercourse under its section.'[51]

The principles constituted through the institutional initiatives of the ILA and the IIL were simultaneously expounded in international custom, treaty practices, national decisions and the learned views of international law publicists. On the whole, one can safely conclude that the evolutionary trend of international watercourses law has simply defied the award of any particular priority or the structuring of a hierarchy of rights between riparian states, whether such has been espoused under the guise of sovereignty, priority of use or any other doctrinal stipulatation, including the natural and historical rights discourse.

Instead, as the ILC's survey of 'available evidence of the general practice of states' assembled during the drafting stages of the UN Watercourses Convention had concluded, there was an overwhelming support for the doctrine of equitable utilization as a general rule of law for the determination of the rights and obligations of states in this field.[52] Indeed, this recognition was reflected in the eventual framing of Articles 5 cum. 7 of the UN Convention on the non navigational uses of international watercourses which clearly confirmed the right of states to utilize an international watercourse in an equitable and reasonable manner and the duty to take all appropriate measures to prevent the causing of significant harm to other watercourse states.[53]

Natural and historical rights: scrutiny under case law and treaty practices

Outside the theoretical realm, the presentation of disputes involving the utilization of international watercourses as well as the treaty practice of states can serve justice

50 United Nations, Panel of Experts on the Legal and Institutional Aspects of International Water Resources Development (1975) *Management of International Water Resources: Institutional and legal aspects: report / of the Panel of Experts on the Legal and Institutional Aspects of International Water Resources Development*, New York, United Nations Publication.

51 Institute of International Law, International Regulation Regarding the Use of International Watercourses for Purposes other than Navigation, Declaration of Madrid, Preamble, 20 April 1911. (Text in: *Yearbook of the Institute of International Law*, Madrid Session 1911, vol 24, p. 365).

52 International Law Commission (1994) 'First report on the Law of the Non-navigational uses of international watercourses', *Yearbook of International Law Commission*, vol 2, no 1, p 98.

53 United Nations Convention on the Law of the Non-navigational Uses of International Watercourses (1997), note 46, Articles 5 and 7.

in shedding further insight on the status of the law and observations of states in a practical milieu. International and inter-state river uses-related disagreements adjudicated by the ICJ and the US Supreme Court, for example, can constitute a subsidiary evidence of international law under paragraph 1(d) of Article 38 of the Statute of the International Court of Justice, and hence become pertinent.

In the *Gabcikovo-Nagymaros Project* case between Hungary and Slovakia (1997), the ICJ addressed the equal rights theme, albeit in a different context, when it referred to an earlier decision of the Permanent Court of International Justice (PCIJ) with regard to navigational issues of the River Oder (1929). The PCIJ had held that: 'the community of interest in a navigable river becomes the basis of a common legal right, the essential features of which are the perfect equality of all riparian States in the uses of the whole course of the river and the exclusion of any preferential privilege of any one riparian state in relation to the others'.

And on the basis of this precedent, the ICJ concluded 'Modern development of international law has strengthened this principle for non-navigational uses of international watercourses as well, as evidenced by the adoption of the Convention of 21 May 1997 on the Law of the Non-Navigational Uses of International Watercourses by the United Nations General Assembly'.[54]

In the Kansas *vs.* Colorado (1907)[55] interstate proceedings in the USA,[56] a downstream Kansas submitted that Colorado's subsequent appropriation and diversion 'of the waters of the Arkansas River, by greatly lowering and permanently diminishing the normal and average flow of the river' for the purpose of irrigation endangered the foundation of the prosperity of the Arkansas Valley and seriously impaired its established rights relating to manufacturing, navigation and irrigation. Kansas prayed that 'the flowing water in the Arkansas must, in accordance with the extreme doctrine of the common law of England, be left to flow as it was wont to flow, no portion of it being appropriated in Colorado for the purposes of irrigation'.

The Court rebuffed Kansas' extreme position[57] along the spirit of a ruling rendered earlier by the State's own Supreme Court in the Clark *vs.* Allaman case wherein it was held that

> the right to flowing water is now well settled to be a right incident to property in the land; it is a right *publici juris* of such character that whilst it is common and equal to all through whose land it runs, and no one can obstruct or divert it, yet, as one of the beneficial gifts of providence, each proprietor has a right

54 *GabCikovo-Nagymaros Project (Hungary / Slovakia)*, Judgment, ICJ Reports 1997, p 85.

55 *Kansas vs. Colorado*, 206 US 46 (1907).

56 Tarlock's review of the Supreme Court's decisions revealed that the Court's rulings had been premised on a mass of contradictory principles, doctrines, local laws, transcendent national laws and economic impacts of its allocations. Hence, arguments which acknowledge a right of reasonable uses of basin constituencies as well as rules safeguarding prior appropriations must be employed with a scale of caution.

57 *Kansas vs. Colorado*, 206 US 117 (1907).

> to a just and reasonable use of it, as it passes through his land; and so long as it is not wholly obstructed or diverted, or no larger appropriation of the water running through it is made than a just and reasonable use, it cannot be said to be wrongful or injurious to a proprietor lower down.[58]

About a century later, the *Colorado vs. New Mexico* suit (1984) presented a virtually ideal parallel of the legal intricacies that involved the definition of user rights in the Nile basin.[59] An upstream Colorado proposed a diversion scheme and sought in the proceedings an equitable apportionment of the waters of the Vermejo River, originating in Colorado and flowing into New Mexico. Historically, the river's waters had been fully appropriated by farm and industrial users in New Mexico. New Mexico's request for exclusive focus on priority of uses was in principle rejected; the Court reasoned it recognized:

> that the equities supporting the protection of existing economies will usually be compelling . . .; under some circumstances, however, the countervailing equities supporting a diversion for future use in one State may justify the detriment to existing users in another State . . . for example, where the State seeking a diversion demonstrates by clear and convincing evidence that the benefits of the diversion substantially outweigh the harm that might result.[60]

Naturally, states have the liberty to engage in any pact that maintain, forfeit or bargain positions impacting on the rights of utilization of international watercourses even when such treaties fall short of the standards composed under the international legal order. Indeed, the practice of states demonstrates that several schemes had endeavoured to maintain equality, reconfigure a status quo or design an arrangement that proffers one or another of basin states an upper hand in the beneficial uses of a shared watercourse.

For instance, Article VII of the Treaty between the United States and Great Britain respecting Boundary Waters between the USA and Canada affirmed the equal rights of the parties in the use of boundary waters defined in the treaty and established an order of precedence among the various uses of waters regulated under the treaty;[61] but, to partly address USA's argument that 'under the doctrine of prior appropriation, since the United States has been first in use of the waters, it has a right to their permanent use; [and that] the application of the doctrine of

58 *Kansas vs. Colorado*, 206 US 102–103 (1907).

59 *Colorado vs. New Mexico*, 467 US 310 (1984).

60 *Colorado vs. New Mexico*, 467 US 181–182 (1984).

The Court of course admitted its belief that 'the flexible doctrine of equitable apportionment extends to a State's claim to divert previously appropriated water for future uses. But the State seeking such diversion bears the burden of proving, by clear and convincing evidence, the existence of certain relevant factors'.

61 Treaty between the USA and Great Britain Relating to the Boundary Waters and Quesrtions Arising Between the USA and Canada, 11 January 1909, US Treaty Series, No 548.

equitable apportionment requires an equitable sharing of waters in the Columbia Basin between the two countries', the treaty further stipulated its provisions shall not apply to disturb any 'existing uses of boundary waters on either sides of the boundary' and hence safeguarded the acquired rights of use on both states.

The Treaty between India and Pakistan Regarding the Use of the Waters of Indus, on the other hand, represents an obvious example of a situation where a state forfeits historical patterns of use through a consensual scheme.[62] At partition, the Indus system of rivers irrigated 37 million acres of land, of which 31 million lied in West Pakistan, an acreage almost five times that irrigated from the Nile River.[63] India also controlled the head works for some of the principal irrigational canals in Pakistan upon which some 1,700,000 acres of irrigation land depended.[64] Although an Arbitral Tribunal set up to resolve questions arising out of Partition delivered decisions on the basis that there would be no interference whatsoever with then existing flow of the waters, the issue developed into a matter of grave dispute when, among other measures, the Eastern Punjab state of India asserted proprietary rights and temporarily cut off supplies in 1948. A comprehensive long-term proposal was eventually worked out. Articles II and III of an accord brokered by the World Bank allocated the Eastern rivers (Ravi, Sutlej, Beas) of the Indus system for the unrestricted use of India, imposing on Pakistan 'an obligation to let the streams flow' unhindered; similarly, the Western rivers (Indus, Jhelum, Chenab) were set aside for Pakistan's unrestricted uses imposing on India analogous duties of non-interference.

In consequence, Pakistan's established uses of the river system were seriously affected. The Western rivers could not have adequately replaced the country's historic uses of the Eastern rivers.[65] The ensuing circumstances obliged the construction and operation of 'a system of works which will accomplish the replacement, from the western rivers and other sources, of water supplies for irrigation canals in Pakistan which on the 15th of August 1947 were dependent on water supplies from the eastern rivers'.[66]

On the other hand, the earliest dispute involving Mexico and the USA over diversions and irrigational works proposed on certain portions of the Rio Grande River in the states of Colorado and New Mexico presented, at least in the initial stages, a converse example. An insufficient volume of the Rio Grande River flood threatened the sustenance of established patterns of prior use down the stream. Mexico claimed that 'the principles of international law would form a sufficient basis for the rights of the Mexican inhabitants of the bank of the Rio Grande',

62 Treaty between India and Pakistan regarding the use of the waters of Indus, Karachi, 19 September 1960.

63 John G. Laylin (1957) 'Principles of law governing the uses of international rivers, contributions from the Indus basin', *Am Soc'y Int'l L Proc*, vol 51, p 20.

64 Laylin (1957), note 63, p 26.

65 Scott Barret (1994) 'Conflict and Cooperation in managing international water resources', *Policy Research Working Paper 1303*, World Bank Research Department.

66 Treaty between India and Pakistan regarding the use of the waters of Indus, note 62, Article IV.

whose 'claim to the use of the water of that river is incontestable, being prior to that of the inhabitants of Colorado by hundreds of years'.[67]

Eventually, however, the disagreement was settled along equitable lines, but in entering the accord in 1906, the US cautiously reserved that its undertaking shall not be construed as conceding, 'expressly or by implication, any legal basis for any claims hitherto asserted . . . nor does it in any way concede to the establishment of any general principle or precedent'.[68] This declaration had presumably been influenced by pre-existing disputes and a strong statement issued in 1895 by Attorney General Harmon, wherein the US had argued any admission of right permitting Mexico to impose restrictions against the USA with regard to the use of the Rio Grande river would be 'completely contrary to the principle that the USA exercises full sovereignty over its national territory' and hence not justified under 'the rules, principles and precedents of international law'.[69]

By way of a summary, two important points can be discerned from the foregoing discussions of sources of international law.

First, the noticeable trends in international watercourses negotiations to settle disputes on the basis of equal consideration of rights and the application of the principle of equitable uses notwithstanding, states can and in fact had engaged in treaty undertakings where priorities are conferred, special hierarchies maintained, or individual positions attended to. The Indus and Rio Grande river disputes represent typical situations where basin states started negotiations with contrasting claims premised on extreme principles coveted in absolute territorial sovereignty, integrity or self-conception of historical rights of use, but ended up endorsing a far more sensible doctrine that either apportioned the resources or regulated their equitable utilization.

Secondly, outside specific treaty frameworks, the rules of customary international law articulating a far less preclusive set of norms prevail. Neither USA's initial proposition in the context of the Rio Grande River dispute that maintained as the fundamental principle of international law the 'absolute sovereignty of every nation, as against all others, within its own territory', nor India's submission which, shortly before the Indus river negotiations, 'reserved full freedom to extend or alter the system of irrigation within India . . . (and) draw-off such quantities of water as needed, subject to such agreement as could be reached with Pakistan'[70] can seize significant legal credence under contemporary international law. As stated above, customary international law on the use and management of shared watercourses has long discarded the idea of complete freedom of riparian states over parts of shared river courses situated in national jurisdictions. The sovereignty of every state with regard to territorial waters is but constrained by equally co-existing rights of other states.

67 International Law Commission (1986) *Yearbook of International Law Commission*, vol 2, no 1, p 106.

68 Convention between the USA and Mexico concerning the equitable distribution of the waters of the Rio Grande for irrigation purposes, Washington, 21 May 1906.

69 International Law Commission (1974) *Yearbook of International Law Commission*, vol 2, no 2.

70 International Law Commission (1986) *Yearbook of International Law Commission*, vol 2, no 1, p 109.

The normative stipulations of the international legal regime applicable to the Nile basin could not be any different. A call for the perpetuation of the status quo now prevailing on the basis of the natural-historical rights conception – *ipso facto* preserving sizeable proportions of the Nile floods for exclusive downstream uses – defeats one fundamental tenet of international law: the sovereign right of each watercourse state to make use of part of a system of international waters lying within its jurisdiction on the basis of equity and a reciprocal restriction on freedom of actions. A rights hypothesis essentially premised on such notions, if espoused to safeguard present patterns or rationalize prospective uses in Egypt or Sudan will effectively deprive upstream inhabitants of the same advantages in the development of the Nile water resources. No single statement of the successive resolutions of the IIA, the ILA and works of the ILC or subsequent evolution of international law on the subject has recognized the inherent supremacy of rights of any state over a watercourse, nor admitted any formulation that affords comparable privileges.

Claims based on considerations of *distinctive* factors: further analysis

On the other hand, downstream user-right conjectures of exceptional entitlements may have evolved as upshot of complex climatic setting that reigned across the far northern half of the Nile basin. A parched land endowed with a mean annual rainfall barely transcending 18mm,[71] Egypt, and in some ways, northern Sudan could barely compare with water resource endowments in the central lakes region and several parts of the Ethiopian highlands plateau. In fact, after the main Nile and the Atbara rivers confluence shortly north of the Sudanese capital, the Nile pours through narrow valleys, cliffs, barren lands and about six cataracts without receiving floods from any tributary. The annual flood of the river is affected by climatic conditions and rain patterns in the north-western Ethiopian mountains and the Equatorial Lakes plateaus.

It followed, and quite naturally so that Egyptian preoccupation had since the days of King Menes about 3000BC focused on the optimal utilization and defence of its only natural means of existence.

Throughout its evolutionary development, international watercourses law has endeavoured to accommodate particular vulnerabilities of riparian states within a broader framework of principles governing the use of common resources. After all, basin states are rarely bestowed with identical sets of hydrologic endowments. Moreover, because of historical, economic and political factors, the nature and scale of development of infrastructures for the beneficial uses of shared river courses had often flaunted greater variations across jurisdictions. The Nile region is not an exception.

71 Current statistics revealed that the annual rainfall in Egypt is a mere 1 bcm/yr and can withdraw ground waters not exceeding 7.5bcm/yr.

Peculiar susceptibilities induced by the uneven distribution of hydraulic resources or historical uses are regulated, corrected or adjusted primarily through the conclusion of bilateral or basin-wide treaty frameworks and to a degree, through the employment of rules and principles of international water courses law.

As noted above, as early as 1911, the Madrid Declaration of the IIL had already precluded any proposition of absolute autonomy of a state over international water courses, a theory subsequently employed to augment the position that no actions undertaken by one state should prejudice reasonable and equitable utilizations of the same resource by other states. The pronouncement under the Madrid Declaration accorded no special credence either to any claim of beneficial uses of international river courses, or to any state on considerations of its particular geographical circumstances or prior uses, and hence pioneered a principle curtailing the sovereign discretion of states.

Evidently, though, the system of international law could barely function fairly and equitably if states, situated in incongruous settings with respect to the natural endowments of water resources and scales of hydraulic developments are treated, and in consequence, accorded, the same rights under all circumstances. The presumptions of equality of rights and fundamental principle acknowledging each riparian state's entitlement to equitable utilization do certainly admit several peculiarities which would be particularly relevant in the context of one basin state but not necessarily the other. While the scale of influence accorded to any such peculiarity would vary from case to case, modern international law has generally evolved along such course.

For instance, the Draft Resolution on the Utilization of International Waters (Salzburg Resolution–1961) of the IIL foresaw that disagreements would ensue even under circumstances where states admit the equality of rights; the Resolution suggested resolving differences on the basis of equity, 'taking into consideration the respective needs of the states as well as other circumstances relevant to any particular use'.[72] The ILA's Resolution of Dubrovnik (1956) affirmed a state's right of sovereign control over international waters within its own boundaries which must be exercised with due regard of its effects on co-riparians;[73] and in weighing the benefits accruing against injuries sustained by other states, the resolution introduced several factors which must be taken in to account including the right to reasonable use, the extent of dependence, comparative economic and social gains, pre-existing agreements and pre-existing appropriation.

Two years on, the New York Resolution of the ILA (1958) introduced a core principle acknowledging that 'each co-riparian is entitled to a reasonable and

72 Institute of International Law, Resolution on the Use of International Non-Maritime Waters, Salzburg, 11 September 1961, Article III (Text in: *Yearbook of the Institute of International Law*, Vol 49, II, Salzburg Session, September 1961 pp 381–4).

73 International Law Association, Statement of Principles, Resolution of Dubrovnik, 1956, Article V.

(Text in: International Law Association, Report of the 47th Conference, Dubrovnik 1956, pp 241–3).

equitable share in the beneficial uses of the waters of a drainage basin'; and further enunciated that what amount is reasonable and equitable share is determined 'in light of all the relevant factors in each particular case'.[74]

The Helsinki Rules of the ILA (1966), a forerunner framework of the UN watercourses convention, not only re-confirmed each basin states' entitlement to a reasonable and equitable share in the beneficial uses of waters of an international drainage basin, but it also refined and further introduced sequences of factors taken into consideration to determine reasonable uses: the list munificently included the extent of the basin geography in each state, hydrological contributions, climate, past utilization, in particular existing utilizations, economic and social needs, population, comparative means of satisfying economic and social needs, availability of other resources, avoidance of unnecessary waste in utilization, practicability of compensation to adjust conflicts and the degree to which needs of a basin state are satisfied without causing substantial injury to a co-basin state.[75]

The latest development of the law under Article 5 cum. 6 of the UN Watercourses Convention (1997) refined the earlier pronouncements and introduced a list along with a set of new trimmings. The Convention recognized states shall, in their respective territories, utilize an international watercourse in an equitable and reasonable manner; a range of factors which would be relevant in arriving at equitable and reasonable utilization were listed: it included geographic, hydrographic, hydrological, climatic and ecological factors, social and economic needs, population dependent on the watercourse, cross-state effects of uses, existing and potential uses of the watercourse, conservation, and the availability of alternatives of comparable value to a particular planned or existing use.

Evidently, the legal readings proffered above impress that particular susceptibilities of downstream Nile, whether emanating from hydrological facts or vulnerable dependence on provisions of the sole water course, as well as the ensuing expressions of natural-historical rights articulated to preserve prior uses are accommodated, if in some form, under the system of international law. Indeed, a mere consideration of these facts places certain restrictions on the sovereign prerogative of upstream states.

Yet, caution should be motioned as well that the conceptual references proposing to validate downstream claims of rights on the grounds of extreme dependency, prior/historical uses, or unavailability of alternative water resources could not be considered as standing separately and operating as such under the system of international law. These specific factors are only accommodated within the context of a broader framework of a prevailing principle: the right to equitable and reasonable utilization. Indeed, as the US Supreme Court had noted in the *Colorado vs. New Mexico* interstate case (1984), no state is entitled to any priority

74 International Law Association, Agreed Principles of International Law, Resolution on the Use of the Waters of International Rivers, New York, 1958.
(Text in International Law Association, Report of the 48th Conference, New York, 1–7 Sept ember 1958, pp viii–x).

75 International Law Association (1966), note 45, Article IV, V.

simply because a river originates in its jurisdiction, in so much as it cannot claim a right to an undiminished flow of a river merely by virtue of its first use.[76] Natural conditions vesting in Egypt or northern Sudan negligible volumes of precipitation in marked distinction to upstream affluence, or even more vitally, an ages-long practice of prior utilization embedded in the social and economic necessities of the downstream polities would no doubt compose imperative factors to consider; yet, each element has to compete with a dozen of other factors lined under articles 6 of the UN watercourses convention. The right in equity of each contending national interest is computed on the basis of consideration of the *whole*.

In bilateral or multilateral discourses, while states will naturally highlight only such circumstances as would prop up their respective positions, neither the Convention nor the norms of customary international law had afforded any given factor an *inherent prominence*. In fact, during the preparatory works of the UN Watercourses Convention, the ILC had rightly confirmed that 'no priority or weight is assigned to the factors and circumstances listed, since some of them may be more important in certain cases while others may deserve to be accorded greater weight in other cases'.[77]

As a result, the merit accorded to any condition varies, depending on particular reading of the circumstances in each basin state, determined, as stipulated under Article 6.3 of the UN Watercourses Convention, by reference to its importance in comparison with that of other relevant factors. As the ILC had earlier observed, the note of lists was based on the recognition that no automatically applicable fixed sets of factors or a given formula for ranking or weighing the factors can be devised that would fit all situations. While such a process would seem to presume intensive negotiations between the stake holding parties involved, it is manifest, for purposes of the present analysis that the Convention's quest for equitable utilization has proceeded on the basis of accommodating all the relevant factors together, not merely the *specially selected few*.

In the context of the Nile River where historically nearly all its waters have been apportioned for exclusive uses down the stream, this does not simply involve investigation of hard facts relating to seniority of user-rights or hydrologic contribution of flows by each basin state. The quest also entails consideration of socio-economic necessities in each of the riparian states, scales of dependency on the river system, cross-effects of uses against each others' interests, the nature and level of existing and potential uses and finally, the availability of options of comparable value to existing and proposed uses.

From the foregoing exposition of the normative standards, it follows that a rights hypothesis of any nomenclature that tries to single out, as a controlling factor, the prior use patterns or geographic, economic or social peculiarities featured along downstream Nile would fail to meet the reasonable and equitable uses threshold established under international law. And as such, the conception of peculiar

76 *Colorado vs. New Mexico*, 467 US 191(1984).

77 International Law Commission (1994) *Yearbook of International Law Commission*, vol 2, no 2, p 101.

circumstances invoked by Egypt or Sudan procures only a limited result in shielding existing downstream claims of share in the Nile waters.

Once the principle has been established that every watercourse state is entitled qualitatively and quantitatively to equitable share in the uses of a watercourse, a final task remains to determine if the contemporary pattern of utilization in the Nile basin can also be portrayed as such.

Hence, the issue of concentration in the subsequent sections would revolve on the theme of whether Sudan and Egypt are availing themselves of no more than their respective equitable shares in the Nile River resources, and where not, on revealing the specific legal effects that ensue from the state of facts thus presented.

Noticeably, the planning and development of water infrastructures has in the past decades been a hugely under-considered commission in upstream Nile because of several factors including colonial epoch geo-political manipulations, post-independence instability and the dearth of fiscal and technical resources.

Whatever the conventional causes of upstream underdevelopment, generally, it could be admitted that on the basis of the principle, neither Egypt nor the Sudan could be denied a right to present reasonable use of the Nile and be called upon to instantly suspend the institution of water use facilities in order to reserve for upstream states' future uses of such waters. A state's right to equitable shares is always protected.

However, this cannot imply that any scale of downstream utilization, particularly when it exceeds the equitable uses threshold, would not be discontinued.[78] Obviously, only an extensive assessment of empirical data and all the specific factors can proffer answer to the question of whether downstream development of the Nile resources has surpassed the equitable uses standard.

Similarly, what scale of upstream diminution of flows of the Nile strikes the equitable uses measure, hence designating such appropriation as inequitable cannot be established in the abstract. Both key analyses will be undertaken in Parts 10 and 11.

For the moment, it suffices to conclude that with the advent of strong momentum challenging existing water allocations and a progressively swelling upstream proclivity in carrying out water control works unilaterally, any downstream postulate preserving the status quo would need to demonstrate congruence with the basic tenets of the equitable utilization theory; lest the proposition will lack clout and risk juridical disregard.

78 In its commentary on the Helsinki Rules (1966), the ILA opined it is clear that existing uses should be given some degree of protection but not so much as to freeze development of an international watercourse system. Thus, such a use should be allowed to continue so long as the factors justifying it are not outweighed by factors indicating that it should be modified, phased out, or terminated (with the payment of compensation, where appropriate) in order to accommodate a competing use that is incompatible.

Also in: International Law Commission (1986) *Yearbook of International Law Commission*, vol 2, pp 141–2.

Stated in a different way, Egypt and Sudan shall credibly demonstrate that the existing pattern of utilization withdrawing some 88 percent of the total 84bcm mean annual flow of the Nile waters does not preclude potential upstream recourse to significant utilization of the flow-regime, and as such, constitutes a legitimate exercise of the right to equitable utilization.

In greater specifics, Chapter 9 would elaborate riparian perspectives with regard to the definition of user rights that particularly relate to the equitable utilizations principle.

9 Customary rules of international watercourses law

Overview of riparian positions and new perspectives in the Nile Basin

Introduction

The opening decade of the twenty-first century marked a slight regression in traditional positions of downstream Nile exhibiting certain scales of resilience in the definition of national user-right policies. This meagre flexibility in contemporary rights perceptions could be attributed to several factors. Upper riparian onslaught against existing use-regimes has been sturdy; the psychological impetus induced through progressive evolution of rules and principles of international watercourses law has been significant. But, most notably, a basin-wide diplomatic process, launched in February 1999 under the auspices of the Nile Basin Initiative has driven user-right dialogues to unprecedented heights.

Along with seven upstream riparian states, Sudan and Egypt continued to engage in negotiations of the Transitional Institutional Mechanism of the Nile Basin Initiative (TIM-NBI). The regional initiative has been mandated to set in place a Commission and endorse an Agreement on the Nile River Basin Cooperative Framework, based on a vision 'to achieve sustainable socio-economic development through equitable utilization of, and benefit from, the common Nile Basin water resources'.[1]

Still, in spite of the slight shifts in perspectives and high-profile political pledges to labour on the attainment of equitable utilization of the Nile River resources, the winding stages of the negotiations on the Cooperative Framework have been held back by serious impediments, and particularly so in the course of 2008–12. Egypt and Sudan echoed national water security concerns and hence conditioned the approval of pending initiatives subject to specific guarantees recognizing prior uses sustained through colonial treaties and the natural/acquired rights arguments. Along the downstream Nile, equitable considerations enunciated under the proposed legal platform have been embraced only in a context that upholds the absolute integrity of established rights.

Discernibly, the preceding part had revealed that the natural-historical rights argument, calling for perpetuation of the pattern of uses now prevailing, is an

1 Meeting of the Council of Ministers of the Nile Basin States, Dar-es-Salaam, Tanzania, 22 February 1999.

indefensible juristic proposition. Such a scheme defeats a fundamental tenet of public international law – the sovereign right of each watercourse state to co-utilize international waters.

Hence, except where specific treaties may have provided for a separate catalogue of rights, basin-wide riparian discourse will greatly rely on the crucial utility of customary rules and general principles of international law. This applies both with respect to articulating rights, prescribing obligations or resolving user-right disputes. The UN Watercourses Convention would yet have to garner enough ratification to enter into force and hence proffers a restricted utility in this respect, although several of its provisions represent restatement of international custom.

In so far as custom is concerned, while early developments of the legal regime of international watercourses law had witnessed certain incompatible and vaguely defined theories, several principles had waned in time, giving way for other widely received notions. In contemporary state and institutional practice, two doctrines have attained supremacy. The first rule entitled riparian states to exploit international watercourses in an equitable and reasonable manner. A second principle cautions states to take appropriate measures in the development of transboundary rivers such that significant harm is averted against the stakes of other watercourse states.

Today, the two principles are indisputably regarded as cornerstones of the regime of international watercourses law. They have been referred to in international, regional and bilateral institutional initiatives working on the collective management, protection and use of shared watercourses. Indeed, the references to the principles both under the Agreed Minutes of the Transitional Institutional Mechanism of the Nile Basin Initiative (NBI) and the Agreement on the Nile River Basin Cooperative Framework constitute one patent demonstration of this trend.[2]

In this part, though, a substantive exposition of the two core principles of international watercourses law would first be preceded by a brief presentation of the development and synthesis of contending right-claims in three basin states – Ethiopia, Sudan and Egypt; this scrutiny of national policies would particularly highlight the positions endorsed with regard to the right to equitable utilization and the obligation not to cause significant harm principles.

In this context, an attempt will be exerted to ellucidate two vital queries: given the concentrated diplomatic engagement of the Nile basin states in the last decade, what measure of significance has contemporary rules of international watercourses law captured in the basin? And, to what extent has progressive development of the law influenced national policies and strategies on the use and management of the Nile basin water resources?

Considering the comprehensive presentation in Chapter 8 on the natural-historical rights, featuring diverse aspects of downstream perspectives, a question may

2 The Agreement on the Nile River Basin Cooperative Framework was opened for signature at Lake Victoria Hotel, Uganda, on 14 May 2010 for a period of one year until 13 May 2011. This act formally initiated transformation of the Nile Basin Initiative into a permanent Nile River Basin Commission. Ethiopia, Rwanda, Tanzania and Uganda signed the Cooperative Framework on the opening day; Kenya followed suit on 19 May 2010 and Burundi on 28 February 2011.

be posed with regard to the added value of the analysis on the issues composed above.

The chief objective of this presentation is to expose the juridical rift manifested in contemporary legal approaches in the Nile basin states and draw insight into the degree of stakes involved in future negotiations pursued under the framework of customary rules of international watercourses law. The study would also attempt to direct attention to the issue of why, in spite of the concentrated riparian actions and a fragile gesture of regime change in the last decade, ambiguities that characterized early developments of international watercourses law sustained to still impact riparian dispositions in the Nile basin region.

The synthesis of recent riparian perspectives: Ethiopia, Sudan and Egypt

In the second half of the past century, one significant upshot of the intense riparian engagements throughout the world has been that the quintessence of basic canons of international watercourses law has captured refined form and import. This progressive evolution of international law has markedly influenced national policies and strategies respecting the use and management of shared water courses in the Nile basin as well.

Indeed, while it is admitted that domestic political and socio-economic considerations have continued to hamper tangible cooperative initiatives, water diplomacy in the basin has steadily evolved from archaic approaches of flat rejection to a reciprocal acknowledgement of at least some general principles that define riparian rights and obligations.

Yet, ambiguities that characterized early development of the system of international watercourses law itself had continued to elude a homogeneous reading of the pertinent principles; the trilateral discourse in the Nile basin, particularly involving Ethiopia, Egypt and Sudan features one fitting demonstration of this verity.

Across the Nile region, particular stipulates of two landmark water sharing agreements – concluded between Great Britain and Egypt (1929) and Egypt and the Sudan (1959) – have symbolized, to all intents and purposes, the focal points of the history and legal politics of the Nile River. Propped by conceptions of exclusive privilege founded on the natural-historical rights, the treaties laid the legal and institutional basis on which significant floods of the Nile have been dedicated for preferential utility in the lower-reaches of the basin.

Not surprisingly, a larger upstream group had ridiculed the agreements on multiple legal grounds. The relative import, in international law, of pre-emptive hydraulic infrastructures installed along the downstream Nile were disputed; attempts have also been exerted to institute upstream user-rights through the employ of both political rhetoric and formal declarations preserving present and future rights of utilization.

In a purely juridical parlance, the basin states have likewise tried to structure the defense of user rights along the spirit of two seemingly incompatible principles: the right to equitable utilization and the duty not to cause significant harm.

Ethiopia: reconstructing competing rights of utilization

For several decades, the state of Ethiopia had yearned for greater scales of economic interest in the Blue Nile segment of the basin. Between 1900 and 1955 alone, Ethiopia pursued an impervious policy against British colonial schemes that had connived to put in place a series of water-control and conservation works across the region.

While Ethiopia may have been entangled in the diplomatic and legal politics of the Nile since the earliest decades of the twentieth century, a forbidding dearth in policy, fiscal facility and technical competence inhibited far-reaching developments in its jurisdiction. For the most part of the past century, Ethiopia was therefore obliged to formulate user-rights policies in less concrete fashion and mostly concentrated on *reacting* to specific downstream schemes targeting the development of parts of the Nile River basin.

For this reason, the virtual merit of one of the earliest diplomatic correspondences, effected in 1914, where the Ethiopian Government pledged to safeguard 'not only existing but also future rights to the use of the water for own irrigation purposes'[3] should be viewed in its political rather than practical context.

Indeed, in a period where key players of the hydro-legal discourse – Great Britain, Egypt and later, Sudan – had conceived the prior appropriation rule as *ipso facto* establishing incontestable rights of use, Ethiopia stalked distantly not only in presenting an organized institutional facility that oversees the development of its water sector, but also in composing comprehensive strategies for legal defence of water uses rights.

Along with other states in the upper-reaches of the basin, therefore, Ethiopia failed to emulate Great Britain's and Egyptian strategies in any meaningful respect. No consistent objectives had been set, water-sector institutions were constantly remade in the context of political turmoil and periodic purges; Ethiopia produced little or no institutional and expert memory with a clear set of priorities and was beleaguered in its efforts in attracting international support.[4]

Against the background of the Anglo-Ethiopian Treaty (1902), it was discussed earlier that Ethiopia had engaged in sequences of bilateral negotiations with Great Britain, Sudan and Egypt. For the British, the chief objective of the diplomatic exercise had revolved on the issue of securing concessionary rights for building a dam on the Lake Tana.

Proposals submitted in a series of communications exchanged in the course of 1900–1955, including the specific draft agreements and technical memorandum on water rent proposed for example in May 1935, and re-submitted 1946 and 1951, were all rejected on various grounds. Ethiopia reasoned that the prescriptions stipulated an unequal regime of riparian rights; the bilateral associations had been orchestrated in a manner that barely considered its own stakes on equal footing.[5]

3 Doughty Wyllie to Lord Kitchener, 27 June 1914, FO 371/15388.

4 John Waterbury (1997) 'Is the Status Quo in the Nile Basin Viable', *J World Aff*, vol 4, p 294.

5 J.E. Killick, British Embassy, Addis Ababa to J.H.A Watson, African Department, Foreign Office, London 29 September 1956, FO 371/119063.

In the past, Ethiopia's legal claims over the Nile River had taken various formulations. The recognition afforded in contemporaneous legal jurisprudence notwithstanding, its arguments typically endeavoured to proclaim and preserve present and future rights of use. The national approach also adopted a rights postulate particularly, but not exclusively accentuating its hydrographic contributions to the river basin system. The legal pursuit had not been attended by specific quantitative assertions, comprehensive surveys or the institution of water infrastructures that could have competed with or potentially pre-empted downstream patterns of prior use.

Despite decades of Ethiopia's engagement in hydro-political discourses, the greatest steer in the articulation of rights of use was instigated in the mid 1950s, with the incidence of a high-profile Egyptian and Sudanese negotiation on the Aswan High Dam and allocation of the Nile waters.

At least in the immediate future, the introduction of the Aswan High Dam diminished the relative import of schemes that had previously proposed to institute water control works upstream. When completed, the dam not only symbolized national prestige and economic power, but it also positioned Egypt and Sudan to command full physical possession of the Nile floods.

This new development reintroduced the contentious issue of riparian entitlement with respect to the natural and conserved flows of the Nile waters.

It is true that full utilization of the Nile waters has been achieved progressively and only over extended periods since the construction of the dam facility. Still, the fact remained that nearly all the *surplus waters* conserved in the dam had been appropriated for downstream developments long before Ethiopia (as well as the rest of the upstream states) could have impressed Egypt or Sudan through accelerated survey and implementation of irrigational and power generation programs.

For a greater part of the twentieth century, the upstream Nile remained either unable or unaware of the precise claims, nor the legal means for defending future stakes in the resource. Confronted by threats of full appropriation of the Nile waters made possible by the Aswan High Dam and baffled by a general legal misconception that priority in uses afforded priority in rights,[6] both Ethiopia and later, Great Britain (belatedly acting on behalf of its upstream colonies) strove to deal with the ultimate contingency by staking forward claims of *future rights* through diplomatic procedures.

Ethiopia ventured to preserve its interests by issuing a string of formal reservations that articulated the country's agitation against a concerted downstream disregard; from time to time, Ethiopia attempted to proclaim that its rights shall not be established by simple default, before the problems relating to the division of the Nile waters were pleasingly settled.

6 Yet, the British Foreign Office's manuscript on the state of international law prepared on the basis of information obtained from works of prominent legal publicists, including Oppenheim (international law 3rd edn), Clyde Eagleton and Fenwick concluded differently. The works of the authors convinced the FO to promote the theory that from the point of view of the law, it appeared open to doubt whether a claim can be advanced that a state has no right to utilize the upper waters of a river to the detriment of a neighboring state down the stream.

J. F. S. Philips, Foreign Office to P.R.A Mansfield, British Embassy, Addis Ababa, 25 June 1956, FO 371/ 119062.

Against downstream strategies of utter exclusion, Ethiopia's initial moves simply replicated Great Britain's diplomatic counsel tendered on the subject in 1955.[7] Previously, Great Britain had undertaken to defend the water rights of upstream colonies by informing the Egyptian Government, 'of [their] interest in respect of Uganda and Tanganyika in the event of any Sudan-Egyptian agreement [on the sharing of the Nile waters]'.[8] A British proposal communicated to Egypt had already declared that 'the division of the Nile waters between Egypt and Sudan should be made on a proportionate basis, and not in terms of absolute quantities, [hence] affording each country a right to a stated proportion of the natural flow at Aswan'.[9]

The diplomatic enterprises intended to afford upper riparian states a legal premise on the basis of which multilateral divisions shall be worked as part of a durable settlement of user-rights. The declarations had also hoped to avert legal uncertainties with respect to riparian rights of share in the resource; they contemplated to preserve upstream entitlements over unquantified shares by *pre-emptively* denying Egypt and Sudan of the opportunity to acquire exclusive user-rights through continued utilization of the waters so impounded.

Hence, in 1956, Ethiopia's Ministry of Foreign Affairs was obliged to issue its first formal communiqué; released shortly after publication of the Sudanese Government's pamphlet on 'The Nile Waters Question', the proclamation depicted 'a clear and immediate reservation of Ethiopian rights'[10] both for irrigational and hydro-electric power projects.

7 Only six months before Great Britain ended its administrative position in the Sudan, it formally advised the Ethiopian Government to 'inform the Egyptian and Sudanese Governments that they [Ethiopia] reserve their right to an appropriate share in the Nile waters'. Bailey to Welson, Washington, 2 May 1956, FO 371/119054.

Mr Shuckburgh's advice to the Ethiopian Ambassador had also been restated in the annex of: Addis Ababa to Foreign Office, 11 May 1956, FO 371/119061.

On 2 November 1955, the British Government reminded Egypt that while it had no objection the two downstream states enter in to bilateral negotiations for the division of the Nile waters, it formally reserved rights of the East African territories and that any such talks shall be undertaken subject to the understanding that the two states would be prepared to consider the claims of the East African Territories in a subsequent separate negotiation.

8 African Department, 13 June 1955, FO 371/113733.

9 W.H. Luce, Governor General Office, Khartoum to T.E. Bromley, African Department, Foreign Office, London, 5 May 1955, FO 371/113763.

Formal text of the British reservation:

'It will be seen that Kenya, Uganda, and Tanganyika territory, like Egypt and the Sudan, need the use of additional Nile water in order to fulfil the irrigation projects which they have in mind. In volume they will certainly be small . . . nevertheless, the acquisition of additional supplies of water is a matter of vital interest to the British east African territories, and in view of the attention now being paid by the Egyptian and Sudanese governments to the question of the division of surplus Nile waters, her Majesty's Government wish to draw to the notice of the Egyptian government the interest of the British East African territories in this question and formally reserve their rights to negotiate on their behalf with the Egyptian and Sudanese governments at the appropriate time for the agreed share of the water.' Text of Note presented by her Majesty's Ambassador in Cairo to the Egyptian Government, 22 November 1955, FO 371/119062.

10 P. R. A. Mansfield, British Embassy, Addis Ababa, to J. F. S. Philips, Foreign Office, London, 27 April 1956, FO 371/ 119061; P.R.A Mansfield to John, British Embassy, Addis Ababa, 27 April 1956, FO 371/119061.

In the midst of confusions in Ethiopia, two schools of thought reigned with regard to the most effective way of establishing Ethiopia's right of share in the Nile waters. After consultations with legal scholars in Italy and Geneva, the Ministry of Foreign Affairs was convinced that the Blue Nile communiqué alone was insufficient and hence a clear statement advocating absolute sovereignty had to be called for.[11] Reflecting on contemporaneous jurisprudence of the US Supreme Court, the British Embassy in Addis Ababa reflected that 'the apparently respectable doctrine of absolute sovereignty applied in recent cases would anyway seem to award Ethiopia considerable shares by any international arbitration in consequence of the application of international principles'.[12]

In reality, however, user-rights claims premised on the absolute sovereignty principle had barely corresponded with Ethiopia's engagements of the time in relation to Great Britain, Egypt or the Sudan. Given its beleaguered position in the trilateral discourses, Ethiopia's efforts had instead focused on preserving its equal footing in the negotiations.

On the other hand, the Ministry of Works reluctantly endorsed a very realistic approach, advocating the doctrine of equitable apportionment, but failed to formally commit Ethiopia to any canon of international law.[13]

Throughout the subsequent decades, the two *extreme* orientations restated in government branches had been able to sway and fundamentally influence the juridical fibre of the rights discourse adopted in Ethiopia.

In conclusion, one can submit that with the exception of occasional political rhetoric highlighting unfettered rights of utilization, Ethiopia's mainstream user-right orientation has mostly endeavoured to formulate prescriptive rights to *certain but unspecified* shares in the volumes of the Nile flows.

In contrast to claims by a few legal scholars, a systematic interpretation of Ethiopia's past reflections and official statements could not be construed as mirroring the absolute territorial sovereignty principle with regard to the definition of its rights of utilization.[14]

In fact, in the aftermath of the Aswan High Dam, Ethiopia had steadily tuned its claims on the basis of principles that advocated equity and sovereign equality in the uses of shared watercourses.

11 P. R. A. Mansfield, British Embassy, Addis Ababa to J. F. S. Philips, African Department, Foreign Office, London, 1 August 1956, FO 371/ 119062.

12 Mansfield (1956), note 11.

13 Mansfield (1956), note 11.

14 Probably on the basis of a country paper presented in 1977 in the UN Water Conference at Mar Del Plata, Ethiopia's call for 'good neighborliness in the basin' and 'a right to proceed unilaterally with water development projects' had been interpreted by Waterbury as implying a call for the exercise of unabridged rights of utilization. John Waterbury (2002) *The Nile Basin, National Determinants of collective action*, New Haven, London, Yale University Press, p 46, 71.

Similarly, Godana submitted that Ethiopia espoused the 'absolute territorial sovereignty' argument as of 1978.

Bonaya A. Godana (1985) *Africa's Shared Water Resources, Legal and Institutional Aspects of the Nile, Niger, and the Senegal River Systems*, London, Lynne Rienner, p 36.

Quite a few other authorities cited works of the two authors.

In spite of such juridical orientations, concrete progress had been missing in Ethiopia's water-control infrastructures, beleaguering, over time, the nation's legal and hydropolitical status. In contrast to extraordinary developments down the stream, decades after decades, the water sector lingered in a frozen state. The earliest negotiations on the Tana Dam schemes, although pursued by a series of technical investigations, had never transpired; and while one of the earliest surveys by the US Bureau of Reclamation was published in 1964, no single-major component of the projects had been carried out.

Over a span the last fifty years too, although numerous irrigational and drainage projects had been identified by about ten studies, most were undertaken at master plan and reconnaissance levels and only a few had been pursued on pre-feasibility and feasibility levels.[15]

Ethiopia decried several factors, most notably fiscal and technical limitations as root causes of the sheer underdevelopment. Waterbury submitted one real mechanism for challenging the status quo by a 'crucial actor' in the upper basin materially hinged on Ethiopia's ability to stimulate growth that proffers the wherewithal for financing water development projects without resorting to the international community.[16] Inopportunely, Ethiopia's economic state did not permit noteworthy development of the key national resource until very recently.

Apart from technical and economic limitations, Ethiopia also lamented the absence of regional cooperation as contributing to the low level of development of the immense land and water resources potentials in the Blue Nile segment of the basin.[17]

In 1972, the National Water Development Commission (NWDC) estimated that for three decades, Ethiopia would require 18.7bcm/yr of Nile waters, about 22 percent of the river's total mean annual flood, for its irrigation, domestic uses and out-of-basin diversions.[18]

Against the background of Imperial-epoch strategies that had lacked vigour and constancy, the Commission advised the Ethiopian Government to frame a clear policy guideline in respect of the use of its international rivers; it advocated design of a two-pronged stratagem that would seek to pre-emptively use the river, work in

15 Federal Democratic Republic of Ethiopia (2006) 'Ethiopian Nile Irrigation and Drainage Project, Consultancy Service for Identification of Irrigation and Drainage Projects in the Nile Basin in Ethiopia', Final Report, Ministry of Water Resources, Addis Ababa, p II.

16 John Waterbury (1997) 'Is the Status Quo in the Nile Basin Viable', *J World Aff*, vol 4, p 296.

17 Federal Democratic Republic of Ethiopia, 'Ethiopian Nile Irrigation and Drainage Project, Consultancy Service for Identification of Irrigation and Drainage Projects in the Nile Basin in Ethiopia', p 2, Appendix 1.

18 National Water Development Commission (1972) 'Note on the Blue Nile', Addis Ababa, p 21 (unpublished)

On the other hand, Ashok Swain noted that Ethiopia had instead asked for 6bcm/yr of water to irrigate land in catchment areas of the Blue Nile. Ashok Swain (1997) 'Ethiopia, the Sudan and Egypt. The Nile River Dispute', *Journal of Modern African Studies*, vol 35, no 4, p 680.

John Waterbury cited an old study of the US Bureau of Reclamation to report Ethiopia's needs at about 4–5bcm/yr Waterbury (2002), note 14, p 128.

concert with upper-stream states to weaken the legitimacy of the 1959 agreement and unequivocally state Ethiopia's position in regard to the resource.[19] It was presumed that the pressing threat to Ethiopia's long-term interests would ensue from the Nile waters Agreement, renegotiated in 1959 between the states of Egypt and the Sudan.

In some measures, Ethiopia subscribed to the Commission's early counsel and has since adopted strategic positions that diluted the continuity and legitimacy of the status quo now prevailing in the Nile basin.

With the advent of a new regime in 1991, Ethiopia's water development policies and national strategies were reorganized with a candidly critical theme, scorning the status quo in the basin as objectionable and unsustainable. Legal, financial and technical hurdles notwithstanding, the issues of restructuring relations with the downstream Nile and developing full potentials of the Blue Nile basin were settled high on the government's agenda. The themes were particularly highlighted in the statement of Ethiopia's Foreign Affairs and National Security Policy and Strategy (EFANSPS. The extreme susceptibility of the country's rain-fed agricultural economy, sustained in an increasingly erratic climatic setting has urged policy makers to endorse that an intensified use of irrigation shall play the most crucial role in stabilizing, enhancing and diversifying agricultural output.

The Ethiopian Water Resources Management Policy (EWRMP) was adopted in 1998–1999. The Policy advocated the use of water harvesting techniques and the construction of small-, medium- and large-scale dams to generate hydropower and sustain an irrigated-agriculture economy since, numerous master plans, pre-feasibility and feasibility studies had been undertaken in succession on the principal courses, tributaries and sub-tributaries.

Two vital executive instruments of the Policy, the Ethiopian Water Sector Strategy and a 15-year Water Sector Development Programme (WSDP) have been completed and set in place in 2001 and 2002 respectively. The WSDP particularly identified specific irrigational and hydropower components, with a planned irrigation target of 274,612 hectares over a 15-Year Period (2002–2016).[20]

On the other hand, Ethiopia's Foreign Affairs and National Security Policy and Strategy underscored the country's predisposition to develop its resources, particularly in the field of hydropower and irrigation, 'without affecting Egypt's fundamental interests' and through 'the balancing of interests'.[21] The obvious impacts of the projected development under the WSDP, both on the quality and quantity of flows of the Nile River, it had been presumed, would be accommodated within the broader entitlements of rights under the principle of equitable utilization.

On the bilateral stage, Ethiopia ventured to improve long-standing hostilities by knotting two general conventions with the Sudan and Egypt.

19 National Water Development Commission (1972), note 18.

20 Ministry of Water Resources (2002) 'Water Sector Development Program, Irrigation Development Programme Report', Addis Ababa.

21 The Federal Democratic Republic of Ethiopia (2000) 'Foreign Affairs and National Security Policy and Strategy', Ministry of Information, Press & Audio-visual Department, Addis Ababa, p 124.

Under the Ethio-Sudanese Accord on Peace and Friendship signed in Khartoum on 23 December 1991, both states underlined the importance of the right to equitable utilization, without causing appreciable harm to one another.

On the other hand, an Ethio-Egyptian Framework for General Cooperation, signed in Cairo in July 1993 confirmed that issues of the Nile water utilization shall be worked out in detail through discussions by experts of both sides on the basis of 'rules and principles of international law'. The parties furthermore agreed to refrain from engaging in any activity related to the Nile waters that may cause 'appreciable harm' to the interests of the other party. In either case, the Ethio-Egyptian agreement fell short of referring to any of the old treaty regimes previously concluded, nor to a prevailing principle of the right to equitable utilization.

In summary, the sovereign aspiration of the state of Ethiopia with respect to the Nile water resources has essentially been founded on a fundamental legal assumption that any limitation against freedom of use of the river stems only from its own perceptions of the pertinent principles of international law.

Ethiopia's reading of the specific rules of international law has nonetheless varied in some measures. If implicitly, the Water Resources Management Policy scorned downstream claims of historical entitlements and accentuated that unilateral measures pursued by individual states would by no means serve as a basis for defining user-rights. To avert unwarranted riparian rivalry, the WRMP recommended that the basic principles developed under international law and more specifically the principle of equitable and reasonable uses laid down under the Helsinki Rules should be endorsed in the allocation of transboundary waters.[22] The document ridiculed past disinclinations wherein downstream states had repeatedly failed to sanction such 'basic principles of universal acceptance'.[23]

On the other hand, the constructive utility of partaking in regional schemes and most notably the Shared Vision and the Subsidiary Action Program of the Nile Basin Initiative have also been highlighted, but Ethiopia's drive remained neither too light nor over-enthusiastic.[24]

During the VIIIth Nile-2002 Conference held in Addis Ababa, for instance, the Government of Ethiopia reasserted its long-stated position that no international

22 UNESCO-WWAP, World Water Assessment Program (2004) 'National Water Development Report for Ethiopia', Addis Ababa, pp 225–6, <http://unesdoc.unesco.org/images/0014/001459/145926e.pdf> last accessed December 2010.

23 UNESCO, World Water Assessment Program (2004), note 22.

24 On a handful of occasions, Ethiopia labelled some of such early initiatives as nothing more than a mere talk stages where 'downstream states declare and acquire recognition of their prior development works on the Nile, and register their claims'.Ministry of Water Resources (1993) 'Local and Transboundary Rivers, Current International Relations', Addis Ababa, p 6 (unpublished).

In a Country Paper presented to a forum of basin states in 1997, Ethiopia highlighted that the 'role that international organizations can play cannot be overemphasized' and indicated that it would be 'necessary to be cautious as to what should be done before investing energy and time since the end result could be slipping back to where one has started from with all the efforts gone down the drain'. Nile 2002 Conference (1997) 'Comprehensive Water Resources Development of the Nile Basin: Priorities for the New Century', Proceedings of the Vth Nile 2002 Conference, Country Paper Ethiopia, 24–28 February, Addis Ababa, p 43.

agreements on water and allocation exist between itself and neighboring countries and hence that it would work on legal and institutional frameworks regulating uses in the Nile basin on the basis of 'equitable sharing of the resource among the basin states'.[25] Indeed, it is up to Ethiopia to force the issue of renegotiating the 1959 status quo against a totally unwilling Egypt.[26]

Hence, within the basin's cooperative enterprises, Ethiopia persevered to spearhead and press the need for devising comprehensive solutions to long-standing riparian issues of dispute. Reinforcing previously articulated claims, Ethiopia warned its participation or lack of one in regional dialogues should neither prejudice nor generate any uncertainty with respect to its right to 'such amount it regards as its legitimate share any time in the future'.[27]

Ethiopia also called upon 'all co-basin states to acknowledge each other's legitimate rights to beneficially use the waters of the Nile River, in view of their own portions of the river basin and quantities of water generated thereof, and in accordance with generally accepted principles of international law'.[28] The legal regime on which downstream states customarily based their claims for preferential rights, when 'put to the test of contemporary international law', Ethiopia held, would 'fail to be tenable since they ignore the inalienable entitlements of each watercourse states . . .'.[29]

In consequence, all basin states were asked to 'recognize unequivocally the principle of equitable entitlement to the use of the Nile waters',[30] a core legal doctrine that assumed priority over the 'no significant harm' rule.[31]

25 Nile 2002 Conference (1996), Proceedings of the IVth Nile 2002 Conference, Country Paper: Egypt, 26–29 February, Kampala, p C-24.

26 John Waterbury (1997), note 16, pp 296, 297.

27 Ministry of Water Resources (1993), note 24, p 6.

Furthermore, country papers submitted in 2000 and 2002 underscored that 'the unevenness in the utilization of the Nile waters will continue to create mistrust among nations unless tackled appropriately and on time' and that 'Ethiopia is legally and morally right to use its share of the Nile River'. Nile 2002 Conference (1997) 'Comprehensive Water Resources Development of the Nile Basin: Priorities for the New Century', Proceedings of the Vth Nile 2002 Conference, Country Paper Ethiopia, 24–28 February, Addis Ababa, p 1.

Ethiopia also demeaned attempts by the downstream states to 'protect the status quo . . . by ignoring the *equitable rights* of upstream countries or by continuously expanding water resources projects', and threatened that such conduct 'might encourage unilateral measures in other parts of the basin which may lead to undesirable results'.

Nile 2002 Conference (1997), p 37.

28 Nile 2002 Conference (1992) 'Framework for cooperation between the Nile River co-basin states: Nile 2002 Conference on Comprehensive Water Resources Development of the Nile Basin, The Vision Ahead', Proceedings of Nile 2002 Conference, Country Paper: Ethiopia, 29 January – 1 February, Khartoum, p 10.

29 Ministry of Water Resources, 'Ethiopia's Technical Advisory Committee Proposal, Application of the Principle of Equitable Utilization and the Duty not to Cause Appreciable Harm in the Context of the Nile', Annex 10, p 3 (unpublished).

30 Nile 2002 Conference (2000) Proceedings of VIIIth Nile 2002 Conference, Country Paper: Ethiopia, 26–29 June, Addis Ababa, p 9.

31 Nile 2002 Conference (1997), note 27, p 40.

In the particular context of Ethiopia's relations with the downstream Nile, the juridical fervour has furthermore advocated that no rule of international law as such exists to *proscribe* a late-coming riparian states' recourse to unilateral utilization of the Nile River.[32]

Prompted by such legal contemplations and some scales of economic renaissance, Ethiopia took certain pragmatic measures not only in drawing a broader outline of national policies, but also in laying down specific arrangements for the development of projects that anticipated to enhance the river's utility across its jurisdiction. In the first decade of the twenty-first century, Ethiopia's relative stability and fiscal command demonstrated that the absence of specific cooperative arrangements or international financial provisioning can no longer deter its water resources development enterprises.

Indeed, the commissioning of a thread of costly hydro-electric power projects – the Tekeze I (300MW), Gilgel Gibe I (180MW), Gilgel Gibe II (420MW), Tana Beles (460MW), Fincha-Amerti Nesh (100MW) as well as the launch of construction on Gilgel Gibe III (1870MW) and the Grand Ethiopian Renaissance Dam (6,000MW) schemes, just in the past decade alone, could be displayed as a case in point.

Considerations of 'equitable use': the downstream juridical pose

For several decades, Sudan and Egypt have been fairly convinced that Ethiopia had neither firm plans nor the means for pursuing consequential developments on the Blue Nile River. Under the 1959 Nile waters treaty, both states expressed intent to jointly consider the claims of other riparian states at some future time and deduct their respective shares if any such consideration results in acceptance.[33]

In practice, however, both states harboured stiff reservations and endorsed British-era strategies to forestall threats potentially originating from Ethiopia's prospective uses of the Nile River. With the passage of time, Waterbury wrote, 'the original spirit of the 1959 Agreement had mostly been lost . . . the shares in absolute terms have now become sacrosanct, absolute floors below which neither country will go'.[34]

Hence, Egypt and Sudan maintained parallel poses both with regard to the theoretical definition of existing use rights and current discourses in the basin. The absolute integrity of the existing water allocations regime has been called for without fail.

32 Prime Minister Meles Zenawi succinctly recapitulated the country's enduring proposition of right of use of the Nile floods: 'if we had the resources, we could store the water, irrigate our lands and provide for our livelihoods . . . the issue is whether we can use *some* of the this water (stored at Aswan) for irrigation purposes'. He concluded *no treaty* would bar Ethiopia, warning 'if and when we get the resources, we will use it'.

TV-2 Documentary, Sunday 28 October 2007, 'Reise til vannets fremtid', Norway, Oslo; ETV televised interviews 2010 and 2011.

33 United Arab Republic and Sudan Agreement for the Full Utilization of the Nile Waters, 8 November 1959, Cairo, Article IV.

34 Waterbury (2002), note 14, p 75.

For long, Sudan's mainstream hydro-political deportment remained hugely fixated with its past. In nearly all official dealings, Sudan replicated strategies adopted by its mentor, Great Britain and its northerly neighbour, Egypt.

Of course, Sudan recognized the sheer scale of dependence of its agricultural economy, greatly relying on yields of the Blue Nile inundating from the Ethiopian highlands – over which it has neither territorial nor hydro-structural control. Water-control works carried in Ethiopia, it had been promoted since the heydays of the Tana Dam negotiations in the 1920s, would tender suitable facilities that heed to Sudan's multifarious hydraulic concerns – most notably in the regulation of floods and prevention of dam siltation. Yet, Ethio-Sudanese negotiations had never been pursued to fruition.

Instead, throughout the 1950s where the historic Nile waters agreement was detailed and eventually sanctioned, Sudan held negotiations with Egypt behind closed doors and in complete disregard of the physical contributions, prospective stakes and stated legal claims of Ethiopia and the East African states.

Admittedly, the need for broader and cooperative schemes has been accentuated in all angles, including Sudan and piecemeal advances were attained on a basin as well as sub-basin levels. Indeed, today, Sudan has stronger political concerns in developing cooperative arrangements with Ethiopia in its own best interest and should endeavour to sway Egypt join discussions with Ethiopia without imposing preconditions on the use of the amounts already allocated.[35]

Barely, though, this has been the case. In spite of the general recognition of natural riparian rights, the basic inventory of Sudanese water-uses policy remained very apprehensive of water security concerns.

As Sudan struggled in contemporary basin-wide initiatives endorsing the right to equitable and reasonable uses, its development enterprise persisted on prompting a policy of expanded utilization of the Nile waters, vulnerably swelling its dependence on the sole resource.[36] The country's expansive uses counted on the hitherto allocated waters, increased conservation and optimal consumption, and beyond, looked for additional waters in future negotiations. In either case, Sudan regarded nearly a fourth of the mean annual floods of the Nile as its legitimate share.

Evidently, in the early 1990s, the dynamic transformation of the global political order and power-relations has incidentally affected the Nile basin states and more significantly, the evolution of the international watercourses law regime. This development has in turn influenced traditional downstream perceptions in some measures.

35 Dante A. Caponera (1993) 'Legal Aspects of Transboundary River Basins in the Middle East, the Al Asi (Orentes), the Jordan and the Nile', *Natural Resources Journal*, vol 33, p 661.

36 Hence, in 1996, the Sudanese Government announced that Sudan has virtually consumed its Nile Waters share of 20.5bcm/yr, taking in to account the storage and irrigation projects currently under execution.

Nile 2002 Conference (1996) Proceedings of the IVth Nile 2002 Conference, Country Paper: Sudan, 26–29 February, Kampala, p C-26.

The increasingly international orientation of Sudanese water-uses policies articulated in the Ethio-Sudanese Accord on Peace and Friendship signed in Khartoum could be a case in point.

Under the bilateral arrangement, Sudan conditionally embraced the principle of 'equitable utilization' 'without causing appreciable harm to one another'. In the series of joint assemblies of the delegates, however, Sudan endeavoured to cautiously append only such *factors* as are listed under the Helsinki Rules and the ILC's early drafts of the UN Watercourses Convention that augmented its positions in the eventual assessment of the equitability of uses.

In May of 1992, a joint declaration of the first convention of water and irrigation ministries of the Ethio-Sudanese Technical Advisory Committee recognized that 'pre-existing agreements' in the basin should not hamper 'the right to equitable share and use' of other riparian states. The Joint Committee pledged to examine facts that impede equitable allocation and agreed to diffuse such setbacks as may protract the reciprocally beneficial uses of the river's resources.[37]

In the fourth meeting held in Addis Ababa years later, however, Sudan backtracked and its delegation refused to address and discuss the fate of prior and acquired rights shielded under the 1959 Nile Waters Agreement. This unenthusiastic development diffused Ethiopia's crave for a new water-sharing regime which it considered was the chief object of the joint undertaking. In tandem with established patterns, Ethiopia accused Sudan of concentrating on less-pressing issues, including the exchange of hydrological and meteorological data and watershed management.

In spite of the charges so levelled, a joint communiqué of the states reaffirmed their agreement that 'existing arrangements in the Nile basin could not be peremptory to the rights of other states in the basin to equitably utilize the Nile waters'.[38] At the same time, the statement warned that developments should be carried 'without causing any appreciable harm to the interests of other co-basin states'.[39]

This guarded endorsement of the equitable uses principle by the Sudanese government can be regarded as affirmative development in the context of bilateral relations and technical negotiations of the states. Ethiopia maintained a new water-sharing agreement would be mandatory although the parties disagreed over the specific list of conditions that should be considered in evaluating the equitability of uses of the Nile waters.[40] Figures explicit in existing uses, Ethiopia submitted, should not be afforded an absolute protection and in fact, would constitute merely *one* of the many factors that shall be considered in the determination of equitable allocation of the international watercourse.[41]

37 Ministry of Water Resources (1992) 'Minutes of the Ethio-Sudanese Joint Meeting on Nile Waters Resources Cooperation', Addis Ababa, p 3 (unpublished).

38 Ministry of Water Resources (1992), note 37.

39 Ministry of Water Resources (1994) 'Minutes of the Fourth Regular Meeting of the Ethio-Sudan Technical Advisory Committee on Nile Water Resources Cooperation', Addis Ababa, p 9 (unpublished).

40 Ministry of Water Resources (1994), note 39, p 5.

41 Ministry of Water Resources (n.d.), note 29.

A gradual digression in Sudan's extreme water-uses policy was also reflected in the country's energetic participation in regional cooperative forums, including the Nile Basin Initiative. The basin-wide enterprise has been working on a legal and institutional framework since the 1990s with the object of establishing the equitable and sustainable utilization of the Nile water resources. A downstream state with greater stakes in the preservation of the status quo, Sudan reiterated the development, conservation and use of the Nile basin should be pursued in an integrated, sustainable and environmentally sound manner, through a basin-wide cooperation, for the benefit of all and with recognition of the principle of equitable entitlement without causing appreciable harm.[42]

In spite of the sequences of oblique admissions that appeared to accommodate Ethiopia's calls for equitable utilization, neither Sudan nor Egypt had consented to formally relegate the status quo in the Nile basin. As noted earlier, the contemporary uses regime has been preserved through the application of such conceptions as the natural historical rights, prior appropriation and the no significant harm notions and a string of colonial-epoch treaties.

Obviously, broadly framed political pledges to equitably utilize the resource for the benefit of all riparian states have been undertaken on multiple occasions; selected water-control projects were also sanctioned jointly and a few have been carried out on the basis of explicit consent of the partaking states – Egypt, Ethiopia and Sudan.

Yet, the case-by-case approach failed to evolve into a concrete cooperative scheme with clearly defined legal and institutional structures and to address rights of utilization on the basis of ordered principles.

On the other hand, Egypt's reflections have been a great deal analogous with the positions adopted by Sudan. In contemporary riparian deliberations, the principle of equitable utilization has been too entrenched to ignore that Egypt, traditionally a staunch adherent of the historical rights and no significant harm notions, had to acknowledge the doctrine's eminence in successive basin discourses. Particulars of its national approach have, however, varied.

In 1996, Egypt admitted the right of each watercourse state to equitable utilization of the Nile River is accommodated, subject to the stipulation that such causes no appreciable/significant harm to its own interests.[43] It alleged the exercise of the right in equity under international law presumes a process carried out in 'a cooperative manner and with prior consultations'.[44] Egypt also reiterated that several of the upper riparian states are still bound to respect existing (colonial and post-colonial) treaties, conventions, rules and principles of international law.[45]

In relation to upstream Nile, Egypt's strategic contemplation primarily concentrates on the potential utility of existing water-control facilities and future conservation projects carried in the upper-reaches of the river. Intellectual discourse had

42 Nile 2002 Conference (1996), note 36, pC-30.

43 Nile 2002 Conference (2000), Proceedings of VIIIth Nile 2002 Conference, Country Paper: Egypt, Addis Ababa, p 8.

44 Nile 2002 Conference (2000), note 43, p 53.

45 Nile 2002 Conference (2000), note 43, p 53.

in the past argued that reservoirs upstream would offer greater advantages in the long term for the integrated management of the Nile from which Egypt stands to gain more than any other riparian.[46]

Yet, while Egypt remained committed to cooperation at a basin and sub-basin levels and a scope for harmonization of national interests has in fact been admitted as feasible, in practice, its national strategy craved to confine upper-basin developments to a rain-fed agriculture and utmost, to the generation of hydro-electric powers; upstream irrigational agriculture was ascribed only a supplementary function.[47]

Besides, with regard to the vital issue of the allocation of Nile waters, Egypt and Sudan opted to overlook Ethiopia's insistence that the Nile basin had already been furnished with adequate hydrologic data that warrants an immediate consideration of equitable resource sharing. Upstream allegations that data gathering for purposes of planning and management had hitherto been employed to prolong water allocation schemes were generally disregarded.[48]

To recapitulate, the contemporary legal discourse in the Nile basin has been espoused on unprecedented scale of cooperation, representing, in some form, a marked shift in national strategies. The growing influence of customary rules of international law can be discerned from the broader outlines of national riparian policies. This can be regarded as a positive development.

On a closer scrutiny, however, one cannot help but perceive that formidable barriers still linger. In the first instance, downstream riparian interests have been premised on diverse legal stipulates and theories. And even when articulating user rights on the basis of commonly recognized principles, in reality, national policies contemplate to realize entirely disparate objectives.

So far, this state of affair has turned the resolution of conflict-of-uses scenarios in to a more complex undertaking and explicates why, in spite of the high-level political and technical negotiations in the past decade alone, a breakthrough could not have come on the single most important stipulation of the Nile Basin Cooperative Framework.

Recent developments within the framework of the Nile Basin Initiative

On 26 June 2007, the Nile Council of Ministers (Nile-COM), the highest decision-making organ of the Nile Basin Initiative represented through water and irrigation ministers of the states, concluded in Uganda negotiations on the substantive and procedural contents of the proposed 'Agreement on Nile River Basin Cooperative Framework'. The regional design has for long contemplated to adopt a comprehensive legal instrument and to set up the Nile Basin Commission. This unprecedented historical discourse wrapped a painstaking decade-long diplomatic enterprise that kicked off in 1997.

46 Caponera (1993), note 35, p 660.
47 Nile 2002 Conference (2000), note 43, p 46.
48 Nile 2002 Conference (1997), note 27, p 40.

In the final phase of the negotiations in 2007, extensive diplomatic shuttling and political efforts had been exerted; in spite of the conscientious deliberations, however, the assembly of the Council of Ministers failed to harmonize riparian positions. Within the Nile Council of Ministers of the NBI, divergences overhang with respect to certain key provisions of the proposed instrument prepared by the Panel of Experts and hence, outstanding matters had to be referred to the respective heads of states for further scrutiny and concessions.

After months of recess since 2007, negotiations were re-launched, hosting various rounds of political and technical congregations of the Nile Council of Ministers (Nile-COM) as well as the Joint Nile-Technical Advisory and Negotiators Committee (JN-TANC) in Kinshasa (May 2009), Alexandria (July 2009), Kampala (September 2009), Dar es Salam (December 2009) and Sharm El Sheikh (April 2010).

Inspired by a common design of achieving equitable uses of the Nile river resources, the Nile basin states put forth huge efforts to synchronize the diversely entrenched riparian policies and mend the unbridgeable gaps that persevered to elude the institution of the first-ever comprehensive legal regime in the region. But, it stalled without success.

In a paradoxical set of historical coincidences, a landmark decree advocating the complete abolishment of the protected uses regime in the Nile basin was eventually proclaimed in no other country but Egypt itself. On 13 April 2010, an Extra-Ordinary Meeting of the Nile-Com held in Sharm El Sheikh voted a landmark resolution to proceed, at a later date, with a formal signature of the proposed Cooperative Framework based on decisions held in Kinshasa in May 2009; the resolution was passed in spite of the outstanding discrepancies in national positions of the partaking states.[49]

Subsequently, the instrument was opened in Kampala, Uganda for signature from 14 May 2010, for a period of not more than one year.[50] Against Egypt's declared anticipation that 'the upstream countries (would) reverse their decision to sign a unilateral framework agreement so that negotiations continue',[51] the agreement had since been signed by six states: Uganda, Tanzania, Kenya, Ethiopia, Rwanda and Burundi. Article 42 had stipulated that the Cooperative Framework shall enter into force on the sixtieth day following the date of the deposit of the sixth instrument of ratification or accession with the African Union. This process marks the beginning of a formal transformation of the NBI in to a permanent Commission.

49 Nile Basin Initiative (2010) 'Ministers of Water Affairs End Extraordinary Meeting over the Cooperative Framework Agreement', Press Release, 14 April. <http://www.nilebasin.org/index.php?option=com_content&task=view&id=161&Itemid=102> last accessed December 2010; note that there had been discrepancy from the first draft of the Framework which contemplated the signature to take place between 1 August 2009 and 1 August 2011.

50 Nile Basin Initiative (2010) 'Agreement on the Nile River Basin Cooperative Framework opened for signature', Press Release, 14 May. <http://www.nilebasin.org/index.php?option=com_content&task=view&id=165&Itemid=102>, last accessed December 2010.

51 Mohamed El-Sayed (2010) 'Dangers on the Nile', *Al-Ahram Weekly Online*, April Issue 995. <http://weekly.ahram.org.eg/2010/995/eg3.htm>, last accessed December 2010.

The preamble of the Agreement on the Nile River Basin Cooperative Framework promoted the need for integrated management, sustainable development and harmonious utilization of the Nile water resources. On substance, the instrument reproduced several foundation principles of international water courses and environmental laws, including the right to equitable and reasonable utilization and the duty not to cause significant harm.

Enclosed in 44 articles, all but one provision of the text had been endorsed through consensus of the partaking states.

The deep conceptual controversy that had occupied a centre stage in nearly all institutional and academic enterprises both with respect to the definition as well as the standing of principles of international watercourses law had simply been pushed to the side. This complex responsibility shall now be inherited by the Nile River Basin Commission (NRBC), a political unit essentially composed of a Conference of Heads of States and Governments and the Council of Ministers.[52]

In an unprecedented tempo of diplomatic unison in Sharm El Sheikh, seven riparian states in the upper-most reaches of the Nile, including Ethiopia adopted similar position on all contents of the Cooperative Framework that projected to scrap pre-existing arrangements outright. Egypt and Sudan reacted without delay, and reiterated that the position so adopted at the Extra-Ordinary Meeting of the Nile-Com 'reflects the views only of the states'.[53]

Instead, a substitute proposal for direct launching of the Nile Basin Commission, within the framework of which further negotiations on the remaining pieces of the Cooperative Framework Agreement would be undertaken, failed to garner upstream favour.

Two disproportionately represented groupings of basin states, following geographical divisions in the upper- and lower-reaches of the river deviated on the substantive framing of one important stipulation, Article 14 of the Cooperative Framework. It addressed issues of water security. Article 14 of the text read:

> Having due regard to the provisions of Articles 4 and 5, the Nile Basin States recognize the vital importance of water security to each of them. The states also recognize that the cooperation, management and development of waters of the Nile River System will facilitate achievement of water security and other benefits. The Nile Basin States therefore agree, in a spirit of cooperation:
>
> a. To work together to ensure that all states achieve and sustain water security, and
> b. Not to significantly affect the water security of any other Nile Basin State.

52 The Commission would have to establish a system of authoritative procedures for the notification, evaluation and determination of whether states, pursuing national developmental aspirations, are acting within the confines of their equitable shares, and for dealing with consequences thereof; in the long term, its responsibilities could also involve instituting a mechanism for a comprehensive review of conflicting riparian plans and for balancing interests on the basis of equitable considerations.

53 Nile Basin Initiative (2010), note 49.

The stipulation had been preceded by two explicit provisions: Article 4 on the right to equitable and reasonable utilizations and Article 5 on the obligation not to cause significant harm.

A novel concept, no doubt, Article 14 introduced a water-security regime, defined under Article 2(f) of the same instrument as 'the right of all Nile Basin states to reliable access to and use of the Nile River System for health, agriculture, livelihoods, production and environment'.

The stipulation did not indicate what the significant added-value of such an inclusion would be in further elucidating riparian rights per se, and particularly so in light of the presentation of several, well-recognized principles of international law under various headings of the same instrument.

If only obscurely, the undertaking under Article 14 had struggled to restate the inconvenient marriage of two principles of international water law the theories of equitable utilization and the duty not to cause significant harm. Against a background of an asymmetrical scale of Nile waters utilization, the new scheme appeared to sanction each watercourse state's right to such unquantified waters as would help achieve its water security, without significantly prejudicing the established uses (or water security regimes) of other states.

Admittedly, the concept of water security had already surfaced in several development researches and had received widespread attention in contemporary water-related studies.[54] In contrast, in juridical discourses, the concept has barely evolved in to a clear-cut legal standard, although a few studies had been conducted in the past. This makes it difficult to trace its precise position within a riparian rights discourse traditionally premised on other commonly recognized principles of international law.

The idea of water security is principally associated with developmental thoughts that endeavoured to address issues of human security in a wider context of human development assessed through the employ of several indexes. In introducing debate on human security, the UN Human Development Report (2006) argued the aim had been 'to look beyond narrow perceptions of national security, defined in terms of military threats and the protection of strategic foreign policy goals and towards a vision of security rooted in the lives of people; water security is an integral part of this broader conception of human security'.[55]

Closely resembling to the legal discourse on human rights to water, the concept of water security was conceived as targeting 'that every person has reliable access to enough safe water at an affordable price to lead a healthy, dignified and productive life, while maintaining the ecological systems that provide water and also depend on water'.[56]

54 Development threats associated with the provision of water security had been the focus of successive United Nations meetings since the UN Water Conference in Mar del Plata (March 1977) and the International Conference on Water and the Environment in Dublin (January 1992); they were also addressed in the Ministerial Declaration of The Hague on Water Security in the 21st Century (2000).

55 United Nations Development Programme (2006) *Human Development Report 2006, Beyond scarcity: Power, Poverty and the Global Water Crisis*, New York, Palgrave Macmillan, p 3.

56 United Nations Development Programme (2006), note 55.

If, in propounding under Article 14 that all states shall achieve and sustain water security, the Cooperative Framework had merely intended to highlight the deep state of trepidation that shall ensue in circumstances where individuals and riparian communities are deprived of a right of access to water, and hence to forestall threats against development through a plain articulation of rights and obligations, then, this compromise is largely superfluous.

The subsequent sections would argue that indeed human security imperatives associated with the access to and availability of water are already parts of the regulatory framework of the mainstream international watercourses law regime. For instance, the economic and social needs of watercourses states, one of the numerous factors and circumstances applied to determine the equitability of utilizations, is in some measure concerned with this particular theme.

As a result, there would appear no compelling rational for introducing a separate *rights regime* under Article 14 and thereby ignite an interminable disagreement that imperils the whole cooperative scheme where identical protections can be afforded under stipulations governing equitable utilization and the duty not to cause significant harm; unless, of course, in so providing, a distinct motive had been conceived from the outset.

Even then, the inclusion a dubious concept of water security with little precedent in international legal relations did little to inveigle Egypt or Sudan into fully espousing the Cooperative Framework in its present form. In spite of the explicit reference to a right to equitable uses and duty not to cause significant harm, Sudan and Egypt failed to perceive that downstream rights would be shielded adequately under the new scheme. The reference of downstream rights had been directed at a string of claims of historical-natural rights institutionalized through colonial and post-colonial pacts concluded in 1929/1959. Both states held that an arrangement under the new Cooperative Framework short of preserving the existing status quo would be wholly objectionable.[57]

Instead, a counter-proposal submitted by Egypt provided that Article 14b should be reformulated to read that the Nile Basin states shall work together 'not to adversely affect the water security and current uses and rights of any other Nile Basin state'.

It is important to note that the need for incorporating such a safeguarding provision has been espoused against the background of a bilateral accord negotiated in 1959 wherein Egypt and Sudan had already apportioned some 74 of the total mean annual flow of 84 billion cubic meters of Nile waters just between themselves.

Paradoxically, the arduous diplomatic calisthenics of the last decade by the Nile basin states had projected to twirl the focus of riparian discourse on *re-allocation* of the appropriated waters, pre-existing treaties notwithstanding.

57 Ironically, in 1993, Caponera explained that on account of their relative vulnerability to upstream water withdrawals and possible benefits of comprehensive water control schemes instituted in the upper-reaches, Egypt had to begin negotiations without placing preconditions on the other parties such as those contained in the philosophy of the 1959 Agreement. Egypt would have to make some concessions to upstream riparians and it shall view the new relationships with these countries, and particularly with Ethiopia, as an arrangement opening a new era. Caponera (1993), note 35, p 660.

Indeed, under the Egyptian proposal, Article 14 of the Cooperative Framework intended to dole out more than the conventional objectives of the water security concept reiterated in human development paradigms. The broader security contemplated, i.e. the security of all pre-existing uses, was readily apparent both in the framing of Article 14 and the subsequent declarations.

Egypt's Minister of Irrigation and Water Resources shortly before the 2011 Arab revolution, Nasredin Allam, declared his country would not sign the agreement before two vital conditions are met: 'commitment to an early notification mechanism before the construction of any projects in upstream countries and that all decisions (in the Commission) should be taken by consensus, not by majority'.[58] In the meantime, if upstream countries states unilaterally insist on signing an agreement, the Minister reiterated, Egypt will not abide by it and any such initiative will not have legal impact on its *share* of the Nile water; the Cooperative Framework must clearly recognize Egypt's and Sudan's historic shares of the Nile waters.[59]

Unsurprisingly, the downstream proposition instilled chilly temperament on the basin's diplomatic tempo and reignited a fresh round of dissonance in the hydropolitical discourse. Several basin states, including Ethiopia, Tanzania, Kenya and Uganda renewed their rejection of the status quo mantra. In tandem, upper riparian states reiterated their entitlement within the frame of existing institutional mechanisms as are founded on widely recognized principles of international law.[60]

58 Mohamed El-Sayed (2010), note 51.

59 Mohamed El-Sayed (2010), note 51.

60 While this can only be implied in the participation of the states in the Nile Basin Initiative, a general restatement of their formal positions is provided here as a supplement.

In Tanzania, the Water Resources Management Strategy highlighted options for utilization of Lake Victoria waters, a chief source of the White Nile River, for irrigational and vital human needs on the basis of 'equitable and reasonable utilization of an international water body'. (Nile 2002 Conference (1996) Proceedings of the IVth Nile 2002 Conference, Country Paper: Tanzania, 26–29 February, Kampala, p C-39).

During the 19th Nile Council of Ministers meeting held in Nairobi – Kenya on 28 July 2011, Hon Professor Mark J. Mwandosya (MP), Minister for Water, Republic of Tanzania stated 'For Tanzania, the significance of equitable and sustainable utilization of trans-boundary water resources is extremely crucial . . .'.

Uganda's Water Action Plan prepared during the period of 1993/94 appraised long-established principles on transboundary waters, and argued a case for 'a rational and equitable utilization of the Nile waters'. (Nile 2002 Conference (1996) Proceedings of the IVth Nile 2002 Conference, Country Paper: Uganda, 26–29 February, Kampala, p C-345.)

In 2011, Hon. Maria Mutagamba, Minister of Water and Environment of the Republic of Uganda underlined that '. . . Uganda, being both an upstream and downstream country and with about 98 percent of its water resources lying wholly in the Nile River Basin, attaches a lot of importance to trans-boundary cooperative management of shared water resources'. (The 19th Nile Council of Ministers meeting held in Nairobi – Kenya, 28 July 2011.).

Kenya, on the other hand, had previously urged for the role of international organizations and particularly the United Nations to formulate rules and guidelines on the utilization of international water courses in 'an equitable and reasonable manner.' (Nile 2002 Conference (1997) Proceedings of the Vth Nile 2002 Conference, Country Paper, Kenya, 24–28 February, Addis Ababa, p C-53.)

In July 2011, Hon. Charity Kaluki Ngilu, Minister for Water and Irrigation, Kenya underscored

To counter the upstream states' defying stance, the post-Mubarak Egypt resorted to high-profile diplomatic lobbying to appeal for delays in the ratification of the Cooperative Framework Agreement in basin states until such time when a civilian government is *elected* in Egypt; the campaigns also projected to sway the legal and institutional momentum.

Despite the complexities and legal stalemate, however, Egypt and Sudan continued to partake in regular meetings of the regional initiative. During the nineteenth Nile-COM assembly in 2011, for instance, Professor Hesham Kandil, Egypt's new minister, acknowledged that the challenges are real and will not be solved in a short span of time, but affirmed Egypt will continue to uphold the NBI objectives and looks forward to settlement of the differences within a general frame that requires upstream states not to cause significant harm.

Conclusions

It remains difficult to foretell what the future holds in relation to the Nile basin's legal and institutional discourse; but it is profusely manifest that the process has already reached a point of no return. Such measures of cooperative spirit and juridical achievement had simply been unprecedented.

True, the Nile basin is a geographical region of huge contrasts. Given the scales of socio-economic dependence, climatic setting and the profundity of fiscal and physical outlays procured in downstream Nile, the water security concerns tossed both in Egypt and Sudan cannot be simply overlooked. On the other hand, it is plain that upstream states had endured a history of grave inequity for several decades. The Cooperative Framework presents the perfect setting, both diplomatically and legally, to rectify past inequities, to address distinctive downstream concerns and engage in a collaborative spirit on the basis of rules and principles of customary international law.

Apart from considerations of comity in neighborly relations, international law proffers the most objective basis in tackling the current impasse in the Nile basin

that '. . . it is important that a permanent institution be established in order to safeguard the gains achieved (under the NBI) and to steer the basin to the next level. In this regard, there is a sense of urgency to conclude the outstanding issues within the Cooperative Framework Agreement to ensure that all the basin states are on board'. (The 19th Nile Council of Ministers meeting held in Nairobi – Kenya, 28 July 2011.)

In far less conciliatory terms, the state of Burundi, situated further upstream in the Nile river system, argued in exporting nearly all its waters, it should be entitled to 'a mutually advantageous cooperation with countries situated down the stream.' (Nile 2002 Conference (2000) Proceedings of VIIIth Nile 2002 Conference, Country Paper: Burundi, 26–29 June, Addis Ababa, p 35.)

Quite recently, Hon. Jean-Marie Nibirantije, Minister of Water, Environment, Land Management and Urban Planning of Burundi was more explicit in stating his country's position when he submitted that '. . . . our respective Governments must have a strategic vision of *water sharing*, keeping in mind that the Nile water is a common good to be protected . . . sustainable management of the Nile water by riparian countries is an imperative task and can be achieved, only through active and close cooperation in respect of each partner state's interests'. (The 19th Nile Council of Ministers meeting held in Nairobi – Kenya, 28 July 2011.)

and for expounding specific rights recognized under the Cooperative Framework Agreement.

In contemporary legal developments, Egyptian and Sudanese legal positions have not only been the most extreme but also the most vulnerable, especially in relation to Ethiopia, for no rule of international law would eventually sustain existing uses in the basin without some qualifications.

This juridical discernment explains why it has been difficult for upstream states to subscribe to the Egyptian arrangement proposed under Article 14b, nor to any alternative scheme that falls short of reorganizing the basin status quo in one form or another. Upper riparian states insisted, and quite convincingly so, that years of participation in a series of protracted dialogues had been triggered by a reasonable buoyancy that in the long-run the diplomatic process would yield some concrete gains.

The long-term service of common riparian interest would require Egypt and Sudan – historically the largest users of the Nile waters – to dodge extreme versions of the status quo niche espoused in the past; they also need to demonstrate that the regional forum represents just more than a mere time-buying diplomatic workout.

While historical and fiscal considerations may have hindered the effective utility of the river in the upper-reaches of the river so far, hence serving downstream interests incidentally, this state may not necessarily hold in the future. Under obviously changed economic and political circumstances, the current impasse on the Cooperative Framework Agreement should not corner upstream countries into harbouring deep-seated convictions which concentrate on unilateralism as the only tool of compelling serious negotiations. In the lower-reaches of the river, the long-term security to national interests very much lay in a fitting compromise volunteered today, both in terms of anticipations and legal justifications.

Against a backdrop of the foregoing presentations on riparian perceptions and positions, the analyses in the Chapters 10 and 11 would be committed to a juridical investigation of the claims on the basis of the equitable and reasonable utilization and the duty not to cause significant harm rules.

In the last legs, the discussions would particularly concentrate on presentation of the specific developmental, social, economic and population factors in the three basin states – Egypt, Sudan and Ethiopia – and endeavour to submit a scrupulous assessment of these facts in a bid to reflect on the states' right-entitlements.

10 The application of fundamental principles of customary international watercourses law

The Nile context

Introduction

Outside the bounds of consensual treaty regimes, the autonomy of watercourse states remains relatively unrestricted; riparian states can freely engage in the utilization of transboundary rivers subject only to such limitations as are imposed on considerations of a corresponding right invested in co-basin states.

While milestone steps have been undertaken with a view to concluding negotiations on the Cooperative Framework Agreement, the Nile region has continued to elude comprehensive legal and institutional mechanisms to date. Only two states in the basin, Kenya and Sudan, voted in favour when the UN General Assembly adopted the Convention on the Law of the Non-navigational Uses of International Watercourse in 1997, but fell short of ratifying it. Even now, the Convention has not yet garnered enough ratification to come into force.[1]

One immediate upshot of this legal setting has been that pending conclusion of a basin-wide scheme, riparian conduct in the region would continue to be regulated by the dictates of customary rules and general principles of international watercourses law.

In contemporary state and institutional practice, two doctrines of customary international law would appear to have attained supremacy: a first rule prescribes the right of each watercourse state to equitable and reasonable uses, while a second rule stipulates duty not to cause significant harm on the uses of co-basin states. As noted before, the two principles have been regarded as cornerstones of international watercourses law today.

The basic right of each watercourse state to utilize transboundary waters in equitable and reasonable manner has seldom been disputed. The reading of Article 5 cum. 6 of the UN Watercourses Convention has not only affirmed this right, but it also provided for a list of the relevant factors and circumstances taken into account to determine equitable entitlements.

1 When the General Assembly adopted the Draft Resolution on the Convention on the Law on Non-navigational Uses of International Watercourses in 1997 by a recorded vote of 103 in favour and 3 against, with 27 abstentions, Ethiopia, Egypt, Rwanda and Tanzania abstained, Kenya and Sudan voted in support, Burundi voted against, and Eritrea and Uganda were absent.

However, several of the factors listed under Article 6 of the Convention are either too broad or vaguely framed, posing risks of potential incompatibility or incomprehensibility. Of course, any juridical process that seeks to strike a balance between contending interests and establish an equitable uses regime would presume intensive negotiations between the parties involved.

In specifics, this part will try to converse on the substance and connotation of the doctrine of equitable utilization in the context of particular settings of the Nile basin.

On the basis of detailed hydrological and developmental facts presented in Ethiopia, Egypt and Sudan, the book shall first investigate whether the limited flow regime presented in the Nile is such that all reasonable uses outlined in national water resources development strategies or implemented in pursuance of the stated right to equitable utilization could be realized to their full extent without involving conflicts of uses.

The crux of this matter lies in a venerable debate under international law that involves the issue of how the concept of international watercourse has been perceived as a physical unit of regulation, and by inference, which particular components of the entire water balance of river basins constitute the objects of common riparian appropriation.

Where a conflict of uses appears inevitable, the scrutiny would also address the questions of what explicitly the equitable uses principle entails as a means of reconciling competing riparian interests and how its functioning affects contemporary legal settings, perceptions and practices in the basin.

Scarcity, contending interests and equity in the Nile basin

In the last two decades, the Nile basin has grown into a center stage of concretely contending riparian interests, aspirations and development strategies. The ominous implication of a competitive course over a *scarce* natural resource is self-evident: the realization of the stated rights through unilateral implementation of massive development programs in any one of the late-coming upstream states, withdrawing certain volumes of the Nile waters, will eventually impact on the patterns of use along downstream Nile.

Conventionally, resource scarcity has been understood as a function of demand and supply; legally, the incidence of new demands contending for Nile waters in the upstream reaches may oblige all watercourse states concerned to *reconsider* existing uses and *share* the resource in a reasonable and equitable fashion.

In the first instance, though, the issue of scarcity will presume a fitting exposition of one vital fact directly associated with hydrological features of the resource and which bears impact on riparian entitlements – including the right to equitable utilization and allocation: does the Nile River present an adequate water flows regime so as to circumvent riparian competition in the beneficial uses of the watercourse?

Piercing details remain still wanting both with respect to the total volumes of water available and the various categories of use to which the Nile has been hitherto committed. This is an archetypal phenomenon in many basins and in fact, only 'a few countries know how much water is being used and for what purposes, the quantity and quality of water that is available and can be withdrawn without serious environmental consequences'.[2]

The limitations notwithstanding, the issue remains of vital concern for one important reason: if existing data reveal that the flow regime of the Nile is in fact limited, it follows that not all uses implemented in pursuance of the stated right to equitable utilization could be realized to their full extent without involving conflicts of uses. On account of *scarcity* of the total discharge, some needs in certain basin states, although critical will remain unmet, hence calling for a complex task involving the *redrawing* of riparian entitlements on the basis of the equitable utilization principle.

On the other hand, should it be submitted that the Nile River is endowed with ample waters to satisfy both current and future requirements of the basin states, a conflict of uses scenario will scarcely arise, obviating the need for engaging in the definition of equitable entitlements, at least in the immediate future.

This exacting analysis would be only indispensable. In establishing equitable entitlements under the UN Watercourses Convention, the evaluation process will, among others, take account of hydrological and hydrographic factors in each of the watercourse states.[3] Arguments relating to the right to equitable apportionment and by inference, whether a conflict between various riparian beneficial uses will actually arise are *ipso facto* affected by the overall quantity of water presented in each particular basin state or a river course. Depending on the conceptual approach adopted, such *total* volume accounted for joint riparian appropriation may refer to a meagre precipitation mass presented by a river channel or water endowments of the whole riverine basin.

This semantic exercise with regard to the definition of the physical scope of river courses is not entirely academic; it has a practical significance. It involves whether basin states should settle on a constricted notion of an international river course – in the traditional sense of *successive* or *contiguous* rivers so as to treat the Nile as a synonym of the surface water-body flowing in the *channel beds* of the two major branches – the Blue and White Nile rivers, or otherwise adopt the broader *drainage basin* approach.

Existing records had enlightened that the average discharge of the Nile River course – a physical process that operates on the surface and excludes both soil moisture, underground infiltration and the amount consumed by biotic environment, has greatly fluctuated over the years and seasons.[4] Bearing for variations in flood and drought years and the cycle of years selected for computation, the

2 The International Bank for Reconstruction and Development/The World Bank (2009) *World Development Report 2010, Development and Climate Change*, Washington, DC, World Bank, pp 125–140.

3 United Nations Convention on the Law of the Non-navigational Uses of International Watercourses, Adopted by the General Assembly of the United Nations on 21 May 1997.

4 Apart from national reports of the pertinent government ministries, the author chose to solely rely on information provided by professionals closely associated with hydrometeorology and hydrology and directly draw on their authority so as to minimize risks of statistical inconsistency widely observed in legal and hydropolitical literatures.

lowest and highest yearly flows during the period covering 1869–1945 had ranged between 45 bcm/yr and 137bcm/yr. During 1963–1991, the flow had varied between as low as 32bcm and as high as 140bcm/yr. Allowing for a longer span of time extending from 1900 to 1959, the mean annual flow draining into the Lake Nasser reservoir was accounted as standing at 84bcm/yr.[5]

In shielding water-quotas set under the 1959 treaty where Egypt and Sudan had been allocated some 74 of the 84bcm mean annual surface flow of the Nile, for instance, Egypt had habitually defended that its current shares represent, when compared 'to the natural flow of the river', only about 'six to eight percent of the total rainfall over the Nile basin'; it submitted that '. . . much is lost, some through evapo-transpiration . . . while yet, more seeps into the ground creating groundwater'. The 'bulk' drains to the sea, and hence Egypt's previous Water and Irrigation Minister Mahmoud Abu Zied reflected, what it actually utilizes is 'very little when compared to the potential'.[6] While the National Water Resources Plan-2017 admitted that at some point in time demand would outgrow available supply in Egypt, the general policy framing has been premised on a hydrological understanding that the Nile River is an abundant source of water.[7]

In consequence, in diplomatic, hydraulic and treaty negotiations, Egypt advised the Nile basin states to make use of the 'vast opportunity to increase their supply of the Nile water', by setting aside 'current disputes over the Nile . . . focused on *less than* five percent of the Nile valley's total water potential',[8] with an estimated annual precipitation of 1600bcm/yr.[9]

These include: H.E. Hurst, R.P. Black, Y.M. Simaika (1946) 'The Nile Basin, The Future Conservation of the Nile', vol VII, Physical Department Paper no 51, SOP Press, Cairo; Mohamed Kamal Ali (1997) 'The Projects for the Increase of the Nile Yield with Special Reference to the Jonglei Project', Water Conference, Mar De Plata, vol 4, no 31, pp 1815–16; A.B. Abalhoda (1993) 'Nile Basin General Information and Statistics', ICOLD 61st Executive Meeting, Cairo, pp 7–13.

5 Yet, Egypt's total supply has been augmented by re-use of return flows from municipalities, industry, and agriculture which accounted for a total of 4.5bcm/yr under patterns existing in the 1980s and which was projected to rise to about 12bcm/yr in the 1990s. This raises the usable supply close to 70bcm/yr of Nile waters. Kingsley E. Haynes and Dale Whittington (1981) 'International Management of the Nile, Stage Three?', *Geographical Review*, vol 71, no 1, pp 21–2.

6 Mahmoud Abu Zied (1999) 'Managing Turbulent Waters', *Al-Ahram Weekly Online*, September Issue 447, <http://weekly.ahram.org.eg/1999/447/spec3.htm>, last accessed December 2010.

Apparently, only a small amount of water drains to the Mediterranean Sea and even that occurs through seepage from the northern Delta lakes and through the barrages of Edifna and Faraskur on the Rosetta and Damietta distributaries.

7 Arab Republic of Egypt (2005) 'National Water Resources Plan for Egypt 2017', Ministry of Water Resources and Irrigation, Planning Sector, Cairo, p I-5.

8 Mahmoud Abu Zied (1999), note 6.

9 Similarly, Ambassador Aziza Fahmi, formerly a Deputy Assistant Minister for International Legal Affairs at the Egyptian Ministry of Water Resources argued that Egypt is actually using only 55.5bcm out of a total of 1900bcm of water resources in the Nile basin.

Aziza M. Fahmi (1999) 'Water management in the Nile, opportunities and constraints', published in *Sustainable management and rational use of water resources*, Institute for Legal Studies on International Community, Rome, p 137.

Similar positions had been reiterated by a series of Egyptian analysts and experts interviewed

Apparently, this model of computation presumed that all components affecting water equilibrium in a given basin constitute proper objects of riparian competition and use. This included considerable ratios of direct precipitation characteristically belonging to the surface on which it falls (dampening the soil or forming disconnected pools or springs), the amount intercepted in evaporation and evapotranspiration, all aspects of underground infiltration (including flows which will not drain back to the surface, and eventually to a common terminus), as well as the surface-flow of a river itself.

Against Ethiopia's objection that basin precipitation shall not form a basis in equitable allocations, the downstream proposition appeared to have counted in the available yield of the Nile River every flowing quantum of the resource, whether or not such is capable of being put to any direct beneficial uses in the riparian states. A broader drainage basin conception had been utilized to rationalize existing patterns of *water uses* as making up petite proportions of the entire riverine constitution and hence to ridicule upstream calls for fairer resource redistribution as uninformed or ill-conceived.

It is obvious that not all water resources of a basin can be brought within the category of utilizable resource. In fact, threats of scarcity have already prompted initiatives in new agricultural techniques, water engineering and hydrology where the conservation and efficient management of water resources have been highlighted in many parts of the basin, including Egypt and Ethiopia. As Whittington observed, the importance of such driving forces as water savings and conservation for the future supply and demand balance of water in the region has not gone unnoticed.[10] Most states are making expanded irrigation using Nile waters and planned increases in irrigation area far outstrip available water supplies, even assuming more water efficient irrigation technologies are adopted; indeed, in their quiet moments, the water resources professionals and policy makers in the Nile basin acknowledge that their plans for expanded irrigation cannot come to pass even with full basin-wide cooperation and more efficient irrigation technologies.[11]

by Al Jazeera's TV Documentary. 'Struggle Over the Nile – Masters No More, Al Jazeera English 2011'.

Ethiopia's objection that basin precipitation shall not form a basis in equitable allocations and that rain falling across the Blue Nile basin (which does not form part of the utilizable flow of the Nile River) merely constitutes a *national resource* was submitted by Asfaw Dingamo, Ethiopia's Minister of Water Resources, in Al Jazeera TV Documentary: 'Struggle Over the Nile – Masters No More, Al Jazeera English 2011'.

10 Dale Whittington (2004) 'Visions of Nile Basin Development', *Water Policy*, vol 6, p 11;

Prime Minister Meles Zenawi advocated the ideal solution in meeting current water shortfalls lies in adopting scientific conservations and dam-building works implemented in Ethiopia's deep gorges; every year, a huge volume of Nile waters is lost to excessive evaporation both in Egypt and Sudan due to the flat landscape and arid constitution of the areas in which downstream dams had been built. He argued the 'billions of cubic meters of waters' thus saved, if attended by a slight lowering of the operational level of the Aswan High Dam, can present water flows enough to meet not only the irrigational and hydropower requirements of Ethiopia, but also additional waters needed in further downstream developments.

Televised Interview, Ethiopian Radio and Television (2011).

11 Dale Whittington (2004), note 10.

If only circuitously, this analysis had rightly presumed that the utilizable water of a river course typically subjected to riparian negotiations and apportionment is not the same as the totality of water resources availed in a particular river basin. While considerations of environmental protection, conservation and management have no doubt laid focus on broader endowments and geographical stretches of river basins, the utilization of waters of an international river course have routinely been computed on the basis of a mass of flood eventually presented by the river bed of the main channel.

This vital geographical reality, which also bears impact on legal issues of equitable use and apportionment, explains why as a shared resource, the Nile River should be viewed as endowed with a very limited potential; it cannot proffer an adequate water-flows regime capable of circumventing future riparian competitions across the basin.

Legal characterization of 'international river course'

Traditionally, the international river expression had been employed to signify that the stakes of two or more states are involved. However, national conceptions and practices characterizing its scope have varied considerably. Should an international river – the geographical range over which the regime of international watercourses law applies – extend over a drainage basin, river basin, hydrographic basin or any other analogous physical constituency, or remain strictly confined to the channel-waters of a successive or contiguous river traversing across or forming a boundary between two or more states?

Geographical investigations, focusing on the natural hydraulic cycle of water systems have long established that the hydrology of a basin involves close physical interaction and interdependence between rivers, feeding streams, connected underground waters, lakes, marshes as well as wetland constituencies. The contemporary practice of states, principally swayed by considerations of cooperative management, protection and sustainable development of shared watercourses has progressively endorsed a conceptual framework that underlines this physical relationship between various components of a basin system, and thus, tended to highlight a basin-wide approach.

In advocating the broadest possible geographical scope for the law of international water courses, Birnie et al. argued in a widely referenced publication *International Law and the Environment* that while a broader interpretation may result in limitations on the use of a very substantial proportion of a state's internal river systems and catchment areas, a narrower approach all the same risks seriously impeding the efficient environmental management of transboundary flows.[12]

If the same conceptualization of rivers as a unity or interconnectedness, as opposed to the ordinary focus on the hydrological flows of river channels, has also

12 Patricia Birnie, Alan Boyle and Catherine Redgwell (2009) *International Law and the Environment*, New York, Oxford University Press, p 536.

moulded thoughts in international legal discourses aiming at the regulation and equitable allocation of shared watercourses remains less certain. Charles Bourne reflected:

It is one thing . . . to assert that international law, recognizing the interdependence of co-basin states, imposes an obligation on them to take heed of the injury their utilizations of water may inflict on each other; it is another to claim that international law requires co-basin states to plan development of a basin as a unit, taking into account all relevant factors within the territorial limits of the basin and ignoring everything pertaining to areas outside those limits.[13]

McCaffrey, former special rapporteur of the ILC that drafted the United Nations Watercourses Convention, observed that historically, and indeed until very recently, state practice in the field of international water courses was concerned, almost exclusively, with international rivers and lakes shared (i.e. traversing) between two or more states; a factually accurate definition of the term, based on the hydrologic cycle would include not only the main surface water channel and the water contained therein, but also other components of a water course system, in particular, tributaries and groundwaters.[14]

Caponera's much earlier view corresponds with this assertion: at the beginning of its development, the law relating to international watercourses had essentially been concerned with the question of boundary demarcation between sovereign states; theories of international water law unanimously recognized that the international character of a river emanates from its successive or contiguous nature. Only navigation on the main courses of international waterways was the object of consideration at the international level; yet, from the beginning of the twentieth century, new norms of water utilization evolved on international rivers for hydropower generation and irrigation, lately followed by international treaties and practice that adopted the international rivers and lakes system expression to extend international rules to tributaries, canals and secondary courses as well as to main streams.[15]

These views, expanding the physical scope of river courses, had particularly been influenced by growing geographical knowledge with regard to hydrologic and geologic conditions and requirements of integrated development of resources on the basis of community of interests. In relation to groundwaters, for instance, it has been maintained that they constitute a vital part of the unbroken cycle of water movement, continually replenishing the supply of fresh waters and hence, that the amount of groundwater moving to a watercourse is taken into account both when framing principles of international law and calculating the total volume of flow of the watercourse.[16]

13 Patricia Wouters (1997) *International Water Law, Selected Writings of Professor Charles B. Bourne*, London/The Hague, Kluwer Law International, p 3.

14 Stephen C. McCaffrey (2001) *The Law of International Watercourses: Non-Navigational Uses*, New York, Oxford University Press, p 35.

15 Dante A. Caponera (1992) *Principles of Water Law and Administration, National and International*, Rotterdam, A.A. Balkema, pp 184–5.

16 International Law Commission (1979) *Yearbook of International Law Commission*, vol 2, no 1, p 150.

On the other hand, several states had been particularly apprehensive that a broader legal characterization of the river concept not only entails wider environmental responsibility, it also impinges on the substance of core rights recognized under the international legal order. Opinions in a few international legal literatures had swerved undecidedly; initiatives to readily expand limits of the territorial scope of international regulation to tributaries, distributaries, underground water systems, lakes, seasonal floods and other water bodies connected to head-courses have constantly provoked agitation. Practice as presented below, and demonstrated during preparatory works of the ILC on the UN Watercourses Convention, as well as in the immediately preceding decades revealed that several states would be willing to admit such limitations against territorial sovereignty only by virtue of express treaty stipulations.

Typically, states situated in downstream positions had tended to advocate a broader scope of the international watercourses regime that not only 'provides protection against overreaching by . . . upstream neighbours',[17] but also acknowledges the hydraulic integrity of the main channels, tributaries, distributaries, smaller streams, lakes and underground water systems. On the other hand, upstream states generally endeavoured to confine the physical bound and limit the effect of international norms, including rules governing equitable allocation, to narrowly defined waters flowing along a river channel.

One of the earliest formal theses of the argument that advocated the hydraulic harmony of transboundary rivers was articulated in 1815 by Wilhelm von Humboldt of Prussia, where he argued, at the Congress of Vienna that a river must be envisaged as a unity. A century later, his opinion was literally reiterated by President Theodore Roosevelt when he promoted the view that each river system, from its headwaters in the forest to its mouth on the coast should be treated as a single unit.[18]

On the other hand, the core spirit of a countering-position espoused the historical concept of an international watercourse as merely referring to one which passes successively through or runs along the boundary of two or more sovereign territories. Among others, Griffin's memorandum composed in the 1950s for the US State Department argued that while it is evident that all interconnected waters of a basin are affected by international interest – including tributaries entirely situated within a single state, it does not necessarily follow that the rules of international law will always apply in the same way to all parts or all uses of the water.[19]

Quite too often, for instance, groundwater systems embody significant constituents of a river hydrology, but their regulation as parts of international water courses had not been without controversy. Fuentes' article on 'The utilization of international groundwater in general international law' summarized the contemporary opinion as follows: 'in general, writers recognize the lack of well-developed

17 International Law Commission (1979), note 16, p 153.

18 Wouters (1997), note 13, p 4.

19 William L. Griffin (1959) 'The use of international drainage basins under customary international law', *American Journal of International Law*, vol 53, no 1, p 77.

principles or norms regulating the utilization of transboundary groundwater'; the author referred to Albert Utton's work, which accentuated that the development of international law and legal institutions for managing the resource and for resolving disputes is in its infancy, concurring with Caponera's position that references in international treaties to underground waters are too limited to propose them in terms of customary international law.[20]

On the other hand, limitations associated with their status as subsidiary sources of international law notwithstanding, a fairly settled authority of national precedents was established in India in the Krishna Water Disputes Tribunal (1973), the Narmada Water Disputes Tribunal (1978) and Godavari Water Disputes Tribunal (1979).

No doubt, increasing knowledge with regard to the physical attributes of river systems has influenced juridical discourses across several river basins. In many instances, modern planning techniques had embraced comprehensive approaches, particularly in dealing with the conservation and management of transboundary rivers on the basis of the totality of water resources and ecology presented in a basin. This naturally makes sense. A wider basin constitutes the most ideal unit for investigating meteorological, hydrological and climatic facts of a particular region; it provides the essential factual basis for organizing and executing contending water resources development projects optimally and comprehensively.

Such a general predisposition in pro-conservation and management approaches or certain state practices notwithstanding, though, it would remain erroneous to propose solely on the basis of such accounts that customary international law has similarly considered the whole physical feature of a basin and basin-flows as proper units of international legal regulation.

Quite on the contrary, since the turn of the twentieth century, there had been a general impression among jurists, the treaty practice of states and certain institutional initiatives that the river basin conception did not form the physical unit for the application of legal rules of international law. In his earliest analysis on the permanent interdependence of the physical facts of a basin, Smith submitted in the 1930s that while the geography of a basin were to be the basis of the legal rules applicable to its development, such cannot be claimed as a positive rule of international law, but was merely put forth as a view of what the law ought to be, a reasonable inference supported by the general trend of practice.[21]

A great many treaties, mostly but not entirely composed in the first half of the twentieth century, had adopted a narrower definition of a river course, tending to highlight the territorial sovereignty of states. The core arguments had generally espoused that hydrologic and management considerations alone cannot compose an adequate explanation to transform feeding streams and other water bodies wholly situated in a states' territory into 'international' units of legal regulation.[22]

20 Guy S. Goodwin-Gilland and Stefan Talmon (1999) *The Reality of International Law, Essays in honor of Ian Brownlie*, Oxford, Oxford University Press, p 185.

21 Wouters (1997), note 13.

22 Treaty between the United States and Great Britain Respecting Boundary Waters between the United States and Canada, US Treaty Series No 584.

In 1992, the UN Economic Commission for Europe Convention for the Protection and Use of Transboundary Watercourses and International Lakes (UNECE) provided a legal framework for regional cooperation on shared water resources. Article 1 of the Convention defined transboundary waters as any surface or ground waters which mark, cross or are located on boundaries between two or more states. This perspective espoused with respect to the physical scope of regulation of river courses appeared to represent a discernible departure from the wider stipulations provided both under the Helsinki Rules and the Berlin Rules. Still, while the UNECE Watercourse Convention has remained the principal multilateral treaty governing environmental protection of European watercourses and represented the first framework convention for dealing with international waters, several treaties negotiated under its framework had instead chosen to extend their regulation over broader geographical areas.[23]

On the other hand, the second half of the twentieth century witnessed an overwhelming count of bilateral and regional legal arrangements and resolutions setting out norms and institutional frameworks for the regulation of shared river courses by subscribing to an approach that bears resemblance to the drainage basin conception.[24] Traditional approaches such as successive or contiguous rivers

Article VI of the 1909 Treaty signed between the USA and Great Britain (representing Canada) with a view to regulating the use of boundary rivers delineated the physical scope of the treaty as applying *merely* over boundary waters, which it defined consists of 'waters from main shore of lakes and rivers and connecting waterways, or portions thereof' along which the international boundary between the two states passes. The definition excluded aspects of the boundary rivers including 'tributary waters which in their natural channel would flow in to such lakes or rivers and waterways or the waters of rivers flowing across the boundary'.

The Treaty on the River Plate Basin (1969) called for physical integration of the basin development and promotion of projects of common interest, but an annexed resolution maintained the contiguous and successive international waters formulation, apparently undermining the original thesis. (Done at Brasilia, 23 April 1969, between Argentina, Brazil, Bolivia, Paraguay and Uruguay.)

The convention between the Federal Republic of Nigeria and the Republic of Niger (1990) declared that its articles shall govern the equitable development, conservation and use of the water resources 'in the river basins which are *bisected* by, or form the *common frontier* between' the contracting parties. (Agreement between the Federal Republic of Nigeria and the Republic of Niger Concerning the Equitable Sharing in the Development, Conservation and Use of their Common Water Resources, Maiduguri, 18 July 1990.)

23 Birnie, Boyle and Redgwell (2009), note 12, p 538. A few examples included the 1994 Danube Convention, the 1994 Agreements on the Meuse and Scheldt and the 1999 Rhine Convention.

24 Some examples included: The Act Regarding Navigation and Economic Cooperation between the States of the Niger Basin (1963), Done at Niamey, 26 October 1963, (Benin, Cameroon, Chad, Guinea, Niger, Nigeria and Burkina-Faso), UN Treaty Series, Vol 587, No 8506, p 9. (The Niger Basin regime for collective utilization and regulation of the shared resource covered all aspects of utilization of 'the river Niger, its tributaries and sub-tributaries');

The Southern African Development Community (SADC) Protocol on Shared Watercourse Systems, SADC Protocol on Shared Watercourse Systems, Done at Johannesburg, 28 August 1995. (The Protocol's rules would apply over the 'geographical area determined by the watershed limits of a system of waters, including underground waters, flowing into a common terminus'.)

The Convention Relating to the Status of the River Gambia (1978), Done at Kaolack, 30 June 1978. (Guinea, Senegal and Gambia; the physical scope of its application extended to the 'Gambia river and its tributaries.)

were generally regarded as 'too restricted a basis . . . in view of the need to take account of the hydrologic unity of the water system'.[25]

Principally, this trend was advocated in the practice of international legal societies working on the progressive development and codification of rules and principles of international law.

Over the years, two notable bodies – the International Law Association (ILA) and the Institute of International Law (IIL) – as well as regional and bilateral treaty frameworks had ventured to conceptualize international rivers with a particular prudence and reservation. The institutional perspectives are chronologically presented and analysed as follows.

A declaration issued by the IIL to regulate the uses of international water courses for purposes other than navigation (1911) obliquely adopted a narrower conceptual approach with regard to rivers, although the preamble had made some reference to the notion of physical interdependences. It recognized that limitations against rights of utilization of riparian states are applied in respect only of streams 'forming a frontier between two states' or 'traversing successively the territories of two or more states'.[26] Five decades on, the Salzburg Resolutions reframed the contour of regulation to encompass all uses of waters 'which are part of a river or a watershed extending upon the territory of two or more states'.[27]

Likewise, the Resolution of Dubrovnik (1956) by the ILA initially adopted a restrictive characterization of an international river as 'one which flows through or between the territories of two or more states'. However, in a distinct

Other older treaties included:

Agreement Between Great Britain, France, and Italy respecting Abyssinia, London, 13 December 1906.

(The tripartite pact concluded formally stretched the prior hydraulic interests of Great Britain in 'the Nile basin, and more specifically as regards the regulation of the waters of that *river* and *its tributaries*'.)

The Exchange of Notes between the UK and Italy Respecting Concessions for a Barrage at Lake Tana and a Railway Across Abyssinia from Eritrea to Italian Somaliland, Rome, 14 and 20 December 1925;

(Under Article III, Great Britain promised to uphold Italy's exclusive sphere of economic influence in western Ethiopia provided that the Italian government 'recognizing the prior hydraulic rights of Egypt and Sudan, will not engage to construct on the head waters of the Blue or White Niles or *their tributaries or effluents* any work which might sensibly modify their flow in to the Nile'.)

Agreement between the Belgian Government and the Government of the United Kingdom of Great Britain and Northern Ireland regarding water rights on the boundary between Tanganyika and Ruanda-Urundi, London, 22 November 1934. (The agreement governed the use of those rivers and streams which form part of the boundary between the Tanganyika territory and Ruanda-Urundi or which flow from one of those territories into the other.)

25 International Law Commission (1976) 'First report on the Law of the Non-Navigational uses of international watercourses', *Yearbook of International Law Commission*, vol 2, no 1, p 185.

26 Institute of International Law, International Regulation Regarding the Use of International Watercourses for Purposes other than Navigation, Declaration of Madrid, Preamble, 20 April 1911.

27 Institute of International Law, Resolution on the Use of International Non-Maritime Waters, Salzburg, 11 September 1961.

discernment of legal implications of this phrasing, the Resolution recommended states to endeavour join hands in making 'full utilization of a river . . . from a point of view of the river basin as an integrated whole'.[28]

In 1958, a resolution of the same institution, that apparently influenced the later courses adopted by the ILC radically changed the restrictive approach maintained earlier. The declaration introduced the basin conception as the foundation of all legal analyses. Hence, a drainage basin was described as 'an area within the territories of two or more states in which all the streams of flowing surface water . . . drain in to a common outlet . . . '. The agreed principles of international law that set out substantive rights and duties of riparian states, the resolution further held, should treat a river in a drainage basin 'as integrated whole, and not in a piecemeal'.[29]

Apparently, this rationalization propounded by the ILA had been one of utilitarian than a reiteration of custom. The Association reasoned that in the face of rapid population increase and scarcity, water resources should be used to produce the greatest economic benefit, hence adopting the view that cooperative development of a basin based on the study of all possible uses of waters of a basin will almost invariably produce greater benefits than a scheme based on a study of only one part, or of one use, of the waters.[30]

This tone expanding the geographical range of regulation of international law appeared sturdier under the Helsinki Rules of the ILA (1966). The Rules equated international drainage basins to all physical stretches 'extending over two or more states determined by the watershed limits of the system of waters, including surface and underground waters, flowing in to a common terminus.[31]

However, it was admitted the ILA's characterization of international drainage basins contradicted the definitional explanations afforded during the working sessions of the Helsinki Rules, wherein a watercourse had merely been considered as referring to 'a channel for water, i.e., a river or at most, a system of rivers and lakes'.[32] Despite the obvious utility of a broadly comprehensive definition of a watercourse and its clear endorsement in international policy, Birnie et al. submitted, this remains a relatively recent approach, only partially reflected in state practice.[33]

28 International Law Association, Statement of Principles, Resolution of Dubrovnik, 1956.

29 International Law Association, Agreed Principles of International Law, Resolution on the Use of the Waters of International Rivers, New York, 1958.

30 Wouters (1997), note 13, p 5.

31 International Law Association (1966); the International Law Association explicitly recognized the applicability of the Helsinki Rules to groundwater in its Seoul Groundwater Rules of 1986.

The Seoul Groundwater Rules recognized that even groundwater that has no significant connection to surface watercourses can be international in its effects and thus, should be international in its management. International Law Association (2004), Berlin Conference, Water Resources Law, Fourth Report p 11.

<http://www.internationalwaterlaw.org/documents/intldocs/ILA_Berlin_Rules-2004.pdf>, last accessed December 2010.

32 Wouters (1997), note 13, p 269.

33 Birnie, Boyle and Redgwell (2009), note 12, p 537.

Still, the latest congregation of the ILA held in Berlin (2004) with a view to considering new developments in international watercourses law carried forward the drainage basin concept.[34] The ILA acknowledged its approach was different from and broader than the nearest equivalent term in the UN Convention which dealt solely with surface watercourses and tributary groundwater and hence too restrictive since the same obligations apply to groundwaters as apply to surface waters, regardless of whether the ground waters are interconnected with a watercourse, or largely independent of any watercourse.[35]

Legal dilemmas confounding the International Law Commission

Mystified by divergent practice and conception of states, one of the daunting tasks inherited by the ILC when, in 1970, it undertook on the study of the law of non-navigational uses of international watercourses had been to identify with a particular specificity the physical reach of international watercourses. Both the Commission and the Sixth Legal Committee of the United Nations General Assembly admitted discrepancies in theories and state practice and were caught by a dense quandary of whether or not to extend the spatial scope of rivers to river basins as such.

The employ of the drainage basin concept as a basis for discussions involving the physical cover of river courses was not considered when the UN General Assembly commissioned work on the systematic development of the UN watercourses convention. During the early drafting deliberations and particularly in response to the UN Secretary General's circular issued in January of 1975 inviting all member states to communicate comments on the ILC's questionnaires, two groups of states appeared to adopt contrasting positions.

A cluster, predominantly comprising states in downstream positions, including Argentina, Barbados, Finland, Indonesia, the Netherlands, Pakistan, Philippines, Sweden, Venezuela and USA espoused the drainage basin framing to determine the scope of the commission's work on the uses of international watercourses.[36] On the other hand, a number of states participating in the Commission's works in various capacities, and notably Austria, Brazil, Colombia, Poland, Spain, France, Turkey and Nicaragua voiced strong support for the definition embodied in Articles I and II of the Regulation of 24 March 1815 . . . and the Final Act of the Congress of Vienna of 9 June 1815.[37] Under the instruments, only constituents of an

34 International Law Association (2004), Berlin Conference, Water Resources Law, Fourth Report, Article 3.
<http://www.internationalwaterlaw.org/documents/intldocs/ILA_Berlin_Rules-2004.pdf>, last accessed December 2010.

35 International Law Association (2004), note 34, p11.

36 International Law Commission (1976) *Yearbook of International Law Commission*, vol 2, no 2, p 157.

37 Article 108 of the Final Act provided that 'The powers whose states are *separated* or *crossed* by the same navigable river engage to regulate, by common consent, all that regards its navigation . . .'; reprinted in Edward Hertslett, *Commercial Treaties and Conventions between Great Britain and Foreign Powers 3*.

international watercourse that 'separated or cut across the territory of two or more states', were considered as objects of international treatment.[38]

In effect, this framing had endeavoured to exclude 'the physical portion of land contained within the *divortium acquarum* of an international river'.[39] Canada favoured the same approach, but hinted its concern that a 'legal definition should be a workable starting point, and not a limiting factor that would preclude consideration of any appropriate geographical unit when specific, concrete problems are considered'.[40] Likewise, the Federal Republic of Germany espoused a parallel position, qualifying in its note that 'it should not be overlooked that the supply of water to countries below a stream may depend just as much on water withdrawals from a national tributary as from the international watercourse concerned.'[41]

Under circumstances where expressions eluded a steady pattern of state perception even among the very few states actively involved in the Commission's deliberations, the UN body's undertaking was gridlocked for several years in the successive stages of the preparatory works. The Commission was unable to choose between formulating the rules on the basis of a narrow classical notion of international watercourses (successive/contiguous rivers) which some argued represents the time honoured and traditional definition, on the one hand, and the territorial conception of a drainage basin which warranted a greater degree of intrusion over larger portions of sovereign territories of basin states, on the other.

Hence, the Commission's admission of the difficulty encountered in choosing from among scores of irreconcilable theories and its eventual declaration that the concept of drainage basin did not illicit 'support from a significant group of riparian states'[42] could not have come as a surprise. For the obvious reasons reiterated earlier, the opposition had been firm and the precedent inconsistent.

The first draft of the UN Watercourses Convention specified the application of the legal regime to the use of waters of international watercourses, but failed to plainly declare whether such phraseology also comprises groundwaters, adjoining small-surface runoffs and major tributaries. As late as in 1991 when the drafting process had reached advanced stages, members of the ILC's Drafting Committee were more divided: 12 were in favour, and 5 or 6 against including groundwater in the concept of watercourse.[43] Even more uncertain had been the Special Rapporteur's account issued in the same period, which, although based on a wider logic, admitted that 'he saw no reason to extend the proposed legal regime to cover groundwater in general, despite its importance in hydrology'.[44] The reference to groundwater was deleted, but eventually reinstated in some form in the final edition of the Convention.

38 International Law Commission (1976) *Yearbook of International Law Commission*, vol 2, no 2, p 157.
39 International Law Commission (1976), note 38, p 153.
40 International Law Commission (1976), note 38.
41 International Law Commission (1976), note 38.
42 International Law Commission (1979) *Yearbook of International Law Commission*, vol 2, no 2, p 164.
43 International Law Commission (1991) *Yearbook of International Law Commission*, vol 1, p 66.
44 International Law Commission (1991), note 43, p 58

Hence, Article 2 of the UN Watercourses Convention (1997) defined the notion of international watercourse as 'a system of surface waters and groundwater, constituting by virtue of their physical relationship a unitary whole, and normally flowing into a common terminus'.

The expression, an outcome of a continuous process of consensus and compromises, consciously avoided employing any of the rivalling phrases hitherto discussed. But on substance, it would appear that the Convention had significantly tilted to the basin notion. McCaffrey concluded: 'the definition takes into account the fact that most fresh water is underground and that most of this groundwater is related to or interacts with surface water'.[45]

The Convention's definition applying over all surface waters and tributary ground waters is still narrower than the wider connotations implied in the ILA's latest declaration under the Berlin Rules, where, for instance, ground waters had been included without qualifications.

Hence, under the Convention, ground waters which on account of their geological features do not discharge substantially or flow back to the surface river system are excluded. The restriction implicit in the common terminus proviso which highlights that basin water bodies are hydrologically interrelated, would also appear to leave out from the dominion of river courses some key hydrologic components of the water balance, such as water volumes retained as soil moistures and significant masses of a river flow consumed by biotic entities.

As indicated above, although the Convention's stipulation tilted to the drainage basin concept, apparently, its draft failed to please a few adherents of the drainage basin approach. During the preparatory deliberations, for instance, Egypt battled the Commission's choice of terminology, registering an official reservation against the proposed resolution. Anxious over the impending effects of the definition discussed above, Egypt argued it does not believe 'the expression international watercourse is inconsistent with the very concept of the basin of an international river'. It submitted that an international watercourse is in fact 'a part of it (a basin) and therefore the use of this new term cannot under any circumstances affect the rights and obligations acquired under bilateral or regional international agreements or the established norms and relations among states on various international river spaces'.[46]

In the subsequent decades, Egypt's challenge against the Convention's stipulation had been reiterated at the highest levels of government: 'with the definition of the basin used . . . the agreement (i.e. the Convention) talks only of the channel while we believe it should talk of the basin as a whole so as to cover all resources, and not just the water in the river', Mahmoud Abuzeid, former Minister of Water Resources and Irrigation argued.[47]

45 Stephen McCaffrey (2001) 'The Contribution of the UN Convention on the Law of the non Navigational uses of International Watercourses', *Int J Global Environmental Issues*, vol 1, p 251.

46 United Nations General Assembly (1997), Convention on the Law of Non-navigational Uses of International Watercourses, Session 51, Meeting 99, Agenda Item 144, May 21, Proceedings.

47 Mahmoud Abu Zied (1999), note 6.

To summarize, one can observe that in spite of the divergences in opinion, one fact has lingered sufficiently evident. Neither the UN General Assembly, when authorising the ILC to work on the codification and progressive development of a new watercourses regime, nor the Commission itself had concluded that an international water course is the practical or notional equivalent of international drainage basin.[48] In fact, during the commissioning stages, the General Assembly had rejected Finland's explicit request to cross-refer to the Helsinki Rules that embraced the basin conception. In the face of conflicting theories, the Commission chose to 'accept the ambiguity of the term international watercourse and determine to what extent the Commission and states are prepared to resolve the problems that arise from the physical aspects of the hydrographic process in dealing with specific uses of fresh water'.[49]

However the Commission may have opted to couch the concept, it is obvious right from the outset that none of the alternatives presented could have attracted support from a significant group of states. While the role of the UN Watercourses Convention in influencing riparian discourse cannot be understated, perhaps, this partly explains why the Convention, a little more than a decade since it was adopted by the General Assembly, has yet to garner enough ratification to bring its dictates to force. The post-adoption practice of states had simply continued to epitomize discontent and hesitation with regard to some key principles and definitions incorporated in the Convention.

Hence, the sheer scale of inconsistency and dearth of resolve demonstrated in the treaty practice of states and institutional initiatives proves that customary international law has not yet evolved to a stage where a basin hydrology can *ipso facto* be treated as a single object of international regulation for purposes of equitable utilization and allocations. Despite a broader support for the drainage basin concept in modern treaty practices and works of international bodies, Birnie et al. concluded the evidence of disagreement in the ILC suggests that it is premature to attribute customary status to this concept as a definition of the geographical scope of international water resources law.[50] This implies that riparian obligations implicit in a wider depiction of the physical scope of a river course cannot be readily admitted except in circumstances where bilateral or regional treaties have expressly provided to that effect.

'International watercourse' under the Nile Cooperative Framework Agreement

The conceptual uncertainty under international law has transpired to affect new developments with respect to the cooperative management and equitable allocation of shared watercourses, including in the Nile basin. While all components of

48 International Law Commission (1976), note 38, p 156.
49 International Law Commission (1979), note 16, p 158.
50 Birnie, Boyle and Redgwell (2009), note 12, p 539.

a hydrographical system, even those which might appear autonomous [such as independent groundwater systems and glaciers], are actually interrelated . . . the existence of those natural links was not enough to dictate the regime applicable to watercourses, although it was a fact which could not be ignored, particularly in view of the Commission's efforts to progressively develop the law.[51]

In consequence, a juridical proposition that assimilates the Nile flow regime as the practical equivalent of the whole heap of precipitation that falls across the basin would not only be contested for dearth of legal authority under international law, it would also lack clear precedent in any state practice. Notable references to the USA-Mexican, USA-Canadian river disputes, particular decisions of the interstate river dispute tribunals in India and the extensive review of numerous treaties and conventions compiled by the ILC as evidence of state practice corroborate this fact; no single state has ever claimed an uncontested right to significant proportions of the *surface flow* of a river course solely on the basis of the fact that quantitatively, its water utilization represents a small proportion of the entire water balance presented in a basin.

Therefore, it is not surprising that the Nile Basin Cooperative Framework Agreement had endeavoured to instil a very cautious approach in this respect. Article 1, on the scope of the Cooperative Framework, introduced its regulations would apply to the 'use, development, protection, conservation and management of the Nile River Basin and its resources'. However, two distinct terms were employed in connection with the geographical area of the application of rules and principles contained in the Cooperative Framework, depending on the specific functions contemplated.

Article 2(a) on 'use of terms' provided that the 'Nile River Basin', representing the 'geographical area determined by the watershed limits of the Nile River system of waters', should be used only in connection with issues of 'environmental protection, conservation or development'.

On the other hand, a new notion was introduced under Article 2(b), the 'Nile River System', which embodied 'the Nile River and the surface waters, and ground waters which are related to the Nile River'; this terminology, the Cooperative Framework Agreement announced, should be used 'where there is reference to utilization of water'.

As a result of such distinction, where issues pertaining to the right of each riparian state in the Nile basin to equitable uses and allocation are considered, the CFA had intended to do away with wider connotations of the drainage basin approach espoused both under the Helsinki and Berlin Rules of the ILA. Implicit in the stipulation and the very unprecedented design of introducing two definitional terms would also appear to be that the particular object of regulation of the CFA had been confined to waters of the Nile River, which, although embodied in the Nile River channel, surface waters and tributary groundwaters, would in actuality represent only such flows as would be eventually availed in the riverbed of the Nile river proper. Both conceptually and in practice, this important categorization

51 International Law Commission (1991), note 43, p 61.

discards downstream legal propositions which equated the Nile flow regime, the quantum-basis on which future equitable apportionments are worked out, as the equivalent of the whole mass of precipitation falling across the river basin.

Equity and contending interests in the Nile

So far, the discussion had endeavoured to reveal the debates under international law that involved the issue of how the concept of international watercourse had been perceived as a physical unit of regulation and by inference, which particular components of the entire water balance of river basins constitute the objects of common riparian regulation and appropriation.

The objective of this theoretical converse has been to reveal the prevalence of potential scarcity and a conflict of uses scenario between contending riparian interests, and to highlight that the Nile River would probably not present an adequate water-flows regime capable of circumventing riparian competition in the beneficial uses of the watercourse.

The profundity of uses of the resource affecting both social and economic structures in the basin and potentially generating a complex conflict of uses setting cannot be grasped adequately without framing the subject in a wider perspective. This involves a brief presentation of resource projections and actual water resource developments on the ground.

One of the major issues discussed in connection with efforts of promoting cooperation in the Nile basin, Caponera observed, was the allocation and management of water resources in a region characterized by water deficiency.[52] Specifics of hydrologic data submitted earlier had enlightened that the mean annual discharge of the Nile River had ranged between 81bcm/yr and 84bcm/yr as measured at Aswan. In 1997, FAO's publication on irrigation potential in Africa estimated that across the Nile basin, the gross irrigational water requirements stands at 124bcm/yr, far beyond the river's mean annual supplies, of which 19.9bcm/yr was in Ethiopia, 38.5bcm/yr in Sudan and 57.4bcm/yr in Egypt.[53]

Contending interests in Egypt, Sudan and Ethiopia

In Egypt, where the national economic activity has concentrated along the north–south strip of the Nile valley and its immediate reaches, agriculture accounted for some 13.1 percent of the GDP and involved nearly a third of the nation's labour force in 2010; in 2000, FAO estimated that agricultural water withdrawal draining an area of some 3.3 million hectares had accounted for 59bcm/yr, representing 86 percent of the country's total renewable water resources,[54] a vastly significant pro-

52 Caponera (1993), note 15, p 629.

53 FAO (1997) 'Irrigation potential in Africa, a basin approach', *Land and Water Bulletin*, p 4.

54 FAO, FAO's Information System on Water and Agriculture, Geography, climate and population, Egypt (Tables 1, 4), <http://www.fao.org/nr/water/aquastat/countries/egypt/index.stm>, last accessed December 2010; Al-Ahram, the *Egyptian Weekly Online* (Issue 979, 31 December 2009) reported that the total yearly water consumption in Egypt is about 78bcm/yr per year: the differ-

portion of which has been availed by the Nile River. Agriculture also contributed 30 percent of Egypt's commodity exports (13.7 percent of the total GDP), making it among the top revenue-generating sectors.[55] Over a span of a similar period, industry, withdrawing 6 percent of the total water resources, accounted for a staggering 37.7 percent of the GDP, and employed 17 percent of the labour force.[56] Municipalities utilized 8 percent of the total waters; navigational uses largely constituted the 3,500km waterways along the Nile River, Lake Nasser, and numerous canals in the Delta, along with the generation of hydropower, made up a slightly lesser percentage, withdrawing a mere 4bcm/yr of waters.[57]

Evidently, in terms of impact produced on the overall national wealth and the sheer size of population drawn in, irrigational and industrial uses are hoisted high among others to vitally assume equivalent positions.

Against a backdrop of an unsuitable climatic condition and vulnerable hydrologic settings, Egypt has for years pursued an irrigation expansion policy that advocates the attainment of food security and a major exporting status of certain farm produces as cherished themes of the national security agenda.[58]

Perceptibly, such policy perspectives have had a global drift and particularly so in regions characterized by higher scales of water scarcity, including the Nile basin. An important factor influencing the management of water in arid regions had been the predominant understanding of food security in such countries, i.e. the access by all people at all times to enough food for an active and healthy life. While the aim has been clear, there are different understandings as to how to reach at this goal; a widely held interpretation of food security had concentrated on self-sufficiency, implying independence from the international market.[59]

Egypt, one of the world's largest food importers, refutes its present agricultural strategy has been based on food self-sufficiency as such, but on maintaining food

ence between water budget of 58bcm/yr and the actual consumption, about 20bcm/yr is covered by recycling agricultural drainage, abstraction from shallow aquifers, and treatment of municipal sewage.

On the other hand, FAO's report estimated that considering average water requirement of 13,000 cubic meters per hectare per year in the Nile Valley and the Delta, about 4,420,000 hectares can be irrigated using 57.4bcm/yr of Nile waters.

55 Egypt State Information Service, Agriculture <http://www.sis.gov.eg/En/Story.aspx?sid=835>, last accessed December 2010.

56 FAO, FAO's Information System on Water and Agriculture, note 533; Central Intelligence Agency, The World Fact Book: Egypt <https://www.cia.gov/library/publications/the-world-factbook/geos/eg.html>, last accessed December 2010.

57 FAO (2005) Egypt Basic statistics and population, *FAO Water Report 29*, Table 1. <http://www.fao.org/nr/water/aquastat/countries/egypt/index.stm>, last accessed December 2010.

58 In an interview with the *Weekly Al Ahram*, Irrigation Minister Abu Zeid announced that 'agriculture shall be the basis of all of Egypt's growth and prosperity' and projected to achieve this without increasing 'Egypt's share of the water under the 1959 Agreement'.

Egypt has been *self-sufficient* in nearly all agricultural commodities with the exception of cereals, oils and sugar; and these exceptions made the country one of the world's largest food importers.

59 Jutta Brunnee and Stephen J. Toope (2002) 'The Changing Nile Basin Regime: Does law matter?' *Harv Int'l LJ*, vol 43, no 1, p 121.

security, by capitalizing on its competitive advantages.[60] Such advantages take account of opportunities afforded in regional and global markets.

Yet, in a region where an uneven distribution of water resources has been a typical phenomenon, the effect of such policies where water could have been exported from water-abundant to water-scarce areas of the Nile basin in the form of cereals has barely been employed in practice, nor endorsed in political discourses. In a spirit that ostensibly targeted the achievement of food self-sufficiency, Egypt continued to produce for export and local consumption large quantities of basic staples and agricultural commodities – including wheat, sugar cane, rice, potatoes and cotton, although in some cases such produces attract comparatively lower values at the international markets.

This could generate dire effects on the long-term sustainability of the agriculture system as such; but most importantly, the negative impact of huge water abstractions on the region's water balance and respective entitlements of the riparian states had triggered serious apprehension across the upstream Nile.

Egypt's agricultural expansion picked added momentum in the 1990s, following the launch of new desert reclamation projects. The new schemes called for expanded patterns of utilization and further strained existing provisions of the water resource base.

Hence, when the National Water Resources Plan was adopted, two vital points had been highlighted: the first involved imperative steps that should be taken to safeguard its existing water resources in the future under conditions of growing population and a more or less fixed water availability scenario;[61] a second measure called for the adoption of conservatory measures and diplomatic efforts to obtain 'new water resources through cooperation with the Nile basin riparian states to increase (its) water supply'.[62]

In both cases, the Nile River resources will continue to be subjected to extended scales and types of beneficial interventions in Egypt. This will not only impact on the social and economic welfare of considerable proportions of the basin's

60 For instance, in 1997, some 29 percent of Egypt's import bill had reportedly been dedicated for this purpose.

Arab Republic of Egypt (2005) 'National Water Resources Plan for Egypt 2017', Cairo, Ministry of Water Resources and Irrigation, Planning Sector, p II-31.

61 Arab Republic of Egypt (2005), note 60, p XVIII.

To cope with increasing challenges of water scarcity, the National Plan outlined three interrelated measures:

1. Developing additional water resources (through increased groundwater withdrawal of up to 3.5bcm/yr in the western desert; rainfall, flash flood harvesting and use of blackish groundwater; and cooperation with the Nile basin states that may lead to additional inflow into Lake Nasser);

2. Measures targeting better use of existing resources (which anticipated irrigation improvement projects, potential increase of agricultural drainage reuse to 8.4bcm/yr in 2017, potential increase of treated waste water re-use to 2.5bcm/yr by the year 2017, the introduction of new crop varieties such as early maturing, salt tolerant seeds and shifting of cropping patterns to less water consuming crops); 3. Measures targeting the protection of water quality and environment.

62 Nile 2002 Conference (2000) Proceedings of VIIIth Nile 2002 Conference, Country Paper: Egypt, Addis Ababa, p 53.

constituencies, but also generate conflict with the present and projected uses by other communities in the same region.

On the other hand, in Sudan where a significant percentage of its physical landscape situates within the Nile basin, nearly all economic activities of import are directly impacted by the availability and sustained flow of the Nile River and its tributaries. While rain-fed agriculture continued to cover the largest area, it is irrigated land, extending over a total equipped area of 1.9 million hectares that actually contributes more than half of the total volume of agricultural production in the country.[63] In 2000, Sudanese water withdrawals, both from surface and groundwaters, stood at 37.32bcm/yr per annum, i.e. 56 percent of the nation's total renewable water resources; non-Nilotic streams yielded only insignificant fraction: 7bcm/yr. Agricultural uses constituted the largest, 36.07bcm/yr, followed by municipal (0.99bcm/yr) and industrial uses (0.26bcm/yr).[64]

The position of an agriculture-driven economy, greatly depending on the munificence of the Nile River system, is further revealed in the verity that in 2002 the sector had engaged some 57 percent of the two nations' 41 million inhabitants and accounted for about 90 percent of the country's non-oil export earnings.[65]

Sudan had acknowledged long before the ceding of the South that it had virtually consumed its Nile Waters *share* of 20.5bcm/yr (measured in mid Sudan), taking into account the storage and irrigation projects under execution.[66] Among other themes, its national policies in the sector have aimed at maintaining its divide under a bilateral agreement concluded with Egypt.[67]

Both in Egypt and the Sudan where the maximum estimated irrigation potential extends up to over five million hectares – the best and marginal soils included – growing population pressures have prompted policy makers to labour on revitalizing irrigational and water control infrastructures and to place the agricultural sector as a vital column of the development drive. As a result, drastic rises in the respective water requirements of the two riparian states would be expected in the future. Realization of the national projections in both states would clearly overwhelm nature's ability to provide for the individual need of each of the eleven riparian states in the basin.

In contrast to Egypt and Northern Sudan, Ethiopia is endowed with considerable surface water resources that range between 110bcm/yr and 122bcm/yr, with a 0 percent dependency ratio on out-of-territory supplies. Ethiopia's Blue

63 FAO, FAO's Information System on Water and Agriculture, Geography, climate and population, Sudan <http://www.fao.org/nr/water/aquastat/countries/sudan/index.stm>, last accessed December 2010; FAO (2005) Sudan, Basic statistics and population, *FAO Water Report 29*, Table 1.

64 FAO (2005), note 63.

65 FAO (2005), note 63.

66 Nile 2002 Conference (1996) Proceedings of the IVth Nile 2002 Conference, Country Paper: Sudan, 26–29 February, Kampala, p C-26.

67 Nile 2002 Conference (1997) 'Comprehensive Water Resources Development of the Nile Basin: Priorities for the New Century', Proceedings of the Vth Nile 2002 Conference, Country paper: Sudan, 24–28 February, Addis Ababa, p 58.

Nile basin region alone accounts for 50 percent of the total average annual runoff and over 40 percent of the national agricultural production.[68] In 2002, agriculture utilized a meagre 5.2bcm/yr of waters, and in 2008, economically active citizens engaged in the sector (both irrigated and rain-fed) represented 37 percent of its 80.3 million population; municipal and industrial water withdrawals made up for 0.33 and 0.02bcm/yr of waters respectively.[69]

On the other hand, on a national scale, the total area equipped for irrigation was a mere 289,000 hectares in 2001,[70] of which only 160,000 hectares was actually developed,[71] with account also taken of the fact that a considerable percentage of irrigational schemes in Ethiopia had traditionally been developed outside the Nile sub-basin.[72]

However, the potential remains great; the country's irrigation potential in the Nile sub-basin (constituted of the Blue Nile, Baro-Akobo and Tekeze-Atbara sub-basins) extends over 2,219,700 hectares; on the basis of an average irrigational water requirement of 9,000 cubic meters per hectare, irrigated agriculture alone would require a total of 19.98bcm of waters a year (FAO Water Report 29 (2005)).

In the last two decades, Ethiopia has progressively eyed on the great potentials of its irrigational and hydropower endowments. For long, achievements in the field of agriculture – a vital sector that has hitherto generated nearly all its export earnings – has been negatively impacted by a mix of factors. Farming practices remained prehistoric and in smallholdings; in several constituents, rainfall has been scarce and the patterns unpredictable; drought, attended by intermittent famine has raged year after year resulting in a constant state of deprivation. By the turn of the last millennium, Ethiopia was barely irrigating more than 200,000 hectares of farmland although nationally a total of 3.7 million hectares had been identified as 'potentially irrigable'.[73]

68 Federal Democratic Republic of Ethiopia (1999) 'Abay River Integrated Development Master Plan Project', Ministry of Water Resources, Addis Ababa, Phase 3, vol 1, p 13.

69 FAO (2005), FAO's Information System on Water and Agriculture, Geography, climate and population, Ethiopia <http://www.fao.org/nr/water/aquastat/countries/ethiopia/index.stm>, last accessed December 2010.

FAO (2005), Ethiopia, Basic statistics and population, *FAO Water Report 29*, Table 1.

70 Federal Democratic Republic of Ethiopia (1999), note 68.

71 Nile 2002 Conference (2000), Proceedings of VIIIth Nile 2002 Conference, Country Paper: Ethiopia, 26–29 June, Addis Ababa, p 55.

72 According to the Water Ministry's report, the total irrigational area developed at the national level is about 200,000 hectares, 60–70 percent of which is situated in the Awash basin. Schemes along the Nile basin account for 29 percent of the total irrigated land, notably represented through the Fincha Sugar Project covering 6,200 hectares, with further expansion of 3,100 hectares and some 30,000 hectares of land developed under small-scale schemes, both private and public. Federal Democratic Republic of Ethiopia (1999), note 68, p 99.

Since the indicated period though, Ethiopia's irrigational utilization of the Nile waters has been propped by new agricultural openings attached to the Tana Beles and Tekeze hydropower facilities, the Koga dam and Lake Tana Area projects.

73 Ministry of Water Resources (2002) 'Water Sector Development Program, Irrigation Development Programme Report', Addis Ababa (unpublished).

As a result, a plan for rapid agriculture-based industrialization which projected to exploit the land, water and peasant labour resources of an agricultural society has been highlighted as a vital policy frame to revive the momentum of the national economic development enterprise. Among others, the institution of a series of hydro-electric power facilities and irrigational schemes had been identified as the most pressing undertaking of the government.

A convenient stage for implementation of this national objective was set in place with the commissioning of studies for integrated master plan projects of the twelve major national basins, encompassing areas along the Blue Nile, Baro-Akobo and Tekeze sub-basins, attended by the identification of irrigational and drainage projects.

Apparently, even within the frame of Ethiopia's current development drives which foresaw great potentials of large-, medium- and small-scale irrigation schemes, the waters required to meet irrigational needs would remain minuscule. Hence, in the instant future, Ethiopia's undertakings would not gravely affect downstream water balances; the incidence of consequential conflicts between various categories of uses in Egypt, Sudan and Ethiopia would remain less forthcoming.

This is confirmed by Ethiopia's water resources study conducted in 1999 on the 'Abay (Blue Nile) River Basin Integrated Development Master Plan Project'. The report evaluated effects of possible utilization scenarios of the master plan period and concluded that 'since the scale of developments proposed remains small relative to water availability, the impacts will be limited'.[74] The reduction of flows at the border with the Sudan would be no more than 6 percent of the mean annual discharge, i.e. 3.1–3.3bcm/yr, which, although of concern to downstream riparian states, would be offset, at least in the case of Sudan, by favourable impact in sediment load if a mainstream dam were to be constructed.[75] Under the Master Plan, two alternative irrigation development scenarios extending over a 50 years period (1999/2000–2048/49) had been contemplated, projecting to develop a total area of 235,000–350,000 hectares in successive phases.[76]

However, it must be noted circumspectly that the master plan had to restrict its conclusions merely to the impact of *one scenario* of development that selects from a broader list of identified projects. Naturally, if the national development scheme had been based on a setting that represented the implementation of all identified projects or the maximum possible development based on a comparison of water resources and irrigable areas at a sub-basin level, Ethiopia's abstraction of the Blue Nile waters would puff up, distressing downstream flows of the river in greater measures.[77]

74 Federal Democratic Republic of Ethiopia (1999), note 68, p 197.

75 Federal Democratic Republic of Ethiopia (1999), note 68, p 200.

76 Federal Democratic Republic of Ethiopia (1999), note 68, p 197.

77 The total net-area identified under potential large- and medium-scale irrigation in the sub-basin had been 526,000 hectares. The FAO had already provided a higher estimate. The potential irrigable area in the three sub-basins of the Nile in Ethiopia has been computed at 2,210,700 hectares, of which the Baro-Akobo sub-basin accounted for 905,500 while the Blue Nile and Tekeze-Atbara sub-basins represented 1,000,500 hectares and 312,700 hectares respectively.

Apart from potential agricultural uses, the Blue Nile basin has also been featured as the major pedestal of Ethiopia's future hydroelectric power supplies. In the last decade alone, Ethiopia has increasingly portrayed itself as poster-child of the hydropower sector. Growing stipulations in industrial, commercial and domestic units both in Ethiopia and the neighbouring markets (of Sudan, Kenya and Djibouti) has provoked the government and its utility firm – the Ethiopian Electric Power Corporation – to aggressively embark on the institution of massive power-generation and transmission schemes. Any considerable growth, transformation and sustainability of its agrarian mode of production depended on the production and accessibility of low-cost energy supplies to the agricultural communities, cottage manufacturing and both small and large-scale industries.[78]

As is the case in agricultural uses, water withdrawal for purposes of generating hydropower can potentially impact the quality, quantity and timing of waters received downstream, and stimulate a conflict of uses scenario. This is particularly so when, for instance the specific nature and design of projects requires diversions and renders the waters unavailable for downstream uses. Of course, the effect depends on the particular sketch of the schemes and not merely on the presence of hydropower infrastructures in upstream locations.

On the basis of a development scenario depicted under an older report of the US Bureau of Reclamation issued in the mid 1960s and a set of variables and assumptions, Guarisso and Whittington concluded that the execution of the Karodobi, Mabil, Mendela and Border projects alone, with an annual active storage capacity of 51bcm/yr and electric generation capacity of over 25 billion kwh, would not impact on Sudanese or Egyptian uses of Nile waters.[79] The solution proposed showed that the objectives of Ethiopia's hydropower production and Egyptian and Sudanese agricultural water uses are not necessarily conflicting; instead, the authors argued, the three riparian states would benefit from the increased regulation of the Blue Nile floods in Ethiopia.[80]

Of course, the projected model assumed the impacts *only* of developing hydropower schemes in Ethiopia as depicted under the Bureau's scientific studies; as noted earlier, the realization of Ethiopia's full irrigational potentials would clearly generate a different set of circumstances. This would obviously be far greater than the Bureau of Reclamation's plan, which had anticipated including small-scale projects that cover only 433,754 hectares of land and withdraw about 6bcm/yr of Nile waters.

For this reason, while the effects of Ethiopia's uses have been considered in the context only of pending development ventures – hence providing a far less gloomy

78 As a result, in addition to existing facilities of the Fincha-Amertinesh, Fincha 4th Unit, Tis Abay I/II, Tekeze I and Tana-Beles hydropower installations, several single and multipurpose projects including the Grand Ethiopian Renaissance Dam, Tekeze II, Mendaia, Border, Mabil, Fettam, Upper-Guder, Aleltu-East, Chemoga Yada and Aleltu-West have been proposed on the mainstream and tributaries of the Nile in Ethiopia. Some are already in the implementation phases.

79 Giorgio Guarisso and Dale Whittington (1987) 'Implications of Ethiopian Water Development for Egypt and the Sudan', *International Journal of Water Resources Development*, vol 3, no 2, p 109.

80 Guarisso and Whittington (1987), note 79, p 112.

picture, the implementation of the nation's full irrigational potentials will eventually entail the removal of greater volumes of Nile waters; in such context, the incidence of conflict of uses in the Nile basin region would not merely be a sheer possibility, it will linger as an ominous factual state of riparian concern.

Conclusions

Should the existing patterns of utilization in the Nile basin region be sustained without some measures of adjustment, the circumstance will *factually* preclude potential upstream recourse to significant uses affecting the Nile flow regime.

On the other hand, the continued implementation of development schemes in upstream Nile, and particularly in Ethiopia will at some point encroach on the water requirements of established uses; a conflict between competing riparian uses is but inevitable.

Hence, as Waterbury had noted, not only should those states most concerned with supply reach some sort of equilibrium of supply and demand among themselves, but also that they must accommodate in some fashion those least concerned.[81]

Legally, the prevalence of conflicting riparian uses, whether actual or projected, compels basin states to *resort* to recognized procedures and *reconsider* existing patterns and future plans with a view to accommodating each state's reasonable entitlements. Such conflicts are settled and entitlements adjusted on the basis of guidelines provided under the principle of equitable utilization.

In organizing individual riparian rights in the Nile basin, though, an issue of vital consideration pounds immediately: what explicitly does the equitable uses principle in fact entail as a means of reconciling competing riparian uses? And how does its functioning affect contemporary legal settings, perceptions and practices in the Nile basin?

These issues cannot be settled merely by reiterating that the doctrine constitutes a settled rule of customary international law. The substantive contents of this canon must be elucidated.

The principle of equitable and reasonable uses

As elucidated in the preceding chapters, an overwhelming body of case law, institutional initiatives and state practice had endorsed the equitable uses principle as one of the established canons of international custom. In fact, during the early commissioning of its undertakings in the progressive development and codification of international water courses law, the ILC had itself admitted that the chief issue with respect to some of the basic principles had barely been one of whether 'they existed as such', but rather how they should be formulated under the convention to regulate future conduct effectively.[82]

81 John Waterbury (2002) *The Nile Basin, National Determinants of Collective Action*, New Haven, Yale University Press, London, p 1.

82 International Law Commission (1983) *Yearbook of International Law Commission*, vol 2, no 1, p 157.

The introduction of this principle under the UN Convention on the Non-navigational Uses of International Watercourses has widely been regarded as 'codification of prevailing principles of international law following from customary international law, and evidenced by general state practice and general principles of law'.[83] In fact, with the exception of the 'no significant harm' doctrine, no other more-widely accepted principle has existed in the law of non-navigational uses of international water courses.[84] In 2004, the revised rules of the ILA adopted at the Berlin Conference reasserted the rule of equitable utilization as expressing the primary rule of international law, whether customary or conventional, regarding the allocation of waters among basin States.[85]

From the outset, thematic works of the ILC had been stirred by a fundamental perception that 'a state's right of use of waters of international watercourse systems within its borders is recognized'; the rules and principles accommodated under the Convention with a view to deflecting conflicts in the beneficial use of shared watercourses are founded on the principle of equality of rights and the application of equitable share concept in one form or another.[86] The parity of rights of states has been regarded 'a postulate of international law so basic that it is unchallengeable'.[87]

In defining rights and constraining the freedom of each state in engaging in the development of shared river courses, the equitable uses principle had contended with various theories applied in the realm of international watercourses law.

Conceptually, the equitable uses principle represents a plodding evolutionary growth of an older doctrine pronounced by the Institute of International Law (IIL) about a century ago. In 1911, the Madrid Declaration of the IIL highlighted the reciprocal feature of riparian rights where it enunciated that 'the permanent physical dependence of riparian states on each other precludes the idea of autonomy of each state in the section of the natural watercourse under its section'.[88] A limited-sovereignty approach had been adopted; by virtue of this theory, no transboundary river may be subjected to either an exclusive appropriation or to a discretionary riparian action that deprives the legitimate interests of other states.

Since the early opening of the twentieth century, the essence of the doctrines of equitable utilization and equality of rights of states had been specifically applied in several federal interstate river disputes – the pioneering case being the Kansas *vs.* Colorado (1907), and further enriched through the jurisprudence of the US Supreme Court.[89]

In the 1960s, Sir Waldock Humphrey, a previous Special Rapporteur of the ILC, remarked that 'some broad principles have now come to existence though

83 International Law Commission (1983), note 82, p 170.
84 International Law Commission (1983), note 82, p 75.
85 International Law Association (2004), note 34, p 16.
86 International Law Commission (1983), note 82, p 163.
87 International Law Commission (1980) *Yearbook of International Law Commission*, vol 2, no 1, p 163.
88 Institute of International Law (1911), note 26.
89 *Kansas vs. Colorado*, 206 US (1907).

their precise formulation may still remain to be settled'. He stated six important principles; one of which read that 'where one state's exercise of its rights conflicts with the water interests of another, the principle to be applied is that each is entitled to the equitable apportionments of the benefits of the river system in proportion to their needs and in light of all the circumstances of the particular river system'.[90]

In 1997, a milestone decree of the International Court of Justice (ICJ) in the *Gabcikovo-Nagymaros Project* case recapitulated the core spirit and contemporary state of the principle which had been previously echoed by the ILA, IIL, regional initiatives, learned views of legal publicists and most notably, the UN-sponsored conferences on water and the environment.

In the *Gabcikovo-Nagymaros Project* case involving Hungary and Slovakia, the ICJ held Czechoslovakia failed to respect the proportionality required by international law by unilaterally assuming control of a shared resource, thereby depriving Hungary of its 'right to an equitable and reasonable share' of the natural resources of the Danube.[91] The Court referred to a previous jurisprudence of the Permanent Court of International Justice (PCIJ) in the *River Oder* case wherein it was held that the 'community of interest' in a navigable river is the basis of a common right, the essential features of which are 'the perfect equality of riparians' in the use of the river and the 'exclusion of any preferential privilege' of any one riparian state.[92] The ICJ concluded modern international law as evidenced through the adoption of the 1997 UN Watercourses Convention had 'merely strengthened' the principle enunciated in the *River Oder* proceeding.[93]

In like tune, McCaffrey submitted that on the basis of state practice, at least three of the general principles embodied in the Convention correspond to customary norms; the list included the obligation 'to use an international water course in an equitable and reasonable manner', 'to use such watercourses in such a way as not to cause significant harm to other riparian states', and the duty 'to notify planned measures'.[94]

Quite evidently, contemporary norms regulating the conduct of states in relation to the non-navigational uses of international watercourses have evolved considerably. The effect has been that the basic principles have steadily derided the legal

90 J. Brierly (1963) *The Law of Nations*, Oxford, Clarendon Press, p 231; International Law Commission (1986) *Yearbook of International Law Commission*, vol 2, no 1, p 127.

91 *Gabcikovo-Nagymaros Project (Hungary/Slovakia)*, Judgment, ICJ. Reports 1997.

92 *Gabcikovo-Nagymaros Project* (1997), note 91.

93 *Gabcikovo-Nagymaros Project* (1997), note 91, p 56, para 85.

94 Stephen McCaffrey (2001), note 45, p 260.

Yet, another report of the Special Rapporteur of the ILC had articulated that while there had been no objection to the inclusion of an article on 'cooperation' under the broader framework of which 'notification of planned actions' would appear to fall, there was in fact divergence of views on the existence of a duty to cooperate under international law. In any event, the report concluded that the 'duty' constitutes one of conduct, general obligation to act in good faith with regard to other states in the utilization of international river courses in pursuing a common goal. International Law Commission (1987) *Yearbook of International Law Commission*, vol 2, no 2, p 21.

credence of certain extreme user-right perceptions previously espoused under the banner of absolute territorial sovereignty and absolute territorial integrity.

Today, no state can claim unqualified rights of utilization of an international watercourse under the guise of sovereignty. The principle of equitable and reasonable utilization describes the interdependence of states in a water community; it operates to limit state sovereignty, and rejects claims of absolute and unlimited rights of upstream riparian states in much the same way as states on the lower-reach of international rivers may no longer claim established and unconditional rights on the basis of the principle of absolute territorial integrity.[95]

Indeed, while the specific essence of the legal regime of watercourses may still call for some elucidation, several principles of international custom and most notably, the doctrine of equitable utilization have evolved to restructure rights, define riparian intercourse and dictate restriction against the territorial autonomy of states. For this reason, Professor Berber's earliest account that outside some areas of Europe and perhaps North America, there are no customary rules governing water relations between independent states except for those which may be inferred from the principle of good neighbourliness and general consideration for each other will now constitute *but* an obsolete juridical postulate.[96]

Composition of the 'equitable and reasonable uses' doctrine

A vital question, however, remains: how is the legal standard so embedded in the equitable and reasonable uses expression characterized? What rights and duties does it essentially entail?

Any analytical investigation that anticipates to validate whether the contemporary patterns of use across the downstream Nile operate within the confines of the equitable utilization doctrine and endeavours to reflect on the specific rights of the basin states naturally urges the fulfilment of two conditions: a presentation on the substance of the principle itself, and a scrupulous reading of the relevant factual and legal circumstances prevailing in the basin.

The right of each watercourse state to reasonable and equitable share in the uses of the waters of an international river had been restated both under the Helsinki Rules on the Uses of the Waters of International Rivers (1966)[97] – a non-binding resolution adopted by the ILA at the fifty-second conference held in Helsinki (revised at the Berlin Conference in 2004),[98] as well as the UN Convention on the Law of the Non-navigational Uses of International Watercourses (1997).

95 Dante A. Caponera (1985) 'Patterns of Cooperation in International Water Law: Principles and Institutions', *Nat Resources J*, vol 25, p 568.

96 F. J. Berber (1959) *Rivers in International Law*, London, Stevens and Sons, pp 70–80.

97 International Law Association (1966) 'Helsinki Rules on the Uses of the Waters of International Rivers', London, ILA Publication, pp 7–55.

98 International Law Association (2004), note 34.

Article IV of the Helsinki Rules declared 'each Basin State is entitled, within its territory, to a reasonable and equitable share in the beneficial uses of the waters of an international drainage basin'.[99]

Likewise, under Article 5, the UN Watercourses Convention established that 'watercourse states shall in their respective territories utilize an international watercourse in an equitable and reasonable manner'. International watercourses shall be used and developed with a view to attaining optimal and sustainable utilization thereof and benefits there from, taking into account the interests of the watercourse states concerned, and consistent with adequate protection of the watercourse. The Convention further dictated that watercourse states shall participate in the use, development and protection of an international watercourse in an equitable and reasonable manner, which includes both the right to utilize the watercourse and the duty to cooperate in the protection and development thereof.

The exact definition of the legal standard embedded in the 'reasonable and equitable manner' expression is not unproblematic. In fact, its ambiguous constitution had been one of the reasons why the duty to cooperate and negotiate was inserted as a supplementary requirement so as to help determine the extent of the respective riparian rights involved.

Various comments submitted during the drafting of the proceedings of the Working Group of the Whole of the United Nation General Assembly Sixth Committee and the ILC observed that the basic tenets underlying the doctrine of equitable utilization had been recognized in numerous international agreements between states located in all parts of the world. An extensive survey of the treaty practice of states demonstrated an entrenched recognition of the equality of rights and equitable entitlement of riparian states in the use of shared watercourses.

99 The emphasis on the beneficial uses of the waters expression is reminiscent of the early debates of the drafting process wherein one line of perspective had argued that what is to be *shared* in equitable and reasonable manner is not the *waters* of an international watercourse as such, but the *benefits* in the uses of such watercourses.

A counter-argument submitted that water is a commodity in short supply, and while the means of distributing waters are many and varied, what states actually have a claim in and would be allocated is water, although they could give up some part of that claim in return for something else, for instance electricity.

International Law Commission (1984) *Yearbook of International Law Commission*, vol 2, no 2, p 94.

In the 1960s, Hutchins defined the concept of beneficial uses, at least as applied in the USA, as requiring not only that the *purpose of use* (irrigation, mining, manufacturing, etc.) be a beneficial one, but also that the *methods* of diverting water, conveying into the place of use and applying it into the land or machinery for which appropriated waters are to be as efficient as is reasonable under the circumstances.

A few western state statutes had listed purposes for which water may be appropriated; several instances are known in which courts have held certain purposes of use to be non-beneficial in the sense that they cannot support a valid appropriation of water: e.g. diversion of water for the sole purpose of drainage; a bare claim of water for no object other than speculation; inadequate casting of water over sagebrush land to increase growth of native grass; winter flooding to produce an icecap to promote moisture retention; carrying of debris in months in which the water is needed for irrigation. Wells A. Hutchins (1962) 'Background and modern developments in water law in the USA', *Nat Resources J* vol 2, p 418.

In attempting to define the substance, successive basin frameworks had enclosed explicit references to the equality of rights and equitable entitlements of the partaking states, or articulated specific rights or shares in flow-volumes. Some schemes merely made oblique references to the notion by providing, for example, for 'the sharing of benefits of the waters', or 'limiting the freedom of unilateral action of upstream states', by 'recognizing the correlative nature of rights of basin states', or by authorizing each riparian state a 'right to divert up to half of the volume of the waters'.

Other treaty regimes organized under similar considerations enunciated 'the territorial sovereignty of states subject to a correlative duty not to injure the interests of a neighboring state', or had simply introduced a 'condition of prior approval by all parties against such projects as would likely modify the characteristics of the regime of a river'.

The language and approaches adopted in various treaty schemes had naturally varied. The Commission held that the unifying theme in several of the arrangements had been the recognition of equal and correlative rights of the parties to the uses and benefits of the international watercourse in question.[100]

Equity/equality of rights *vs.* 'identical' division of waters

During one of the series of the continental shelf delimitation proceedings, the ICJ pronounced that equity does not necessarily imply equality. There can never be any question of completely refashioning nature, the Court reasoned, and equity does not require that a state without access to the sea should be allotted an area of continental shelf, any more than there could be a question of rendering the situation of a state with an extensive coastline similar to that of a state with a restricted coastline. Equality is to be reckoned with in the same plane and it is not such natural inequalities as these that equity could remedy.[101]

In contrast to the Court's proposition, international watercourses law has been directed by different considerations which among others puts prime emphasis on natural inequalities and thrives to adjust the imbalances engendered through such conditions. In fact, in the case concerning the *Continental Shelf (Tunisia/Libyan Arab Jamahiriya)*, the same Court admitted that while the legal concept of equity is a general principle directly applicable as law, when applying positive international law, the Court may choose among several possible interpretations of the law the one which appears, in the light of the circumstances of the case, to be closest to the requirements of justice.[102]

Admittedly, contemporary international law acknowledges the equality of rights and equitable entitlement of each basin state in the uses of shared river courses. But the rules are set far from implying a right to identical divisions of flows of a

100 International Law Commission (1986) *Yearbook of International Law Commission*, vol 2, no 1, pp 103–4.

101 *North Sea Continental Shelf (1969)*, Judgment, ICJ Reports, pp 49–50, para 91.

102 *Continental Shelf (Tunisia/Libyan Arab Jamahiriya) (1982)*, Judgment, ICJ Reports, p 60, para 71.

river or to equal share of the uses. Indeed, under the conceptual framing, the point of departure has barely been one of evenly dividing flows of a watercourse, but recognizing rights equal in kind which sanction each state with a general sovereign privilege of utilizing parts of a transboundary river situating in the respective jurisdictions.

Hence, the ILC did correctly observe when asserting that the notion of equality of rights – a premise on which equitable computations have been conceptually founded, does not connote that each state shall receive identical shares in the uses of the waters.[103] In fact, in actual apportionment scenarios, a right in equity may place states further beyond a strict parity with regard to shares in the waters or beneficial uses of international watercourses. It can well result in one co-basin state receiving a right to use water in quantitatively greater amounts than its neighbours in a basin; the idea that underlies equitable sharing is the provision of maximum benefits to each basin state from the uses of the waters with a minimum detriment to each.[104]

It is in this spirit that the UN Watercourses Convention had called upon watercourse states to consult cooperatively and in good faith to determine the equitability of uses on the basis of several factors and circumstances. Indeed, a cursory glance at the diverse set of factors and circumstances detailed under Article 6 of the Convention bears out that neither customary rules nor the Convention had sought to bring about a regime of equal apportionment of river flows or uses and benefits; instead, the stipulation had been inspired by the need for attaining reasonable and equitable uses and benefits in each of the watercourse states.

Hence, without prejudice to the liberty of states to enter into specific agreements providing otherwise, the precise scope of each riparian state's equitable entitlements, whether this relates to domestic consumption, industry, irrigation, electricity, navigation or fishery, will essentially be an upshot of the *cumulative review* of each of the factors and circumstances depicted under Article 6 of the Convention.

The fundamental reasoning for adopting an approach that sustains an apportionment model premised on considerations of broader equity than equal division of waters is obvious. Very rarely do riparian states stand on level plains in terms of social, economic or hydrological settings, as well as measures of uses of shared watercourses. Egypt, for instance, is a barren landscape with meagre basin mean annual rainfall ranging between 0 and 120mm/yr. A home to an overwhelming population of 80.4 million (2010),[105] Egyptian affluence mobilizes a gross national income of some $146.9 billion, including a sophisticated

103 International Law Commission (1986), note 100, pp 103–4.

104 International Law Association (1966), note 97.

105 Central Intelligence Agency, The World Fact Book, Egypt <https://www.cia.gov/library/publications/the-world-factbook/geos/eg.html>, last accessed December 2010.

World Water Assessment Program (2003) *The United Nations World Water Development Report: Water for People, Eater for Life*, Barcelona, UNESCO Publishing/Berghahn Books, p 74.

irrigational economy that stretches over 3.3 million hectares, depending nearly exclusively on the munificence of about 54bcm of the Nile floods each year.[106]

In sharp contrast, with a population count of 23 million, Uganda is located right at the heart of the equatorial rainfall region; in relation to its physical ratio, Uganda is endowed with a massive total renewable water resources of 66bcm/yr. Agriculture withdraws a mere 0.12bcm annually, and in 1998, its irrigation was confined to a mere 9,000 hectares of land.[107]

In drawing an overarching principle that equitably applies across the board, therefore, international law has to contend with such sets of conditions that affect each particular basin or basin state in entirely distinctive ways.

For this reason, while any claim advocating the inherent superiority of rights or specific category of uses would be instantaneously rejected, the right to equitable entitlement is nonetheless conceived as admitting a range of peculiarities that are particularly relevant in one basin state, but not the other. The divergent setting of riparian states suffices to render arithmetic propositions of equal divisions less appealing, except where specific agreements have been involved.

In a geographical milieu where nature's provision is uneven and the patterns of resource utilization exhibit greater scales of contrast, the principle of equity is meant to embody a model that conveys broader fairness in each political constituency of a basin. The institution of a quasi-equality status as between a number of states is surely incidental, but justifies a differential treatment that cannot be avoided.

In ensuring the protection of equal rights of basin states and in determining the equitability of uses, legal and political discourses are basically restricted to depend on the intricate assessment of numerous factors and circumstances formulated in broader languages both under the Helsinki Rules (as revised) and the UN Watercourses Convention.

Detailing factors determining the equitability of uses in the Nile basin: the challenges

For more than a century now, the Nile River has constituted the object of a convoluted legal and diplomatic history. For most part of the first-half of the twentieth century, significant user-right conflicts involving the resource had been confined to a lower-reach rivalry between Sudan and Egypt, linking Ethiopia and Uganda only incidentally. Two landmark historical episodes – the collapse of colonialism and the institution of the Aswan High Dam – insinuated the rise of active riparianism in the upper-reaches of the region. This spurred diplomatic tussles for the establishment of prospective rights of use (upper riparians) and a hegemonic control of the river (by lower riparians).

106 FAO (2005), Egypt, Basic statistics and population, *FAO Water Report 29,* Table 1; FAO, FAO's Information System on Water and Agriculture, Geography, Climate and Population <http://www.fao.org/nr/water/aquastat/countries/egypt/index.stm>, last accessed December 2010. World Water Assessment Program (2003), note 105, p 194.

107 World Water Assessment Program (2003), note 105, p 194.

Successive basin initiatives had been launched time and again negotiating on diverse issues of common riparian interest, but to no avail. Although Article 6.2 of the UN Watercourses Convention had called upon states to enter into consultations in a spirit of cooperation with a view to determining the equitable entitlement of each watercourse state, to date, the substantive scope of rights of the Nile basin states remained self-prescribed. The basin endured without all-inclusive institutional mechanisms for proper planning, use, management and conservation of its resources. No comprehensive set of legal safeguards exist to avert potential riparian conflicts.

While Sudan and Egypt had endeavoured to synchronize their patterns of use on the basis of two legal frameworks instituted in 1929 and 1959, water-resources development policies in the two leading *recipient* states and in Ethiopia remained largely national both in design and outlook. For the most part, their approaches concentrated on stipulations of short-term domestic considerations – a state of fact which presents the least-ideal setting for cooperative computation of equitable rights and optimum management of the basin resources.

In consequence, in a legal and hydropolitical milieu where states operated on the basis of a self-conceived depiction of rights, the normative prescriptions of international law ordering certain standards would become even more vital.

In this context, the limited guidelines proffered by the Helsinki/Berlin Rules and the UN Watercourses Convention for evaluating the equitability of existing and potential uses or for establishing specific riparian entitlements would help offset the depressing drawbacks noticed in the Nile basin region as the result of the dearth of basin-wide arrangements.

With regard to the utility of principles of international law, though, partly, the specifics are where the gridlocks have constantly permeated. The description and practical implementation of the equitable uses theory presumes a delicate interpretative undertaking and involves more than a unilateral and often disputed declaration by riparian states characterizing any given pattern of utilization as equitable.

While the Tribunal in the Lake Lanoux arbitration had held that under general principles of international law, it is for each state to evaluate in a reasonable manner and good faith the situations and the rules which will involve it in controversies, the Tribunal had also anticipated that a state's evaluation may well be in contradiction with that of another state.[108] The imminent partiality involved in a one-party process rationally foretells that any unilateral assessment or assertion will be challenged instantaneously, engendering an unending series of claims and counterclaims.

Of course, in cases of disputes, the parties will normally seek to resolve it by negotiation or, alternatively, by submitting to the authority of a third party; yet, the Tribunal concluded, one of them is never obliged to suspend the exercise of its jurisdiction just because of a dispute.[109] This could encumber the chances of arriving at a just allocation of the beneficial uses of international watercourses.

108 Lake Lanoux Arbitration (1957) France/Spain, Arbitral Tribunal set up under a compromise dated 19 November 1956 pursuant to an Arbitration Treaty of July 10, 1929, para 16.

109 Lake Lanoux Arbitration (1957), note 108.

Somewhat, the relevant provisions of the Helsinki Rules and the UN Watercourses Convention have tried to lessen the undesired consequences of riparian states' subjective propensity by providing for a broader list of factors and circumstances that aid in establishing equity. It had been anticipated that even while admitting the equitable uses principle as the most suitable rule, basin states with substantial interests in the utilization of international watercourses could still engage in serious water-use disputes.

Article 6.1 of the UN Watercourses Convention provided the utilization of an international watercourse in an equitable and reasonable manner requires taking into account all relevant factors and circumstances, including:

(a) Geographic, hydrographic, hydrological, climatic, ecological and other factors of a natural character;
(b) The social and economic needs of the watercourse states concerned;
(c) The population dependent on the watercourse in each watercourse state;
(d) The effects of the use or uses of the watercourses in one watercourse state on other watercourse states;
(e) Existing and potential uses of the watercourse;
(f) Conservation, protection, development and economy of use of the water resources of the watercourse and the costs of measures taken to that effect; and
(g) The availability of alternatives, of comparable value, to a particular planned or existing use.

Several of the components incorporated under Article 6 are reiterations of factors and circumstances listed under Article V of the Helsinki Rules on the Uses of the Waters of International Rivers.

In like manner, Article 4 of the Agreement on the Nile River Cooperative Framework has reproduced, with some notable modifications, the basic stipulation of the UN Watercourses Convention.

Naturally, each constituent of a river basin is endowed with a distinctive set of geographical, hydrological, human and socio-economic features that impinge on its standing *vis-à-vis* the rest of riparian states. In the nature of things, therefore, the list of factors and circumstances that impact on the equitability of uses can hardly be thorough. The ILC observed that while the index represents an express formulation, the wide diversity of international waters and the human needs they serve makes it impossible to compile an exhaustive list,[110] with some order of priority.

On the other hand, the articles had offered a broadly couched, non-exhaustive list of factors and circumstances; this can constitute a challenge, potentially impeding the effectiveness of any commission that strives to ascertain the equitability of riparian uses or claims.

The same challenges could manifest in the context of the Nile basin as well; the region is a home to diverse communities placed in unequal stages of social and

110 International Law Commission (1984) *Yearbook of International Law Commission*, vol 2, no 2, p 96.

economic development; the basin also exhibits a highly contrasting hydrologic and climatic constitution. This implies that riparian perspectives would diverge not only with respect to the index of factors that should be *particularly* stressed in any given negotiation, but also with regard to the issue of whether *additional factors* should also be considered to suitably complete any such undertaking. Conceivably, such limitation in the structure of the norms tells why during the early stages of negotiations on the UN Watercourses Convention, several states had treaded great lengths to ridicule the provision's formulation.[111] A few states maintained that if the article was meant to be meaningful, fundamental criteria or factors that would apply in virtually all situations should have been considered.[112]

Yet, it is evident, and so had the ILC held persistently that no mechanical formula (of factors and circumstances) that applies across the board to all river courses could be feasibly devised. In fact, in many instances, basin institutions had properly envisaged the scale of complexity involved and sought the solution elsewhere. Some had heeded the increasing challenges by taking clear stands in recent years in favor of strengthened cooperation among basin states which aimed at a rational utilization of shared water sources; multiple, often conflicting uses, and a much greater total demand have made imperative the implementation of an integrated approach to river basin development.[113]

Apart from such limitations, however, it can be submitted that a fairly sufficient detail provided under Article V of the Helsinki Rules and Article VI of the UN Watercourses Convention had provided concrete guidelines for an enhanced understanding of the content, nature and interpretation of the legal standard embodied in the doctrine of equitable utilization.

Shaping equity

No provision in the Convention has provided for a clear set of guidelines as to how the blend of factors and circumstances should be applied in a particular circumstance to give effect to the notion of the right to equitable utilization.

With regard to the relative weight accorded to each factor or circumstance, however, Article 6.3 of the UN Watercourses Convention and Article 4.4 of the Cooperative Framework Agreement, verbally emulating Article 5.3 of the Helsinki Rules, stipulated that such would be decided by reference to its importance in comparison with other relevant factors; in establishing what is reasonable and equitable use, all relevant factors are to be considered together and a conclusion reached on the basis of the whole. The obvious hurdle that arises in connection with the multiplicity of the factors had barely been addressed, tempting some

111 In the view of some states, 'the article, as presented, did not provide much guidance for solving problems as it was too long, too complicated, and repetitive, and mixes both subjective and objective factors'.

International Law Commission (1983), note 82, p 86.

112 International Law Commission (1984), note 110, p 96.

113 International Law Commission (1983), note 82, p 86.

authors to capriciously propose arithmetic figures as substitutes for each of the factors listed under Article 6.1.

In anticipation of the problem, the working committee of the ILA commented: '. . . no factor has a fixed weight nor will all factors be relevant in all cases. Each factor is given such a weight as it merits relative to all other factors . . . and no factor occupies a position of preeminence *per se* with respect to any other factor.'[114]

Similarly, this elucidation was reiterated in the jurisprudence of the ICJ. The Court explained: '. . . while it is clear that no rigid rules exist as to the exact weight to be attached to each element in the case, this is very far from being an exercise of discretion or conciliation; nor is it an operation of distributive justice'.[115]

In the Nile basin context, the exigent issue relates to how the factors and circumstances so listed band together to reconcile conflicting uses and to bring about a fair and reasonable settlement of claims and rights. To evaluate the divergent interests of eleven riparian states on the basis of some eight generally sketched criteria will no doubt constitute an intricate commission. Disagreement is inevitable not only in selecting any given factor, but also in relation to the particular weight that should be accorded to such factors identified.

Apparently, the intention has been that the Nile Basin Commission (NBC), acting through one of its organs – the Council of Ministers – shall take the prime responsibility in this regard. The Commission would act on the basis of recommendations of the Technical Advisory Committee and make decisions regarding equitable uses in each riparian country based on the list of factors provided under Article 4 of the Cooperative Framework Agreement.[116] Naturally, the Commission would need to establish detailed procedures that facilitate the effective implementation of the principle of equitable utilization in real scenarios.[117]

Of course, the pursuit of equity will not necessarily meet all riparian development aspirations and particularly so when a resource is in short supply. As Special Rapporteur Schwebel explained, '. . . an accommodation of . . . conflicting needs will by definition result in the *full* needs of one or usually both states not being met . . . which may well entail harm in the factual sense to one or both states'.[118]

The physical scale and patterns of utilization of the Nile River resources has been depicted above. Water withdrawn by the basin states for domestic consumption and sanitary purposes would most probably remain the least-contested, although there exists no clear legal authority for ascribing such uses a position of *pre-eminence.*

On account of qualitative, quantitative and temporal impacts, it is the utilization of waters in irrigation, industry and perhaps the development of hydropower that will occupy a center stage in competitive uses.

114 International Law Association (1966), note 97.

115 *Continental Shelf (Tunisia/Libyan Arab Jamahiriya)*, note 102, p 60, para 71.

116 Agreement on the Nile River Basin Cooperative Framework (2010), Articles 26.5, 24.12, 16.a.

117 Agreement on the Nile River Basin Cooperative Framework (2010), note 116, Article 4.6.

118 International Law Commission (1986), note 100, p 131.

Allowing for a restricted flow-regime of the Nile River, it was previously indicated that long-established irrigational uses in Egypt and Sudan will be in some scales of conflict with new agricultural schemes in Ethiopia; likewise, farming practices in the lower-reaches of the river can be negatively impacted in consequence of Ethiopia's implementation of hydropower facilities which could store and release waters at imperfectly timed periods.

In considering to accommodate Ethiopia's, and by corollary upstream states' claims for an equitable allocation, a contextual application of the various factors and circumstances will naturally present more than a few complex issues, many of which stem from the very framing of Article 6 of the UN Watercourses Convention itself.

In scrupulous detail, Part 11 will go through some of the most important factors and circumstances listed and address complex legal issues that ensue in connection with their application. The selective approach has been justified by the fact that not *all* variables would be necessarily crucial in the context of particular constitution of the Nile River basin. In fact, as the ILC had observed, in spite of the extended list of factors, it would be geography, hydrology, climate, existing utilization and economic and social needs that are normally emphasized in any enterprise on equitable determinations.[119]

119 International Law Commission (1979), note 16, p 163.

11 Analysis of factors and circumstances affecting the equitability of uses in the Nile Basin

'Geographic, hydrographic, hydrological, climatic, ecological and other factors of a natural character'

The utilization of an international watercourse in an equitable and reasonable manner within the meaning of Article 5 requires taking into account all relevant factors and circumstances, including 'geographic, hydrographic, hydrological, climatic, ecological and other factors of a natural character'.

The reference under Article 6.1.(a) to natural factors generally embraces those which influence certain important characteristics of a river, such as quantity and quality, rate of flow, periodic fluctuations, etc.; geographic factors denote the extent of a river in the territory of each watercourse state; hydrographic facts relate to measurement, description and mapping; while hydrological elements take account of water flow and distribution, including contribution of each watercourse state to the waters of a river.[1] Under the sub-article, the intention had been to include every possible physical feature that has some relationship to basin waters.[2]

In devising a procedure for the distribution of the beneficial uses of international watercourses among states, successive literatures had endeavoured to narrow down the most controlling variables under the caption of 'geographic, hydrographic, hydrological, climatic and ecological' conditions to essentially three headings. These are the extent of a river in the territory of each watercourse (geographical), the contribution of each watercourse state to the waters of a river (hydrological) and climatic settings affecting the basin. This is particularly evident in the formulation of geographical, hydrologic and climatic factors under distinct sub-provisions in Article V of the Helsinki Rules.

In consequence, in the context of the Nile basin, the factor analysis would concentrate on presenting a general outline of data on the overall volume, flow contribution and spatial distribution of waters of the river in the respective territories of the three basin states of Egypt, Sudan and Ethiopia; this shall be attended by a reflection on the relative legal weights accorded to each factor under the Convention and customary international law.

1 International Law Commission (1994) *Yearbook of International Law Commission*, vol 2, no 2, p 101.
2 International Law Commission (1979) *Yearbook of International Law Commission*, vol 2, no 1, p 162.

This enterprise will specifically endeavour to address one important question: how do the particular factual settings relating to hydrology, geography and climate translate in relation to issues of determination of the respective equitable entitlements of the three basin states?

Hydrological factors

Meteorological events that provide crucial precipitation to the White and Blue Nile, Tekeze and Baro-Akobo river systems are distinct; the annual floods not only rise and fall at different seasons of the year, they also fluctuate at different paces, affecting the relative contribution of each of the particular sub-basins in any given period.

In spite of the colossal length it traverses across central, east and north Africa, the Nile River has not only been endowed with a very limited flow-regime, the resource is also distributed disproportionately across the region, exhibiting extremes of surplus in some parts and water deficiencies in others.

Allowing for a longer span of time, the mean annual flow has been widely accounted as standing at 84bcm/yr. Two geographical areas contribute significant proportions of the deluges: the Ethiopian highlands (through the Baro-Akobo-Sobat river system, the Blue Nile river system, and the Tekeze-Atbara river system) and the Great Lakes Region (through the White Nile river system).

Hydrologically, Ethiopia, Egypt and the Sudan are placed in contrasting positions of eminence particularly in relation to seasonal flood regimes, water flows, distribution and mean annual contribution to the Nile River system.

Sudan is endowed with a total renewable water resources of 64bcm/yr. out of which internally produced surface waters, including provisions of the Nile basin system make up 28bcm/yr.[3] Egypt, on the other hand, produces a meagre 0.5bcm/yr of internal surface waters and 1.3bcm/yr of internal groundwater while its total renewable water resource has been computed at 58.3bcm/yr, with account taken of its stated *legal rights* to supplies of the Nile floods. In terms of internally derived water-resource endowments, therefore, Egypt and Sudan linger in a highly vulnerable position, respectively appraised for 97 percent and 77 percent dependency ratios on out–of-territory supplies.

In contrast, Ethiopia produces 40bcm/yr of internal groundwaters and its total renewable water resource, generated exclusively within its territories, stands at more than 110bcm/yr.[4]

The Nile receives no water supplies throughout its course in Egypt and northern Sudan. In fact, 310km north of Khartoum where the Nile is joined by the third and last stream from Ethiopia – the Tekeze-Atbara river system – the Nile acquires no additional floods from any tributary throughout its entire downstream route towards the sea.

3 World Water Assessment Program (2003) *The United Nations World Water Development Report: Water for People, Eater for Life*, Barcelona, UNESCO Publishing/Berghahn Books, p 70.

4 World Water Assessment Program (2003), note 3.

On the other hand, while Southern Sudan is endowed with a fair mass of internally produced surface waters attributed to huge precipitation that falls in central and southern regions, only a portion of its internal waters originate in its territory; even then, its net contribution to the Nile River system has been seriously curtailed because of the particular ecological setting of the Sudd region. Methodically, the hydrological pattern is explained as follows.

The White Nile channel starts in the African Lakes Region and arrives in southern Sudan carrying along 26.5bcm/yr of waters; inside Sudan, the river receives about 4.8bcm/yr of torrential waters from some inland tributaries (the Asua, Kaia and Kit rivers). However, the combined flow is emptied into a huge marshland in the impassable Sudd, a desolate region in the lower-middle reaches of the country composed of a vast expanse of an over-flowing area covering tracts between Bor and Lake No. On crossing the Sudd swamps, therefore, the White Nile River becomes a relatively insignificant stream, losing as much as 50 percent of its waters through seepage, evaporation and enormous transpiration.[5]

At Lake No in Sudan where the marshes end, the White Nile is joined by a large tributary – the Bahr el Ghazal which collects internal waters from a different but outsized inland/shared catchment area along the south-western border regions between Sudan and Congo. While the Bahr el Ghazal collects as much as 15.1bcm/yr waters, its volume is similarly discharged into the flat swamps of the Sudd, hence losing nearly all its waters before it arrives at its outlet near Lake No. The White Nile system eventually receives a mere 0.5bcm/yr of waters from the Bahr el Ghazal.

Furthermore, at various junctions, several small and seasonal streams inundating within the territories of Sudan including the Pibor, Dinder and Rahad provide waters to major tributaries of the White Nile (like the Baro-Akobo-Sobat river system) and that of the Nile Proper (the Blue Nile River and the Tekeze-Atbara rivers). Still, not only do these major tributaries pour directly from Ethiopia, nearly all the small, highly seasonal rivulets that in the Sudan supply water flows to the major tributaries too have their headwaters located in Ethiopia. This verity dwindles Sudan's aggregate contributions to the overall flow regime of the Nile River system.

As a result, out of the roughly 24bcm/yr of net water-flow of the White Nile River that arrives at Aswan, with account also taken of some losses along the way, the input of Sudanese internal waters represents a very insignificant proportion. About 15bcm/yr of the bulk water of the White Nile is derived from the Equatorial Lakes Region; and the Baro-Akobo branch of the Sobat River, itself constituted of several rivulets in Ethiopia, further contributes a net outflow of 9.2bcm/yr. The only potent tributary of the Sobat from within Sudan, the Pibor River, whose headwater is also located in Ethiopia, draws a mere 2.8bcm of water annually.[6]

5 Garstin, who described the region as 'melancholy to an indescribable degree', argued the volume of water lost in the marshy plain ranges between '50–80 percent of the supply it received from the Lakes'.

William Garstin (1909) 'Fifty Years of Exploration, and Some of its Results', *The Geographical Journal*, vol 33, no 2, p 137.

6 A.B. Abalhoda (1993) 'Nile Basin General Information and Statistics', ICOLD 61st Executive Meeting, Cairo, pp 7–13.

In relation to the Blue Nile River, two highly seasonal runoffs in Sudan – the Dinder and Rahad – with headwaters likewise located in Ethiopia, supply a mere 4bcm/yr of waters; the Blue Nile's total annual inundation between Sennar and Khartoum is 54bcm/yr, or 48 bcm/yr at Aswan,[7] the bulk-flow of which is produced in north-western and central highlands in Ethiopia.

Ethiopia's contribution through the three head streams – the Baro-Akobo (Sobat), the Blue Nile and the Atbara-Tekeze river basins – is computed at 68.7bcm/yr of waters at Aswan, i.e. about 82 percent of the entire Nile flow.

Sudan's net flow contribution to the Nile proper system cannot be worked out with precision simply because of the great display of hydrological interdependence between most of its major internal tributaries and their headwaters in the Ethiopian highlands. However, it is evident in the facts presented that Sudan, with a 77 percent dependency ratio on out-of-territory supplies, would be situated in an exceptionally incomparable stature in relation to Ethiopia. Only a small proportion of the remaining 18 percent of the mean annual discharge of the Nile crossing its borders in the north derives from within its territories.

The question then is: how does this factual setting translate in relation to issues of determination of the respective equitable entitlements of the three basin states? What legal implication does it insinuate that the Nile River hardly receives additional floods throughout its downstream course in parts of Sudan and whole Egypt?

As one constituent element of factors, the precise *role* of the relative hydrologic contribution of each basin state is probably difficult to singularly trace in the treaty practice of states. Often, even when apportionment proceedings are based on the equality-of-rights principle, a variety of factors and circumstances are blended together. On the other hand, when allocation regimes are either silent or framed in general expressions as regards the basis on which they had been established, no explicit information would usually be availed specifically indicating that the relative contribution of each watercourse state to the flow-regime of a river has in fact played a vital role, although in some cases, this is only implicit.

In contemporary state practice, sharing waters on the basis of the equality of rights and equitable use principles has no doubt tended to assume a predominant position. There are plenty of instances where basin states had simply divided water flows equally (50–50) or other similarly quantified methods, in which case the need for engaging in a rigorous analysis of each of the factors and circumstances had been obviated.[8] Still, the patterns of state practice have been paradoxical.

7 A.B. Abalhoda (1993), note 6, p 14.

8 Under Articles II and III of the treaty concluded between India and Pakistan regarding the use of the waters of Indus, for instance, India had simply been allocated the Eastern rivers (Ravi, Sutlej, Beas) of the Indus system for its unrestricted use, imposing on Pakistan 'an obligation to let the streams flow' unhindered, while the Western rivers (Indus, Jhelum, Chenab) were set aside for Pakistan's unrestricted uses, imposing on India analogous duties of non-interference.

Treaty between India and Pakistan regarding the use of the waters of Indus, Karachi 19 September 1960.

Similarly, against a background of dispute between seven federal states that had battled for a share of a river on the basis of 'prior uses' and 'future rights of use', the Colorado River Compact

It is evident that Ethiopia cannot claim an absolute priority in the beneficial uses of the resources of the Blue Nile simply because the Nile River pours from its jurisdiction in significant proportions, in much the same as Egypt and Sudan cannot legally demand the river to flow as in its natural state because they have had deeply entrenched interests represented through a pattern of pre-existing uses. As such, water contribution is only one factor; a claim for settlement of dispute solely on the basis of water contribution would amount to the application of the absolute territorial sovereignty theory which is already denied as being a rule of international water law.[9]

In this regard, a very solid but far too enlightened jurisprudence was presented in decisions of the US Supreme Court. In the *Colorado vs. New Mexico* case (1984), the Court's ruling declared: 'the mere fact that the Vermejo River originates in Colorado does not automatically entitle Colorado to a share of the river's waters. . . . Equitable apportionment of appropriated water rights turns on the benefits, harms, and efficiencies of competing uses and thus, the source of the river's waters is essentially irrelevant to the adjudication of these sovereigns' competing claims'.[10]

Unfortunately, in this particular proceeding, the Court's finding on 'appropriated waters' cannot be utilized perfunctorily on account of two important rationales: first, the Court drew its rules from a blend of common law, local customs, precedents and practices, particularly those applied extensively in the western United States, many of which are not congruent with contemporary rules and principles of international law. Second, should the source of a river be irrelevant in equitable apportionment of appropriated waters, it then follows that there would be no point in explicitly incorporating hydrological factors as one of the variables affecting the determination of equitable entitlements both under the Helsinki Rules and the UN Watercourses Convention.

In the past decades, Ethiopia had endeavoured in diplomatic and legal discourses to broaden the legal horizon of its position through the express employ of hydrological factors as a basis for far-reaching claims of rights. Two landmark communiqués, formally issued on 7 February 1957[11] and on 23 September 1957,[12] laid the essential foundation of a perception that dominated the national hydro-legal discourse throughout the succeeding decades.

(1922) apportioned the Colorado River on an essentially equal (quantitative) basis between each of the seven constituents, the volume of waters each contributes to the river's flow notwithstanding.

Colorado River Compact (1922), Done at the City of Santa Fe, New Mexico.

Under the Nile waters agreements (1929, 1959), the allocation regime had been founded on different rationales, and heeded no regard to the respective flow contributions of Egypt and the Sudan.

In the Euphrates–Tigris basin, Turkey contributes nearly 67 percent of the entire watercourse, but planned to consume only 30 percent of the total flow. Ibrahim Kaya (2003) *Equitable Utilization, The Law of non Navigational Uses of International Watercourses*, Aldershot/Burlington, Ashgate Publishing Co, p 103.

9 Ibrahim Kaya (2003), note 8, p 103.

10 *Colorado vs. New Mexico*, 467 US 310 (1984).

11 Ministry of Foreign Affairs (1956) Press Communiqué, Addis Abba Ethiopia, *Ethiopian Herald*, 6 February.

12 Counselor of American Embassy at Cairo (Ross) to the Department of State (1957), Aide Memoire of 23 September 1957, encl in Dispatch No 342, 8 October 1957 (MS Department of State, file 974.7301/10–857).

The 1957 diplomatic declaration issued in Cairo stated:

> . . . Ethiopia alone supplies 84 percent of those waters, as well as the immense volume of alluvium fertilizing the lower reaches of the Nile. In view of this fact and the overwhelming importance which such waters and soils represent with reference to the total water and other resources of Ethiopia, the Imperial Ethiopian Government finds it important once again to make clear the position and rights of Ethiopia. . . . Ethiopia has the right and obligation to exploit the water resources of the Empire . . . and must, therefore, reassert and reserve now and for the future, the right to take all such measures in respect of its water resources and in particular, as regards that portion of the same which is of the greatest importance to its welfare, namely, those waters providing so nearly the entirety of the volume of the Nile, whatever may be the measure of utilization of such waters sought by recipient states situated along the course of that river.

Under circumstances where Ethiopia had not been consulted as regards the Nile discussions in the 1950s, the note explained:

> Ethiopia, alone the source of nearly the entirety of the waters involved, must, once again, make it clear that the quantities of the waters available to others must always depend on the ever increasing extent to which Ethiopia, the original owner, is and will be required to utilize the same for the needs of her expanding population and economy.

The welfare of the inhabitants of downstream states on the banks of the Nile would be a 'privilege' Ethiopia would be contributing to through 'her natural resources'.

The formal reservation tried to emphasize Ethiopia's perception of a privileged legal position ensuing from its being a major source of the Nile floods.

Since, Ethiopia's mainstream legal position continued to espouse nearly the same approach. During the fifty-first working session of the Sixth Legal Committee convened as Working Group of the Whole to negotiate on the final pieces of the draft UN watercourses convention in 1996, for example, Ethiopia presented a proposal that catches 'the contribution of water by watercourse states to an international river' as a self-standing sub-provision under Article 6 of the Convention. The move was rejected presumably because the general reference to 'hydrological' factors under Article 6.1.a had already covered the theme.

Ethiopia's aspiration was nonetheless fulfilled under the Agreement on the Nile Basin Cooperative Framework. Although Article 4.2.(a) has already stated that in ensuring equitable utilization of the Nile River, the basin states shall take in to account 'geographic, hydrographic, hydrological, climatic, ecological and other factors of natural character', an independent sub-provision – Article 4.2.(h) – provided explicitly that 'the contribution of each basin state to the waters of the Nile River system' shall likewise be considered as one of the factors affecting equitable apportionment. This development, restating the same variable twice under a single provision, signifies the increased weight attached to the source of waters of a river course as one of the *controlling* factors.

In summary, it is important to once again note that the weight accorded to any given factor is decided by its importance in comparison with that of other relevant factors which must be considered *together* and a conclusion reached on the basis of the *whole*.[13] This does not imply that all factors and circumstances are attributed an absolutely equal standing in any given circumstance. Some are more important than the others and as a rule, the circumstances of each particular basin shall help identify which.

In this context, states could be presumed to have varying scales of sovereign interest over natural endowments presented in meagre quantities. With respect to shared watercourses, such interests may assume exceptionally vital import in certain unique circumstances, as in cases when, in a display of distinctive geographical realities, the water flow of a river is furnished by one or two riparian states *only*.

In referring to the Nile basin, it could be submitted that the near-absolute hydrological dependence of the states of Egypt and Sudan on floods of a river essentially derived from a single co-riparian state – Ethiopia, proffers a compelling rationale to acknowledge that among the factors, the *relative contribution* of each of the three basin states would assume a prevailing credence both in comparison to several other variables as well as in the eventual assessment of equitable benefits.

Geographical and climatic factors

Similarly, the extent of a river course and the climatic constitution (including rain patterns, seasonality and evaporation) in the territory of each watercourse state have been depicted as some of the relevant factors considered both under the UN Watercourses Convention and the Helsinki Rules.

Before the South Sudan's independence, about 79 percent of the entire territory of Sudan – covering a staggering 1,978,506sq.km, and more than a third of the physical landscape in Ethiopia and Egypt, respectively stretching over 365,117 and 326,751sq.km – are placed within the watersheds of the Nile basin system. A huge proportion of the entire Nile basin (64 percent) had been confined within the Sudan alone. Both in Egypt, Ethiopia and particularly in Sudan, the Nile traverses colossal distances, covering areas of arid, semi-arid and tropical climate.

Sudan receives a scanty mean annual rainfall of 416mm and an average basin rainfall of about 500mm, with a climate ranging between extremes of a dry setting in Northern Sudan and a tropical rain pattern in the South where rain-fed

13 International Law Association (1966) 'Helsinki Rules on the Uses of the Waters of International Rivers', ILA Publication, London pp 7–55, Article 5.3; United Nation Convention on the Law of the Non-navigational Uses of International Watercourses (1997), Article 6.3.

agriculture is practised.[14] The annual precipitation varies from about 20mm in the arid and semi-arid northern third of the country to 400–800mm in the fertile central clay plains and 1,200–1,500mm in the extreme South.[15]

On the other hand, the Blue Nile (Abay) basin alone – one of the three distinct sub-basins in Ethiopia providing floods to the Nile system – accounts for 25 percent of its population, 20 percent of Ethiopia's land area and 50 percent of its total average annual runoff, extending over 199,812sq.km.[16] The Tekeze and the Baro-Akobo sub-basins extend over 90,001 and 74,102sq.km respectively.

In Ethiopia, the Blue Nile basin receives a mean annual rainfall of 1400mm; on the basis of climatic conditions, four readily defined areas have been described in the region: two areas of the sub-basin are characterized by a relatively high rainfall, largely providing the main perennial cropping and surplus grains; certain districts in the north-west and north-east are endowed with a relatively low annual rainfall, representing the main drought-prone constituencies that have hitherto posed problems with respect to food self-sufficiency.[17]

In contrast, in Egypt, a hugely significant proportion of its population settles in close vicinity of the fertile banks of the Nile River, stretching from a northern tip of the Aswan High Dam all the way to Cairo, the delta region and Alexandria. The average precipitation in Egypt has been computed as low as 51mm/yr.

Relatively, geographical and climatic considerations provide objective facts on the basis of which equitable entitlements may be worked out. But, neither international law nor the practices of states have been explicit in elucidating the correlation that should exist between geographical/climatic facts of a particular basin state and its relative entitlements of rights under the law.

The general legal impression would appear to be that the geographical breadth and adverse climatic setting of a riparian state are associated with enhanced entitlements in equitable rulings. After all, Article V.1.3 of the Helsinki Rules had singled out the climate affecting the basin as independent factor, and Article 4.2.(i) of the Cooperative Framework Agreement has explicitly stressed that the determination of equitable and reasonable utilization of the Nile waters shall take, among others, 'the extent and proportion of the drainage area in the territory of each basin state'.

Yet, given the facts presented above, how precisely each of these variables translates into real and quantifiable measures of rights in the context of procedures dealing with equitable sharing of waters/enefits and the extent to which they influence any such decision-making process is where the serious enigma rests. A

14 FAO (2005), FAO's Information System on Water and Agriculture, Geography, Climate and Population <http://www.fao.org/nr/water/aquastat/countries/sudan/index.stm>, last accessed December 2010.

15 Asim I. Mogharby (1982) 'The Jonglei Canal, Needed Development or Potential Eco-disaster?', *Environmental Conservation*, vol 9, no 2, p 141.

16 Federal Democratic Republic of Ethiopia (1999) 'Abay River Integrated Development Master Plan Project', Ministry of Water Resources, Addis Ababa, Phase 3, vol 1, p 13.

17 Federal Democratic Republic of Ethiopia (1999), note 16, p 46.

clear set of precedents is wanting in this respect as well and legal literatures had been barely specific.

Without any prejudice to the independent stature of the factors as such, reason would tend to order that the assessment of geographical and climatic elements would make better sense when such facts are blended with other considerations, including but not limited to size of population dependent on the watercourse in a basin, existing and potential uses and the scales of social and economic dependency on the shared watercourse.

In this perspective, a provisional conclusion can be drawn within a broader framework of the analysis of factors that affect equitable utilization across the basin.

First, the arid climatic constitution and absolute dearth of alternative fresh water resources would clearly favour Egypt's position, and if on a much lesser degree, the state of Sudan. Although Egypt and Ethiopia are similarly exposed to concentrated demographic pressures of a population living in the respective basin constituencies of an equivalent stretch, an extremely unfavourable climatic setting situates the former in a relatively enhanced standing. Climatic conditions, however, may work against Egypt, particularly in connection with the construction of major water-control works such as reservoirs, where evaporation and waste have been exceedingly high.

On the other hand, in Sudan, an oversized breadth of the basin's geography could signify a higher scale of economic, social and demographic impact of the resource across its jurisdiction and as such, it positions the country in a *proportionately* elevated stature in contrast to its two neighbours to the north and east.

Social and economic needs of the watercourse states concerned

A second important factor, restated both under the Helsinki/Berlin Rules and the UN Watercourses Convention and which utilization of an international watercourse in equitable and reasonable manner requires taking into account is the social and economic needs of the watercourse states concerned. The same variable has been listed as one of the nine broad factors and circumstances under Article 4 of the Cooperative Framework Agreement.

Any enterprise that considers social and economic factors with a view to establishing equity would readily heave multifaceted issues whose solutions may not necessarily be evident in a simple reading of the provision.

What is the geographical scope of economic and social needs of watercourse states that should be considered in computing the equitability of uses of international watercourses? And which particular facts of development (or perhaps, underdevelopment), presumably fulfilled through utilization of a shared resource, should be selected for assessment and eventually, determination of equitable apportionment based on consideration of the social and economic needs of watercourse states? How should each constituent element of competing social and economic interests of basin states be set on a balancing scale and prioritized? In equitable determinations based on the social and economic factors, would a general reference to the stages of economic development of the system states be legally warranted?

Generally established in a political process, the 'identification of social and economic needs of watercourse states is a subjective criterion and controversial by nature';[18] it is difficult to state with sufficient lucidity and certainty.

For the present purpose, though, some conventional indicators in development and poverty studies which draw on facts relating to national incomes, population growth, agricultural development, existing and potential cultivable areas, food security, employment and access to improved sanitation/drinking waters can be employed as feasible indexes; the indicators can help reflect on the impact of shared watercourses on a riparian country's level of social and economic state.

Admittedly, such a presentation of details cannot be comprehensive; development facts are susceptible to frequent changes, not to mention that even when considering a limited quantum of resource base, theoretically, national aspirations of needs that can be derived from shared river courses can simply be infinite. As the ILC had noted, the open-ended nature of the economic and social needs criteria under Article 6 would naturally pose problems for the needs of states are unconfined, increasing, instead of diminishing with each particular level of satisfaction.

Moreover, even where the social and economic values of a resource can be ascertained within reasonable bounds, as much a challenge remains in interpreting any such conclusion as may be drawn from the extra-legal development standards, and in translating the same in to some measurable privilege under international law.

Neither the commentaries furnished on the Helsinki/Berlin Rules nor the UN Watercourses Convention tendered sufficient illumination in this regard. In the following sections, a narrower focus of the presentation would be directed at submitting and assessing only such *selected* indexes of development as would help reveal the social and economic utility of the Nile in the territories of the three basin states of focus.

The territorial scope of *needs* covered

Under Article 6.1.(b), the reference to economic and social needs of a watercourse state whose satisfaction is projected through utilization of a transboundary river encompasses both constricted aspirations focusing specifically on the growth requirements of the *basin* itself, and corresponding necessities of the *whole riparian state* as such. That no territorial limitation had been implied in the definition of the principle is evident under the pertinent instruments, which stipulated that 'watercourse states shall, in their respective territories, utilize an international watercourse in an equitable and reasonable manner'.

Chiefly drawing on existing developmental realities across many drainage basins, this reading merely reasserts a broadly acknowledged observation that 'comprehensive

18 Katak B. Malla (2005) *The Legal Regime of international watercourses, progress and paradigms regarding uses and environmental protection*, Stockholm, University of Stockholm, p 357.

river basin development plan must always take account of competing projects, demands and service areas within wider boundaries than merely those of the basin; natural and social factors may indicate a wider area for optimum growth'.[19]

Of course, in addressing issues of equitable apportionment under the Convention, recourse to a comprehensive assessment of the respective levels of social and economic development of the states not significantly *linked* nor particularly *depending* on particular uses of an international river course would not be legally warranted. As Tanzi and Arcari had observed, the factor at hand is not intended to deal with the stage of economic development of riparian states (as such), but rather to cover the degree of their dependence, both in social and economic terms, on the use of the watercourse and its waters.[20] This is achieved through a cross-comparison of the relative needs of basin states sharing the resource.

This interpretation confirms the countrywide dimension of the right of states to utilize river resources for the common good of their entire communities, the geographical location of the waters notwithstanding. In practice, this involves not only that a river's waters can be diverted outside the watershed limits of a sub-basin, but also that water can be subjected to social and economic utilities quite distantly from the physical sites and population centres of the 'parent' drainage basin, whatever the technical means employed to realize such objectives.[21]

In limited contexts, decisions of the ICJ had the occasion to reflect on both issues raised above. In several maritime delimitation proceedings involving equitable use determinations, the Court referred to 'economic circumstances/potentials' of contested resources, but discarded arguments relating to a general comparison of the stages of development of states as indefensible legal proposition.[22]

In the *North Sea Continental Shelf* case (Germany, Denmark and the Netherlands), for instance, the ICJ held that delimitation of the continental shelf between the

19 J.D. Chapman (1963) *The International River Basin Proceedings of a Seminar on the Development and Administration of the International River Basin*, Vancouver, University of British Columbia, p 2; R.E. Clark (1967) *Water and Water Rights*, Indianapolis, Vol II, pp 427–9.

20 Attila Tanzi and Maurizio Arcari (2001) *The UN Convention on the law of international watercourses*, London/ The Hague/ Boston, Kluwer Law International, p 132.

The author drew on Fuentes' arguments wherein it was submitted that the inclusion of these factors should not consist in the comparison of stages of economic and social development of the states concerned; the question about the needs of the parties is a question about *degrees* of dependence from waters and watercourse utilization. Ximena Fuentes (1996) '*The Criteria for the Equitable Utilization of International Rivers*', *British Yearbook of International Law*, vol 67, p 344.

21 After a detailed survey of several legal authorities, though, the Krishna Water Disputes Tribunal concluded: 'the preponderance of opinion seems to indicate that diversion of water to another watershed may be permitted, but normally, in the absence of any agreement, the prudent course would be to limit diversion to the surplus waters left, after liberally allowing for the pressing needs of basin areas; in general, basin regions are more dependent on the water than other areas.' Government of India, Krishna Water Disputes Tribunal (1973) *The Report of the Krishna Water Disputes Tribunal with the Decision*, vol II, para 406.

22 However, it must be noted beforehand that maritime decisions represent a distinct legal regime whose evolution had been influenced by a set of facts that are not necessarily congruent with the progressive development of international watercourses law.

parties in the North Sea is governed by the principle that each coastal state is entitled to a just and equitable share; and in balancing the factors in question, the Court explained various aspects must be taken into account, some of which are related 'so far as known or readily ascertainable, to the physical and geological structures and natural resources of the continental shelf areas involved'.[23] This economic logic had been premised on the notion of the 'unity of deposits' in the continental shelf itself,[24] but did not transcend to the consideration of exterior circumstances of the parties to the dispute.

This conclusion was endorsed more explicitly in a subsequent ruling involving Tunisia and Libya, wherein, Tunisia pleaded that general economic circumstances of the disputing states should be duly considered in equitable determination procedures. Tunisia endeavoured to draw the Court's attention to its relative poverty *vis-à-vis* Libya in terms of the absence of natural resources, including agriculture and minerals; likewise, it highlighted the abundance of oil and gas wealth as well as agricultural resources in Libya.

The Court categorically declined to heed to Tunisia's claims. It submitted that such economic considerations cannot be taken into account in equitable delimitation of the continental shelf areas; while the presence of oil-wells in an area to be delimited may, depending on the facts, be an element to be taken into account in the process of weighing all relevant factors, the economic arguments submitted are virtually *extraneous* factors since they are variables which unpredictable national fortune or calamity, as the case may be, might at any time cause to tilt the scale one way or the other; a country might be poor today and become rich tomorrow as a result of an event such as the discovery of a valuable economic resource.[25]

By refusing to consider such a standard and cautiously limiting the significance of the application of economic factors exclusively in the context of the particular area delimited, the Court refused to draw itself into an essentially political discourse under the guise of equitable delimitation/apportionment of maritime territories. Fuentes observed that as such, the Court's reluctance did not originate in the 'extra-legal nature of the economic criteria', but from its perceived reservation on 'how these factors should operate in the process of delimitation so that the decision does not intrude in to a political realm'.[26]

Yet, the Court's disinclination in considering the economic positions of states in the maritime delimitation proceedings does not necessarily warrant, at least in the context of the UN Watercourse Convention, that some scrutiny of national economic settings and relative resource endowments should be circumvented under all circumstances. As noted above, broader national exigencies of a riparian state in economic and social services can be fulfilled through proper utilization of a river course situated in a particular basin.

23 *North Sea Continental Shelf (1969), Judgment, ICJ Reports*, paras 93–94,

24 *North Sea Continental Shelf (1969)*, note 23, para 97.

25 *Continental Shelf (Tunisia/Libyan Arab Jamahiriya) (1982), Judgment, ICJ Reports*, pp 77–8, paras 106–7.

26 Fuentes (1996), note 20, p 342.

This implies that certain facts involving the comparative stages of development of basin states (as for example in the scales of irrigated agriculture, level of food security, access to improved drinking water, the provision of hydro-electric power, etc.) will help provide indications in balancing and prioritizing the competitive requirements of the states. Furthermore, as opposed to the ICJ's rulings in the maritime delimitation cases, it is already established that the availability of alternative resources 'outside of a basin' (such as alternative energy endowments like oil, gas or additional sources of water) will certainly count in equitable apportionment of transboundary river courses.[27]

A national jurisprudence of courts or arbitral tribunals specifically conversing on the issues had not been plentifully availed; a few decisions, involving interstate disputes in the Indian federation had the occasion to tender an illustration of both the perspectives and legal stakes involved.

In addressing one of the issues discussed above, the Krishna Water Disputes Tribunal summarized the pertinent propositions of the contending states as follows:

> Mysore contends that diversion outside the basin is illegal and that only in-basin needs should be considered in determining a state's equitable share; Maharashtra asserts that transfer of water to another watershed for purposes of both power-generation and irrigation is lawful and that, while in-basin needs only should be considered in determining a state's equitable share, a state should be permitted to divert its share of the water outside the basin; Andhra Pradesh contends that out-of-basin needs are a relevant factor and that diversion outside the basin for irrigation needs only should be permitted.[28]

Drawing on a widespread practice of several states, the Tribunal held and very unambiguously, that diversion of water of an interstate river outside the river basin is legal.[29] And in so ruling, needless legal disputes involving the issue of whether or not the out-of-basin requirements of riparian states potentially satisfied through the employ of waters of a particular basin should be considered as relevant factors was rendered moot. The Tribunal's dictum reasoned:

> a state is one integral unit, and its interests encompass the wellbeing of all its inhabitants within its territory, including areas outside the river basin; without prejudice to interests of a (local) state or of any of its inhabitants in the waters of the inter-state river and river valley, the relevant consideration is the interest of the state as a whole and all its inhabitants and not merely the interest of the basin areas of the state.[30]

27 Under Article 6 of the UN Watercourses Convention, for instance, equitable determinations must take account of circumstances relating to hydrology and climate as well as the availability of alternatives (in agriculture, energy development, etc.), of comparable value, to particular planned or existing uses. The availability of other resources has also been alluded to under the Helsinki Rules.

28 Government of India, Krishna Water Disputes Tribunal (1973), note 21, para 393.

29 Government of India, Krishna Water Disputes Tribunal (1973), note 21, para 401.

30 Government of India, Krishna Water Disputes Tribunal (1973), note 21, para 402.

By the same token, Bourne submitted:

> . . . in view of the present engineering skill which makes it possible to transfer water of one river basin to another, one has to consider the use of waters of an area rather than of a particular drainage basin. In determining what is equitable share in the waters of a river, the most relevant factor is the use that can be made of it by the riparian states and so diversions to or from a river system ought to be embraced in this definition.[31]

The point is therefore self-evident and hardly calls for a supplementary reflection. However, certain challenging issues linger: which particular facts of development (or perhaps, underdevelopment), presumably fulfilled through the utilization of a shared resource should be selected for assessment, and eventually, determination of equitable apportionment based on consideration of the social and economic needs of watercourse states? And whether any such value of water relates to securing opportunities of direct employment, the preservation of food security, the provisioning of power, obtaining export revenues or for industrial water consumption, how should each constituent element of competing social and economic interests of basin states be set on a balancing scale and prioritized? As illustrated above, a mere recourse to scrutinize and compare the general social and economic positions of the states would simply be inadequate.

Harmonizing indexes of social and economic development

Admittedly, the task is not uncomplicated; in this section, a narrower focus would be directed at presenting a general reflection of riparian needs and domestic challenges associated with demographic pressures, food security, access to water and opportunities of employment. The discussion would be accompanied by a limited analysis of particulars relating to existing agriculture, future developments in cultivable areas and the generation of water-propelled energy sources.

Traditionally, the Nile River has been subjected to varied categories of beneficial uses. In 2008, the Egyptian economy mustered an annual gross domestic product of $162.2, respectively three and six times larger than the corresponding feats in Sudan and Ethiopia.[32] Industry, relying on waters of the Nile basin accounted for

31 He concluded, though, that the ILA and IIL documents do not expressly confer the right to utilize waters outside its basin; their whole tenor showed that states have such right in certain circumstances.

Patricia Wouters (1997) *International Water Law, Selected Writings of Professor Charles B. Bourne*, London/The Hague, Kluwer Law International, p 19.

32 The respective GDP figures were accounted as $162.2 (Egypt), $55.9 (Sudan, shortly before separation of the South), $25.5 (Ethiopia); the GNI per Capital was – Egypt (1,800), Sudan (1100) and Ethiopia (280).

The World Bank Group (2010) World Bank 2008 World Development Indicators Database, April 2010 <http://ddpext.worldbank.org/ext/ddpreports/ViewSharedReport?REPORT_ID=9147&REQUEST_TYPE=VIEWADVANCED>, last accessed December 2010.

a staggering 37.7 percent of the GDP, but employed only 17 percent of the labour force.[33] On the other hand, agriculture, depending nearly exclusively on provisions of the Nile River, contributed 13.1 percent of its GDP, 30 percent of commodity exports and involved nearly a third of the nation's labour force in 2010.[34] The sector accounted for 95 percent of the total net water demand in Egypt.[35]

A nation with an estimated population of 84,474,000 (2010) growing at a rate of 1.8 percent per annum,[36] part of the broader response to swelling susceptibilities prompted by demographic pressures has been addressed through increased urbanization, the building of new desert urban centres and expansion of off-valley irrigation schemes. In 1946, the total cultivated area stood at 2.52 million hectares (6 million feddans) and the outer limit of cultivation had been estimated as 3.15 million hectares (7.5 million feddans), requiring about 58bcm/yr of waters at Aswan.[37] In 2005, Egyptian agriculture, including lands reclaimed since 1952, extended over 3.38 million hectares (8 million feddans),[38] withdrawing about 59bcm/yr of Nile waters.

Egyptian agricultural development has generally proffered huge opportunities in direct and indirect employment.[39] The sector's growth also permitted Egypt to attain food self-sufficiency in several crops and agricultural products and reduce the gap by up to 75 percent in several strategic crops including sugar, poultry, dairy, fish and meat.[40]

33 Egypt State Information Service, Agriculture, <http://www.sis.gov.eg/En/Story.aspx?sid=835>, last accessed December 2010; FAO (2005) Egypt, Basic statistics and population, *FAO Water Report 29*, Table 1; FAO, FAO's Information System on Water and Agriculture, Geography, Climate and Population <http://www.fao.org/nr/water/aquastat/countries/egypt/index.stm>, last accessed December 2010;

Central Intelligence Agency, The World Fact Book, Egypt <https://www.cia.gov/library/publications/the-world-factbook/geos/eg.html>, last accessed December 2010.

34 Egypt State Information Service, note 33.

There has been some digression though: in 1960, the same sector represented 40 percent of the GDP, according to the Ministry of Water Resources and Irrigation; the agricultural sector represented 17 percent of the GDP and provided employment to 40 percent of the population in 2005.

Arab Republic of Egypt (2005) 'National Water Resources Plan for Egypt 2017', Ministry of Water Resources and Irrigation, Planning Sector, Cairo, p I-6.

35 Arab Republic of Egypt (2005), note 34.

36 The World Bank Group (2010), World Bank 2008 World Development Indicators Database <http://ddpext.worldbank.org/ext/ddpreports/ViewSharedReport?REPORT_ID=9147&REQUEST_TYPE=VIEWADVANCED>, last accessed December 2010; In contrast, the National Water Resources Plan estimated that in the year 2017, the population of Egypt is expected to grow to 83 million. Arab Republic of Egypt (2005), note 34, p XVIII.

37 H.E. Hurst, R.P Black and Y.M. Simaika (1946) 'The Nile Basin, The Future Conservation of the Nile', Vol VII, Physical Department Paper no 51, Cairo, SOP Press, p 11.

38 Arab Republic of Egypt (2005), note 34, pp II-29, 31.

39 For instance, in 2005, cotton production employed one million people during most of the year, constituting the principal source of cash income in many farming households; the textile industry reportedly provided direct employment to half a million workers, and indirectly to several millions more.

Arab Republic of Egypt (2005), note 34, p 2–34.

40 Egypt State Information Service, Agriculture, note 33.

Egypt is extremely vulnerable to water security mainly because of its most downstream geographical position. Yet, a policy that endeavoured to preserve national food security as one cherished pillar of the overall development drive continued to draw considerable political interest. While the Government had admitted that the agricultural strategy is not based on self-sufficiency, but on food security using Egypt's competitive advantage,[41] in practice, Egypt continued to produce large volumes of low-valued basic staples and water-intensive crops. For understandable rationales, the option of resorting to virtual water imports that emphasize on a pure economic logic of obtaining, for same or lesser cost, alternative sources of food supplies other than through intensive home-based agriculture was not conceived as a strictly plausible course.[42] Egypt's approach accentuated the vital social and economic utilities of agriculture both as a source foreign currency and as a means of keeping some of the population down on farm, and hence, reducing population pressures in overcrowded and underserviced urban areas.[43]

On the other side, in Sudan, while rain-fed agriculture continued to still cover the largest area and constituted a vital basis of the social and economic fabric, irrigation extending over some 1,863,000 hectares and composed on just 11 percent of the total cultivated land[44] contributed more than half of the total volume of agricultural production in the north and south.[45] The scale of socio-economic impact of agriculture has also been evident that in 2004, for instance, the sector engaged 57 percent of the total economically active population (estimated 7.9 million), and accounted for about 90 percent of the country's non-oil export earnings.[46] Agriculture represented for about 26 percent Sudan's GDP, preceded by industry (34 percent) and services (40 percent).[47]

41 Arab Republic of Egypt (2005), note 34, pp 2–32.

42 For instance, the UNDP was not conclusively satisfied, at least from a human development perspective that the case for reducing water stress by expanding virtual water trade is not without its problems.

United Nations Development Programme (2006) *Human Development Report 2006, Beyond scarcity: Power, Poverty and the Global Water Crisis*, New York, Palgrave Macmillan, p 3.

Waterbury and Whittington argued that in the long-term, irrigation agriculture would not constitute a feasible alternative for achieving food security and countries in water-stress regions and under demographic pressures would have to exploit the option of pursuing economic development strategies that pay for imported foods.

John Waterbury and Dale Whittington (1998) 'Playing Chicken on the Nile, Implications of micro dam development in Ethiopian highlands and Egypt's New Valley project', *Middle Eastern Natural Environment Bulletin*, vol 22, no 3, pp 158, 163.

43 Jutta Brunnee and Stephen J. Toope (2002) 'The Changing Nile Basin Regime: Does law matter?' *Harv Int'l LJ*, vol 43, no 1, p 121.

44 FAO, FAO's Information System on Water and Agriculture, Geography, Climate and Population, Sudan <http://www.fao.org/nr/water/aquastat/countries/sudan/index.stm>, last accessed December 2010.

FAO (2005) Sudan, Basic Statistics and Population, *FAO Water Report 29*, Table 1.

45 FAO, FAO's Information System on Water and Agriculture, Geography, Climate and Population, note 44.

46 FAO, note 44.

47 The World Bank Group (2010) World Bank 2008 World Development Indicators Database <http://ddpext.worldbank.org/ext/ddpreports/ViewSharedReport?&CF=&REPORT_ID=9147&REQUEST_TYPE=VIEWADVANCED>, last accessed December 2010.

As in Egypt, Sudan too has displayed national policies that concentrated on revitalizing its irrigational and water-control infrastructures; it placed the agricultural sector as a vital column of its development initiative. Hence, along with water withdrawals in industries, the agricultural sector in general and irrigated agriculture in particular would continue to compose critical columns of its economy both in terms of foreign earning, GDP contribution and the size of population involved.

On the contrary, in Ethiopia, irrigated agriculture utilized a meagre 5.2bcm/yr of waters, and in 2008, the count of economically active population in the agricultural sector had been assessed at 30.6 million, i.e. 37.5 percent of its 80.3 million populations – growing at a rate of 2.6 percent per annum.[48] The Blue Nile basin alone, one of the three separate sub-basins that yield waters to the White Nile and the Nile-proper systems, accounted for over 40 percent of agricultural production in Ethiopia,[49] symbolizing an immense prospect in terms of the delivery of economic and social services. In contrast to the national setting in Sudan and Egypt where the services and industry sectors have been placed on the top, agriculture constituted the principal basis of the national GDP (44 percent), followed by services (42 percent) and industry (13 percent).[50]

In spite of its enormous potentials, the Nile had barely influenced Ethiopia's economic development and nationwide, poverty remained a deeply entrenched phenomenon. Although the World Food Summit (1996) pledged to eradicate hunger, food insecurity and malnutrition within a decade,[51] years on, the number of undernourished people stood at 854 million worldwide (2001–03), some 820 million of which were in developing countries.[52] The trend had been declining since, but the same period saw that 2.4 million (i.e. 3 percent of the total population) in Egypt, 7.9 million in Sudan (37 percent), and a staggering 38.2 million people in Ethiopia, representing 46 percent of the total population, had been undernourished.[53]

The challenges of meeting future food requirements have had global dimensions. Conventionally, part of the solution in reducing drought and the incidences of hunger rested on increasing food productivity and improving access, which impact both rural and urban economies, particularly in developing countries. The FAO anticipated a net expansion of irrigated land of some 45 million hectares in 93 developing countries (rising to a total of 242 million hectares in 2030) and projected that agricultural water withdrawals will increase by some 14 percent from 2000 to 2030.[54]

48 FAO, Information System on Water and Agriculture, Geography, Climate and Population, Ethiopia <http://www.fao.org/nr/water/aquastat/countries/ethiopia/index.stm>, last accessed December 2010.

FAO (2005) Ethiopia, Basic statistics and population, *FAO Water Report 29*, Tables 1 and 4.

49 Federal Democratic Republic of Ethiopia (1999) 'Abay River Integrated Development Master Plan Project', Ministry of Water Resources, Addis Ababa, Phase 3, vol 1, p 13.

50 The World Bank Group (2010) World Bank 2008 World Development Indicators Database, note 47.

51 FAO (2006) *The State of Food Insecurity in the World 2006, Eradicating World Hunger — taking stock ten years after the World Food Summit*, Rome, UN FAO, p 2.

52 FAO (2006), note 51, p 8.

53 FAO (2006), note 51, pp 32–7.

54 World Water Assessment Program (2003), note 3, p 193.

Inauspiciously, though, Ethiopia's total land area equipped for irrigation remained very insignificant. A greater proportion of the national wealth continued to derive from a subsistence-level rain-fed mode of agricultural production.

Concluding observations

On the basis of a very limited overview of the economic and social implications of the Nile River in Egypt, Sudan and Ethiopia, certain conclusions can be drawn in relation to the determination of equitable apportionment.

Two words of caution, though: first, equitable apportionment decisions do not merely involve objective socio-economic considerations at all times and in all situations; often, other countervailing factors including international comity and the principle of good neighbourliness will play a part.

Second, in illustrating the relative positions of the Nile basin states, the stated facts and the projected benefits do not in any way purport to present the whole measure of social and economic values of water in the sub-region, nor the alternative means of satisfying such needs. In the nature of a primarily legal research contemplated, the reflections have been but condensed.

As noted above, in Egypt and parts of Sudan, the practice of irrigational agriculture is deeply entrenched, significantly impacting both the organization and functioning of social and economic structures. In fact, in Egypt, the effect transcends far beyond mere irrigated lands and crops grown, to define its very existence. Together, irrigational agriculture and industry make up more than half of the national GDP and engage a corresponding figure of the national labour force in direct and indirect employments. Likewise, the sector has been responsible for significant proportions of national export revenues and is a key resource base of raw materials supplied to industries. Egypt's total cultivated area tops similar developments both in the Sudan and Ethiopia.

In consequence, any initiative aiming at equitable determinations by stressing the social and economic values of the Nile waters will naturally ascribe the aforesaid facts bigger weight. This becomes compelling given Egypt's extreme vulnerability deriving from its arid climatic constitution and the dearth of substitute resources to satisfy domestic, irrigational and industrial water requirements.

Of course, increasing trends have been perceived wherein the service and industry sectors tended to occupy a more vital position in Egypt's national economic setting. This corresponds with an earlier prediction by the United Nations Development Program which concluded that a broader drift is discernable where urban centres and industry would increase their demand for water, while agriculture continues to lose out.[55] Legally, this verity may engender dire consequences.

To the extent that there is little correlation between industries and agricultural water withdrawals in Egypt (in the sense that industrial outputs do not depend

55 United Nations Development Programme (2006), note 42, p 17.

substantially on inputs supplied by agricultural raw materials),[56] and the national economy diversifies, a larger proportion of the GDP, employment and foreign exchange earnings would be extracted from other sectors. This sinks the traditional supremacy of the agriculture-based development drive in Egypt and in consequence, its entitlement.

By most rational accounts, though, such a scenario may not bring about significant effects on quantitative aspects of waters withdrawn at a *national* level. In relative economic terms, however, the new progress can shrink Egypt's excessive reliance on bulk-flows of the Nile waters to satisfy social and economic requirements of its population. Emerging sectors that consume a good-deal less volume of Nile waters have increasingly contributed greater proportions of the national wealth. With regard to the issue of equitable use determinations, such a course affects Egypt's standing negatively, in relation to Sudan and Ethiopia.

A similar leaning has also been observed in Northern Sudan where, while agricultural remains a dominant sector of the national economy, its share has increasingly declined recently because of decreased agricultural production and the increased exploitation and export of mineral oil.[57]

While Egypt commands a sophisticated irrigation economy that stretches over 3.38 million hectares and its position will be accorded greater measures of protection on account of multifarious impacts of irrigation agriculture on the national economy, paradoxically, Sudan and Ethiopia can also stand on the *gaining* side on the basis of their social and economic under-achievements. In the past decades, both states have performed poorly in some indexes of human development and as such they can submit for superior claims based on these considerations.

Successive studies commissioned by various agencies of the United Nations had indicated that Ethiopia and Sudan have the most abysmal records in several indicators of human development, including the count of populations living under defined poverty lines, food security, nutritional status, access to improved water resources and sanitation.

Naturally, uncertainties involving food production engender the gravest threat to human existence. In Egypt, of course, agricultural development has trekked far beyond corresponding progresses in Sudan. Even worse, Ethiopia had been completely missing from the atlas of irrigated agriculture.

As illustrated earlier, Egypt, a downstream riparian situated just in a middle of a parched region has already attained food self-sufficiency in several crops and agricultural products; it has also managed to reduce the gap in several strategic crops including sugar, poultry, dairy, fish and meat by up to 75 percent.[58]

56 Within the industry sector, though, the food industry sub-sector and the textile/woods/paper industry sub-sector, heavily depending on the provision of raw materials in the agriculture sector, constitute two of the largest contributors of total 'industrial output' respectively at 24 percent and 13 percent. The rest is divided between petroleum, engineering, chemical/pharmaceutical, cement/building material, and mining industry sub sectors.

Arab Republic of Egypt (2005), note 34, pp 2–38.

57 FAO, Information System on Water and Agriculture, Sudan, note 44.

58 Egypt State Information Service, Agriculture, note 33.

Considering the demographic pressures and adverse climatic constitution, Egypt's accomplishment in the provision of one basic component of social and economic necessities is but extraordinary.

The state of affairs is not fundamentally unrelated in the Sudan. In spite of problems of drought and rainfall variability, irrigated agriculture remained 'a central option to boost the economy in general and increase the living standard of the majority of the population'.[59] Sudan has generally been self-sufficient in basic foods, with important inter-annual and geographical variations and wide regional and household disparities in food security prevailing across the country.[60]

In contrast, Ethiopia – the second most populous state in Africa just overtaking Egypt – has undergone enormous economic and demographic strains caused by the uninhibited expansion of its human population and sheer underdevelopment of its massive resources.

Ethiopia's classically agrarian economy is based on small-holding subsistence farming and covers nearly half of its GDP. For several decades, the agricultural sector failed to sustain national food security. Sequential episodes of drought, famine and extreme water insecurity raged in the preceding decades, with certain overwhelming consequences.

As a modern nation, Ethiopia depended heavily on imports and food aids to address its food security concerns. The FAO observed 'food insecurity, as a result of persistent drought among other reasons, has been the order of the day for a very long period in Ethiopia; even during good years, the survival of some 4–6 million people depends on international food assistance'.[61]

Between the periods covering 1999–2004, more than half of all households in the country had reportedly experienced at least one major drought shock.[62] Rainfall variability and extreme changes in water flow recurred – destroying assets, undermining livelihoods and reducing the growth potential of whole economies: variability has diminished Ethiopia's growth potential by about a third, according to the World Bank.[63]

As part of a broader development strategy, successive schemes have been put in place projecting to reduce social and economic vulnerability; these included the introduction of irrigation agriculture, the generation of hydropowers and enhanced investments in physical, institutional and human infrastructures associated with the water sector.

Admittedly, national strategies that targeted on increased agricultural production and secure supply of food stuffs had occupied a center stage of the political discourse for quite a long period, with varying degrees of success. However, the concrete gains of engaging in large-scale irrigated agriculture had been stressed only in the last decade. Several specifics of the national strategy presumed various types of beneficial interventions in the main Nile and its tributaries in Ethiopia.

59 FAO, Information System on Water and Agriculture, Sudan, note 44.
60 FAO, note 44.
61 FAO, Information System on Water and Agriculture, Ethiopia, note 48.
62 FAO, note 48.
63 United Nations Development Programme (2006), note 42, p 15.

Agriculture constitutes a basic requirement of life and irrigated agriculture plays a significant role in this regard. Hence, Ethiopia's demonstrated susceptibility to successive droughts and famines and its part-dependence on the provision of external aid evinces but the augmented use that should be made of the Nile River water resources with a view to satisfying the social and economic challenges of its population. As the Krishna Water Disputes Tribunal had rightly noted, the use of water resources for irrigation to the fullest extent possible is an essential condition for diversifying agriculture and increasing crop yields.[64]

This presumes the institution and implementation of policy, regulatory and physical measures in the agricultural sector providing for the immediate provisioning of basic food stuffs and in the long term, the inputs required for industrial growth, as well as the means for mobilizing finance, labour and foreign exchange earnings. Egypt and the Sudan have performed fairly well on these counts and particularly so in agricultural food self-sufficiency. Ethiopia, on the other hand, will need to trek quite a long way before it can situate itself on a balance in meeting the *like needs* of its population.

In the context of prospective water allocations involving the three states, therefore, this particular verity of *underdevelopment* justifies a heightened priority accorded to Ethiopia's claims based on considerations of social and economic needs.

Moreover, Ethiopia's position will be reinforced since its development drive, at least in the immediate future, concentrates on the provisioning of a primary necessity of existence, i.e. the delivery of foodstuffs. This also has a human rights dimension. The right to food is indivisibly linked to the inherent dignity of the human person and is indispensable for the fulfilment of other human rights enshrined in the International Bill of Human Rights.[65]

Hence, while Ethiopia and parts of Sudan struggled with the steps needed to ensure the fundamental right of citizens to *freedom from hunger*, a large swathe of commercial plantations both in Egypt and Sudan, annually withdrawing billions of cubic meters of Nile waters, constituted vital pillars of the socio-economic welfare, but far beyond the means required for direct fulfilment of natural wants. A consideration of prime importance in equitable decisions should be that an occupation that inclines on preservation of the human existence as such cannot be treated on equal footing with essentially profit-motivated or export-oriented ventures that lay in the heart of downstream economic drive.

Conceptually, this argument draws a parallel rationalization from comments furnished by the ILA on Article 14 of the Berlin Rules (revising Article VI of the Helsinki Rules), where between competing categories of uses of international watercourses, vital human needs had been accorded an undisputed priority.[66]

64 Governments of India, Krishna Water Disputes Tribunal (1973), note 21, para 139.

65 United Nations (1999) 'The Right to Adequate Food (Art 11)', CESCR General Comment No. 12, Adopted at the Twentieth Session of the Committee on Economic, Social and Cultural Rights, 12 May, Document E/C 12/1999/5.

66 International Law Association (2004), Berlin Conference, Water Resources Law, Fourth Report, p 11.

Admittedly, the legal context in which the ILA raised the issue of vital human needs had been entirely different, and this is borne in mind. The ILA's category of vital human needs to which precedence was accorded included such waters as may be needed for immediate human consumption such as drinking, cooking and washing, and for other uses necessary for the immediate sustenance of a household, such as watering livestock and kitchen gardens.[67] Of course, the comment did not explicitly embrace 'basic food requirements' under its list of natural wants, and while there seems no compelling reason why this should not be so, the Association's concluding observation acknowledged that waters used for commercial irrigation, mining, manufacturing, the generation of power or for recreation do not fall under the concept of vital human needs. Simply, basic food requirements had not been in the list of exclusions.

Consequently, on the basis of the general theoretical underpinning of the ILA's annotations, one can further draw a broader perspective that equitable decisions based on the economic and social necessities of the Nile riparian communities should draw a distinction between two types of competing demands. On the one hand stood ordinary requirements intended for the satisfaction of natural wants, which should be accorded precedence; and on the other side are extraordinary requirements which, although crucial to the general enhancement of social and economic welfare of riparian communities (as in the creation of jobs, export revenue, etc.), are not absolute requisites for the immediate sustenance of human existence, and hence receive only a secondary consideration.

Population dependent on the watercourse in each basin state

The extent of 'population' covered

In 2010, the population in Ethiopia, Egypt and the Sudan would reach 211 million, representing nearly 50 percent of the total inhabitants in the Nile basin; by the year 2030, the figure would surge to 339 million.[68]

The impact of demographic facts was incidentally touched in the preceding sections principally concerned with expounding the social and economic values of the Nile waters in the riparian states of focus. The analysis had proffered a limited indication on the potential needs and relative degrees of dependence of populations of the Nile watercourse states on the shared resource. In this part, the investigation would concentrate on a broadly related theme, raise certain specific issues of concern and reinforce the legal dialogue presented above.

Both Articles 5.2.6 of the Helsinki Rules (as revised), Article 6.1(c) of the UN watercourses convention and Article 4.2.(c) of the Cooperative Framework

67 International Law Association (2004), note 66.

68 In the same year, the total count of population in the basin countries was estimated at 422.2 millions. (Eritrea 5.2, Burundi 8.5, Rwanda 10.2, Uganda 33.7, Kenya 40.8, Sudan (including South) 43.1, Tanzania 45.0, DR Congo 67.8, Egypt 84.4, and Ethiopia 84.9), <http://esa.un.org/unpp/>, last accessed December 2010.

Agreement have correspondingly provided that one important element that should be taken in to account in connection with the determination of equitable and reasonable utilization is the count of population dependent on the watercourse in each watercourse state.

At first glance, the population factor seems to offer an objective standard; in reality, though, the employ of such a parameter in equitable use determination procedures is liable to heave the same hurdles of comprehension as in above: should the expression population dependent on the watercourse be understood as merely referring to population of a particular basin area in which a watercourse situates? Or, of the basin state at large? And, in considering population as a factor, should there be some qualification requiring the presence of direct correlation between population facts on the one hand and a pattern of dependency, existing or potential, in the uses of a river course, on the other?

In the context of economic and social needs of states in waters of international watercourses, it had been held that the relevant geographical scope of economic interests satisfied through utilization of a river course should not be limited to the basin of a state as such, but also to areas outside of a basin.

An analogous view is reiterated here as well: in addressing issues related to population dependent on a transboundary river, the relevant consideration would embrace, as the Krishna Tribunal had outlined, 'the interest of the state as a whole and all its inhabitants, and not merely the interest of the basin areas of the state.'[69] Bourne submitted that the most beneficial use-thoughts will take into account the interests of larger population living outside of a basin, for science has removed the geographical limitations upon the utilization of water resources, and given man the capacity to transport water and energy generated by water to wherever he needs and uses them most economically and beneficially – even to places far outside the drainage basin.[70]

Yet, a rational approach in equitable and reasonable use deliberations instructs that the population element under Article 6.1 should not be construed in absolute terms, in the sense that every single inhabitant of a riparian state would *ipso facto* count, but only as referring to the total number of the riparian populace whose needs, present or projected, can be satisfied through utilization of a shared river course. In view of the uneven demographic strains and competitive stakes of states across a basin, this distinction is but simply crucial. In fact, this prerequisite explains the guarded phraseology under Article 6.1 of the Convention which did not provide that equitable procedures should consider the size of population in 'each watercourse state', but rather the 'population dependent on the watercourse in each water course state'.

Obviously, in this regard, the approach espoused under the Convention draws a logical appeal; while river courses constitute shared natural amenities, this verity could not be overstretched to imply that such resources alone could tender the

69 Government of India, Krishna Water Disputes Tribunal (1973), note 21, para 402.
70 Wouters (1997), note 31, p 19.

solution to every developmental predicament of riparian populations. Industries, the expansion of services, mineral reserves and rainfall can similarly furnish the basis for alternative sources of national wealth and by inference, provide the means for satisfying economic and social needs of watercourse states.[71] In fact, as Batstone put it, as states become industrialized, an increase in population does not necessarily reflect in a corresponding enlargement of irrigational needs; and in circumstances where 'states receive adequate rainfall for some part of their agriculture, it would seem strange if a section of the population supported by rain-fed farming or dependent on nomadic grazing should swell claims to water.'[72] The point is that the scope under Article 6.1(c) of the Convention is limited.

Precedents are not plenty where water allocation regimes had been instituted on the basis a combined reading of several variables that also highlight population-related facts. During the early stages of negotiations on the 1959 Nile Waters Agreement between Egypt and Sudan, population size had been proposed as one of the factors on the basis of which the total flow of the river should be apportioned. In his widely referred article titled: 'The utilization of the Nile waters' (1959), Batstone's study on the circumstances surrounding the conclusion of the treaty reflected on positions of both Egypt and Sudan, espoused in relation to the significance attached to the population variable. Sudan opted not to accord any consideration to pre-existing uses, in which case the absolute population ratio between Egypt and Sudan (roughly 2:1) would have given Egypt two-thirds and the Sudan one-third of the total flow – a division in a proportion of 56:28bcm/yr. Naturally, Egypt objected because of the sacrifice this would entail to its superior scale of uses.[73] Yet, population facts were too important not to heed to. Egypt was willing to consider a per capita division only with regard to the surplus waters (15bcm/yr) proposing to effect the allocation in a proportion of 72:8bcm/yr, to which the Sudan objected.[74]

As pointed out above, while the division of shared watercourses on a basis of population seems to offer a comparatively objective standard as opposed to many other variables, Batstone held reservation against the approach adopted during the Nile treaty negotiations. One concern related to the constant fluctuation of population; he argued population figures are

> too changeable a factor, and not sufficiently related to irrigation needs and riparian interests to provide a sound basis for determining international water rights. It is the land which is watered, not the people . . . and it seems in accordance with general principles of law that rights to water should attach to riparian territory than to a fluctuating population.[75]

71 It is worthy to note that in fact, Article V.2 (g) of the Helsinki Rules had provided 'the comparative costs of alternative means of satisfying the economic and social needs of each basin state' as one of the relevant factors considered in the determination of reasonable and equitable share, although it was subsequently dropped under Article 13 of the Berlin Rules (2004).

72 R. K. Batstone (1959) 'Utilization of the Nile Waters', *Int'l & Comp LQ*, vol 8, p 548.

73 Batstone (1959), note 72, p 547.

74 Batstone (1959), note 72, p 547.

75 Batstone (1959), note 72, p 548.

Evidently, since the 1950s, international law has evolved quite considerably to ascribe population facts vital credence in equitable use decisions. Batstone's view failed to contemplate that existing equitable and reasonable uses can generally be subjected to re-evaluation or modification where circumstances justifying their continuation are no longer present on account of changed conditions with regard, for instance, the size of population. Still, one aspect of his observations deserves a particular attention: that there must exist a genuine link between population facts and existing/potential dependence on the waters of an international watercourse.

Dependence: aspects of human development contemplated

Certainly, the *link* requirement is not devoid of complications and particularly so when one notes how diversely water affects humanity. Throughout history, human progress has depended on access to water and on the ability of societies to harness the potential of water as a productive resource. Water for life in the household and water for livelihoods through production constitute two important foundations of human development.[76] And within the confines of riparian resource endowments, states have constantly endeavoured to enlarge human development through the realization of these potentials: national frameworks have been drawn, water resources management strategies designed and water infrastructures put into service.

Obviously, water permeates all aspects of human development; the impact would grow in the future whether the benefits accruing to riparian populations relate to domestic utilization required to sustain basic life, to water irrigational fields, to propel the generation of power or to provide for industrial consumptions.

Therefore, in appraising the size of population dependent on an international watercourse, the diverse and entwined functions of water poses serious methodological and practical challenges, and particularly so in computing human development gains directly associated with the utilization of shared watercourses. The trouble can further complicate when the human rights dimension of uses of international watercourses is also considered: as Attila noted the concept of dependence referred to under Article 6 encompasses not only the size of the population dependent on the water course, but also the degree of its dependence.[77]

This entails that even with a general outline of full development scenarios of transboundary river courses at hand, a thwarting hurdle will remain in measuring and eventually presenting a complete picture of the direct impacts of an international watercourse on the respective populations of basin states. In establishing the size and intensity of population dependency, for instance, should one merely concentrate on objective facts relating to total cultivated and potentially cultivable lands utilized for the production of crops essential for the

76 United Nations Development Programme (2006), note 42, p 2.

77 Attila Tanzi and Maurizio Arcari (2001) *The UN Convention on the Law of International Watercourses*, London/The Hague/Boston, Kluwer Law International, p 131.

maintenance of food security, the generation of export earnings or the supply of industrial raw materials?

Or, instead, should the emphasis recline on waters withdrawn for domestic requirements? Now that over a billion persons lack access to basic water supply and adequate sanitation and hence that universal access to water has been championed as a fundamental human right,[78] should the stress be directed at the quantified balance of access or deprivation, in each riparian state, of water supply sufficient and continuous for personal and domestic uses?

Or, in a world where one in two people, 2.6 billion in all lacks access to adequate sanitation, and productivity losses linked to water and sanitation in developing countries amount to 2 percent of GDP – rising up to 5 percent in Sub-Saharan Africa,[79] should any statistical scrutiny relating to the figure of population dependent on watercourses take due account of the prospective utility of rivers in this regard? And all the same, couldn't population impacts, or in other words, the scales of necessity or dependency be measured in terms of, for instance, the relative prospects of the provision of water and sanitation in reducing the incidence of diseases and afflictions?

Or, in appraising the population dependent on an international watercourse, should one rather reflect on other non-consumptive uses of waters as in the generation of power and benefits that accrue to riparian communities in the form access to electricity services?

The human development list can simply pile. Of course, the current investigation will present only a very limited perspective; it cannot claim to submit on every aspect of development indexes associated with the utilization of the Nile River and its tributaries and, a propos, inform on the scales of population dependency in the basin. Without prejudice to the inevitability of considering the full-scale implications of the resource in concrete water-sharing negotiations, therefore, the analysis would endeavour to contextually provide a fractional interpretation of the pertinent developments and potentials in the Nile basin.

Certainly, the most visible impact of the Nile waters in meeting challenges associated with human development relate to the ever-expanding functions of the river system in sustaining agricultural productivity and in feeding growing populations.

In the past decades, intensive agriculture and industrial water requirements have continuously increased in Egypt, pushing the demand for water to a level that reaches the limits of the available supply. One of the three most-populous nations in Africa, the Egyptian population is densely concentrated in the Nile valley and the delta: 97 percent of its inhabitants (i.e. about 80 million) live on just 4 percent of the total land in Egypt.[80]

78 United Nations Economic and Social Council, Committee on Economic, Social and Cultural Rights (2002), General Comment No 15, Twenty-ninth session, 11–29 November, Geneva

79 United Nations Development Programme (2006), note 42, pp 6, 7, 35.

80 Arab Republic of Egypt (2005), note 34, p XVIII.

Of course, this unique pattern of demographic settlement does not in itself signify that inhabitants of the sub-basin rely in entirety on the Nile floods for the satisfaction of all necessities. Yet, the absolute dearth of alternative water resources in Egypt bluntly illustrates that agriculture, industry, access to safe drinking water and sanitation of the Egyptian population profoundly depend on provisions of the lone national resource.[81] In 2004, for instance, agriculture, relying on irrigational waters provided by the Nile engaged 8,594,000 inhabitants, i.e., 31 percent of the total economically active population in Egypt, which for the same period stood at 27,902,000.[82]

Apart from opportunities of direct employment, if one also considers the impact of irrigated agriculture on the preservation of national food security, perceptibly, the total size of residents bracketed as dependent on the Nile waters for the provision of the single most important human necessity – foodstuffs – will shoot up. Decades of advances in the agricultural sector has enabled Egypt to attain food self-sufficiency in several crops and agricultural products, with some exceptions in certain agricultural commodities.

Similarly, in 2001, the industrial sector, most visibly represented through the food industry sub-sector and the textile, woods and paper industry sub-sectors withdrew a net Nile waters of about 4bcm/yr,[83] and had employed 22 percent of the national labour force, then estimated at 20.6 million.[84]

Again, in 2008, some 43 percent of Egypt's 81.5 million populations lived in predominantly urban areas.[85] Municipal water withdrawals satisfying diverse necessities of both urban and rural inhabitants constituted 5.3bcm/yr, the largest fraction of which was derived from the Nile surface water system.[86] As part of municipal water service delivery, 100 percent of the Egyptian urban population and 97 percent of the rural population had already been afforded with access to improved drinking water sources as early as in 2002.[87] In the same way, by 2010, Egyptian population with access to improved sanitation facilities reached between 90 and 100 percent in urban centres and about 90 percent in rural areas.[88]

81 Of the 68,300km³ of waters withdrawn in 2000, Nile surface waters made up 86 percent, followed by ground waters in aquifers in the western desert independent from the Nile (11 percent), and mixed sources (6 percent).

FAO (2005), Egypt, Basic statistics and population, *FAO Water Report 29*, Table 1 <http://www.fao.org/nr/water/aquastat/countries/egypt/index.stm>, last accessed December 2010.

82 FAO (2005), note 81.

83 These sectors heavily rely on the agricultural sector for the provision of industrial raw materials.

84 Arab Republic of Egypt (2005), note 34, pp 2–26.

85 World Health Organization (2010) 'World Health Statistics 2010', France, p 160.

86 FAO (2005), note 81.

87 World Health Organization (2010), Egypt – Health Profile <http://www.who.int/gho/countries/egy.pdf> last accessed December 2010.

88 World Health Organization (2010), note 87; Official estimates in Egypt confirm that only 50 percent of the urban population has access to sewerage services with flush toilets, while the corresponding value for rural areas is less than 10 percent. The rest of the population uses various types of improved sanitary facilities. Arab Republic of Egypt (2005), note 34, pp 2–36.

Of course, this arduous presentation of figures cannot purport to reveal the full scale of dependence of the Egyptian population on the Nile water resources. In fact, there are a plethora of other sectors, including for instance, inland transport and tourism, that in some form or another rely on the Nile waters and hence sustain the daily occupation of significant counts of the populace. There are also population interests that are only indirectly affected in a chain process involving cross-sector interactions. On the basis of a few indicators of human development, the limited effort in this section has only endeavoured to provide a glimpse of the total number of inhabitants dependent on or affected by the presence of the Nile water resources.

The Egyptian polity is simply addicted to the Nile waters both in sustaining the national economy and meeting several indexes of human development; indeed, the Nile pervades every aspect of its existence.

If anything, these vital facts confirm that neither the current nor any projected utilization of the Nile waters in Sudan or Ethiopia can exhibit a faintly resembling scale or intensity of population dependency that matches the state of affairs in Egypt.

Hence, with some notable exceptions, clearly, the population dependency factor under Article 6 of the UN Watercourses Convention will place Egypt in particularly higher position in future riparian discourses on equitable water allocation. Unlike in Ethiopia or Sudan where the resource base could be diversified, in Egypt, the fulfilment of nearly all basic services concentrates on a lone resource.

This conclusion does not of course imply that national stakes are inconsequential in Sudan or Ethiopia; the assessment is but only relative. Indeed, significant proportions of the respective populations in the two riparian states too depend on current or future utility of the Nile waters in meeting vital needs in a range of social and economic stipulations, although on a much lesser measure.

On the other hand, when one considers the intensity of population dependence in Sudan, it is clear that agriculture is not entirely dependent on the Nile waters as is the case in Egypt; yet, in both Sudan and Ethiopia, the Nile looms large as a key national resource of little substitute. The river can potentially fulfil a range of imperative functions that allay the ill-effects of deprivation and underachievement.

As revealed previously, Sudanese agriculture dominates its economic landscape both in terms GDP contribution and employment. In 2004, the sector engaged 57 percent of the total economically active population (or the national labour force) which then stood at 13,806,000.[89] However, unlike in Egypt, rain-fed agriculture characterized by a small farm size, labour-intensive cultivation techniques and low input levels covered by far the largest area, yielding significant percentages of the crop production in the country.[90] While irrigated agriculture composed just about 11 percent of the total cultivated area and depending exclusively on the Nile floods produced more than half the total volume of agricultural production,[91] it engaged a far lesser number of population as compared to rain-fed farming, and

89 FAO, Sudan, Basic statistics and population, note 44.
90 FAO, note 44.
91 FAO, note 44.

hence, in comparison, the total count of population dependent on the Nile waters in the sector has been very petite.

Yet, Sudan has an irrigational agricultural potential that exceeds the facility both in Egypt and Ethiopia; and although it has generally achieved self-sufficiency in several basic food crops, full utilization of its cultivable land potentials could further involve millions of inhabitants in the agriculture sector.

A significant percentage of the Sudanese population lives in the Nile sub-basin; this is only predictable given that the Nile sub-basin stretches over 79 percent of the entire Sudanese territory. Naturally, this verity evinces that the Nile River and its tributaries will occupy a critical position in fulfilling several aspects of future development requirements of the Sudanese population.

Despite a concentrated pattern of demographic settlement and relative ease of access to the vital resource, poverty remained a deeply entrenched phenomenon in the Sudan. Over two-thirds of the population and under the most favourable assumptions, around 50–70 percent are estimated to live on less than $1/day.[92] And while 43 percent of its population lived in urban areas in 2008, only 60–65 percent had access to improved drinking water resources in urban centres and 50–55 percent in rural settlements in 2010. Similarly, improved sanitation facilities had been afforded only to 50–55 percent of the urban population and 15–20 percent of the population in rural areas.[93] Sudanese use of the Nile waters for industrial purposes, estimated at 0.26bcm/yr in 2000, is but another manifestation of the sheer scale of underutilization of the supply, resulting in a lesser number of population dependent on the resource.

It is admitted that the total count of Sudanese population directly depending on the Nile water resources is very small; in relative terms, the trend will most probably remain the same on a balance, if for any other reason because Sudan has only as half the total population as Ethiopia or Egypt. This verity of lesser dependency affects its stature in equitable decisions.

Yet, it is equally evident that any prospective exploitation of the resource can swell the size of population affected by the Nile, both in meeting the aforementioned necessities of decent human existence and in achieving general economic development. In equitable use decisions, estimates of projected benefits accruing to a nation are as important considerations as current patterns of resource utilization.

The circumstances are not fundamentally unrelated in Ethiopia, except that unlike in the Sudan, Ethiopia has yet to contend with recurring problems of food security affecting millions of its population every year.

Ethiopia's agricultural sector is not dependent on the Nile waters; nor was the nation's socio-economic setting fundamentally wrought by the presence of the resource. By and large, the river's utility reclines in future utilizations.

While Ethiopia is endowed with nine major river basins flooding an aggregate

92 FAO, note 44.

93 World Health Organization (2010), Sudan – Health Profile, <http://www.who.int/gho/countries/sdn.pdf>last accessed December 2010.

runoff ranging between 110–122bcm/yr, by far, the Nile sub-basin region visibly impends in all dialogues of national resource planning and development. Climatic, physical and demographic facts are to account. The Ethiopian section of the Nile basin stretches over a total of 36,881,200 hectares of land, i.e. about a third of its entire landscape, with annual run off of 84.5bcm/yr which represents 69 percent of the total run off in the country.[94]

In a national context, this statistical verity depicts but a profound value of the resource, and explains why, in spite of the presence of other water sources, the analysis concentrates on vast potentialities of the river in meeting several aspects of domestic development challenges.

In Ethiopia, virtually all food crops derive from rain-fed agriculture and although the count of economically active inhabitants engaged in the agricultural sector had been estimated at 30.6 million in 2008, the irrigation sub-sector accounted for only 3 percent of the total food production.[95] Irrigated land in the Nile sub-basin represented a mere 84,640 hectares,[96] an insignificant proportion of the total economic irrigation potential assessed at 1,312,500 hectares in 2001. In consequence, the overall figure of population directly depending on the Nile to meet agricultural water requirements has been extremely meagre.

However, this image of underutilization would change in the context of maximum utilization scenarios; indeed, the Nile has immense prospective utility in addressing Ethiopia's long-standing concerns of national food security. Irrigation can supplement rain-fed agriculture and constitute a basis of livelihood for millions of people in the basin.

Even then, though, the size and intensity of population dependency will not compare strongly with the status in Egypt simply because of the availability of alternative water resources, including a fairly regular pattern of rainfall across several constituencies, and limitations on the maximum acreage of irrigation.

In Ethiopia, industrial, municipal and hydro-electrical power uses are new sectors where the vast potentials of the Nile River would likely be exploited on unequaled scales; in 2002, industrial and municipal uses withdrew only 0.021 and 0.333bcm/yr respectively.[97] In 2010, 95–98 percent of the urban residents, representing 17 percent of the entire population, had access to improved drinking water sources and 20–25 percent in rural areas; similarly, the figure of population with access to improved sanitation facilities had ranged between 20 percent and 25 percent in urban areas and less than 10 percent in rural settlements.[98]

94 FAO, Information System on Water and Agriculture, note 48; FAO, Ethiopia, Basic Statistics and Population (2005), *FAO Water Report 29*, Table 4.

95 FAO, note 48.

96 Constituted of 47,020 hectares in the Blue Nile, 13,350 in the Baro-Akobo and 24,270 in the Tekeze-Atbara sub-basins. This figure does not of course include new irrigational openings along the Tana Beles and Tekeze multipurpose dam schemes inaugurated since FAO's study in 2005. FAO, note 48.

97 FAO, note 48.

98 World Health Organization (2010), Ethiopia – Health Profile, <http://www.who.int/gho/countries/eth.pdf>last accessed December 2010.

Hence, concrete development initiatives aiming at alleviating the chronic concerns of underdevelopment will entail enhanced utilization of the Nile waters resources in Ethiopia. Naturally, the projected dependency of population will vary from one sector to another, involving, in certain instances as huge a population as in Egypt or Sudan. This can be the case in future provisions of safe drinking waters and improved sanitation services. Such projections, planning on improved management of the Nile water resources with a view to addressing specific socio-economic requirements are taken into consideration in the eventual determination of equitable entitlements based on the size of population dependent on an international watercourse.

Similarly, population dependency can be evaluated on the basis of different developmental considerations: the degree of electrification and access to energy sources generated through the employ of Nile waters.

Conceivably, the energy sector – a crucial precondition of nearly all aspects of human developments detailed above, is where Ethiopia's increasing dependence on the Nile waters will be visibly witnessed both as a source of electric power and foreign exchange earnings. After years of neglect and stagnation, the energy sector and particularly the generation of hydro-electric power has experienced a discernible comeback in just the past decade.

Three major factors have reportedly accounted for the accelerated investments in Ethiopia's hydro-electric power infrastructures: expanding demand associated with rural and urban electrification, industrial growth and the gradual transformation of parts of subsistence agriculture into a sector that semi-processes commodities; unstable costs of fossil fuels in world markets; and an increasing perception of the vital link that exists between economic growth, human development and the provision of reliable energy supplies.

Given the distressed state of the energy sector in Ethiopia, this national enterprise is but only obliging. In 2004, the electrification rate had been a mere 15 percent in Ethiopia, expanded to 32 percent only in the last three years, 30 percent in the Sudan and 98 percent in Egypt. During the period under investigation, only 1.5 million people had no access to electricity in Egypt, in sharp contrast to 25.4 million people in the Sudan and 60.5 million in Ethiopia.[99] In consequence, the per-capita electricity consumption – an important indicator of living standards in any given society – displayed a huge disparity in the three basin states: 1,465 kilowatt hours in Egypt, 116 kilowatt hours in Sudan, and 36 kilowatt hours in Ethiopia.[100]

Oil and gas have been the primary sources of energy in Egypt, while 80 percent of the energy sources in Sudan and 90 percent in Ethiopia were derived from biomass and waste. Hydropower sources contributed less than 1.1 percent both in Sudan and Ethiopia.[101] The total existing hydro-electric power capacity in Egypt, installed on various points of the Nile course is 2.81GW, making up for some 16 percent of the gross electricity generated nationally.[102]

99 United Nations Development Program (2007) *Human Development Report 2007/2008, Fighting Climate Change: Human Solidarity in a Divided World*, New York, Palgrave Macmillan, pp 302–5.

100 United Nations Development Program (2007), note 99.

101 United Nations Development Program (2007), note 99, p 306.

102 Arab Republic of Egypt (2005), note 34, pp 2–46.

Against such a background of sheer underdevelopment, Sudan had since undertaken the massive Meroe Dam scheme with an installed capacity of 1250MW; Ethiopia, on the other hand, implemented a radical policy turn assertively trying to feature itself as the continental poster-child of the hydropower sector.

The national strategy advocated the construction of a series of small-, medium- and large-scale dams to generate hydropower and sustain an irrigated-agriculture economy. As noted before, several master plans, pre-feasibility and feasibility investigations had been successively undertaken on the principal course, tributaries and sub-tributaries.[103]

The overtone of this latest initiative which gradually transformed the national energy profile is self-evident: Ethiopia planned to recompense national setbacks by exploiting its untapped hydropower endowments in much the same intensity as irrigation has been practised in Sudan and Egypt.

For a nation where 60.5 million its populace lives without access to electricity, the challenges are simply multifarious; in any event, the point remains that when such schemes are put into service, the national enterprise will enlarge the direct dependence of millions of Ethiopians on resources of the Nile.

Of course, the population impact transcends far beyond, for power is a key element in nearly all aspects of social and economic developments. In equitable determination procedures, therefore, both direct and indirect accounts of the impacts of a resource shall be taken in to consideration in computing the size of population dependent on an international water course. This fact places Ethiopia in a far greater position than its westerly and northerly co-basins – Egypt and Sudan.

Existing and potential uses of a watercourse and effects of uses on other water course states

Introduction

Both Article 6.1.(d)/(e) of the UN Watercourses Convention and Article 13.2.(d)/(e) of the Berlin Rules (revising the Helsinki Rules) similarly provided that the equitable and reasonable utilization of an international watercourse requires taking into account all relevant factors and circumstances including existing and

103 Ministry of Water Resources (2002) 'Water Sector Development Program, Irrigation Development Programme Report', Addis Ababa

In particular, the Water Sector Development Program identified specific hydropower components stretching across various parts of the Nile basin: already, the Nile basin in Ethiopia hosts the Fincha-Amerti (100MW), Fincha 4th Unit (33), Tis Abay I/II (11.5 and 75MW), Tekeze I (300MW) and Tana Beles (460MW) hydropower facilities.

Construction on The Grand Ethiopian Renaissance Dam, the largest ever feat in the sector, was launched in 2010. Several single and multi-purpose projects including the Tekeze II, Mendaia-Border-Mabil, Fettam, Upper Guder, Aleltu East, Chemoga Yada, Aleltu West and Neshe have also been proposed / initiated on the main stream and the Nile tributaries.

potential uses of the watercourse and the effects of the use or uses of the watercourses in one watercourse state on other watercourse states.[104]

That both existing and potential uses of an international watercourse are protected is plainly beyond issue; they refer to a factual scenario embracing schemes of resource utilization that are already operational and to projections of what states can make out of such resources in light of their physical endowments. However, the legal issues that ensue are not as uncomplicated.

Both conceptually and in the particular contexts of the Nile basin, the most essential themes of legal dispute can be summarized as follows. What do existing and potential uses actually entail? Does the framing of existing uses, contemplated under the Convention, extend to any physical scale of utilization, including out-of-basin diversions, embarked in a wake of formal reservations of future uses by other co-riparian states? Does the reference of potential uses merely involve an objective assessment of the facility availed by a resource, or does it otherwise impose restrictions against speculative benefits in the form of immediacy, certainty and even capacity, and hence require that riparian states come up with a definite formulation of national plans of river development? And finally, in cases of conflict between existing and potential uses of basin states, what measure of credence does each factor command in the overall context of equitable use determination?

Article 6.2.(e) of the UN Watercourses Convention obliges that equitable use decisions shall take account of 'the effects of the use or uses of the watercourses in one watercourse state on other watercourse states'. What specific meaning this stipulation aspired to convey cannot be discerned without difficulty, nor was ample annotation furnished under the pertinent literatures of the ILA or the ILC.

Generally, though, it can be noted that cross-riparian effects of uses are reciprocal in nature and can manifest in a variety of forms. In an effort to construct the provision in a fitting context, the present analysis would illustrate this rule not just in isolation, but by relating it to contemporary developmental settings in the Nile basin. This involves the demonstration of downstream–upstream effects of both existing and potential uses and examination of the legal basis on which their status and relationship has been determined.

For the moment, it suffices to note that the Nile River presents a unique structure of resource development pattern across the basin, fundamentally oriented in a downstream perspective. The pertinent rules of international law expounding on existing and potential uses are but indispensable in illuminating the specific legal stipulates on the basis of which upper riparian states may submit claims to test the continuity of the status quo in the basin, and where new or broadened uses are contemplated, to demand for the reassessment or adjustment of existing patterns of uses.

104 Article 4.2(d) and (e) of the Agreement on the Nile River Basin Cooperative Framework simply replicated provisions of the UN Watercourse Courses Convention, while Article V.2.4 of the Helsinki Rules provided only 'past utilization of the waters of the basin, including in particular existing utilization' as one of the factors considered.

Existing *vs.* potential uses: the focus on irrigated agriculture

As detailed in the preceding sections, both in Egypt and Sudan, existing uses touch upon every facet of life and still command greater prospects of expansion; in contrast, in Ethiopia, the resource's utility rests largely in the context of future utilization.

About 93 percent of the total water consumption along downstream Nile has been dedicated to a single vital sector – irrigation agriculture;[105] inevitably, future extractions in Ethiopia, too, will focus on the extensive production of food crops. In light of such developmental settings, therefore, it is only sensible to direct the discussion of legal issues associated with existing and potential uses in a perspective that particularly stresses the extent of cultivated and cultivable irrigational lands in the basin.[106]

In 1997, the gross irrigational water requirements in the Nile basin was estimated as standing at 124bcm per year, of which 19.9 was in Ethiopia, 38.5 in Sudan and 57.4 in Egypt.[107] This particular assessment was preceded by sequences of technical investigations that extended over the whole course of the twentieth century.

In the mid 1960s, the US Bureau of Reclamation initiated studies on the potential development of the waters of the Blue Nile river basin in Ethiopia. In 1952, the mission undertook field reconnaissance surveys and a preliminary report identified several areas as feasible for irrigation through direct diversions and the construction of storage reservoirs.[108] The Bureau's final report of investigation published a decade later identified several irrigational projects across the Blue Nile basin extending over an area of 433,754 hectares, with a total water requirement of some 6.3bcm/yr.

On a separate development, the National Water Development Commission predicted in 1972 that for three decades, Ethiopia would require 18,789bcm/yr of Nile waters, i.e. 22 percent of the river's total mean annual flood for irrigations, domestic uses, and out-of-basin diversions.[109]

105 Nile 2002 Conference (2000) Proceedings of VIIIth Nile 2002 Conference, Country Paper: Egypt, p 46; Also in FAO (2005) Egypt, Basic Statistics and Population, *FAO Water Report 29*, Tables 1 and 4; agricultural water withdrawal of 54bcm/yr represents 93 percent of its total renewable water resources (which is 68.3bcm/yr).

106 Only such data as are provided by the FAO and pertinent government ministries of the basin states would be utilized; by so doing, the Book obviates unwanted controversies relating to the extent of 'potentially cultivable lands', which, depending on the reference adopted, (e.g., 'ease of access', 'best soil', 'marginal soil', etc.) could be inflated or otherwise kept within minimum bounds.

107 FAO, Irrigation potential in Africa, note 532.

108 United States Department of Interior, Oscar L. Chapman, Secretary, Michael W. Straus, Commissioner, Bureau of Reclamation, Reconnaissance Report, Blue Nile River Basin, Ethiopia, From T.A Clarck et al, Washington, DC (August 1952).

109 National Water Development Commission (1972) 'Note on the Blue Nile', Addis Ababa, (unpublished);

Ashok Swain noted Ethiopia had instead asked for 6bcm/yr of waters to irrigate land in catchment areas of the Blue Nile. Ashok Swain (1997) 'Ethiopia, the Sudan and Egypt – The Nile River Dispute', *Journal of Modern African Studies*, vol 35, no 4, p 680.

In a medium term, Ethiopia's Water Sector Development Program launched at a much later epoch identified specific irrigational components with planned irrigation targets of 274,612 hectares over a 15-year period (2002–2016).[110] And in 1999, the Ministry of Water Resources in Ethiopia had already published a comprehensive technical report of the 'Abay (Blue Nile) River Basin Integrated Development Master Plan Project'. Under the Master Plan, two alternative irrigation development scenarios extending over a 50-year period (1999/2000–2048/49) projected to develop a total area of 235,000–350,000 hectares,[111] withdrawing about 6 percent (3.1–3.3bcm/yr) of the mean annual discharge of the Blue Nile River.[112] The study also identified that potential large and medium scale irrigation in the sub-basin extends over a total net area of 526,000 hectares.[113]

In contrast, in 2005, FAO's estimate of the eventual irrigation potential in the Blue Nile sub-basin put the figure at 1,001,500 hectares; the irrigation potential in Baro-Akobo and Tekeze-Atbara sub-basins of the Ethiopian Nile system had been assessed at 905,500 and 312,700 hectares respectively.[114] Of this, only 84,640 hectares was utilized to date depicting a huge gap between existing facilities and potentials.

On the other hand, in Egypt, early investigations undertaken by Hurst, Black and Samaika confirmed that in 1946 the total cultivated area stood at 2.52 million hectares; the outer limit of cultivation was 3.15 million hectares, requiring about 58bcm/yr of waters at Aswan.[115] Half a century on, the Ministry of Water Resources and Irrigation accounted that Egyptian agriculture extended over 3.38 million hectares,[116] withdrawing about 59bcm/yr of Nile waters.[117] In 2005, Egypt's ultimate irrigation potential was assessed as standing at 4,420,000 hectares.[118]

John Waterbury cited an older study of the US Bureau of Reclamation to report that Ethiopia needed 4–5 bcm/yr; John Waterbury (2002) *The Nile Basin, National Determinants of Collective Action*, New Haven, London, Yale University Press,p 128.

110 Ministry of Water Resources (2002), note 103.

111 Federal Democratic Republic of Ethiopia (1999), note 49, p 197.

112 Federal Democratic Republic of Ethiopia (1999), note 49, p 200.

113 Federal Democratic Republic of Ethiopia (1999), note 49, p 245.

114 FAO, FAO's Information System on Water and Agriculture, Ethiopia, note 48.

Based on a water requirement of 9,000 cubic meters per hectare set by the FAO, the agricultural potential in Ethiopia would require a total base supply of 19.98bcm/yr of Nile waters.

115 H.E. Hurst, R.P. Black and Y.M. Simaika (1946) 'The Nile Basin, The Future Conservation of the Nile', Vol VII, Physical Department Paper no 51, SOP Press, Cairo, p 11.

116 Arab Republic of Egypt (2005), note 34, pp II-29, 31.

117 Egypt State Information Service, Agriculture; FAO, Egypt, Basic Statistics and Population, note 33.

FAO's study estimated that considering average water requirement of 13,000 cubic meters per hectare per year in the Nile Valley and the Delta, about 4,420,000 hectares can be irrigated using 57.4bcm/yr of Nile waters.

Al-Ahram, the *Egyptian Weekly*, reported (Issue No 979, 31st Dec 2009) that the total yearly water consumption in Egypt is about 78bcm/yr; the difference between water budget of 58bcm/yr and the actual consumption, about 20bcm/yr is covered by recycling agricultural drainage, abstraction from shallow aquifers and treatment of municipal sewage.

118 Egypt State Information Service, note 33.

In Sudan too, irrigation constitutes a vital basis of the social and economic fabric, extending over some 1,863,000 hectares.[119] In 2005, the FAO appraised irrigational prospects in the Nile sub-basin constituency of Sudan as standing at 2,784,000 hectares.[120] In 2000, Sudanese water withdrawals from surface and groundwaters stood at 37.32bcm per annum, i.e. 56 percent of the nation's total renewable water resources. Agricultural uses constituted the largest, 36.07bcm/yr.[121]

Existing uses: what does the concept presume?

The UN Watercourses Convention placed both existing and future uses under a single stipulate, but did not provide what each of these concepts constitutes. Of course, Article 5 had recognized the right of each water course state to utilize transboundary rivers in an equitable and reasonable manner and this had been read to conjecture that in cases of conflict between existing patterns and potential uses, a possibility of future assessment or adjustments will always be implicit.

Still, the provision falls short of enlightening which specific aspects of existing or future uses are protected, if they should be protected, and the circumstances under which they may be subjected to evaluation and modification.

The notion of an existing use generally presumes a state of fact, that waters of transboundary river courses have been put to some beneficial uses. The Helsinki Rules tried to elaborate on a technical characterization of what the concept represents: 'an existing use is a use that is in fact operational, and is deemed to have been existing use from the time of initiation of construction directly related to the use, or where such construction is not required, the undertaking of comparable acts of actual implementation'.[122] In this regard, the reference applies 'to the extent of water actually appropriated in connection with such use'.[123]

Physical scope of *protected* existing use regimes

The first query that immediately obtrudes in connection with existing uses is concerned with the legally permitted physical latitude of such utilizations: how expansively can an existing use of a riparian state enlarge, physically, and still be considered in the assessment of equitable use determinations? Is there a conceptual threshold beyond which a basin state's use may not merit a measure of legal credence in the assessment of factors and circumstances?

While the concept of equality of rights in the beneficial uses transboundary rivers can generally be construed as connoting certain limitation on the discretion

119 FAO, Information System on Water and Agriculture; FAO (2005) Sudan, Basic statistics and population, *FAO Water Report 29*, Table 1 and 4, note 44; also in – Nile 2002 Conference (2000), Proceedings of the VIIIth Nile 2002 Conference, Country Paper: Sudan, 26–29 June, Addis Ababa, p 46.

120 FAO, note 44.

121 FAO, note 44.

122 International Law Association (1966), note 13, Article VIII.1.

123 International Law Association (1966), note 122.

of states, no single resolution on international watercourses law provided expressly to such effect, specifically in connection with existing uses; nor had the issue drawn significant attention in juridical discourses, except with the ILA.

The ILA admitted favor both for existing and potential uses, but the ambiguity remained with regard to how such rights of potential uses can be implemented in practice, particularly in cases where a resource had been preemptively appropriated.

The UN Watercourses Convention did not place express limitation on the physical scope of uses except for what may be inferred from the operation of the equitable uses doctrine itself. It is by no means certain if a basin state's right of equitable utilization under Article V of the Convention presumes a wider proposition that each riparian state is due to bound to adopt a measure of forethought so that its utilization does not intrude into a possible (present or future) share entitlements of a co-basin state.

If only implicitly, Article VII of the Helsinki Rules sheds some light on status of the theme under international law. It started by providing that 'a basin state may not be denied the present reasonable use of the waters of an international drainage basin to reserve for a co-basin state a future use of such waters'.

Generally, this rule impresses that a riparian state is under no obligation to limit the physical scope of its utilization of a transboundary river even where such a course encroaches on the presumed but unutilized shares of a co-basin state. Hence, it would be supposed that only present, and perhaps, explicit needs of other basin states can restrict a riparian state's present disposition to exploit a shared resource. The rational that lie behind such a stipulation could be that as a valued common amenity, water should not lay to waste at the present in order that the future, and perhaps, speculative uses of other states may be preserved.

The ILA's reading under Article VII in which only present reasonable uses had been emphasized and where the reservation of future uses was possibly disallowed is probably influenced by the absence of an express provision in the list of factors and circumstances under the Helsinki Rules formally recognizing potential uses on a par with existing uses. Unlike a corresponding formulation of the contemporary regime under the Berlin Rules and the UN Watercourse Convention, the pertinent provision under Article V.2.(d) of the Helsinki Rules had a drafting shortcoming, and spoke only of 'the past utilization of the waters of the basin, including in particular existing utilization'. A matching reference to potential uses, a conceptual underpinning that could have set restrictions on the physical scope of utilization of riparian states, had simply been missing.

Yet, it can be maintained that under Article VII of the Helsinki Rules, a basin state will not be authorized carte blanche to engage in the utilization of shared river courses simply because no co-riparian had come forward with immediate needs or definite plans for utilization of the same resource. Even in the absence of pressing competitions or predisposition to use, it is only commonsensical to hold that the physical scope of utilization and entitlement by each basin state should be circumscribed.

This can be inferred from the very foundational theory of international water courses law itself which recognized the right of every state to make use of the waters flowing across or bordering its territory, subject to limitations imposed on account of a comparable right of use accorded to other states.

More specifically, though, one can note that under Article VII, the physical scope of existing uses had been qualified by the insertion of 'reasonable use' expression, a steering tenet whose application confines the freedom of states in the utilization of shared resources. Hence, what a basin state may not be denied is not *every use*, but only a *present reasonable use*; a pattern of utilization by a riparian state that imperils another basin state's prospective opportunities by a pre-emptive appropriation of substantial floods of a stream cannot be considered as a present reasonable use.

For this reason, while states may choose to embark on unlimited scales of exploitation of a communal resource and indeed, more than a few had so undertaken, as such, they engage in such courses only at own peril. Not every aspect of such existing uses will be eventually protected and in consequence, eligible for consideration in equitable uses decisions.

In practice, however, a condition of present reasonable use under Article VII of the Helsinki Rules will only have a limited significance; this is because in specific circumstances, the maximum threshold of use that could have been set through the employ of the reasonable uses standard is itself difficult to ascertain. However, the point remains that the physical scope of a state's right of utilization is not entirely unlimited. Basin states must impose self-restraint or perhaps risk the consequences that are implicit in an extended utilization of a shared river course in their jurisdiction.

It is true that the Tribunal in the *Lake Lanoux* case had confirmed that neither customary international law nor general principles of law require a prior consent or agreement between interested parties before a basin state may embark on utilization of a shared river.[124] However, this dictum cannot be interpreted as permitting first appropriators a right of pursuing national developments in a manner that menaces future rights of utilization of other states.

The earliest resolution adopted by the IIL, the Declaration of Madrid on international regulation regarding the non-navigational uses of watercourses (1911), provided slightly closely: 'no establishment (especially factories utilizing hydraulic power) may take so much water that the constitution, otherwise called the utilizable or essential character of the stream shall, when it reaches the territory downstream, be seriously modified'.[125]

Only Article 4 of the 1961 Salzburg Resolution came close to expressly articulating that the autonomy of riparian states is indeed restricted: it read 'each state may only proceed with works or use the waters of a river or watershed that may affect the possibilities of use of the same waters by other states on condition of preserving for those states the benefit of the advantages to which they are entitled

124 Lake Lanoux Arbitration (1957) France/Spain, Arbitral Tribunal set up under a compromise dated November 19, 1956 pursuant to an Arbitration Treaty of July 10, 1929, paras 167–69.

125 Institute of International Law (1961), Resolution on the Use of International Non-Maritime Waters, Salzburg, 11 September, Article III.

by virtue of Article III, [equity] as well as adequate compensation for any losses or damages incurred'.

The rule did not say in specifics the legal consequence that ensues if a basin state fails to oblige by proceeding with extensive appropriations of a shared river course. Yet, the idea remained that a condition preserving the like benefits to which another co-riparian state would be entitled by virtue of the application of equitable uses principle had been anticipated.

Existing uses *vs.* formal reservations of future uses

Elements of a legal regime that set out bounds on the physical scope of existing uses can also be discerned from a distinct, but essentially related perspective. This involves a reflection on two sets of conflicting concepts under public international law presenting a case for and against a right of *preserving*, through formal declarations, waters of a transboundary river course for future uses.

Given the typical constitution of the diplomatic discourse and resource development patterns across the Nile basin, a discussion on such a theme is only indispensable. Egyptian and Sudanese agriculture had undergone both technically and physically through various stages of evolutionary growth in the 1920s, 1950s and 1990s. This stimulates interesting issues particularly in relation to downstream agricultural expansions adopted in the wake of *upstream objections*, and the legal effects, on existing uses, if any, of formal upstream declarations venturing to preserve future rights of utilizing the Nile waters.

The ILA had the occasion to specifically address the validity, under international law, of reserving future rights of use.

In sketching a vague principle under Article VII presented above,[126] the ILA confessed it had been confronted with two conflicting extremes with respect to the equitable sharing of waters: the dilemma of assuring each watercourse state the use of certain waters by reservation even where such waters cannot be utilized at the present, on the one hand, and backing the position that no water should be reserved for future uses since to do so might interfere with current uses of the water or uses which come from time to time.[127] The ILA ridiculed both positions on the basis of different rationales discussed below.

The first approach which proposed to set aside certain portions of a river's floods for future utilization in fact bears a strong semblance to the decades-long diplomatic enterprise of the upstream Nile and most notably Ethiopia. As indicated earlier, Ethiopia had habitually argued that large scale developments in Egypt and Sudan, appropriating significant waters of the Nile, could affect neither its rights nor its presumed shares should it choose to embark on the development of the resource at a subsequent stage.

126 It must be noted that Articles VII and VIII do not have a parallel stipulation under the Berlin Rules (2004), nor under the 1997 UN Watercourses Convention.

127 International Law Association (1966), note 13.

The ILA submitted that such an approach may have a visceral appeal because of what appears to be its fairness; yet, the Association disparaged this view because of its perceived conviction that 'it would constitute a bad policy to entitle states reserve certain waters when they had no present need for them and could conceivably make use of such waters, if at all, only at some time in future'.[128]

In defense of the argument, the ILA also espoused certain practical concerns relating to the 'unfeasibility' of fixing future water shares with a 'meaningful degree of certainty'.

True, at least with regard to the second rationale, the prevalence of some challenges can be admitted; yet, there is nothing impractical about fixing the respective water requirements of riparian states, including shares set aside for prospective uses. This is only because if such computations appear 'inadequate', 'excessive and wasteful' at a later stage, as the ILA had feared would likely happen, there seems no reason why the whole scheme should not be subjected to reassessment once again, on the basis of various factors impinging on the equitable uses doctrine.

On the other hand, while the ILA's observation may be regarded as a judicious exercise in emphasizing on the present maximum utilization of shared watercourses, the interpretation had obviously failed to heed to two vital perspectives.

First, this argument seemed to insinuate, although not so clearly, that international law does not ascribe any legal credence to formal reservations of riparian states pronounced with a view to maintaining future rights of using a share in the flows of a river. That is certainly controversial.

Second, the ILA's reading overlooked that indeed there are basin states which actually have pressing existing needs for waters of a shared river course, but cannot realize their aspirations simply because of human, fiscal and technical limitations. It can scarcely appeal to equitable considerations to submit that such states shall forfeit an equal right of utilization recognized under international law simply because at the present, they are not in a position to develop a resource.

Probably, in anticipation, the ILA had presumed that the equitable uses principle would operate post facto to accommodate the concerns of such late coming states. The principle could have been possibly understood as providing implicit mechanisms for re-evaluation and adjustment of a status quo that places basin states in inequitable positions through, for example, uneven appropriation of shared water resources.

Yet, to shove aside a fundamental stake of a sovereign state to some uncertain eventuality under the equitable uses doctrine will represent a less plausible approach under international law on account of one conspicuous rationale: academic and state practice had suitably demonstrated that while the equitable uses procedure tenders a fairly pleasing mechanism for resolving river disputes, frequently, it is too complex and uncertain, entails greater risks and functions properly only under certain set of conditions.

128 International Law Association (1966), note 13.

After all, each watercourse state's entitlement to a right to equitable uses cannot in itself insinuate that the fate of late-coming states shall be subjected to an insecure allocations regime presented through a post facto implementation of the equitable uses doctrine, which in some cases can involve adopting measures long after uses of a resource had been deeply entrenched. While a basin state's extensive use does not acquire absolute security solely on account of first appropriation, it is evident that quite too often, established uses are difficult to overturn; a strict perpetuation of guidelines indicated under the equitable-uses principle may not necessarily guarantee that such old uses would be eventually unseated.

Hence, considering the imminent peril engendered through a pattern of large-scale pre-emptive utilization of shared watercourses, incapable or late-coming states should be permitted to resort to remedies afforded in diplomatic measures, including privileges of reserving future rights of use.

This is particularly sensible in circumstances where cooperative regimes are not in place and therefore, formal declarations are employed in the interim to forestall the institution of new use-regimes through expanded withdrawal of waters by other basin states. In the absence of such safeguards, some states, although situated in like standing under international law, can end up eternally precluded of the opportunity of utilizing shared river courses just because accidents of fiscal shortfall at a certain stage of their economic development had forced the resource's underutilization.

Finally, the ILA's perspective can also be disputed on the basis of the very framing of certain relevant provisions of its own resolutions. It was submitted earlier that under contemporary international law, the implementation of the equitable uses principle presumes taking into account several factors and circumstances, one of which is future uses of waters by basin states.

This vital factor had been missing under the Helsinki Rules, but was explicitly incorporated under the UN Watercourses Convention of 1997 and the ILA's Berlin Rules adopted in 2004. In its Commentary on Article 13 of the Berlin Rules which revised developments since the adoption of the Helsinki Rules, the ILA acknowledged that the 'need for water for future uses in the basin states' had as such been implicit in the original Helsinki Rules and argued that it referred to 'the need to consider foreseeable future uses'.[129]

But if such projected but not necessarily present uses in waters of an international watercourse had been regarded as important considerations that required setting aside some waters, this would have entailed that another basin state which could have had a present need for the same resource would be divested of the opportunity to utilize the same. By advocating that, in the context of equitable utilization, part of the waters of an international watercourse may be reserved for future uses, at best, the approach contravened the original premise on which the ILA's rule had been allegedly founded: the maximum present utilization of resources.

This notional dilemma has practical implications. In the past century, the treaty and hydropolitical discourse in the Nile basin and particularly, the trilateral

129 International Law Association (2004), note 66.

communication between the states of Great Britain, Egypt and Ethiopia had witnessed sequences of such formal declarations, venturing to preserve, in one form or another, future rights of utilizing the Nile waters.[130]

One of the earliest historical episodes dates back to a diplomatic correspondence exchanges in 1914; it involved negotiations between Great Britain (representing Egyptian and Sudanese colonies) and Ethiopia on the Lake Tana dam. In explaining Ethiopia's disinclination to acquiesce to British proposals, British diplomats of the time accounted that 'one of the first comments made by . . . the Ethiopian government on the draft agreement [regarding the Lake Tana Dam] . . . was that they wished to safeguard not only their existing but their future rights to the use of the water for their own irrigation purposes'.[131]

Similarly, against a backdrop of negotiations that involved Sudan and Egypt on full utilization of the Nile waters in 1955, Great Britain declared that 'the division of the Nile waters between Egypt and Sudan should be made on a proportionate basis and not in terms of absolute quantities, affording each country a right to a stated proportion of the natural flow at Aswan'.[132] British enterprise had endeavoured to set aside certain portions of the Nile waters although it was manifest that its upstream colonies had no immediate use for the resource. Shortly, the declaration was followed by notice of formal reservation of rights served directly to the stake-holding states.

The British text read:

> . . . in view of the attention now being paid by the Egyptian and Sudanese governments to the question of the division of surplus Nile waters, her Majesty's government wish to draw to the notice of the Egyptian government the interest of the British East African territories in this question, and formally reserve their rights to negotiate on their behalf with the Egyptian and Sudanese governments at the appropriate time for the agreed share of the water.[133]

The diplomatic venture had attempted to afford upstream colonies, which then had neither firm plans nor the fiscal/technical aptitude required for launching water-control works, a conceptual framework based on which a multilateral division would be worked out as part of durable settlement of user-rights. The pre-emptive declaration also hoped to avert legal uncertainties; it projected to preserve a right over unquantified shares for subsequent uses in upstream territories and hence deny Sudan and Egypt the opportunity of acquiring exclusive user rights formed through continued unilateral utilization of waters impounded at the Aswan High Dam.

130 Anglo-Egyptian relations had similarly experienced repeated negotiations between the two states trying to set limits on the extent of existing uses recognized and protected by both states.

131 Doughty Wyllie to Lord Kitchener, 27 June 1914, FO 371/15388.

132 Text of Note presented by her Majesty's Ambassador in Cairo to the Egyptian Government, note 414; Text of Note presented by her Majesty's Ambassador in Cairo to the Egyptian Government, 22 November 1955 FO 371/119062.

133 Text of Note presented by her Majesty's Ambassador in Cairo to the Egyptian Government, 22 November 1955 FO 371/119062.

In his comments on the acts of the British Government, Sir Elihu Lauterpacht explained the formal reservation may be viewed in two ways: one of such may assume that it targets 'the substantive rights of Egypt; and regarded in this way, the statement must be considered as an implied rejection of the doctrine of prior appropriation'.[134] Without exploring the legality of formal reservations under the pertinent rules, he furthermore clarified 'the United Kingdom is in effect declaring that the extent to which the upper riparian territories are entitled to share in the waters of the Nile cannot be conclusively determined by reference to the quantities of water hitherto annually taken by the Sudan and Egypt from the river'.[135]

In the mid 1950s, Ethiopia too pursued the same model espoused by Great Britain, by replicating a British diplomatic counsel tendered on the subject in 1955.[136] A formal communiqué issued by the Ministry of Foreign Affairs outlined the need for calling international tenders with a view to 'opening up new agricultural regions and sources of power' necessitated by 'the impressive growth of the Ethiopian economy . . . increased population and the enormous expansion of internal and external trade'.[137] The letter depicted a 'clear and immediate reservation of Ethiopian rights'[138] both for irrigational and hydro power projects.

Ethiopia's position was reasserted on 23 September 1957 in an aide-memoire circulated to diplomatic communities. The note stated Ethiopia had

> the right and obligation to exploit the water resources of the empire . . . for the benefit of present and future generations of its citizens . . . [and] must therefore reassert and reserve now and for the future the right to take all such measures in respect of its water resources and in particular, as regards that portion of the same which is of the greatest importance to its welfare, namely those waters providing so nearly entirely of the volume of the Nile, whatever

134 E. Lauterpacht (1957) 'The Contemporary Practice of the United Kingdom in the Field of International Law, Survey and Comment II', *International and Comparative Law Quarterly*, vol 6, p 137.

135 Lauterpacht (1957), note 134.

136 Only six months before Great Britain gave up its administrative status in the Sudan, it officially advised the Ethiopian Government, who had all along disapproved the exclusive feat of the negotiations between Sudan and Egypt, to 'inform the Egyptian and Sudanese Governments that they [Ethiopia] reserve their right to an appropriate share in the Nile waters.' Bailey to Welson, Washington, 2 May 1956, FO 371/119054;

Mr Shuckburgh's advice to the Ethiopian Ambassador had also been restated in the annex of: Addis Ababa to Foreign Office, 11 May 1956, FO 371/119061.

On 2 November 1955, Great Britain had already reminded Egypt that, while it had no objection that the two downstream states enter in to bilateral negotiations for the division of the Nile waters, it had formally reserved the rights of the East African territories and that any such talks shall be undertaken subject to the understanding that the two states would be prepared to consider the claims of the East African Territories in a subsequent separate negotiation.

137 Ministry of Foreign Affairs (1956) Press Communiqué, Addis Ababa, Ethiopia, *Ethiopian Herald*, 6 February

138 P. R. A. Mansfield, British Embassy, Addis Ababa, to J. F. S. Philips, Foreign Office, London, 27 April 1956, FO 371/ 119061; P.R.A Mansfield to John, British Embassy, Addis Ababa, 27 April 1956, FO 371/119061.

> may be the measure of utilization of such waters sought by recipient states situated along the course of that river.[139]

Batstone investigated the pre- and post-Nile treaty diplomatic events and objections raised in upstream Nile; he concluded that in the face of a British formal reservation, there is no reason why any increases in irrigation, purporting to appropriate water to which these (upstream) territories have a legitimate claim should be protected under international law as established uses.[140] Hence, any state diverting water to which another state has a legitimate claim and knowing that this second state intends at some future date to make use of this water must be held to act at its own peril.[141]

Reclusive authorities, bracing both sides of the argument, corroborated this position. Adjudicated against a background of an entirely unrelated set of facts, for instance, the US Supreme Court held in *Arizona vs. California* (1963), that the Government's assertion of water rights in the Colorado River, on behalf of five Indian Reservations stretching across the country, to meet present and future requirements of life and irrigation, are legitimate. Arizona argued the US did not have the power to make a reservation of navigable waters by Executive Orders, and in any event, that the amount of water reserved (for current and prospective utilizations) should be measured by a 'reasonably foreseeable needs' of the Indians living on the reservation, rather than by the number of irrigable acres.[142] The Court concluded a volume of water 'intended to satisfy the future as well as the present needs of the Indian Reservations' and 'enough . . . to irrigate all the practicably irrigable acreage on the reservations' should be set aside.[143]

In the *Colorado vs. New Mexico* case (1984) where a ruling had been delivered on the basis of prior appropriations principle, the Court admitted of the possibility of reserving parts of the Vermejo River flow for future utilization in the Colorado, but conditioned its application subject to the satisfaction of certain stringent requirements.[144]

The Court's dictum read that 'countervailing equities supporting a diversion for future use in one State may justify the detriment to existing users in another State' and reiterated its conviction that 'the flexible doctrine of equitable apportionment extends to a State's claim to divert previously appropriated water for future uses'.

Ostensibly, the ruling presumed that while a future right of use could have been acknowledged, it did not exist in abstract, but depends, among others, on

139 Counselor of American Embassy at Cairo (Ross) to the Department of State (1957), Aide Memoire of Sept. 23, 1957, encl in Dispatch No 342, 8 October 1957 (MS Department of State, file 974.7301/10–857).

140 Batstone (1959), note 72, p 544.

141 Batstone (1959), note 140.

142 *Arizona vs. California*, 373 US 595–7 (1963).

143 *Arizona vs. California*, 373 US 601 (1963).

144 Historically, the Vermejo River had exclusively been utilized in farm and industrial uses in New Mexico. In 1975, Colorado proposed to divert some waters of this fully appropriated interstate river.

a riparian state's readiness to commit time and capital on the development of specific plans. In other words, a state would be obliged to demonstrate that it is not engaging in a proposal that only has speculative benefits.

On the other hand, in criticizing a majority's ruling in *Nebraska vs. Wyoming* (1945), a dissenting opinion by Justice Roberts held quite the opposite view:

> water for beneficial use is what counts; no injury results from the deprivation of water unless a need is shown for that water for beneficial consumptive use at the time by the State claiming to have been wrongfully deprived of it. If water is not needed by downstream senior rights, the denial of water to upstream junior rights can result only in waste. No state may play dog in the manger, and build up reserves for future use in the absence of present need and present damage.[145]

Admittedly, the core essence of the decision relates to the issue at hand only circuitously, for, as in many other proceedings, the Supreme Court's decisions had considered long-established national doctrines whose contents did not necessarily mirror stipulations of the regime of international law. Besides, the decision had been rendered in a narrower context that endeavoured to indicate how parties to the dispute should have proven damage in a controversy. Apart from that, the conceptual conclusions had been edifying.

The Court's pronouncement had influenced the outlook perpetuated by Bourne. Viewing the issue from upstream–downstream perspective, Bourne reproduced the ILA's explanation in reluctantly submitting that the 'attitude of the US Court is reasonable for it encourages the utilization of water that would otherwise be wasted'.[146] He noted 'a state that has no immediate use for waters (of a transboundary river) has no ground of complaint under customary international law when a river in its territory is deprived of some or all of its flow by acts done in the territory of another state'.[147] Contrary to the ILA's commentary on the Berlin Rules, he concluded that even the principle of equitable apportionment does not compel a paralysis of present development for the sake of hypothetical future needs.[148] No authority was presented to augment his arguments, though.

In summary, it is imperative to direct attention to two crucial points.

First, only few authorities had specifically dealt with the issue, and hence, it could be difficult to draw a broadly convincing conclusion.

Second, whereas considerations that law should stimulate full utilization of resources had been restated in plentiful occasions and in fact this constitutes a rational proposition, such approach does not necessarily guarantee that the fundamental interests of basin states will be pleased in a manner that accentuates

145 *Nebraska vs. Wyoming*, 325 US 659 (1945).

146 Charles B. Bourne (1965) 'The Right to the waters of International Rivers', *Can YB Int'l L*, vol 3, p 192.

147 Bourne (1965), note 146.

148 Bourne (1965), note 146, p 193.

their parity and fair expectations. After all, natural resources are matters of common interest. In some circumstances, an expansive pattern of utilization in a basin state may prompt irredeemable consequences affecting vital riparian interests of the others, unless the pertinent legal regime is construed in such a mode as to connote that such states are permitted, beforehand, to preserve rights of future uses. The legal regime of international watercourses law is too uncertain on the specific theme to simply conclude that the fundamental stakes of basin states could just be left to post facto workings of the principle of equitable uses.

Therefore, a view should be endorsed which articulates that the physical scope of utilization of basin states is presumed as restricted. This may stem either from the basic concept of the sovereign equality of states under international law or because international law attaches legal significance to formal declarations reserving waters for future uses.

From these conclusions ensue certain legal consequences that particularly affect the multifaceted relations of the Nile basin states.

Hence, while an existing use constitutes one of the several factors considered in determining the equitable allocation of shared waters, in Egypt and Sudan only *certain* parts of such uses will be eventually regarded as existing utilization for purposes of equitable determinations. Indeed, the reference to downstream existing uses will solely encompass the status quo that prevailed nearly half a century ago, shortly before upstream formal reservations had been issued – when the degree of exploitation of the Nile waters was relatively lesser. This in turn entails that along the lower-reaches of the river, certain parts of contemporary utilizations, appropriating huge proportions Nile floods, would remain outside the protected legal regime.

Measure of protection afforded to existing uses

It was presented above that the ILA was confronted with two conflicting extremes with respect to reserving future rights, which it rejected. One view proposed to assure each watercourse state the use of certain waters by reservation even where such waters cannot be utilized at the present; a second perspective backed the position that no water should be reserved for future uses since to do so might interfere with current uses of the water or uses which come from time to time.[149]

In countering the second approach, the ILA submitted it would be unfair to give the first user a vested right in perpetuity in all the waters which it demonstrates it can presently use; such a policy would in all likelihood lead to a use race, resulting in haphazard planning and inefficiency.[150] Conceivably, a state could move quickly to appropriate all the waters of a basin to the complete exclusion of its co-basin states – a result which is hardly consistent with the equal status of basin states.[151]

149 International Law Association (1966), note 13.
150 International Law Association (1966), note 13.
151 International Law Association (1966), note 13.

On a balance, the ILA's analysis intimated that while the stipulation under Article VII implied that no water may be kept back for future utilization, the continued security of existing uses could not be guaranteed under all circumstances; the presumption of protection is but circumstantial. Since no provision under the UN Watercourses Convention has expressly provided for a restriction on existing uses, the same approach would also seem to constitute the position implicitly harboured under the Convention, should a conflict arise between existing patterns of resource development and potential uses by other co-riparian states.

Therefore, in order to accommodate any such new or expanded uses as may be contemplated by new arriving states such as Ethiopia, and by corollary the rest of the upstream Nile states, Article VIII of the Helsinki Rules provided for a guiding principle. It stated 'an existing reasonable use may continue in operation unless the factors justifying its continuance are outweighed by other factors leading to the conclusion that it be modified or terminated so as to accommodate a competing incompatible use'.

No corresponding provision had been incorporated both under the UN Watercourses Convention and the Agreement on the Nile River Basin Cooperative Framework; nor will such an insertion be indispensable in any event. In equitable determinations, the fact that existing uses will eventually be subjected to assessment and adjustment is simply evident from the context and objective of the equitable uses stipulation. After all, both instruments had prescribed that in deciding the equitability of utilizations, an existing use of any basin state, however vital, would not necessarily receive a complete protection; in fact, it constitutes only one of the numerous factors considered cumulatively, and as such, it occupies no particular position of pre-eminence.

Therefore, first appropriators could not legally presume that entrenched uses in shared river courses will be accorded a secure protection in perpetuity. When new users of a resource become 'ready to use the waters or to increase an existing use, then the entire question of equitable utilization of the waters is opened up for review . . . and the rights and needs of the various states would be considered'.[152]

In turn, this implies that in the long term where the rule of equitable utilization is set in motion, Egypt and Sudan could be confronted with the risk of slumping a great deal of the benefits now enjoyed through prior appropriation of the resource. The ILA's underlying maxim discussed earlier, inspiring states to engage in a maximum present utilization of river courses, cannot eventually offer a meaningful salvage for 'no one state could possibly guess what is likely to constitute an equitable utilization at some future time when a particular state's prior appropriation is placed at issue'.[153] Depending on the specifics of each circumstance, a broader process of evaluation involving several factors and circumstances may conclude the continuation of existing uses or may simply oblige modification or termination of all or some aspects of existing beneficial uses.

152 International Law Association (1966), note 13.
153 International Law Association (1966), note 13.

Hence, a prudent approach in national development policies will oblige a degree of forethought with regard to the implications of one's own actions on comparable stakes of other states sharing the same resource.

Finally, now that a detailed description of the equitable uses principle has been presented, a closing remark is obliging with respect to the particular measure of significance (protection) accorded to existing and potential uses in the Nile basin.

In so far as full scale implementation of riparian development strategies engender a conflict of uses scenario, and the foregoing facts on social and economic impacts of Nile River have demonstrated that they will, the present analysis must start by recognizing the unique import of an irrigation based economy along the downstream Nile. It extends over millions of hectares of land and constitutes a hugely discernible fact of life. Equities supporting the sustenance of existing social and economic settings are commanding; hence, an increased consideration should be given to grant them some protection, at least in relation to such uses of the Nile waters as will primarily target satisfaction of natural means of subsistence and such major developments as had been implemented prior to the issuance of upstream reservations. In some form, this can provide the assured minimum downstream entitlement.

However, one must also consider countervailing equities in upstream Nile and particularly the requirements of increased food production. This justifies the imposition of certain measures of detriment against existing uses. Evidently, such a delicate balance can be struck only through procedures afforded in cooperative negotiations, which, in the instant case, are not in place.

In striking the equilibrium, hard physical facts relating to the measure of total irrigated and potentially irrigable lands across the basin can provide important indicators on the basis of which riparian entitlements can be worked out.

Yet, neither existing nor potential uses of international watercourses are necessarily confined to agricultural uses, although the sector has traditionally consumed the largest proportion of the Nile waters. The employ of such a narrower parameter may be convenient for the present purposes, but it is evident that apportionment procedures will always require an informed judgment that takes into account a much larger set of factors and circumstances.

Existing uses and the duty not to cause significant harm

The most inevitable corollary of the convoluted relationship between existing and potential uses and the measure of protection afforded to each factor under international law has been that in certain circumstances, equitable determinations may well entail the non-fulfilment of all needs of watercourse states. The commencement of new uses in pursuance of a right to equitable uses may *ipso facto* lead to a measure of impairment against pre-existing uses.

If such damage should also be regarded as a legal injury and hence involve international responsibility of the harming state has for decades been a source of unfathomable controversy.

Article 7 of the UN Watercourses Convention and a range of regional instruments had provided that in utilizing an international watercourse in their territories, watercourse states shall take all appropriate measures to prevent the causing of significant harm to other watercourse states. Indeed, this principle has remained one of the cornerstone dictates of the international watercourses law-regime.

Over the years, the scope of this obligation and nature of its relationship with the equitable uses doctrine had engendered unending debates.

A chain of international law publicists and the ILC itself had submitted that indeed the principle under Article 7 of the UN Watercourses Convention prescribing a duty not cause significant harm prohibits late coming states from causing harm that exceeds a certain threshold. Such level of harm is set within the context of a process of equitable use determinations of the watercourse concerned.

In other words, a state's utilization of already appropriated waters will involve its international responsibility only when such use exceeds its equitable entitlement; harms inflicted within the limits of the exercise of such a right will not be regarded as infringing the rights of an injured state.

Regardless of the conceptual framing applied, the ILC explained:

> the object should be to make clear that what is prohibited is conduct by which one state exceeds its equitable share or deprives another state of its equitable share of the uses and benefits of the watercourse. To put it in another way, the focus should be on the duty not to cause legal injury (by making a non-equitable use), rather than on the duty not to cause a factual harm. This is not to deny by any means that there is a general duty to refrain from causing harm, in the factual sense, to another state; the point is simply that in the context of watercourses, suffering even significant harm may not infringe the rights of the harmed state if the harm is within the limits allowed by an equitable allocation.[154]

The essential basis of this perspective involves an inveterate controversy that had raged over the decades with regard to the relationship of the two domineering principles of international watercourses law: the equitable uses principle and the rule prescribing duty not to cause significant harm. The correlation between the two principles, coupled with the principle of due diligence, Fitzmaurice concluded, had a long and troubled history.[155]

While several authorities had diversely conversed on this particular theme, a concise summary of a convincing interpretation presented by McCaffrey will be excerpted here. He concluded 'in an effort to strike the balance between the two principles, the ILC's final text had favored equitable utilization too heavily. However the better view appears to be that paragraph 2 of Article 7

154 International Law Commission (1986) *Yearbook of International Law Commission*, vol 2, no 1, p 133.

155 Malgosia Fitzmaurice (1997) 'Convention on the Law of Non-navigational Uses of International Watercourses', *Leiden J. Int'l L*, vol 10, no 3, pp 502–5.

gives precedence to equitable utilization over the no harm doctrine, which is also consistent with actual state practice'.[156] This position was further strengthened through the implicit acknowledgement in paragraph 2 of Article 7, which stated that harm may be caused without engaging the harming state's responsibility and the proposition in Article 10, which stated that any conflict between uses of international water courses is to be resolved by reference to articles 5 to 7, thus denying the latter any inherent preeminence.[157]

In consequence, the right of late coming riparians to utilize resources of an international watercourse would still remain qualified by the duty not to cause significant harm, except as may be allowed under equitable utilization of the watercourse concerned. The focus is on the duty not to cause *legal injury* through a non-equitable pattern of utilization. Against a backdrop of different approaches adopted by various rapporteurs of the ILC itself, this model in which the two principles had been interrelated, McCaffrey accounted in 1987, seemed to be in basic agreement with the whole Commission's views.[158]

Correlation between competing uses of international watercourses

The Nile River resources have traditionally been utilized for diverse purposes. Such uses encompass waters withdrawn for domestic requirements in urban and rural settlements (drinking, cooking, washing, waste disposal and recreational), for economic and commercial uses (industry, construction, transportation, fishery, tourism), to sustain the generation of hydro-electrical power and most importantly, in agriculture (including the irrigation of small-holding and large-scale commercial farms, drainage uses and aquatics food production).

Given the unique setting of water resource developments in the basin, how do the various categories of competing uses of international watercourses correlate? Does any particular utilization enjoy priority over other uses?

Article 10 of the UN Watercourses Convention, reproducing a like stipulation under Article VI of the Helsinki Rules, institutes the basic canon:[159] 'in the absence of agreement or custom to the contrary, no use of an international watercourse enjoys inherent priority over other uses . . . and in the event of a conflict between uses of an international watercourse, it shall be resolved with reference to Articles 5 to 7, with special regard being given to the requirements of vital human needs'.

156 Stephen McCaffrey (2001) 'The Contribution of the UN Convention on the Law of the Non-Navigational Uses of International Watercourses', *Int J Global Environmental Issues*, vol 1, p 255.

157 McCaffrey (2001), note 156.

158 International Law Commission (1987) *Yearbook of International Law Commission*, vol 1, p 67.

159 No corresponding provision has been provided under the Nile Basin Cooperative Framework Agreement; under the statement of general principles, however, Article 3.14 provided that 'water is a natural resource having social and economic value, whose utilization should give priority to its most economic use, taking into account the satisfaction of *basic human needs* and the *safeguarding of ecosystems*'.

The ILC correctly observed that as a matter of existing law, it would be doubtful if one can make a statement of precedence among uses of waters for all systems in the world. In some systems, navigational uses would be of paramount importance and in others, irrigation would surely come next to drinking and domestic uses.[160]

The ILA elaborated the premise on which the historical shift from an approach that accorded supremacy to navigational uses to a new model that practically equates all types of uses had been based; in the past twenty-five years, the ILA held in 1967, technological revolution and population explosion which led to the rapid growth of non-navigational uses have resulted in the loss of the former pre-eminence accorded to navigational uses. Today, neither navigation nor any other use enjoys such a preference; each drainage basin must therefore be examined on an individual basis and a determination made as to which uses are most important in that basin or, in appropriate cases, in portions of the basin.[161]

In factual settings, however, the hypothesis framed under the UN Watercourses Convention that no particular use enjoys inherent priority will barely proffer solid standard in regulating the conduct of the Nile basin states. While theoretically no riparian state may claim the supremacy of any use it had embarked on or intends to institute in the future, the principle did not say how precisely an order of precedence shall be set when conflict of uses looms or in fact ensues and basin states fail to resolve the dispute through amicable procedures.

The Nile has traditionally played critical functions in the fiscal and social welfare of the states of Egypt and Sudan and has picked growing import in a belated economic resurgence of Ethiopia. The extensive but unsynchronized pattern of resource utilization along the downstream jurisdictions, attended by an egocentric predilection in Sudan, Egypt and Ethiopia to place the river at the centre stage of national development policies, attests the increasingly swelling clout the river has commanded in domestic orders.

Inevitably, such developmental course assures conflict between various categories of uses. Conflict could manifest where, for instance, extensive agriculture in downstream regions constrains waters which should be available for other uses elsewhere; or where, water dammed in hydro-electric facilities upstream – normally a non-consumptive utilization – impacts on the quality, timing or availability of flows along a downstream course. Growing urbanization and industrial consumptions have also withdrawn increased volumes of water.

In a purely physical context, the World Water Forum suggested that the responses to increased competition for water are supply augmentation, conservation and reallocation.[162] Yet, even within the narrow confines of the

160 International Law Commission (1983) *Yearbook of International Law Commission*, vol 2, no 1, p 90.

161 International Law Association (1966), note 13.

162 The World Water Assessment Programme (2009) *The United Nations World Water Development Report 3, Water in a Changing World*, London, UNESCO Publishing, p 154.

physical way-outs recommended by the Forum, the schemes will presume comprehensive arrangements between concerned watercourse states, which is still lacking in the Nile basin.

In a legal context, on the other hand, the response to a limited resource base where the flow of a river becomes the object of incompatible riparian policies and competitive uses lies elsewhere. Riparian predicament ensuing from the scarcity of available water resources obliges the need for composing a set of principles and procedures; such rules shall be employed to determine the circumstances and extent to which any particular use may be protected, reconsidered or given up in order to give way for new uses or users.

Generally, water withdrawn for drinking and sanitary purposes represent meagre volumes and rarely raises dispute because of the indispensability of the uses in sustaining human life. On the other hand, both in Egypt and Sudan, consumptive uses in irrigated agriculture overwhelmingly depend on the sustained flows of the Nile. While, in Egypt water used in the industrial sector still remains very modest, along with agriculture, this category of use has continued to constitute a critical column of the national economy in terms of GDP contribution, export revenue and size of population involved.

In contrast, Ethiopia's stakes in the resource rest in future investments in irrigational agriculture, although current policies inclined to direct significant percentages of the national wealth to the development of the energy sector.

It is evident that, if in varying scales, increased utilization of Nile waters in agriculture, industry and the generation of powers will distinctively impact the overall standing of the three riparian states. Water resources development initiatives in the named sectors will remain indispensable in the coming decades as well.

Therefore, any enterprise that endeavours to determine which one of these uses is the most important and hence assured a first charge of the waters will constitute a hugely impracticable commission. Given the enormity of the sank costs, the ingrained social and economic values appended to each of the uses and the vital prospective utilities of the river in some parts, no riparian state will likely give up the perpetuation of one category of use in its jurisdiction nor willingly modify or forfeit a competing use with a view to accommodating another use or comparable interest of other basin states.

While international law seeks to evaluate the key factors that affect the equitability of uses and rank water uses in some order, as such, the pertinent rules do not prescribe precedence between various uses of international watercourses. Hence, in the context of the circumstances so depicted, the stipulation under Article 10 of the UN Watercourses Convention that no use of an international watercourse enjoys inherent priority over other uses would not seem to furnish a particularly useful direction.

The protected position of waters used for *domestic* requirements, including for drinking, household purposes and watering of cattle has generally been strong. In the absence of specific agreement or custom to the contrary, Article 10 of the UN Watercourses Convention provided that *special regard* shall be given to the requirements of vital human needs in the event of a conflict between various uses of an international watercourse. This position restates a very old statement in the jurisprudence of the USA Supreme Court where water uses for drinking and other domestic purposes were accorded priority of the highest order.[163]

In this spirit, Article 3.14 of the Nile Cooperative Framework had likewise provided that water utilization in the basin 'should give priority to its most economic use, taking into account the satisfaction of basic human needs and the safeguarding of ecosystems'.

With regard to other types of uses, however, no principle has been developed nor universally acknowledged that accords any use of river courses *precedence* over the other. In as much as no specific agreement or custom exists in a basin to ascribe irrigational uses, industry or the generation of power a status of preeminence, therefore, the conflict between various categories of uses is resolved by reference to Articles 5 to 7 of the Watercourse Convention.

This again presumes a complex process involving the cumulative evaluation of each of the factors and circumstances affecting the equitability of uses. The weight accorded to any particular use may differ from basin to basin; as Eagleton had noted as early as in the 1950s, 'in a number of cases and treaties, something is said concerning certain uses of the water to be regarded as more important than other uses and consequently, to be given priority of rights. The establishment of such priorities in each situation belongs . . . to equitable apportionment'.[164]

163 Connecticut vs. Massachusetts, 282 US 673 (1931).

164 Clyde Eagleton (1955) 'The use of waters of International Rivers', *Canadian Bar Review*, vol 33, pp 1018, 1025.

12 Conclusions

The twentieth century witnessed an asymmetrical pattern of water resources utilization and developments across the Nile basin. A blend of socio-economic, hydro-political and legal factors coalesced to structure an exceptionally unique form of riparian relationship in the region.

Since the distant past, the Egyptian economic order relied on the provision of Nile waters to meet domestic, agricultural and industrial stipulations. An idiosyncratic relationship between nature's scarce bequest and a national pattern of socio-economic reality inspired constant innovations in irrigational and water management techniques.

Over a course, such advances have not only intensified the economic yields of the river as such, they also swelled the downstream polity's existential vulnerability and user-right perceptions. Paradoxically, the increased control and management of the river also prompted a psychosomatic momentum that impeded Nile water resources development prospects elsewhere in the basin.

More significantly, however, British Nile policies of the early twentieth century and the complex legal hurdles it orchestrated have been accounted as the most important reasons for the virtual underdevelopment of water-control works in the upper-reaches of the river.

Indeed, in the same epoch, Great Britain had put into service river-use policies that accorded greater import to the economic and political well-being of just two downstream constituencies – Egypt and Sudan, with little contemplation for the prospective requirements of the upper riparian countries.

Within the broader framework of imperial necessities, a series of water-control schemes had been contemplated and construction of a few over-year and annual reservoirs were carried out in the course of the 1900s to 1950s. The British colonial administration considered Nile waters conservation and storage plans on a grander scale, projecting to achieve full development of the river's resources throughout the basin; for the most part, the development chart sought to guarantee the foreseeable water requirements of the downstream states.

The contemplations failed mainly because of the absence of stable diplomatic relationships between the riparian parties involved and incompatible riverine policies pursued, and in part, due to the dearth of fiscal and technical facilities.

In consequence, an opportunity that could have fundamentally shaped the basic feature of riparian discourse was aborted. The subsequent decades witnessed a growing Egyptian nationalism that sought to formulate development strategies on a secure water resources base situated close to its frontiers. The construction on the Aswan High Dam in 1955 was a logical upshot of such a national predisposition.

The new dam scheme forestalled the contemplations for storage facilities dispersed across various constituencies of the basin; likewise, it reinvigorated Egypt's proprietary perceptions which repressed any significant utilization of the Nile waters in other parts of the basin.

In the 1990s, changes in the political, economic and demographic landscape of the basin precipitated a greater degree of involvement of the basin communities in the Nile River resources. This setting unveiled new challenge against the legal and developmental status quo.

In upstream Nile, no other country has grappled against the Anglo-Egyptian and later, Egyptian and Sudanese domination for control of the Nile waters as robustly and persistently as Ethiopia. The country's embedded perception of a leading stake in the subject has been stimulated by a range of geopolitical and simple physical facts that as provider of the largest proportions of the Nile deluge every year, it should be entitled to a matching reward in its exploitation.

While Ethiopia remained a self-governing entity even at the height of the British colonial empire in the Nile region in the 1890s, Ethiopia's sovereignty did little to guard it from the knotty British diplomatic callisthenics. By 1902, Great Britain had been able to influence Emperor Menelik to conclude a treaty that was subsequently perceived as restricting Ethiopia's sovereign rights in utilizing the Lake Tana, Baro-Akobo and Blue Nile river systems.

Attended by Ethiopia's own fiscal limitations, inert visionary acumen and political vacillation of its leadership, the Anglo-Ethiopian Treaty moderated opportunities for early development of hydraulic infrastructures across the Ethiopian parts of the Nile basin.

Historically, the Anglo-Ethiopian Treaty of May 1902 occupied a central position in structuring the hydro-legal discourse and relationships between Ethiopia, Sudan and Egypt. Constituted through notes exchanged between the respective governments, the treaty represented a key chapter in the winding phases of London's relentless quest for juridical protection and control of the whole Nile basin region. Throughout the post-treaty and post-independence periods, the pact remained the single most important instrument defining the international rights and obligations of the states of Sudan and Ethiopia.

From the very inception, a key aspect of the treaty under Article III had been perceived by the states parties to the arrangement quite divergently. With a continuously shifting scale of enthusiasm and perspective, the states endeavoured to define, design and carry out Nile River resources development schemes along lines that espoused their respective interpretations.

Throughout its tenure as the overseer of Egyptian and Sudanese interests, London deduced from the treaty that Ethiopia had been bound to completely refrain from laying any water-control work on the Nile and its tributaries. In due course, the perception of rigid monopoly had been moderated to accommodate utilization of the River for *minor* cultivation schemes serving the immediate needs of local consumption.

Ethiopia's views largely deviated. It argued that Emperor Menelik's pledge, more unequivocally conveyed in the Amharic text, only stipulated a duty not to *wholly stop up* the flow of the river without British consent, leaving other less detrimental uses for irrigational, industrial or domestic purposes to its own discretion.

The first imperative issue that should be considered in connection with the application of the Anglo-Ethiopian accord involves the geographical scope of the treaty.

In essence, this concerns the subject matter of how international law perceives the concept of an *international watercourse* as such.

From a strictly geographical perspective, river systems have been treated as physical unities; yet, the international legal order has for long had trouble in forging the correct expression and characterization of rivers in laying a conceptual framework for a global regulation of non-navigational uses of transboundary rivers.

Generally, modern planning practices have tended to adopt river conservation and management approaches on the basis of the *totality* of water resources presented in a basin. This naturally makes sense; a wider basin constitutes the most ideal unit for investigating meteorological, hydrological and climatic facts of a particular region.

However, such a predisposition in pro-conservation approaches and certain state practices notwithstanding, it could not be proposed that the system of international law has similarly considered the whole physical feature of a basin and basin-flows as proper units of international legal regulation. Despite a broader support for the drainage basin concept in modern treaty practice and works of international codification bodies, the evidence of disagreement suggests that it would be premature to attribute customary status to this concept as a definition of the geographical scope of international watercourses law.

As a result, riparian obligations which are implicit in a wider depiction of the physical scope of a river course cannot be readily admitted, except in circumstances where bilateral or regional treaties have expressly provided to that effect.

The Anglo-Ethiopian Treaty is not an exception. In forbidding the construction of any work on or across the Blue Nile, Lake Tana or the Sobat, the treaty could not be conceived as having contemplated to regulate the flows or uses of secondary river courses in the natural drainage basins of the principal rivers.

The other important disagreement relating to the application of the Anglo-Ethiopian Treaty was concerned with the alleged discrepancies in the Amharic and English versions of the accord from which both states had endeavoured to deduce differing substantive obligations.

Great Britain advocated a wider view of Article III that obliges Ethiopia not to arrest the flow of the river in anyway whatsoever without prior authorization, where as Ethiopia deviated, making its case that it is merely bound not to block up or stop up its flow from banks to banks. The first edition guaranteed Great Britain's monopolistic holding of the resource for downstream uses, whereas the latter version appeared to afford Ethiopia a substantial discretion in terms of rights of future utilization of the named rivers.

Both treaty languages were authentic texts; the parties did not provide beforehand for the text that should prevail in cases of variance.

In such eventualities, the Vienna Convention on the Law of Treaties (1969) institutes a fundamental assumption that the terms of a treaty are presumed to have the same meaning in each authentic text. The rule absolves one of the necessities of engaging in routine comparison of multiple texts with a view to carrying out their application.

The presumption is however nothing more than a mere theoretical implement and indeed rebuttable as soon as a plausible claim of difference surfaces. In such cases, any enterprise that seeks to elucidate the terms of a treaty and construct a meaning which can reasonably be presumed as constituting the intended joint volition of the parties must employ tools recognized under the Vienna Convention and the rules of custom. The standard rules of interpretation are contained in Articles 31–32 of the Convention.

Generally, texts are objective proofs of the parties' intentions and the search for common volition should not endeavour to read the treaty as denoting a line contrary to express stipulations. This reference constitutes an implied warning to any undertaking that places an undue emphasis on the intention of the parties as independent tool where texts exhibit plain and simple content.

In conversational dictionary and in the context emphasising its particular use under Article III, neither the expression *arrest* nor its Amharic equivalent could sincerely insinuate a controversial language. A careful reading of this exposition would uphold that the treaty does not bar Ethiopia from engaging in the assembly of hydraulic edifices that propose to merely cause a diminished flow of the headwaters, and not their arrest/block up. On its face, at least, the ordinary meaning of terms of the accord had hardly anticipated to keep out all forms of interference with the flow of the rivers, and hence did not appear to fittingly accommodate long-advocated British, later, Sudanese perceptions.

Yet, however convincing the ordinary interpretation may sound, common sense promptly poses the obvious question of why Great Britain would engage in a treaty scheme that had no reasonable merit in sustaining downstream monopolistic positions. Intensive scrutiny of the contemporaneous diplomatic records attests that in concluding the accord, Great Britain had most likely foreseen an enlarged Ethiopian responsibility, covering not only cases of complete damming but also threats emanating from lesser scales of interference with the river flows. This practical consideration weakens the interpretation of Article III in the ordinary form presented earlier.

Indeed, several extraneous evidences could be adduced indicating directly or otherwise that at least one of the parties could not be presumed to have intended such a formulation as is implicit in the ordinary reading above. A sequence of communications exchanged between Emperor Menelik, Emperor Haileselassie and Great Britain's emissaries in Addis Ababa, depicting the post-treaty observations of states, may confirm this conclusion.

With evidence of two versions subjectively radiating from states' practice and arguably discerned from the reading of treaty texts, further employment of interpretative tools embraced under the Vienna Convention on the Law of Treaties may only be indispensable.

Contextual interpretation principally presumes the reading of a treaty as a whole, ascribing phrases or terms which may be understood in several ways a meaning that best fits the whole context. It also engages the reading and construction of the preamble, annexes, subsequent practices and agreements correlated to the treaty in issue.

Of course, the Vienna Convention on the Law of Treaties does not generously provide for an outright inclusion of all preceding and subsequent manuscripts connected to a treaty as forming part of the context. Still, in the examination of the principal items evidencing subsequent conduct or practice of the Parties, the ILC as well as the ICJ had extensively employed sequences of materials including diplomatic exchanges, internal memos, decrees, declarations, reports, protests and complaints as evidences of acquiescence, admissions or assertions of the parties' understanding of a treaty at issue.

Hence, various manuscripts chronicling historical and diplomatic events that took place between 1902 and 1935 had been extensively utilized with the assumption that they constituted subsequent practice of the parties in the application of the treaty which establishes their agreement regarding its interpretation within the meaning of Article 31 of the Vienna Convention.

The systematic examination of the documents bears out one important conclusion: both parties had reiterated hugely contrasting observations as regards rights supposedly radiating from Article III of the treaty.

In so far as an objective stipulation of the ordinary meaning of the terms at issue, construed in their context is concerned, the historical recital had only substantiated an inconclusive pattern of facts, conceptions and national perceptions that cannot be reconciled with ease. This fact warranted a brief consideration of the object and purpose of the treaty as a last conjunctive tool of treaty interpretation.

What the parties to the treaty might have looked forward to gaining under Article III of the treaty would remain too complex to discern with certainty. The intentions of the parties are subjective abstractions and often, as when there is little structural relationship between various provisions making up a treaty or where a preamble fails to proffer clear communication, the underlying objectives may not be detected readily from a mere reading of the scripts as such.

On the basis of the limited exposition of provisions of the Anglo-Ethiopian Treaty and relatable legal-historical chronicles, it can be gathered that the most important design which prompted the parties to conclude the treaty had been to settle and delineate longstanding boundary issues between the Sudan and Ethiopia. The historical and diplomatic records are too scanty to discern with confidence the specific factors that prompted Emperor Menelik to undertake the obligation under Article III within a broader treaty framework that worked on regularizing boundary issues.

The historical anecdotes tended to confirm that whatever obligation the terms of the treaty stipulated, Ethiopia had deduced that they did not imply the wider construction to which Great Britain had adhered in the immediately ensuing decades.

The early positions of the states cannot claim to be unwavering; Great Britain had maintained a fairly obstinate deportment advocating the treaty as instituting a uses regime that outlaws nearly all forms of interference. However, in framing the treaty text in its present form, the British had simply failed to substantiate such a position by inserting a clear legal stipulation to that effect.

If only inconclusive, the subsequent conduct of the parties has generally put an interpretation of the language of the treaty that harbours a constricted construction of the scope of Article III.

In any event, an intrinsic element of sovereignty of states universally recognized under international law has been the absolute freedom of command over natural resources situated in their jurisdiction; while states may willingly relinquish certain aspects of sovereign prerogatives through treaties, an arrangement requiring a permanent surrender of rights of utilizing a river course could not be presumed from indistinct state of facts.

Apart from legal assessments premised on international rules of treaty interpretation, the continued validity of the Anglo-Ethiopian Treaty had also been challenged on the basis of certain distinct principles of international law.

One of such principles related to unequal treaties. Evidently, the system of international law lacks a theoretical frame applied across the board which could be utilized to adjudge the juridical fate of unequal treaties as such, and in any event, whether the emphasis should be laid on objective contents of treaties or the circumstances of their creation.

On the whole, the weight of legal literatures would appear to hold that pacts concluded between states could not be appraised as unequal merely on account of the circumstances under which they had been negotiated.

A sequence of classical literatures of international law had approached the subject indirectly, and nearly unanimously, held the view that the rule of duress applies only in a limited mode, with respect to constraints, serious physical menace or intimidation, employed against treaty-making representatives of states. The present formulation of Articles 51 and 52 of the Vienna Convention on the Law of Treaties, reflecting on the spirit enshrined in Article 2(4) of the UN Charter, has expanded and propounded this view.

Of course, Articles 51 and 52 of the convention addressed only cases of consent obtained through duress, and not the theme of incongruent treaties as such. Yet, while ordinarily states exercising a genuinely free will could not be expected to surrender legitimate interests without a quid pro quod gain, it is equally evident that not every regime of inequality in treaties fits in the category of pacts procured through the *coercion of a state* by threat or use of force.

Admittedly, the Anglo-Ethiopian Treaty was concluded in an apprehensive political setting, at the height of expansion of European colonialism in Africa. In spite of the edgy ambience that over-clouded the process, the state of affairs impress that Emperor Menelik had not engaged in the frontier haggle with a manifestly impotent stature as to deduce that he was subjected to coercion and that the terms of the treaty were imposed on him against his will. The treaty, although favouring Great Britain's views on issues that really mattered, had been constructed on the basis of recognition of rudiments of sovereign equality.

On the other hand, a formidable defiance of unequal treaties had been procured by a series of United Nations General Assembly resolutions adopted in the 1950s and 1960s. Among others, General Assembly Resolutions 523, 626, 1314, 1515, 1803 and 3281 instituted a systematic framework of conceptual correlation between the principles of sovereign equality, self determination and permanent sovereignty of states over natural resources.

The UNGA resolutions on PSNR laid one facet of the doctrinal and legal regimes that govern the use of natural resources and the measure of discretion afforded to states in the exercise of such rights. The resolutions inter alia declared the permanent sovereign right of every state to freely dispose its wealth and resources in accordance with national interests and in the spirit of economic collaboration.

A significant boost to the stature of the concept was, however, endowed through its genetic organization under another theme of international law: the right to self-determination. Whether permanent sovereignty over natural resources constitutes a basic constituent of the right to self-determination, hence engendering a distinct set of rights with regard to the uses of international watercourses, had been the subject of intensive deliberation in the early UN resolutions and literatures.

One consequence of the prominence of PSNR as a principle of international law and, even more, as a vital constituent of the right to self-determination has been that it could afford states a legal lee in seeking the nullification of treaty undertakings that impinge heavily on rights of utilizing natural resources situated in their jurisdictions.

In its spirit contemplated by Great Britain, the Anglo-Ethiopian Treaty could properly be regarded as artefact of a British authoritative drafting; in this context, it can be presumed as structuring a case of permanent inequality of rights of use over a sovereign state's natural resources.

Complemented by other factors, the state of inequity thus created had gravely jeopardized Ethiopia's development prospects and could afford a ground for calling the nullity of the treaty. A literal implementation of the Anglo-Ethiopian Treaty in the context perpetuated by Great Britain would naturally deny Ethiopia of a vital means of its subsistence. This is hardly consonant with the conditions implicit in the application of the principles of equality and permanent sovereignty of states over natural resources.

A third principle of international law which states have employed to rectify an unequal state of affairs instituted through treaty regimes is the doctrine of *rebus sic stantibus*.

As stated under the Vienna Convention on the Law of Treaties, the canon confers in states a measure of cause for withdrawing from treaty obligations on account of fundamental change of circumstances which has occurred with regard to those existing at the time of the conclusion of a treaty and which was not foreseen by the parties.

It can be inferred from the framing of Article 62 of the Vienna Convention that not every allegation of consequent change can *ipso facto* upset the application of treaty regimes as such. The change must be unforeseen, fundamental in nature and the facts existing at the time of the conclusion of the treaty must have constituted the essential basis of the consent of the parties.

Hence, permanent servitudes such as those purportedly instituted through the Anglo-Ethiopian Treaty would not be abrogated merely on account of the fact that they had tended to be *cumbersome* to one of the parties.

The mass of historical presentations on the Anglo-Ethiopian relations illustrates that the interpretation of certain issues and essential factual settings surrounding the conclusion of the treaty could not be established conclusively. Whatever the implied assumptions, the specific arrangement governing the use of the Nile had been orchestrated to meet Great Britain's colonial-period objectives in the lower-reaches of the basin. Emperor Menelik's dispensation of the various privileges to Great Britain had taken such facts into consideration.

Consequently, the demise of British colonial establishment and the advent of Sudanese self-rule in the mid twentieth century had represented a radical transformation of the status quo fundamentally affecting the position of the parties to the original pact. The outcome of such political developments had been such that the prime raison d'être of Article III of the treaty, i.e. upholding the welfare of British colonial establishment in Sudan and Egypt and the friendly relations between Great Britain and Ethiopia, could no longer be fulfilled through the machination of the same treaty scheme. By virtue of the rules of state succession, Ethiopia would now be urged to discharge the obligation to an essentially different party, a state of fact which itself depicts fundamental changes from the practical anticipations of both Great Britain and Ethiopia within the framework of the treaty.

On this basis, it could be concluded that the disappearance of such a vital condition of the treaty on which its continued functioning had depended and which the parties had not anticipated may afford Ethiopia a ground for calling the abrogation of the agreement on the basis of fundamental change of circumstances.

The Anglo-Ethiopian Treaty is not the *only* legal scheme that structured rights of access and utilization of the Nile waters in the region.

In the late nineteenth and throughout the twentieth century, the basin had also witnessed a complex legal order organized through a string of other contentious pacts, regional customs and self-conceived notions of rights regulating the use, development and management of the Nile river resources.

The *natural* and *historical rights* (or prior uses) expressions constituted the central pillars of entitlements along the downstream Nile; the two conceptions formed the doctrinal platform on which the institutional and water sharing schemes introduced through the Nile waters treaties of 1929 and 1959 had been premised.

In nearly all regional initiatives and diplomatic discourses, Egypt and Sudan maintained a parallel pose, albeit in varying forms. Hence, any upstream development of the Nile impacting on the natural and historical rights, respectively fixed at 55.5 and 18.5bcm/yr under the Nile waters accords, has been held as offensive of the rights so *established.*

The Anglo-Egyptian insistence on preservation of the historical and natural rights of use had not been a sporadic phenomenon; it evolved over a longer span of time. Regardless of how claims based on natural and historical rights may have been framed or espoused, the crucial point in the context of the analysis of basin-wide rights-relations has been assessment of the status of such formulations under international law.

A circumspect delving into the mechanics of the pertinent rules of international law would oblige but to concur with the hypothesis that arguments for *exclusive uses* of the Nile waters premised on the natural-historical rights conception are unconvincingly linked to the pertinent norms of international law. Any defense of downstream rights has to be inferred either from a comprehensive treaty regime or express stipulations of customary international law governing the use of shared water courses.

The mere *entrenchment* of the natural/historic rights clause under the 1929/1959 treaties could not effectively shield downstream rights if the coercive utility of the treaties themselves has been challenged upstream, and particularly in Ethiopia, for want of consent to be bound. A fundamental proposition of customary international law, restated under Article 34 of the Vienna Convention on the Law of Treaties, prescribes that a treaty can neither create obligations nor institute rights for a third state without its consent.

On its face, the natural and historical rights hypothesis may impress some association with certain doctrines of international watercourses law. In some cases, the natural rights conception had been construed as embodying the *natural flow* doctrine, also referred to as the theory of *absolute territorial integrity* vesting in lower riparians rights to the natural (unhindered) flow of international watercourses.

Yet, in the functioning of contemporary international watercourses law, there exists no practical precedence where any state had successfully declared uninfringeable privileges of utilization by virtue of natural rights as such. Today, of course, legal arguments premised on an extreme version of the theory of absolute territorial integrity had long been discredited.

On the other hand, downstream theories advocating a right to special entitlements may have evolved as an upshot of a complex climatic setting that reigns across the far-northern half of the Nile basin region. A parched land with a mean annual rainfall barely transcending 18mm, Egypt and northern Sudan could barely compare with water resource endowments in the central lakes region and the Ethiopian highlands plateau.

Even in the absence of basin-wide treaty frameworks, special riparian vulnerabilities induced by uneven distribution of hydraulic resources or a historical pattern of extended uses could be regulated or adjusted through the employment of rules and principles of international watercourses law. The system of international law could not be labelled as equitable if states situated in incongruous settings with respect to the allocation of water resources or the scales of hydraulic developments are accorded the same rights. The equality of rights and equitable entitlements admits several peculiarities which would be relevant in the context of one basin state, but not the other.

Hence, if in some measure, the particular susceptibilities of the downstream Nile and the resulting legal rhetoric of historical patterns of prior uses are accommodated within the frame of international law. But, the conceptual references proposing to validate downstream claims of rights on the grounds of extreme dependency on a water course, prior or historical uses or unavailability of alternative water resources could not be considered as standing separately under international law. They are considered only within the context of a broader framework of a prevailing principle: the right to equitable and reasonable utilization.

Therefore, natural conditions bestowing in the downstream Nile small volumes of precipitation or even more vitally, an ages-long practice of prior resource utilization embedded in the socio-economic necessities of Egypt and Sudan would have to compete with a dozen of other factors lined under Article 6 of the watercourses convention. The right in equity of contending national interests is computed only on the basis of consideration of the *whole*.

Once it is held that the natural-historical rights argument constitutes an indefensible juristic proposition, riparian entitlements would need to be worked on the basis of broader rules of customary international watercourses law.

The opening decades of the twenty-first century have marked a slight regression in traditional downstream positions which tended to accommodate long-standing concerns of the upstream states. This meagre flexibility in user-right perceptions could be attributed to several factors. A basin-wide diplomatic process, launched in February 1999 under the auspices of the Nile Basin Initiative, has driven user-right dialogues to unprecedented heights. Along with seven upstream riparian states, Sudan and Egypt continued to engage in negotiations of the transitional institutional mechanism of the Nile Basin Initiative.

The regional initiative had been formally mandated to set in place a Commission and endorse an Agreement on the Nile River Basin Cooperative Framework based on a vision to achieve sustainable socio-economic development through equitable utilization of and benefit from the common Nile Basin water resources.

However, both within and outside the framework of the Nile Basin Initiative, Ethiopia, Egypt and Sudan persisted to espouse different positions in relation to the fundamental principles of international watercourses law.

In the past, Ethiopia's right claims over the Nile River water resources have taken various formulations. Its arguments characteristically endeavoured to proclaim and preserve present and future rights of use. The national approach adopted a rights-based postulate which accentuated the nation's hydrographic contributions to the basin system.

Yet, in contrast to claims presented by a few legal authorities, a careful interpretation of Ethiopia's positions and official statements could not be construed as mirroring the *absolute territorial sovereignty* principle with regard to the definition of its rights on the Nile. In practice, in the aftermath of post-Aswan Dam period, Ethiopia had gradually but steadily tuned its claims along the line of principles advocating equity and sovereign equality in the use of internationally shared watercourses.

On the other hand, for several decades, Sudan and Egypt had been fairly convinced that Ethiopia had neither firm plans nor the means for pursuing significant developments on the Blue Nile. Under the 1959 Nile waters treaty, both downstream states expressed intent to jointly consider the claims of other riparian states at some future time and deduct their shares if any such consideration results in acceptance. In practice, however, both states harboured stiff reservations and endorsed British-era strategies to forestall threats potentially originating from Ethiopia's prospective uses of the Blue Nile River.

In regional discourses, Egypt's reflections have been analogous with the positions adopted by Sudan. The equitable utilization principle has been too entrenched in contemporary international law to overlook that Egypt, traditionally a staunch adherent of the historical rights and the no significant harm conceptions, had to acknowledge the doctrine's standing in successive basin-wide forums. Particulars of its national approach, however, have varied.

Egypt generally recognized the right of each watercourse state to equitable utilization of the Nile River, subject to a stipulation that such causes no appreciable/significant harm to its own interests. Likewise, it reiterated that several of the upper riparian states are still bound to respect existing (colonial and post-colonial) treaties, conventions, rules and principles of international law.

On the whole, while positive developments may have been witnessed in the contemporary cooperative discourses in the basin, on a closer scrutiny, one cannot help but perceive that formidable barriers still linger. This explains why, in spite of the concentrated negotiations in the past decade alone, no breakthrough has been forthcoming on certain important stipulations of the Agreement on the Nile Basin Cooperative Framework.

On 26 June 2007, the Nile Council of Ministers, an organ of the Nile Basin Initiative represented through water and irrigation ministers of the riparian states, concluded negotiations on the substantive and procedural aspects of the proposed 'Agreement on Nile River Basin Cooperative Framework'. In spite of outstanding discrepancies in the national position of the partaking states, the Cooperative Framework Agreement was opened for signature from 14 May 2010, for a period of not more than one year. Egypt's declared expectation that 'the upstream countries (would) reverse their decision to sign a unilateral framework agreement so that negotiations continue' was not heeded; the agreement has since been signed by five states: Uganda, Tanzania, Kenya, Ethiopia as well as Rwanda and Burundi.

In an unprecedented tempo of diplomatic unison in Sharm El Sheikh, seven upstream states adopted an analogous position on contents of the Cooperative Framework Agreement that projected to scrap all pre-existing arrangements. Egypt and Sudan reacted without delay, and reiterated that the position adopted at the Extra-Ordinary Meeting of the Nile-COM reflects the views only of the seven states. Instead, a substitute proposal for a direct launching of the Nile Basin Commission, within whose framework further negotiations would be undertaken, failed to garner favour in the upstream block.

Two groupings of basin states, following geographical divisions in the upper- and lower-reaches of the river, deviated on the substantive framing of the single most important stipulation, Article 14 of the Cooperative Framework which addressed issues of water security. The provision stipulated that the Nile Basin

States agree, in a spirit of cooperation to work together to ensure that all states achieve and sustain water security, and not to significantly affect the water security of any other Nile Basin State.

In spite of the explicit references to a right to water security, equitable uses and duty not to cause significant harm, Sudan and Egypt failed to perceive that downstream rights would be adequately shielded under the new scheme. An arrangement short of preserving the existing status quo was held as entirely objectionable.

Admittedly, it would be difficult to predict what the future holds for the Nile basin; but it is copiously evident that the legal and diplomatic discourse in the region has already reached a point of no return. Such a scale of cooperation and legal achievement has simply been unprecedented.

The Cooperative Framework Agreement presents the perfect setting, both diplomatically and legally, for rectifying entrenched perceptions of grave inequity in upstream Nile and for engaging cooperatively on the basis of recognized rules and principles of customary international law. Such rules alone could proffer objective platforms for tackling the current impasse and expounding specific rights stipulated under the Cooperative Framework Agreement itself.

In the context of the contemporary legal developments under the Cooperative Framework Agreement, downstream positions have not only been extreme, they are also the most vulnerable, for no rule of international law would eventually sustain existing patterns of uses without some qualifications. Hence, downstream states would not only need to dodge extreme versions of the status quo niche espoused, they would also have to demonstrate that indeed the regional platform represents more than a mere time-buying diplomatic workout.

So far, historical, political and fiscal considerations have hindered the effective utility of the river in the upper-reaches of the basin; under obviously changing socio-economic and political realities in the region, however, the contemporary state should not corner upstream countries into harbouring deep-seated convictions which concentrate on unilateralism as a means of compelling serious negotiations. Along downstream Nile, the long-term security to national riparian interests would very much depend in a fitting compromise volunteered today, both in terms of anticipations and legal justifications.

Outside the framework of contemporary cooperative initiatives in the Nile basin, the definition of riparian rights essentially depends on customary rules of international water course law, and most notably, the doctrine of equitable utilization. Contending riparian interests in the basin would have to be assessed, balanced and adjusted on the basis of rules and principles of international watercourses law.

While national conceptions may have reflected differing positions on the subject of the *international river* expression, this analysis has proceeded on the basis of a substantiated legal premise that the flow regime availed in the Nile is such that *not all* beneficial uses implemented in pursuance of the right to equitable utilization could be realized to their full extent without involving conflicts of uses.

This takes particular note of the venerable debate under international law which involved the issue of how the concept of international watercourse has been perceived as a physical unit of regulation, and by inference, which particular components of the entire water balance of river basins constitute, legally, the objects of common riparian appropriation.

In this regard, the Cooperative Framework Agreement has endeavoured to instil a very cautious approach. Two distinct conceptions, the *Nile River Basin* and the *Nile River System*, have been employed in connection with the geographical scope of the application of rules and principles contained in the treaty, depending on the specific functions contemplated.

Where conflict of uses is established as inevitable in the Nile basin region, the role of principles of international law focuses on the question of how they could be employed to reconcile competing riparian interests.

An overwhelming body of case law, institutional initiatives and state practice has already endorsed the equitable-uses principle as one of the established canons of international custom. Today, no state can claim unqualified rights of utilization of international watercourses under the banner of sovereignty.

The right of each watercourse state to reasonable and equitable share in the uses of the waters of an international river has been restated in a number of instruments including the Helsinki Rules on the Uses of the Waters of International Rivers (revised at the Berlin Conference in 2004) as well as the UN Convention on the Law of the Non-navigational Uses of International Watercourses (1997).

Equitable entitlement as conceived under international watercourses law does not connote that each state shall receive identical shares in the uses of the waters. In fact, in actual scenarios, equity would place states further beyond a strict parity in sharing the waters or beneficial uses of international watercourses. The fundamental idea that underlies equitable sharing is the provision of maximum benefits to each basin state from the uses of the waters with the minimum detriment to each.

Essentially, the scope of each riparian state's equitable entitlement in the beneficial uses of an international watercourse is an upshot of a cumulative review of each of the factors and circumstances depicted under Article 6.

Whereas Article 6.2 of the watercourses convention requires states to enter into consultations in a spirit of cooperation with a view to determining equitable entitlements, to date, the precise range of substantive rights of the Nile riparian states has basically remained self-prescribed. The basin endures without inclusive institutional mechanism for proper planning, utilization, management and conservation of its resources.

Hence, in a legal milieu where basin states operate autonomously and based on self-conceived depiction of rights, the normative prescriptions of international law become even more pertinent.

The right of each state to use an international watercourse depends upon a just and objective evaluation of all the factors circumstances. The pertinent provisions of both the Helsinki Rules and the watercourses convention have endeavoured to lessen the subjective propensity of riparian states by providing for a broad list of factors and circumstances that should be taken into consideration in establishing equity.

Article 6.1 of the convention provided that utilization of an international watercourse in an equitable and reasonable manner requires taking into account all relevant factors and circumstances including geographic, hydrographic, hydrological, climatic, ecological and other factors of a natural character; the social and economic needs of the watercourse states concerned; the population dependent on the watercourse in each watercourse state; the effects of the use or uses of the watercourses in one watercourse state on other watercourse states; existing and potential uses of the watercourse; conservation, protection, development and economy of use of the water resources of the watercourse and the costs of measures taken to that effect; and the availability of alternatives, of comparable value, to a particular planned or existing use.

Unfortunately, no single stipulation has provided for a clear set of guidelines which explain how the blend of factors and circumstances should be applied in a particular circumstance to give effect to the notion of the right to equitable and reasonable utilization. With regard to the relative weight accorded to each factor or circumstance, however, Article 6.3 of the convention and Article 4.4 of the Cooperative Framework Agreement provided that this would be decided by reference to its importance in comparison with other relevant factors.

The first reference under Article 6.1.(a) involves geographic, hydrographic, hydrological, climatic, ecological and other factors of a natural character. Hydrologically, Ethiopia, Egypt and the Sudan are placed in entirely contrasting positions of eminence, particularly in relation to seasonal flood regimes, water-flows, distribution and mean annual contribution to the Nile River system.

What precise role the hydrologic contribution of each basin played is difficult to trace in the treaty practice of states. Often, allocation regimes are either silent or framed in general expressions as regards the basis on which they have been established, and no explicit information is availed singularly indicating the weight that should be accorded to the relative contribution of each watercourse state.

Evidently, Ethiopia cannot claim an absolute priority in the beneficial uses of the Nile waters simply because the river pours in significant proportions from its jurisdiction, in much the same as Egypt and Sudan may not demand the river to flow as in its natural state merely because they have had a deeply entrenched pattern of pre-existing uses. As such, water contribution is only one factor; a claim for settlement of disputes solely on the basis of water contribution would amount to the application of the *absolute territorial sovereignty* theory which has already been denied being a rule of international water law.

While generally it is true that not all factors and circumstances would be attributed an absolutely equal standing in any given circumstance, some are more important than the others and unique circumstances of each particular basin can help identify which.

In displaying a distinctive set of geographical reality, the water flows of a river can in some cases be furnished only by a few riparian states. In the context of the Nile basin, the near-absolute hydrological dependence of the states of Egypt and Sudan on the natural floods of a river essentially derived from a *single* co riparian – Ethiopia – proffers a compelling rationale for acquiescing that as a factor, the relative contribution of the three basin states should assume a prevailing credence in relation to other variables and in the eventual assessment of equitable benefits.

Apart from hydrological considerations, geographical and climatic factors have also been recited as equally important. The physical extent of a river course and the climatic constitution (including rain patterns, seasonality and evaporation) in the territory of each watercourse state are depicted as some of the factors considered under the watercourses convention.

Neither international law nor the practices of states are very explicit in their messages as to the nature of the correlation that should exist between geographical/climatic facts of a particular basin state and its relative entitlements of rights. A clear set of precedents is wanting and legal literatures have been barely specific.

The general legal impression would appear to be that the geographical breadth and adverse climatic setting of a riparian state in a basin is associated with enhanced entitlements in equitable rulings. In this context, the arid climatic constitution and sheer size of population directly impacted by the availability of the Nile waters would clearly favour Egypt's position, and on a much lesser degree, the Sudan. Although Egypt and Ethiopia are similarly exposed to concentrated demographic pressures of a population living in the respective basin constituencies of equivalent stretch, an unfavourable climatic setting situates the former in a relatively enhanced standing.

On the other hand, in the Sudan, oversized measure of the basin's geography, which could also signify a scale of economic, social and demographic impact of the resource across its jurisdiction, positions the country in a proportionately elevated stature as opposed to its two neighbours.

Another important factor restated the UN watercourses convention and which utilization of an international watercourse in equitable and reasonable manner requires taking in to account is the social and economic needs of the watercourse states concerned.

In presenting the social and economic factors in context, some conventional indicators in developmental and economic studies which draw together facts relating to national incomes, population growth, agriculture, existing and potential cultivable areas, food security, employment and access to sanitation/drinking waters have been employed as some of the feasible indexes. They are hardly comprehensive but could help reflect on the impact of the Nile waters on a riparian state's level of social and economic growth.

The open ended nature of the economic and social needs criteria under Article 6 naturally poses problems for the national aspirations of states are unconfined, increasing, instead of diminishing with each particular level of satisfaction. Even where the social and economic value of a resource can be ascertained within reasonable bounds, as much a challenge would remain in credibly interpreting any such conclusion as may be drawn from the extra legal development standards and in translating the same in to some measurable privilege under international law.

Under Article 6.1.(b), the reference to economic and social needs of a watercourse state whose satisfaction is projected through utilization of resources of a transboundary river encompasses both the requirements of the sub-basin itself as well as the corresponding necessities of the whole riparian state. That no territorial limitation had been implied in the definition of the principle is evident both from the pertinent rules which stipulated that watercourse states shall, in their respective territories, utilize an international watercourse in an equitable and reasonable manner.

Of course, in addressing issues of equitable apportionment, several challenging issues would linger. On the basis of a very limited review of the economic and social implications of resources of the Nile River in Egypt, Sudan and Ethiopia, certain conclusions could be provisionally sketched.

In Egypt and parts of Sudan, the practice of irrigational agriculture has been deeply entrenched, significantly impacting the organization of social and economic structures. In fact, in Egypt, the effect transcends far beyond mere irrigated lands and crops grown to define the nation's very existence. In consequence, any initiative that aims at equitable determinations by stressing the social and economic values of the Nile waters would ascribe such facts a particularly greater weight.

This is without prejudice to discernible drifts in the service and industry sectors which tended to occupy a more vital position in Egypt's national economic setting and hence sink the traditional supremacy of an agriculture-linked development drive in the future. A similar leaning has also been observed in Sudan where, while agricultural remains the dominant sector in the national economy, its share has increasingly declined in recent years because of decreased agricultural production and the increased exploitation and export of mineral oil.

Egypt commands a sophisticated irrigational economy stretching over about 3.38 million hectares and its position has been accorded a measure of protection on account of multifarious impacts of irrigation agriculture on the national economy and social establishment.

Paradoxically, Sudan and Ethiopia could also stand on the gaining side based on the relative positions of their social and economic under-achievements. Both states perform shoddily in several indexes of human development and hence, can submit for superior claims on the basis of such considerations. Ethiopia and Sudan have had abysmal records in several indicators of human development, including the count of total population living under defined income lines, food security, nutritional status and access to improved water resources as well as sanitation.

Naturally, uncertainties involving food security engender the gravest threat to human existence. In Egypt, agricultural development has trekked far above corresponding advances in Sudan. Ethiopia, on the other hand, has completely been missing from the atlas of irrigated agriculture.

Egypt has attained food self-sufficiency in several crops and agricultural products; it has also managed to reduce the gap in several strategic crops. The state of affairs is not fundamentally unrelated in the Sudan. In spite of incidences of drought and rainfall variability, irrigated agriculture remained a central option to boost the economy in general and increase the living standard of the majority of the population. Sudan has been self-sufficient in basic foods, with important inter-annual and geographical variations and wide regional and household disparities prevailing across the country.

In contrast, Ethiopia's classically agrarian economy failed to meet food security concerns and persistent drought has been the order of the day for a very long period.

Agriculture constitutes a basic requirement of life and irrigated agriculture plays a significant role in this regard. Ethiopia's demonstrated vulnerability to successive droughts and occasional famines and its part-dependence on the provision of external aid evinces the augmented use that should be made of the Nile River water resources with a view to satisfying the social and economic challenges of its population.

Egypt and Sudan have performed fairly well on these counts and particularly in agricultural food self-sufficiency. In contrast, Ethiopia would need to trek quite a long way in this respect before it can situate on a balance in meeting the like needs of its population. In the context of prospective water allocations involving the three states, therefore, this particular verity justifies a heightened priority that should be accorded to Ethiopia's claims based on consideration of social and economic needs.

Ethiopia's position could also be reinforced on account of the fact that its development drive, at least in the immediate future, primarily targets the provisioning of primary necessities of existence, i.e. the delivery of foodstuffs. While Ethiopia and parts of Sudan essentially struggle with the steps needed to ensure the fundamental right of citizens to freedom from hunger and malnutrition, a large swathe of commercial plantations both in Egypt and Sudan, withdrawing billions of cubic meters of Nile waters, constituted vital pillars of the socio-economic welfare far beyond the means of direct fulfilment of natural wants. A consideration of prime importance in equitable decisions should be that an occupation that inclines on preservation of the human existence as such cannot be treated on equal footing with essentially profit-motivated or export-oriented ventures that lie in the heart of the downstream economic drive.

Conceptually, this argument draws a parallel rationalization from comments furnished by the ILA on Article 14 of the Berlin Rules where, between competing categories of uses of international watercourses, vital human needs had been accorded undisputed priority.

Another important factor under the Convention considers the size population dependent on the watercourse in each basin state.

At first glance, the population factor would seem to proffer an objective standard; in reality, the employ of such a parameter in equitable use determinations is liable to heave the same hurdles of comprehension.

In addressing issues related to population *dependent* on a transboundary river, the relevant consideration would embrace the interest of the state as a whole and all its inhabitants, and not merely the interest of the basin areas of the state.

A rational approach instructs that the population element under Article 6.1 should not be construed in absolute terms, in the sense that every single inhabitant of a riparian state would *ipso facto* count, but only as referring to the total number of a riparian populace whose needs, present or projected, could be satisfied through utilization of a shared river course. In view of the uneven demographic strains and competitive stakes of states across the Nile basin, this distinction is simply crucial.

Certainly, a requirement of the link between population and water availability is not devoid of complications, particularly noting how diversely water affects humanity. The most visible impact of the Nile waters in meeting challenges associated with human development relate to the ever expanding functions of the river system in sustaining agricultural productivity and in feeding a growing population.

The absolute dearth of alternative water resources illustrates that agricultural, industrial, drinking and sanitational water requirements of the Egyptian population are profoundly dependent on provisions of the lone national resource. Aside from opportunities of direct employment, if one also considers the impact of irrigated agriculture on the preservation of national food security, perceptibly, the total size of population dependent on the Nile waters for the provision of the single most important human necessity, foodstuffs, would shoot up.

Similarly, withdrawal in the industrial sector is further manifestation of the levels of dependence of the Egyptian population on the Nile waters. Indeed, the Nile pervades every aspect of the nation's existence.

This confirms that neither the current nor any projected utilization of the Nile waters in Sudan or Ethiopia could exhibit a resembling scale of population dependency that matches the state of affairs in Egypt.

Hence, with some notable exceptions, the *population dependency* factor under Article 6 of the UN Watercourses Convention would place Egypt in particularly higher position in future riparian discourses on equitable water allocations. Unlike in Ethiopia or Sudan where the resource base could be diversified, in Egypt, the fulfilment of all basic services relies on a lone resource.

This conclusion doesn't, of course, imply that the national stakes are inconsequential in Sudan or Ethiopia; the assessment is but only relative. In fact, a large proportion of the population in the two states too depend on a current or prospective utility of the Nile waters in meeting vital needs in a range of social and economic stipulations, although the scale could be much less.

In Ethiopia, concrete initiatives that have been launched with a view to alleviating chronic concerns of underdevelopment would basically imply an enhanced utilization of the Nile waters resources; the projected dependency of the population would naturally vary from sector to sector, potentially affecting, in certain instances, as huge a population as in Egypt or Sudan. This may be perceived in future provisions of safe drinking waters and improved sanitation services. Such projections would count in any eventual determination of equitable rights based on the number of population dependent on an international watercourse.

The dimension of population dependency can likewise be assessed on the basis of a different developmental consideration: degree of electrification and access to energy sources generated through the employ of the Nile waters. In the last decade, Ethiopia had adopted a radical policy course featuring itself as the continental poster-child of the hydropower sector. Its national strategy advocated for the construction of a series of small-, medium- and large-scale dams to generate hydropower and sustain an irrigated-agriculture economy.

The potential overtone of this initiative is self-evident. For a nation where about sixty million people live without access to electricity, the enterprise would enlarge the direct dependence of millions of Ethiopia's population on resources of the

Nile. In equitable determination procedures, the direct and indirect impacts of the resource are taken in to consideration in computing the size of population dependent on the international watercourse, a fact which places Ethiopia in a far greater position than Egypt or Sudan.

Another vital factor under Article 6.1.(d) that determination of the equitable utilization of an international watercourse requires taking into account involves *existing* and *potential* uses of a watercourse.

The Nile basin presents a very limited resource base; still, riparian states have to contend with a fast-growing demographic pressures and diverse development necessities of their communities. The potential for a conflicting pattern of uses has been but inevitable. On the one hand lingers the enormity of existing utilizations in the lower-reaches of the basin, withdrawing nearly all the mean annual flows of the river, and precluding potential upstream recourse to any significant utilization. On the other hand, the fiscal and technical facilities have constantly improved in upstream Nile and particularly in Ethiopia, attended by greater political predilection to meet social and economic stipulations.

Evidently, the founding of major development schemes in the upper Nile would eventually encroach on already established uses, setting in place the right milieu for conflict between competing riparian interests. How precisely basin states may decide to circumvent the incidence of such a scenario remains uncertain.

Both in Egypt and Sudan, existing uses touch upon every facet of life and still command prospects of expansion; in contrast, in Ethiopia, the resource's utility reclines largely in the context of future utilization.

About 93 percent of the total water consumption along downstream Nile has been dedicated to a single vital sector – irrigation agriculture; likewise, future extractions in Ethiopia would focus on extensive production of crops. In light of such a developmental setting, therefore, it would be sensible to direct discussion of the legal issues associated with existing and potential uses in a context that stresses the extent of cultivated and cultivable irrigational lands in the basin.

The watercourses convention places both existing and future uses under a single stipulate, but did not provide what each of these concepts constitutes. Of course, Article 5 recognizes the right of each watercourse state to utilize transboundary rivers in equitable and reasonable manner, and this had been read to conjecture that in cases of conflict between existing patterns and potential uses, some form of adjustment would always be implicit.

Still, the provision had fallen short of enlightening what specific aspects of existing or future uses are protected, nor the specific circumstances under which they may be subjected to evaluation and modification.

The watercourses convention did not place express limitation on the physical scope of irrigational utilization, except for what may probably be inferred from the operation of the equitable uses doctrine itself. It is not certain if a basin state's right to equitable utilization under Article 5 of the convention presumes a wider proposition that each riparian state is bound to adopt a measure of forethought so that its utilization does not intrude into a possible future entitlements of a co-basin state.

Of course, a basin state may not be authorized carte blanche to engage in the utilization of shared river courses simply because no co-riparian has come forward with immediate needs or definite plans for utilization of the same resource. Even in the absence of pressing competitions or a predisposition to use, it is only commonsensical that the physical scope of utilization and entitlement by each basin state should be circumscribed.

This could be inferred from the broader equitable theories of international water courses law, but more specifically, from Article VII of the Helsinki Rules where existing uses had been qualified by the insertion of *reasonable use*, a steering tenet whose application would presumably confine the freedom of states in the utilization of shared resources. Accordingly, utilization by a riparian state that imperils another basin state's prospective opportunities of making use of its entitlements by, for example, a pre-emptive appropriation of substantial floods of a stream, could not be considered as a present reasonable use.

This would mean that while states may choose to embark on unlimited scales of exploitation of a shared resource, as such, states would engage in such courses only at own peril; not every aspect of such existing uses would be eventually protected and eligible for consideration in equitable-uses decisions.

Another closely related theme investigates complex issues associated with specific downstream measures of agricultural expansions adopted in the wake of *upstream objections*, and the legal effects, on existing uses, if any, of formal upstream declarations venturing to preserve future rights of utilizing the Nile waters.

Ethiopia has consistently argued that large-scale developments in Egypt and Sudan, appropriating significant floods of the Nile, would affect neither its rights nor its presumed shares should it choose to embark on developing the resource at a subsequent stage.

The ILA submitted that reserving future rights of use may have a visceral appeal because of what appears to be its fairness; yet, the ILA disparaged this view because of its perceived conviction that it would constitute a bad policy to entitle states reserve certain waters when they had no present need for them and could make use of such waters, if at all, only at some time in future. In defence of the argument, the ILA espoused certain practical concerns relating to the unfeasibility of fixing future water shares with a meaningful degree of certainty.

While the ILA's observation might well be regarded as a judicious exercise in that it encouraged the present maximum utilization of shared watercourses, the interpretation had obviously failed to heed to certain vital perspectives.

First, the argument seemed to insinuate that international law does not ascribe any legal credence to formal reservations of riparian states effected with a view to maintaining future rights of using a share in the flows of a river basin. That certainly is controversial.

Second, the ILA's reading overlooked that indeed there could be plenty of states which actually have pressing existing needs for waters of a shared river course, but could not realize their aspirations simply because of fiscal, human resources and technical limitations. It would scarcely appeal to equitable considerations to submit that such states shall forfeit an equal right of utilization recognized under international law simply because at the present, they are not in a position to exploit a resource.

What scales of downstream uses would be regarded as existing utilization for purposes of equitable determinations in the Nile basically hinges on the legal categorization of existing uses as such and the juridical effect attached to formal declarations of upstream states reserving waters for future uses.

In countering the approach which espoused that no water should be reserved for future uses under all circumstances, the ILA submitted it would be equally unfair to give the first user a vested right in perpetuity in all the waters which it demonstrates it can presently use. Such a policy would in all likelihood lead to a use race, resulting in haphazard planning and inefficiency; it is conceivable that a state could move quickly to appropriate all the waters of a basin to the complete exclusion of its co-basin states – a result which is hardly consistent with the *equal status* of basin states.

The analysis intimated that while the stipulation under Article VII implied that no water may be kept back for future utilization, the continued security of existing uses could not be guaranteed under all circumstances. The presumption of protection is but circumstantial.

Therefore, in order to accommodate any such new uses as may be contemplated by new-arriving states such as Ethiopia, and by corollary, the rest of the upstream Nile states, the guiding principle endorsed under Article VIII of the Helsinki Rules could be adopted. It stated that an existing reasonable use may continue in operation unless the factors justifying its continuance are outweighed by other factors leading to the conclusion that it be modified or terminated so as to accommodate a competing incompatible use.

No corresponding provision had been incorporated under the watercourses convention or the Cooperative Framework Agreement, nor would such an insertion appear indispensable; that in equitable determinations, existing uses would eventually be subjected to assessment and adjustment is simply evident from the overall context and objective of the equitable uses stipulation. First users could not therefore presume that entrenched uses in shared river courses would be accorded protection in perpetuity. As the ILA's comments had put it succinctly, when new users of a resource become 'ready to use the waters or to increase an existing use, then the entire question of equitable utilization of the waters is opened up for review . . . and the rights and needs of the various states would be considered'.

This implies that in the long term where the rule of equitable utilization is set in motion, Egypt and Sudan could be confronted with the risk of slumping a great deal of the benefits enjoyed at the present through prior appropriation. Depending on the specifics of each circumstance, an evaluation involving several factors and circumstances could conclude the continuation of existing uses or may simply oblige modification or termination of all or some aspects of existing beneficial uses.

Hence, a prudent approach in national policies should compel a considered forethought before embarking on developmental actions that impact on comparable stakes of other states sharing the same resource.

Across the Nile, such a delicate balance could be struck only through procedures afforded in cooperative negotiations, which, in the instant case do not exist. While it is admitted that not *all* aspects of contemporary uses could be threatened with injury, established uses are not automatically prioritized and particularly so when such a course of action condemns other basin riparians to a perpetual state of underdevelopment.

Bibliography

I. Books

Abu-Zeid, M.A. and Biswas, A.K. (1996) *River Basin Planning and Management*, Calcuta, Oxford University Press

Baker, S.W. (1866) *The Albert Nyanza, Great Basin of the Nile and Explorations of the Nile Sources*, London, Macmillan

Berber, F.J. (1959) *Rivers in International Law*, London, Stevens and Sons

Birnie, P., Boyle, A. and Redgwell, C. (2009) *International Law and the Environment*, (3rd edn), New York, Oxford University Press

Brawnlie, I. (2003) *Principles of International Law*, New York/Oxford, Oxford University Press

Brierly, J. (1963) *The Law of Nations*, Oxford, Clarendon Press

Bruce, J. (1790) *Travels to Discover the Source of the Nile, in the Years 1768, 1769, 1770, 1771, 1772 and 1773*, London/Edinburgh, J. Ruthven

Burton, R.F. (1864) *The Nile Basin, Tanganyika to be Ptolemy's Western Lake Reservoir*, London, Tinsley Brothers

Caponera, D.A. (1992) *Principles of Water Law and Administration, National and International*, Rotterdam, A.A. Balkema

Cassese, A. (2001) *International Law*, Oxford University Press, Oxford

Chapman, J.D. (1963) *The International River Basin Proceedings of a Seminar on the Development and Administration of the International River Basin*, Vancouver, University of British Columbia

Clark, R.E. (1967) *Water and Water Rights*, Vol. II, Indianapolis, Alan Smith Co

Coopey, R. and Tvedt, T. (2006) *A History of Water: The Political Economy of Water*, London/New York, I.B. Tauris

Draper, S.E. (2002) *Model Water Sharing Agreements for the 21st Century*, Reston, Virginia, Environmental and Water Resources Institute ASCE

Erlich, H. (2002) *The Cross and the River: Ethiopia, Egypt and the Nile*, London, Lynn Rienner Publishers

Fahmi, A.M. (1999) 'Water management in the Nile, opportunities and constraints', in *Sustainable Management and Rational Use of Water Resources*, Rome, Institute for Legal Studies on International Community Publications

FAO (2006) *The State of Food Insecurity in the World, Eradicating World Hunger-Taking Stock Ten Years after the World Food Summit*, Rome, United Nations FAO

Garretson, A.H., Hayton, R.D and Olmstead, C.J. (1967) *The Law of International Drainage Basins*, New York, Oceana

Gleick, P. H. (1996) 'Water resources', *Encyclopedia of Climate and Weather*, New York, Oxford University Press

Godana, B.A. (1985) *Africa's Shared Water Resources, Legal and Institutional Aspects of the Nile, Niger, and the Senegal River Systems*, London, Lynne Rienner

Goodwin-Gill, G. S. and Talmon, S. (1999) *The Reality of International Law, Essays in Honor of Ian Brownlie*, Oxford, Oxford University Press

Herodotus (1920) *The Histories*, A. D. Godley trans., Cambridge, MA, Harvard University Press

Hertslet, Sir Edward (1984) *The Map of Africa by Treaty*, London, Harrison and Sons

Hussain, K. and Chowdhury, S.R. (1984), *Permanent Sovereignty over Natural Resources in International Law, Principle and Practice*, London, Francis Pinter

Imperial Ethiopian Ministry of Information (2000), *Selected Speeches of His Imperial Majesty Haile Selassie I*, New York, One Drop Books

Kaya, I. (2003) *Equitable Utilization, The Law of Non Navigational Uses of International Watercourses*, Aldershot/Burlington, Ashgate Publishing Co

Lobo, J. (1789) *A Voyage of Father Jerome Lobo: A Portuguese Missionary*, trans. S. Johnson, London

Malla, K.B. (2005) *The Legal Regime of International Watercourses, Progress and Paradigms Regarding Uses and Environmental Protection*, Stockholm, University of Stockholm

Malanczuc, P. (1997) *Akehurst's Modern Introduction to International law*, New York, Routledge

Manner, E. J., and Metsalampi, V. (1988) *The Work of the International Law Association on the Law of International Water Resources*, Helsinki , Publication of Finnish Branch of the International Law Association

Marcus, H.G. (1987) *Hailesellassie I: The Formative Years 1892–1936*, Berkeley, University of California Press

Marcus, H.G. (1995) *The Life and Times of Menelik II, Ethiopia 1844–1913*, Lawrenceville, NJ, The Red Sea Press Inc

McCaffrey, S.C. (2001) *The Law of International Watercourses: Non-Navigational Uses*, Oxford/New York, Oxford University Press

Oppenheim, L. (1955) *International Law, A Treatise*, 8th edn, London, Longmans, Green and Co

Pliny the Elder (1855) *The Natural History*, ed. John Bostock and H.T.Riley, London, Taylor and Francis

Rubenson, S. (1976) *The Survival of Ethiopian Independence*, London, Heinman Educational Books Ltd

Shaw, M.N. (2003) *International Law*, 5th edn, Cambridge, Cambridge University Press

Speke, J.H. (1863) *The Journal of the Discovery of the Source of the Nile*, Edinburgh, William Blackwood and Sons

Tanzi, A. and Arcari, M. (2001) *The UN Convention on the Law of International Watercourses*, London/The Hague /Boston, Kluwer Law International

Teclaff, L.A. (1985) *Water Law in Historical Perspective*, New York, Williams S. Hein Co

Teclaff, L.A. and Utton, A.E. (1981) *International Groundwater Law*, London/Rome/New York, Oceana Pub Inc

The International Bank for Reconstruction and Development/The World Bank (2009) *World Development Report 2010, Development and Climate Change*, Washington, DC, World Bank

The World Water Assessment Programme (2009) *The United Nations World Water Development Report 3, Water in a Changing World*, London, UNESCO Publishing

Tvedt, T. (2004) *The River Nile in the Age of the British, Political Ecology and the Quest for Economic Power*, London/New York, I.B. Tauris

Tvedt, T., Chapman, G. and Hagen, R. (2011) *A History of Water Series II, Volume III, Water, Geopolitics and the New World Order*, London/New York, I.B. Tauris

Ullendorf, E. (1976) *The Autobiography of Emperor Haile Selassie I, My Life and Ethiopia's Progress 1892–1937*, Oxford, Oxford University Press,

United Nations, Panel of Experts on the Legal and Institutional Aspects of International Water Resources Development (1975) *Management of International Water Resources: Institutional and Legal Aspects: Report of the Panel of Experts on the Legal and Institutional Aspects of International Water Resources Development*, New York, United Nations Publication

United Nations Development Programme (2006) *Human Development Report 2006, Beyond Scarcity: Power, Poverty and the Global Water Crisis*, New York, Palgrave Macmillan

United Nations Development Program (2007) *Human Development Report 2007/2008, Fighting Climate Change: Human Solidarity in a Divided World*, New York, Palgrave Macmillan

Waterbury, J. (2002) *The Nile Basin, National Determinants of Collective Action*, New Haven, London, Yale University Press

World Water Assessment Program (2003) *The UN World Water Development Report: Water for People, Water for Life*, Barcelona, UNESCO Publishing/Berghahn Books

Wouters, P. (1997) *International Water Law, Selected Writings of Professor Charles B. Bourne*, London/The Hague, Kluwer Law International

II. Journal articles

Batstone, R. K. (1959) 'Utilization of the Nile Waters', *Int'l & Comp LQ*, vol 8

Bourne, C.B. (1965) 'The Right to the Waters of International Rivers', *Can YB Int'l L*, vol 3

Bourne, C. (1996) 'The International Law Association's Contribution to International Water Resources Law', *Natural Resources Journal*, vol 36

Brunnee, J. and Toope, S.J. (2002) 'The Changing Nile Basin Regime: Does Law Matter?', *Harv Int'l LJ*, vol 43, no 1

Buell, R.L. (1927) 'The Termination of Unequal Treaties', *Am Soc'y Int'l L Proc* 21

Caponera, D.A. (1985) 'Patterns of Cooperation in International Water Law: Principles and Institutions', *Nat Resources J*, vol 25

Caponera, D.A. (1993) 'Legal Aspects of Transboundary River Basins in the Middle East, the Al Asi (Orentes), the Jordan and the Nile', *Natural Resources Journal*, vol 33

Speke, J.H. and Grant, J.A. (1862–63) 'The Nile and its Sources', *Proceedings of the Royal Geographical Society of London*, vol 7, no 5

Cheesman, R.E. (1928) 'The Upper Waters of the Blue Nile', *The Geographical Journal*, vol 71, no 4

Detter, I. (1966) 'The Problem of Unequal Treaties', *Int'l and Comp. LQ*, vol 15

Dupuis, C.E. (1936) 'Lake Tana and the Nile', *Journal of the Royal African Society*, vol 35

Eagleton, C. (1955) 'The Use of Waters of International Rivers', *Canadian Bar Review*, vol 33

FAO (1997) 'Irrigation Potential in Africa, a Basin Approach', *Land and Water Bulletin*, vol 4

Fitzmaurice, M. (1997) 'Convention on the Law of Non-Navigational Uses of International Watercourses', *Leiden J Int'l L*, vol 10, no 3

Fuentes, X. (1996) 'The Criteria for the Equitable Utilization of International Rivers', *British Yearbook of International Law*, vol 67

Garretson, A. (1960) 'The Nile River System', *American Society International Law Proceedings*, vol 54

Garstin, W. (1905) 'Report Upon the Basin of the Upper Nile, with Proposals for the Improvement of that River', *The Geographical Journal*, vol 25, no 1

Garstin, W. (1909) 'Fifty Years of Exploration, and Some of its Results', *The Geographical Journal*, vol 33, no 2

Gess, K.N. (1964) 'Permanent Sovereignty over Natural Resources: Analytical Review of the United Nations Declaration and its Genesis', *Int'l & Comp L Q*, vol 13
Griffin, W.L. (1959) 'The Use of International Drainage Basins under Customary International Law', *American Journal of International Law*, vol 53, no 1
Guarisso, G. and Whittington, D. (1987) 'Implications of Ethiopian Water Development for Egypt and the Sudan', *International Journal of Water Resources Development*, vol 3, no 2
Hardy, J. (1961) 'The Interpretation of plurilingual Treaties by International Courts and Tribunals', *BYIL*, vol 37
Haynes, K.E. and Whittington, D. (1981) 'International Management of the Nile, Stage Three?', *Geographical Review*, vol 71, no 1
Hurst, H.E. (1927) 'Progress in the Study of the Hydrology of the Nile in the Last Twenty Years', *The Geographical Journal*, vol 70, no 5
Hurst, H.E. (1936) 'A Study of the Upper Nile', *Discover*, vol 17
Hurst, H.E. (1948) 'Major Irrigation Projects on the Nile', *Civil Engineering and Public Works Review*, vol 43, no 507
Hutchins, W. A. (1962) 'Background and Modern Developments in Water Law in the USA', *Nat Resources J*, vol 2
H. Concord (1935) 'Supplement to the American Journal of International Law', *Am J Int'l L Sup*, vol 29
Jongei Investigation Team (1953) 'The Equatorial Nile Project and its Effects in the Sudan', *The Geographical Journal*, vol 119, no 1
International Law Commission (1966) *Yearbook of International Law Commission*, vol 2
International Law Commission (1974) *Yearbook of International Law Commission*, vol 2, no 2
International Law Commission (1976) 'First Report on the Law of the Non-Navigational Uses of International Watercourses', *Yearbook of International Law Commission*, vol 2, no 1
International Law Commission (1976) *Yearbook of International Law Commission*, vol 2, no 2
International Law Commission (1979) *Yearbook of International Law Commission*, vol 1, no 1
International Law Commission (1979) *Yearbook of International Law Commission*, vol 2, no 1
International Law Commission (1979) *Yearbook of International Law Commission*, vol 2, no 2
International Law Commission (1980) *Yearbook of International Law Commission*, vol 2, no 1
International Law Commission (1982) *Yearbook of International Law Commission*, vol 2, no 1
International Law Commission (1983) *Yearbook of International Law Commission*, vol 2, no 1
International Law Commission (1984) *Yearbook of International Law Commission*, vol 2, no 2
International Law Commission (1986) *Yearbook of International Law Commission*, vol 2, no 1
International Law Commission (1987) *Yearbook of International Law Commission*, vol 1
International Law Commission (1987) *Yearbook of International Law Commission*, vol 2, no 2
International Law Commission (1991) *Yearbook of International Law Commission*, vol 1
International Law Commission (1994) 'First Report on the Law of the Non-Navigational Uses of International Watercourses', *Yearbook of International law Commission*, vol 2, no 1
International Law Commission (1994) *Yearbook of International Law Commission*, vol 2, no 2
Lauterpacht, E. (1957) 'The Contemporary Practice of the United Kingdom in the Field of International Law, Survey and Comment II', *International and Comparative Law Quarterly*, vol 6
Laylin, J.G. (1957) 'Principles of Law Governing the Uses of International Rivers, Contributions from the Indus Basin', *Am Soc'y Int'l L Proc*, 51
Marcus, H.G. (1963) 'Ethio-British Negotiations Concerning the Western Border with Sudan, 1896–1902', *The Journal of African History*, vol 4, no 1
Marcus, H.G. (1966) 'The Foreign Policy of the Emperor Menelik 1896–1898: A Rejoinder', *The Journal of African History*, vol 7, no 1

McCaffrey, S. (2001) 'The Contribution of the UN Convention on the Law of the Non-Navigational Uses of International Watercourses', *Int J Global Environmental Issues*, vol 1

McCann, J. (1981) 'Ethiopia, Britain and Negotiations for the Lake Tana Dam 1922–1935', *The International Journal of African Historical Studies*, vol 14, no 4

Mogharby, A.I. (1982) 'The Jonglei Canal, Needed Development or Potential Eco-disaster?', *Environmental Conservation*, vol 9, no 2

Molle, F. (2004) 'Defining Water Rights: By Prescription or Negotiation?', *Water Policy*, vol 6

Nicholson, S. (2001) 'Water Scarcity, Conflict, and International Water Law: An Examination of the Regime Established by the UN Convention on International Watercourses', *New Zealand Journal of Environmental Law*, vol 5

Putney, A.H. (1927) 'The Termination of Unequal Treaties', *Am Soc'y Int'l L Proc*, vol 21

Roskar, J. (2000) 'Assessing the water resources potential of the Nile River based on data available at the Nile forecasting center in Cairo', *Geografski Zbornik*, vol xxxx

Sanderson, G.N. (1964) 'England, Italy, the Nile Valley and the European Balance, 1890–91', *The Historical Journal*, vol 7

Swain, A. (1997) 'Ethiopia, the Sudan and Egypt: The Nile River Dispute', *Journal of Modern African Studies*, vol 35, no 4

Wallach, B. (1988) 'Irrigation in Sudan since Independence', *Geographical Review*, vol 78, no 4

Waterbury, J. (1997) 'Is the Status Quo in the Nile Basin Viable?', *J World Aff*, vol 4

Waterbury, J. and Whittington, D. (1998) 'Playing Chicken on the Nile, Implications of Micro-dam Development in Ethiopian highlands and Egypt's New Valley project', *Middle Eastern Natural Environment Bulletin*, vol 103

Weld, H. (1928) 'The Blue Nile and Irrigation', *Journal of Royal African Society*, vol 27, no 106

Whittington, D. (2004) 'Visions of Nile Basin Development', *Water Policy*, vol 6

Wiebe, K. (2001) 'The Nile River: Potential for Conflict and Cooperation in the Face of Water Degradation', *Natural Resources Journal*, vol 41

III. Government reports, papers and proceedings

Abalhoda, A.B. (1993) 'Nile Basin General Information and Statistics', ICOLD 61st Executive Meeting, Cairo

Ali, M.K. (1997) 'The Projects for the Increase of the Nile Yield with Special Reference to the Jonglei Project', Water Conference, Mar De Plata, vol 4, no 31

Arab Republic of Egypt (2005) 'National Water Resources Plan for Egypt 2017', Ministry of Water Resources and Irrigation, Planning Sector, Cairo

Barret, S. (1994) 'Conflict and Cooperation in managing international water resources', Policy Research Working Paper 1303, World Bank Research Department, Washington, DC

FAO (2000) 'Water and Agriculture in the Nile Basin' Nile Basin Initiative Report to the ICCON, Rome

Federal Democratic Republic of Ethiopia (1999) 'Abay River Integrated Development Master Plan Project' Phase 2/3, vol I, Ministry of Water Resources, Addis Ababa

Federal Democratic Republic of Ethiopia (2002) 'Foreign Affairs and National Security Policy and Strategy', Ministry of Information, Press & Audio-visual Department, Addis Ababa

Federal Democratic Republic of Ethiopia (2006) 'Ethiopian Nile Irrigation and Drainage Project, Consultancy Service for Identification of Irrigation and Drainage Projects in the Nile Basin in Ethiopia', Final Report, Ministry of Water Resources, Addis Ababa

Hurst, H.E. (1927) 'The Lake Plateau Basin of the Nile', Ministry of Public Works, Physical Department Paper No 23, Cairo, Government Press

Hurst, H.E., Black, R.P and Simaika, Y.M. (1946) 'The Nile Basin, the Future Conservation of the Nile', Physical Department Paper no. 51, Vol VII, Cairo, SOP Press
International Law Association (1966) 'Helsinki Rules on the Uses of the Waters of International Rivers' (Commentaries), ILA Publication, London, pp 7–55
Ministry of Water Resources (1992) 'Minutes of the Ethio-Sudanese Joint Meeting on Nile Waters Resources Cooperation', Addis Ababa (unpublished)
Ministry of Water Resources (1993), 'Local and Transboundary Rivers, Current International Relations', Addis Ababa (unpublished)
Ministry of Water Resources (1994) 'Minutes of the Fourth Regular Meeting of the Ethio-Sudan Technical Advisory Committee on Nile Water Resources Cooperation', Addis Ababa (unpublished)
Ministry of Water Resources (n.d.) 'Ethiopia's Technical Advisory Committee Proposal, Application of the Principle of Equitable Utilization and the Duty not to Cause Appreciable Harm in the Context of the Nile', Annex 10, Addis Ababa (unpublished)
Ministry of Water Resources (2002) 'Water Sector Development Program, Irrigation Development Programme Report', Addis Ababa
National Water Development Commission (1972) 'Note on the Blue Nile', Addis Ababa (unpublished)
Nile 2002 Conference (1992) 'Framework for Cooperation Between the Nile River Co-basin States: Nile 2002 Conference on Comprehensive Water Resources Development of the Nile Basin, The Vision Ahead', Proceedings, Khartoum
Nile 2002 Conference (1996), Proceedings of the IVth Nile 2002 Conference, Kampala
Nile 2002 Conference (1997) 'Comprehensive Water Resources Development of the Nile Basin: Priorities for the New Century', Proceedings of the Vth Nile 2002 Conference, Addis Ababa
Nile 2002 Conference (2000), Proceedings of VIIIth Nile 2002 Conference, Addis Ababa
Report of the Nile Projects Commission (1920), Printed with the authority of the Egyptian Government, London
Shenouda, W.K. (1993) 'The High Aswan Dam: A Vital Achievement, Fully Controlled Symposium', ICOLD, 61st Executive Meeting, Cairo
Soliman, A. and MacGregor, R.M. (1926) 'Reports of the Nile Commission', Cairo
United Nations (1972) 'Report of the United Nations Conference on the Human Environment', Stockholm
United Nations (1977) 'Report of the United Nations Water Conference', Part 1, Mar del Plata
United Nations (1999) 'The Right to Adequate Food (Art 11)', CESCR General Comment No. 12, Adopted at the Twentieth Session of the Committee on Economic, Social and Cultural Rights, 12 May, Document E/C 12/1999/5. http://www.unhchr.ch/tbs/doc.nsf/0/3d02758c707031d58025677f003b73b9>, last accessed October 2012
UNESCO-WWAP, World Water Assessment Program (2004), 'National Water Development Report for Ethiopia', Addis Ababa, <http://unesdoc.unesco.org/images/0014/001459/145926e.pdf> last accessed December 2010

IV. British foreign office archieves

(The National Archives, Kew, Richmond, Great Britain)

Abyssinia, Record of meetings to discuss the method of negotiation with Abyssinian Government for the Lake Tana Concession. 4 August 1926, FO 371/13099
Addis Ababa to Foreign Office. 17 February 1949, FO 371/73613

Addis Ababa to Foreign Office. 11 May 1956, FO 371/119061
African Department. 13 June 1955, FO 371/113733
Bailey to Welson, Washington. 2 May 1956, FO 371/119054
Bentinck to Ras Teferi. Addis Ababa, 20 December 1920, FO 371/13099
Bentinck to Sir Austen Chamberlain. Suggestions for a Treaty. Addis Ababa, 10 May 1927, Enclosure 2.1, FO 371/12341
Bentinck, Addis Ababa. October 1927, FO 371/12341
Bentinck to Sir Austen Chamberlain. Addis Ababa, 14 December 1927, FO 371/13099
Bentinck to Austen Chamberlain. 9 January 1928, Enclosure 2.1, FO 371/13099
Bentinck to Sir Austen Chamberlain. Addis Ababa, 30 January 1928, FO 371/13099
Bentinck (Charles) to Teferi Mekonnen. Suggestions for a Treaty. 25 July 1929, Addis Ababa Enclosure 1, FO 371/12341
BFOR File 1
BFOR No 4 and 5.
Cairo to Foreign Office. 16 July 1949, FO 371/73619
Counselor of American Embassy at Cairo (Ross) to the Department of State (1957), Aide Memoire of 23 September 1957, encl in Dispatch No 342, 8 October 1957 (MS Department of State, file 974.7301/10-857)
Doughty Wyllie to Lord Kitchener. 27 June 1914, FO 371/15388
Draft Telegram to Cromer. Addis Ababa 16 February 1907, FO 371/14591
Draft of a Note to Be addressed by His Majesty's Ambassador to the Egyptian Minister for Foreign Affairs. April 1949, FO 371/73616
E.B. Boothby to D.L. Busk, London. 5 February 1954, Enclosure FO 371/108264
Field-Marshall Viscount Allenby to Mr Austen Chamberlain, E 10986/192/16, Enclosure 3 in No. 1, Cairo, 29 November 1924
Foreign Office Memorandum, Lake Tana. 31 May 1927, FO 370/1234
G. Schuster, Note on Italian Negotiations for Concessions in Abyssinia. 6 June 1925, FO 371/10872
Governor of Uganda (The) to the Secretary of State for Colonies, Egyptian Proposals for Water Storage in Lake Albert. 15 April 1947, FO141/1191
Harrington to Salisbury. 14 May 1900, FO 403/299
Harrington to Boyle. 27 March 1902, FO 1/40
J. Hugh Dodds to Viscount Allenby, Draft Agreement, Addis Ababa. 26 December 1922, FO 371/8403
H.B Shepherd. Foreign Office Minute, 1929 Nile Water Agreements. 5 September 1956, FO 371/119063
Ilg to Harrington. 18 March 1902, FO 403/322
J.E. Killick to J.H.A Watson, British Embassy, Addis Ababa. 26 September 1956, FO 371/119063
J.E. Killick, British Embassy, Addis Ababa to J.H.A Watson, African Department, Foreign Office, London. 29 September 1956, FO 371/119063
J. F. S Philips, Foreign Office to P.R.A Mansfield, British Embassy, Addis Ababa. 25 June 1956, FO 371/ 119062
Lake Tana, Record of Conversation between Dr. Martin and Murray. 11 November 1927, FO 371/12343
Lord Allenby F.M, High Commissioner [Egypt] to Ziwer Pasha, Cairo. 26 January 1925, (Nile Commission Report 1925 Appendix A)
Memorandum, History of the Lake Tana Negotiation, Foreign Office. 23 January 1923, FO 371/8403

Memorandum on future conservation works. October 1945, CO 537/1521

Minutes on conversation with the Secretary of State. 31 September 1949, FO 141/1414

Mr Ronald, FO Memorandum, Lake Tana. 31 May 1927, FO 371/12341

Outline of the Equatorial Nile Project. 4 December 1948, FO 371/69233

P.R.A Mansfield, British Embassy, Addis Ababa, to J. F. S. Philips, Foreign Office, London. 27 April 1956, FO 371/ 119061

P.R.A Mansfield to John, British Embassy, Addis Ababa. 27 April 1956, FO 371/119061

P.R.A Mansfield, British Embassy, Addis Ababa, to J. F. S. Philips, African Department, Foreign Office, London. 1 August 1956, FO 371/ 119062

Ralph Stevenson to Harold Macmillan, British Embassy, Cairo. 16 May 1955, FO 371/113733

Ramsay Macdonald to Teferi, Foreign Office. 19 July 1924, FO 371/10872

Ramsay MacDonald to Teferi, Foreign Office. 14 August 1924, FO 371/10872

Ras Teferi to Bentinck, Addis Ababa. 26 December 1927, FO 371/13099

Sanderson to Harrington. 28 August 1902, FO 1/47

Sir Barton, Lake Tana Negotiations, Addis Ababa. 18 August 1930, FO 371/14591

Sir Barton to Hon. Arthur Henderson, Addis Ababa. 29 June 1931, FO 371/15388

Sir J. Maffey to Sir P. Lorraine, Khartoum. 26 April 1931, FO 371/15388

Sir John Hathorn Hall to Secretary of the State of Colonies, Lake Albert Dam. 12 May 1946, CO 536/217

Sir M. Lampson, Lake Tana Dam Project, Draft Agreement or Treaty, Cairo. 22 June 1935, Minutes, FO 371/19186

Sir P. Loraine, Cairo. 26 March 1931, FO 371/15388

Sir Ronald Campbell, From Cairo to Foreign Office. 16 July 1949, FO 371/73619

Sudan Government London Office to John Murray, London. 11 October 1927, FO 371/12341

Teferi to Ramsay McDonald, Paris. 26 July 1924, FO 371/10872

Teferi to Austen Chamberlain, Enclosure in Addis Ababa Dispatch 363, Bentinck to Chamberlain, Addis Ababa. 14 December 1927, FO 371/13099

Telegram from Cromer, Cairo. 7–9 March 1907, FO 371/14591

T. E. Bromley to Busk, London. 29 July 1954, FO 371/108264

Text of Note presented by her Majesty's Ambassador in Cairo to the Egyptian Government. 22 November 1955, FO 371/119062

United States Department of Interior, Oscal L. Chapman, Secretary, Michael W. Straus, Commissioner, Bureau of Reclamation, Reconnaissance Report, Blue Nile River Basin, Ethiopia. From T.A Clarck, et al, Washington DC (August 1952)

W.H. Luce, Governor General Office, Khartoum to T.E. Bromley, African Department, Foreign Office, London. 5 May 1955, FO 371/113763

Ziwer Pasha, President of Council of Ministers, to Lord Allenby, Cairo. 26 January 1925, (Nile Commission Report 1925 Appendix A)

V. Periodicals, press and web resources

Abu Zied, M. (1999) 'Managing Turbulent Waters', *Al-Ahram Weekly Online*, Issue 447, <http://weekly.ahram.org.eg/1999/447/spec3.htm>

Central Intelligence Agency. *The World Fact Book*, Egypt <https://www.cia.gov/library/publications/the-world-factbook/geos/eg.html>

Egypt State Information Service. 'Agriculture' <http://www.sis.gov.eg/En/Story.aspx?sid=835>

Egypt (2005) 'Basic statistics and population', *FAO Water Report* 29 (Tables 1 and 4) <http://www.fao.org/nr/water/aquastat/countries/egypt/index.stm>

Egypt State Information Center. <http://www.sis.gov.eg/En/Story.aspx?sid=835>

El-Sayed, M. (2010) 'Dangers on the Nile', *Al-Ahram Weekly Online*, Issue 995 <http://weekly.ahram.org.eg/2010/995/eg3.htm>

FAO (2005) 'FAO's Information System on Water and Agriculture, Geography, Climate and Population', Egypt, (Tables 1, 4) <http://www.fao.org/nr/water/aquastat/countries/egypt/index.stm>

FAO (2005) 'FAO's Information System on Water and Agriculture, Geography, Climate and Population' Sudan, *FAO Water Report* 29 (Table 1 and 4) <http://www.fao.org/nr/water/aquastat/countries/sudan/index.stm>

FAO (2005) 'FAO's Information System on Water and Agriculture, Geography, Climate and Population' Ethiopia, FAO. 'Ethiopia, Basic statistics and population' *FAO Water Report* 29 (Table 1 and 4) <http://www.fao.org/nr/water/aquastat/countries/ethiopia/index.stm>

International Law Association(2004) Berlin Conference, Water Resources Law, *Fourth Report* <http://www.internationalwaterlaw.org/documents/intldocs/ILA_Berlin_Rules2004.pdf>

International Law Commission. 'Law of Non-Navigational Uses of International Watercourse.' (historical summary): <http://untreaty.un.org/ilc/summaries/8_3.htm>

Leila, R. (2009) 'Wading Through the Politics', *Al-Ahram Weekly Online*, Issue 949 <http://weekly.ahram.org.eg/2009/955/eg2.htm>

Nile Basin Initiative (2010) 'Agreement on the Nile River Basin Cooperative Framework opened for signature', Press Release <http://www.nilebasin.org/index.php?option=com_content&task=view&id=165&Itemid=102>

Nile Basin Initiative (2010) 'Ministers of Water Affairs End Extraordinary Meeting over the Cooperative Framework Agreement', Press Release <http://www.nilebasin.org/index.php?option=com_content&task=view&id=161&Itemid=102>

Nkrumah, G. (2004) 'Who Runs the River?', *Al-Ahram Weekly Online*, Issue 685 <http://weekly.ahram.org.eg/2004/685/eg5.htm>

Nkrumah, G. (2004) 'Fresh Water Talks', *Al-Ahram Weekly Online*, Issue 694 <http://weekly.ahram.org.eg/2004/694/eg4.htm>

Rizk, Y.L. (2004) 'War Games', *Al-Ahram Weekly Online*, Issue 711

Rizk, Y.L. (2004) 'Chronicles, War Games', *Al-Ahram Weekly Online*, Issue 711<http://weekly.ahram.org.eg/2004/711/chrncls.htm>

Sudan. 'Irrigated agriculture, Control device for switching water flow to one of the many canals used for irrigation in Al Jazirah, south of Khartoum.' <http://www.country-data.com/cgi-bin/query/r-13379.html>

The World Bank Group (2010) World Bank 2008 World Development Indicators Database <http://ddpext.worldbank.org/ext/ddpreports/ViewSharedReport?REPORT_ID=9147&REQUEST_TYPE=VIEWADVANCED>

UNESCO World Water Assessment Program (2004) 'National Water Development Report for Ethiopia', Addis Ababa <http://unesdoc.unesco.org/images/0014/001459/145926e.pdf>

United Nations Department of Economic and Social Affairs, Population Division (2008) 'World Population Prospects', <http://esa.un.org/unpp/>

Wolf, A.T. (2001) 'International Conference on Fresh water, Transboundary waters, Sharing Benefits, Lessons Learned', Thematic background paper, Conference on International Fresh Water Courses, Bonn <http://www.agnos-online.de/inwent1/images/pdfs/transboundary-waters.pdf>

World Health Organization (2010), Egypt – Health Profile <http://www.who.int/gho/countries/egy.pdf>

World Health Organization (2010), Sudan – Health Profile <http://www.who.int/gho/countries/sdn.pdf>

World Health Organization (2010), Ethiopia – Health Profile (2010) <http://www.who.int/gho/countries/eth.pdf>

World Facts Index, Sudan. 'Irrigated Agriculture.' <http://countrystudies.us/sudan/55.htm>

Wouters, P., Salman, M. A. Salman, and Jones, P. 'The Legal Response to the World's Water Crisis: What Legacy from the Hague? What Future in Kyoto?', p 5 <http://www.africanwater.org/Documents/colorado_draft_4.doc>, last accessed in December 2010.

Index

Note: Documents and Latin words are given in italics. Where a page note is referred to, it appears thus: "149 n2", i.e. note 2 on page 149. A table is indicated by "t", a figure by "f".

E